MELCHIZEDEK

VOLUME 2

TREE OF LIFE REALITIES

EMANATING LIFE FROM
OUR TRUE SELF IN CHRIST

JOHN L. MASTROGIOVANNI, D. MIN.

Compass Rose Press

Published by Compass Rose Press
Las Vegas, Nevada
www.CompassRosePressBooks.com

ISBN Print: 978-1-946892-53-9
ISBN ebook: 978-1-946892-52-2

Library of Congress Control Number: 2023949540

Scripture quotations taken from the Amplified® Bible, Copyright 1954, 1958, 1962, 1964, 1965, 1987 by The Lockman Foundation. Used with permission. (www.Lockman.org)

Scripture taken from the Good News Translation - Second Edition, Copyright 1992 by American Bible Society. Used by Permission.

Scripture taken from *The Message*. Copyright 1993, 1994, 1995, 1996, 2000, 2001, 2002. Used with permission of NavPress Publishing Group.

Scripture quotations taken from the New American Standard Bible®, Copyright 1960, 1962, 1963, 1968, 1971, 1972, 1973, 1975, 1977, 1995 by The Lockman Foundation. Used with permission. (www.Lockman.org)

Scripture taken from the HOLY BIBLE, NEW INTERNATIONAL VERSION®. Copyright 1973, 1978, 1984 International Bible Society. Used with permission of Zondervan. All rights reserved.

Scripture taken from the New King James Version. Copyright © 1982 by Thomas Nelson, Inc. Used by permission. All rights reserved."

Scripture quotations marked NLT are taken from the Holy Bible, New Living Translation, copyright 1996, 2004. Used by permission of Tyndale House Publishers, Inc., Wheaton, Illinois 60189. All rights reserved.

Revised Standard Version of the Bible, copyright 1952 [2nd edition, 1971] by the Division of Christian Education of the National Council of the Churches of Christ in the United States of America. Used by permission. All rights reserved.

THE MIRROR: The Bible translated from the original text and paraphrased in contemporary speech with commentary by Francois du Toit. Scripture taken from THE MIRROR. Copyright 2012. Used with permission of The Author.

TABLE OF CONTENTS

SECTION I

REFRESHING THE UNANSWERED QUESTION: MELCHIZEDEK

PROLOGUE
THE KINGDOM WE CAN'T REMEMBER

"And I have no doubt that every new example will succeed, as every past one has done, in showing that religion and Government will both exist in greater purity, the less they are mixed together."

James Madison
Fourth President of the United States

Part 1: A Skewed Kingdom

There has always been a stark tension between religion, politics, and spirituality. One would suspect that the most obvious example of this would be between religion and politics. Yet, from the perspective of the priesthood of Christ, that isn't actually true. Rather, we find that both religion and politics emerge from the same root: the Egoistic Serpent and the Tree of the Knowledge of Good and Evil. When we view them with a genuine spirituality, the contrast, or better said, *distinction*, would be between this world, which includes both religion and politics, and the realm which Jesus called *above*, which has little to do with anything egoistic, or good or evil.

In exploring the Melchizedekian priesthood, we are reminded that it's a King-Priesthood, combining Kingship (government) and priesthood (spirituality). Please note, we did not say politics and religion. The challenge before us is that we have a propensity to look at the kingdoms of this world and model them into the Kingdom of Heaven. To be frank, the kingdoms of this world and the Kingdom of Heaven are literally universes apart. Pertaining to any of the kingdoms of this world, our High-Priest, King Jesus, was clear. *"Render to Caesar the things that are Caesar's and to God the things that are God's."* (Luke 20:25). Jesus doesn't have a problem with us praying for and being humble citizens in the governments of this world. The problem arises when we render to Caesar what is God's and superimpose on God what is of Caesar. It's become evident that Christendom in the West has homogenized the two and we've demeaned the Christ and His Kingdom. We are like Judas, who thought he was doing both his nation and religion a favor when he gave up Christ to the serpentine political-religious powers of the day.

When we do the same, even in the subtlest of ways, we impose that God wants us to use our spiritual authority to enforce, endorse, and empower a particular kingdom, country, or state. This is the Serpentine intention from the beginning. When we give to Caesar what is God's and vice versa, we unwittingly become an agent who empowers the Luciferic proclamation, *"I will exalt my throne above the stars of God."* (Isaiah 14:13) While on the surface it may seem that God Most High reigns supreme and the Luciferic declaration is an unfulfilled evil desire, the subtilty of spiritual truth unveils something different. In spiritual reality, the proclamation *is the deposition.* It's no different than *"For as a man thinks within his heart, so is he."* (Proverbs 23:7) This doesn't mean the true Divine order has changed in the upper worlds, but it definitely has in *the inner world of the one who conceived the proclamation.* In other words, we all view reality from our own inner world. Accordingly, we see the world around us through that lens and that is our reality. If we see our thrones above the stars of God, then that's reality. When we egoistically partook of the Tree of the Knowledge of Good and Evil, that's exactly what happened.

This is the situation for many of us in the fallen condition. It's a subordination of God Most High to a lesser authority based on right and wrong. The ego rules rather than the nature of God, though we still carry Bibles, wear Jesus shirts, and sing our favorite worship songs. It doesn't mean we removed the true God from the redesigned bureaucracy— though in some nations we've attempted that—we've simply integrated Him into it. This skewed view of ourselves, God, and His Kingdom results in a grotesque caricature of the Creator and His Creation. To the observer, such religion and politics make it seem that this was always the appropriate order. While our perception may be that all the governments of the world are ordained and placed by God, this is a misconception of both Old and New Testaments. Following through on this rationalization, you could say that it empowers the throne of the Serpent and its Tree. The result is the misdirection and misuse of our creative power in Christ. What we've actually done is yield to the Satanic voice in the wilderness and, with the power of the Spirit, turned the stone into bread, proving we are sons of God. Of course, what follows is the natural order of things. With full bellies of self-gratification, we heed the voice further, we bow to the new order, and gain the kingdoms of the world. Now, as proved sons of God, we stand in political power, making the world a better place in His name. Supposedly. The final step, now that the kingdoms of the world are our temple, is that we trip over the very stone that started it all, hurling ourselves from its pinnacle, and rather than angels bearing us up, it's a fallen one that pushes us over the edge (Luke 4:1-12, with a clear modification).

In actuality, the governing factor of the Kingdom of Christ is set forth by the Tree of Life. It doesn't approach any aspect of Creation, including people groups, tribes, or nations, from a good and evil perspective. When it comes to the function of the governments of this world and their respective religions, everything is based on the rule of what's deemed to be good and evil. Granted, some of this world's kings and leaders have been nicer than others, yet that doesn't mean they were an expression of the Tree of Life. In the domain of the Tree of Life, there is only one King, and He doesn't rule through laws or any derivative thereof. Rather, He rules through the nature of the Divine Likeness of Love, Light, and Life, all emanating through the union of His people. In that light, the book of Revelation has a powerful statement at its conclusion:

> *"...flowing from the throne of God and of the Lamb down the middle of the great street of the city. On each side of the river stood the tree of life, bearing*

twelve crops of fruit, yielding its fruit every month.
And the leaves of the tree are for the healing of the
nations."   *(Revelation 22:1b-3/NIV)*

The leaves of the Tree of Life have the power to heal the nations. What a powerful promise and declaration! But what does that imply? Evidently, the other Tree, the one of the Knowledge of Good and Evil, has infected humanity, including their kingdoms and religions, with a heinous illness. The healing of the nations never implied that the two systems were happily merged together and all was well. To the contrary, as mentioned earlier regarding giving to Caesar what is God's, the same can also be said of the two trees. We are not to render, or superimpose, the Tree of the Knowledge of Good and Evil onto the Tree of Life. The two are incompatible, as one clearly results in Death and the other Life. Yet within the realm of Life, there is no Death, meaning the Tree of the Knowledge of Good and Evil may not be what the Serpent said it was, a perspective we will consider later.

The purpose of the following pages is to help us to return our inner life to the Garden of Eden, relinquish our egoistic addiction to the Tree of the Knowledge of Good and Evil, and once again live engrafted with the Tree of Life. Unless we awaken and become conscious to the Tree of Life, we deprive the world and its nations from the revelation of Christ and the healing in its leaves. Remember, after the Adam partook of the Tree of the Knowledge of Good and Evil, God said:

"He must not be allowed to reach out his hand and take also from the tree of life and eat, and live forever."   *(Genesis 3:22b/NIV)*

Clearly, the last thing God wanted was a mingling of the two trees in that form within His Creation. This would only give shape to a disfigured amalgamation. This verboten merger immediately skews our view of God and, inevitably, our view of ourselves, being that we are created in His Image. If our views of ourselves and God are skewed, can you imagine what that does to our view of government and spirituality? Hence, the present state of politics and religion, especially in Christendom.

Nonetheless, God never changed our identity, rather, we changed our perception of it. Remember, it doesn't mean the true Divine order has changed, but it has become something different in *the inner world of the one who conceived it*. It was our choice, which God afforded us. God made sure that our "choice" between the two trees would be a central aspect of our existence, which continues to this moment. As we will discuss further, the essential aspect to godlikeness is *choice*. Choice is what gives authenticity to *love*, which is the central character and substance of what makes God, God. Thus, it is also what makes our Likeness of Him. In contrast, regardless of how good we are in opposition to evil, we are still concealing our true selves behind the fig leaves we plucked from the Tree of Death. The perpetual challenge before us is not only what we think we know, but something far more daunting. It's not what we know, but what we can "remember."

Part 2: The Primordial Memory

"Right now I'm having amnesia and déjà vu at the same time. I think I've forgotten this before."

Steven Wright
Comedic Author

Currently, despite our focused, physical, ego-centric existence—in which we envision financial success, jostling for political power, embracing religious rightness, raising our posterity, and seeking whatever feeds our need for gratification—we are forever plagued with a dim awareness. Like a dream that's hard to remember, or a distant memory of a time forgotten, a momentary inkling arises. A fleeting impression appears, as if an encounter with déjà vu. At times it seems to gently emerge in the back of our thoughts, then, as soon as we attempt to focus on it, it eludes us like mist in a breeze. The faint sensation we detect feels closer than our own breath, yet dissipates as quickly. We seem to be aware of another existence, something from another dimension, possibly an alternate world or parallel universe. This distant impression occasionally casts a shadow, forming several questions deep within, but the questions are as ambiguous as any potential answer. "Who am I? Why do I exist? Why am I here? Where did I come from?"

What plagues us even more than the questions isn't that we don't know the answers, rather, *we can't remember them.* In that transitory moment, the sensation is that "we should know whatever *that* is." Thus, these questions aren't formed from the unknown, but from the *once-known.* We ask because we want to *remember.* But it's not from a distant dream we attempt to invoke, *it's from a troubling dream we struggle to wake from.* We know within the core of our existence that upon waking, we'll remember, and upon remembering, we'll find the knowledge and wholeness we long for. To discover such isn't that we've found a primordial biological source code, but our *actual Source.* In seeking, we ultimately seem to know that if we connect to that Source, we connect to ourselves. You could say that to find the Source is to also remember *our true self.*

Living in this world truly isn't about politics, religion, wealth, or any such thing; it's about trying to grasp the memory we've always known, yet seems to allude us. It's as if being born into this world carries with it a dimly lit memory of a world forgotten. We're not just speaking of a prior life in this world, but a life from another realm. Yet something has happened where we essentially suffer from amnesia.

Mind you, simply being told one has amnesia doesn't restore the memory. In many cases, the one with amnesia doesn't even know they have it. They just know they "don't know" and are puzzled with a deep sense of missing something. Then add to the mix someone who calls them by name and says, *"I know you,"* (Jeremiah 1:5). Next come the pictures of family barbecues, wedding days, vacations, and the like, trying to stir the memory of a life seemly long ago or of another reality. Of course, depending upon how our ego manifests, we don't like admitting that we don't know, so we arrogantly say otherwise. Many times, we reject the notion that we don't remember because of the uncertainty it brings. Instead, we'd rather shape another existence, the illusion of the existence we have now, to ignore the gnawing apparitions. Nonetheless, regardless of how hard we try, the memories plague us like shadows we occasionally catch out of the corner of our eye. From the moment of our first breath to our last, living in this world is simply about a quest to remember and discover *who we always were.*

REFRESHER
IN THE BEGINNING AGAIN

Note: Throughout this book, when bold text or underlined text is found within scriptural references, they have been added by the author for focus and emphasis.

A Suggestion to the Reader

The purpose of this book is to further address the spiritual realization, both in a conceptual and practical manner, that was opened to us in the previous volume, *Melchizedek: Our Gracious King-Priesthood in Christ.* Previously, we laid out the spiritual paradigm of the Melchizedekian priesthood (of which our Lord Jesus Christ is a High Priest), which is in stark contrast to the Levitical priesthood and all religions in general. It is highly recommended for the reader to obtain a copy of the first book and prayerfully study its contents before proceeding. While this refresher chapter briefly summarizes a few key points of what was discussed extensively in the previous volume, it is not meant to be a replacement. It is only a refresher for those who have read book one or have heard its teachings from the author.

The key to all our Christian spirituality and our approach to the Bible comes down to this: **We need to be a Christ-centered people using the Bible as a tool,** *not* **a Bible-centered people hoping and assuming Christ will be a result.** The employment of the latter—being Bible-centered people hoping and assuming Christ will be a result—forms a lens through which we study, conceive, and consent, thus fabricating a misrepresentation of Christ. The result might wear the label of His name, but it's distant from His essence and character. Consider the multitudes throughout the last two thousand years whose lands were invaded, homes taken, and people enslaved, all in the name of Christendom. The irony is that each time this occurred, the so-called Christians had cause, right, and blessing from their god and holy book. While such things were done, the justification was, "We are not like those people who do bad things, we are Christians, we have God's blessing." Many times, with the compounded delusion, the Christians who erroneously supported the emperor (or chancellor, dictator, president, and so on) that led such atrocities would say, "They weren't like us, we know better! We have important teachers and prophets showing us the way." To the contrary, to be Christ-centered as the primary guidance unveils a completely different path to His likeness.

While we will explore the scriptures in this book, its purpose from start to finish is to discover the reality of our true self in Christ and Christ in us. His essence and reality are at the very core of who we are, which is the focal point. To start from anywhere else creates a distorted view of ourselves and God.

Refresher 1: The Dynamics of Biblical Interpretation

While there are several aspects to Biblical interpretation, there are five key aspects that have been practiced since the scripture was conceived and disseminated thousands of years ago.

The first is called *the principle of roots and branches.* This comes from the center of Hebraic thinking with the concept that the scripture is a spiritual document and, as the Apostle Paul states in 1 Corinthians 2:14-15, it must be *spiritually discerned.* The branch is the physical representation of a spiritual root. For example, when the scripture is speaking of a tree, it is not simply speaking of a physical tree, but the multifaceted spiritual properties a tree represents. Thus, the Tree of the Knowledge of Good and Evil has little to do with a physical tree once located somewhere in Mesopotamia. Rather, it's a perennial system representing a state of being that was a catalyst for the "Fall of Man" and our current physical existence. The key point is that the entire Bible, both Old and New Testaments, was written in this fashion. This is not to say that events didn't happen, like the story of Ishmael and Isaac, but they are also a depiction of branches relating to spiritual roots (or qualities). The Apostle Paul said it this way to his non-Hebrew-thinking audience:

"For it stands written, Abraham had two sons, one from the maidservant and one from the freewoman. But, on the one hand, the son of the maidservant was one born in the ordinary course of nature. On the other hand, the son of the freewoman was one born

*through the promise, **which class of things is allegorical.** For these are two covenants, one from Mount Sinai, begetting bondage, which is as to its nature classed as Hagar. Now this Hagar is Mount Sinai in Arabia, and corresponds to the Jerusalem which now is, for she is in bondage with her children. But the Jerusalem which is above is free, which is our Mother."*

(Galatians 4:22-26/Wuest)

The second aspect, which is built on the first, is known in Hebrew as the פרדס (PaRDeS). These are four levels of textual understanding with the intention of opening to us the highest of the four, where spiritual reality and the mysteries of God abide. The word פרדס (PaRDeS) is an acronym of the first letter of each of the four words that describe each level: פשט (p'shat) means *the simple* (or *literal*); רמז (remez) means *the hint;* דרש (d'rash) means *conceptual;* and finally, סוד (sod) means *mystery, hidden,* or *esoteric.* While most of us read the scripture in the literal sense, which is the *simple* approach (including the study of language and culture), we almost always seek, even inadvertently, the underlying *hint* of what it means. In other words, "How can I apply its meaning in my daily life?" However, divine truth and wisdom are not found merely in the simple or hint, but in the world of the *conceptual* and rooted in its source, *the mystery.* When we discover the mysteries of the Kingdom within us, it transforms our concepts of reality and, of course, our day-to-day application. Both Jesus and Paul made this clear, telling us to be overseers and knowers of such mysteries (Luke 8:10; 1 Corinthians 2:7, 4:1). If we come from the standpoint of taking Biblical texts literally and stop there, we might as well say to the Serpent in his tree, "Teach me, my lord." Remember, Jesus and Paul also warned us about falling into the trap of searching the scripture with only a literal or legal interpretation. Jesus warned us that when we take them literally, "we think we have eternal life" (John 8:39). In other words, we may think it, but we are only deluding ourselves. Worse yet, if we think we have life and egoistically delude ourselves, then when we use such knowledge, we do it from a standpoint of death. Paul said it plainly, "The letter or text alone kills" (2 Corinthians 3:6).

Albert Einstein made a profound statement: "No problem can be solved from the same level of consciousness that created it." Herein is the difference between religion and Christlikeness, and our propensity to try to mingle the two. As we pointed out in the prologue, God was clear that He didn't want us mingling both the Tree of Life and the Tree of the Knowledge of Good and Evil. Our consciousness must change and not merely our informational study. It can start with a simple heartfelt prayer like, "Father, open to me how to release my egoistic clutch on the Tree of the Knowledge of Good and Evil, and humbly embrace Christ's Tree of Life." (It may be beneficial to stop at this moment and pray that prayer or something similar.)

The simple and the hint levels point us in the direction of information and action, but they in themselves are not revelatory. Revelation comes from the hidden and disseminates downward through the conceptual, to the hint and the simple. This is evident when Peter tells Jesus that He is the Christ, the Son of the Living God (Matthew 16:13-20). Jesus responds to Peter saying that he received this revelation directly from the Father. Clearly, Peter wasn't doing any textual Torah study at the moment. Another way to consider this is that study will help give definition to the revelation we've encountered. The way revelation comes is through the humility of moving aside our inner egoistic curtain so we can see clearly what has always been right in front of us.

The third aspect is the logic of the scripture. In the western world, rooted in Greek culture, we use a process called Step Logic. The basic idea is that 1 + 1 = 2, 2 + 2 = 4, and so on. Like climbing steps, one concept is built upon the other. However, the Bible (in both Old and New Testaments) is written from an eastern mindset, whose logical process is called Block Logic. This form of logic can be best explained by a child's toy block. If we pick up a block with the letter *B* painted in red on one side, we find related ideas on each of the block's other sides: one side may have two red balls, another a cute red bear cub, another two red keys and a blue key, another with a red numeral two, and on the final side, a red boat. (Of course, there can be other relationships used in their place, these aren't exclusive, but most common.) The correlation between all the sides of the block is that all have a relationship to the letter *B* and thus are related to each other. For example, we have a cute red *bear* cub, because the word *bear* starts with the letter *B*, this also applies to the *boat.* Also, *B* is the second letter of the alphabet, so on another side we have the *numeral two*, and yet on another, *two balls* and *two* of the three keys colored red.

The concept of block logic is that each side tells a functional story about the whole. Thus, in Biblical logic, we cannot separate the mosaic of these correlations. While we can talk about the bear and the boat on each side, we must find the key focus of their relationship, which has nothing to do with one liking honey and the other floating in the ocean. When we read scripture with a step logic point of view, we rarely see the big picture and their correlations. Returning to our example, if we mix our logic, we'll see one side of the block having three keys, two colored red and one blue. So we find ourselves studying and discussing the meaning of the keys and aspects of their colors, rather than their relationship to the letter *B*. If these were Bible verses, we would take *the keys* literally, and through further linear logic study, look for color coded locks to go with them. Missing the point to a greater extent, if we can't find a matching lock side on the block, we assume that God is telling us to find locks on other blocks and see if the colors match. Of course, they don't. If there is a block with a single lock, it's painted green and is on the block with the letter *A*. So we develop a detailed theology of why red and blue keys are made to fit green locks, totally missing the point of the mystery of the letters. In the same way that we discussed the inappropriateness of imposing on God what is Caesar's and mingling the two Trees, it's treacherous to use step logic where forms of block logic are required.

The fourth aspect is grasping that the writers of the New Testament were spiritual Hebrew men who understood God,

Christ, and humanity from that point of view. They were not Greeks, nor were they avid proponents of Greek mythology, philosophy, logic, or its language. However, they understood to whom they were communicating, so they utilized the Greco-Roman worldview to disseminate their revelation. They found aspects of the mythology that fit their revelation and unfolded it to their audience. Unfortunately, in that crossover we can find ourselves stuck in a room of fractured mirrors. When our approach is from the Greco-Roman view, it overshadows the writer's mindset. In the same manner, this mindset isn't to be understood through, or confused with, the Jewish religion; the two are not necessarily the same. It's about a way of perceiving.

The fifth and final aspect are the languages and hermeneutics used to aid in our Biblical interpretation. For most of the Christian world, we read or preach from a translation of the scripture. Over the years, many scholars have done great work in this field, but there is still the old adage, "lost in translation." For those of us who preach or teach, we have a propensity to succumb to our cultural and linguistic world views, imposing them on what we read. Thus, we miss the universal, eternal, contextual views of the writings. While we need not be a scholar of the languages, a basic working knowledge of them, and more importantly, the philosophical and conceptual thinking of those languages, are important.

When I began studying Hebrew, I asked my Hebrew teacher if there was a good English translation that I could use for study purposes. He replied, "Trying to read the Hebrew scripture in another language is like trying to kiss your lover through a brick wall." A year later, I began to understand what he meant. It wasn't looking at the words on a page and translating them into English. It was about the multifaceted view of each letter, word, sentence, and concept that the logic opens. In addition to the language, the actual manuscripts themselves can be an issue, especially when it comes to the Greek New Testament. In some cases, there are significant variances. For example, in the scholarly work of Kurt and Barbara Aland's book, *The Text of the New Testament*, (considered the premier authorities on the subject), they point out these variances and their impact on translation. For example: across the known 300 or so Greek manuscripts of the Book of the Revelation, of the 405 verses, 214 are variant free. This means that 47.2% of the text has variances. In some cases, the changes are minor. However, there are also those where a small, yet significant word is different, drastically changing the meaning. This is why not only the translation used is an issue, but now we have to ask which of the Greek texts were used. In the end, the plumbline that gives us the ability to focus on meaning is what we referred to earlier as being Christ-centered in our interpretation.

Going back to the original point just prior to Refresher 1, the most important approach to our hermeneutics is what a fellow minister calls, "The Jesus Hermeneutic." In addition to the hermeneutical and textual approaches suggested above, the scripture must be viewed with the person of Jesus Christ as the fulcrum. For example, Jesus is very clear regarding the nature of His Father. While some religious views tend to make

27

the Father's actions punitive and retributive, Jesus shows us someone very different. Rather, Jesus brings us a view of the Father as having a justice that's restorative and redemptive.

In the final analysis, learning all these technical aspects are good. They have a way of forcing the intellect, emotions, and even our egos to relax a bit. This way, the potentially unsettling inner transformation and awareness can occur. Remember, new information is not in itself revelation and, in some cases, such *knowledge* can be just as misleading. Our self-centeredness, selfishness—thus our ego, in contrast to our true self, love, and selflessness—will determine the density of the filter of our consciousness and how we progress.

Refresher 2: The Nature of Creation

The physical universe as we perceive it with our five senses is not the fullness of creation. Actually, it's the consequence of what we normally call The Fall. Thus, this corporeal dimension is merely a thin illusion of what creation truly is, right down to the molecular and quantum levels. Some might even say that the quantum level leads us to the border of the upper world. It could be that string theory is the actual border. The proverbial Big Bang is a scientific suggestion of a fragment of limitless creation shattering into space, time, and matter. However, even the consequences of the Big Bang are still ultimately subject to our perception from our inner world. Notwithstanding, that same limitless creation existed long before the shattering (the Bang) and still exists beyond it. You could say that creation is the vastness of all God was, is, and shall be. Creation is the *I Am*, the eternal endless present. The physical world of space, time, and matter is a small consequence of our direct egoistic choice and involvement.

In broad terms, Creation is called *Eden,* meaning *paradise* or *pleasure.* It's an expression that fills all the pleasure the Infinite Creator freely gives. It's the countenance of who the Creator is. Eden wasn't a mere place or location on planet earth, but a state of being in which the non-fallen Creation exists and pre-fallen Creation existed. For Eden to come into being, the Creator, the ultimate Giver, the Source of all Life, had to first create a quality that was *complimentary* to Himself. Therefore, if the Creator is Love (1 John 4:16), whose essence is the Desire to Give (which we also call Light and Life), His first creative expression was to fashion the Desire to Receive. However, when we are conscious of the Tree of the Knowledge of Good and Evil, we usually think in terms of opposites like right/wrong, love/hate, faith/fear, joy/sorrow, and so on. This is not so in the Divine realm where the nature of God disseminates its handiwork. Rather, what may appear as contrasts actually *complement* each other. Thus, the Desire to Give/the Desire to Receive, masculine/feminine, image/likeness, day/night, and so on. Please note, the desires of giving and receiving (and all in between) are not simply human cravings as we currently know them. Eventually, they will become mere carnal desires based on our choice to unite with the Serpent, but not so in the world above. In the Divine realm, they are spiritual "organs" as vast and limitless as the Creator Himself. You could say that Eden is the spiritual

29

embodiment of God, with all its components intimately living, breathing, and beating together.

The most familiar Biblical names for these desires are *Heaven* and *Earth,* which appear in the first verses of Genesis. Heaven, as described in scripture, is giving (the branch to the root), bestowing the light of the sun, the atmosphere which the Creation breathes, and the rain which descends, nourishing the Earth and all within it. In the spiritual root, Heaven is a description of the extension or the giving of God. The word Earth is *the desire to receive pleasure.* It is Creation's reception of what Heaven gives and the returning of its intimate fruit. (Later it will become the broken or shattered aspect of Creation as described previously.) Earth is not a planet, though that's the name we ascribed to the planet we live on about 1000 years ago. The word *Earth* comes from middle English, rooted in the Old Saxon, High German, and Norse languages: *ertha, erda,* and *jorth.* It was related to the goddesses of those mythologies, not just barren land, or the third rock from the sun. Earth is a persona. In Hebraic description it's no different; Earth is a description of a living being. Even the Hebraic roots of the word *Earth* start with the concept of *the Desire to Receive,* which is also the Hebraic definition of "the Soul." Within that *Desire to Receive* was also a "choice" to either receive what the Creator is continually giving, and share it with Him in return, or to simply receive for *itself only.* In sharing and giving back, the Creature is like the Creator. Another way of saying this would be that it's given the choice of Mirroring the Creator, being an emanation of

Him and filling out all Creation in passionate intimacy with His Image and Likeness.

In the same manner that the Heavens bestow rain and the Earth receives it, these qualities are also described in masculine and feminine terms. The word Heaven, describing that which gives, is masculine, and Earth, describing that which receives and gives back, is feminine. The phrase opening the book of Genesis is, *"In the beginning God created..."* As discussed in the first volume, the Hebrew is descriptive of the masculine fattening (or impregnating) the feminine. This is a spiritual description (a root) using the physical analogy (a branch) of a man placing his seed within the womb of a woman and her reception of it. As it gestates, her womb fattens, or expands, as life grows within her. (You can see why in other mythologies, "earth" is a goddess. We will discuss this further later.)

Finally, we see the expression of this in the creature called *The Adam*. After all, The Adam (both masculine and feminine attributes) is created from the ground and is a recipient of the breath of God, which gives them life. The Adam is created with the right to choose to be God's Image (the word for *image* is masculine) and God's Likeness (the word for *likeness* is feminine). We are told God's Image and Likeness are both masculine and feminine, and together they emanate the Creator. These masculine and feminine qualities are not to be confused with physical bodies and their respective genitals. Such physical aspects don't come into the picture until after the Fall and, respectfully, have nothing to do with their

31

spiritual designation. It's interesting to note that when Jesus refers to God's ultimate intention in the World to Come and the restoration of all things, He says that there will be no marriage or giving in marriage (Luke 20:34-36). The point being, the Genesis creation account is not discussing corporeal forms, but spiritual qualities. Thus, Eden was (and still is) a state in which the Creator gives and the Creature/Creation receives and gives back again. This occurs over and over in the endless pleasure of Eternal Life.

Refresher 3: Transformation of Lucifer

The Genesis Creation story tells us that God separated the darkness from the light (Genesis 1:4). This has several ramifications, yet the central feature for such to occur is that aspect of Creation called *Lucifer.* Lucifer, the Latin word for the Hebrew הילל (helel), means *Daystar* or *Morning Star.* Genesis defines what this state of being means. Most of us in the world of lightbulbs, neon lights, and lasers believe that when you turn on a light, darkness is expelled, but this is not actually the case. If, like in the time when Moses was scribing the Torah, you were in the desert at night and it was so overcast that the moon and stars were completely obscured, you would be in total darkness. If you had a flashlight, as we do today, and pointed it into the sky or into the far distance, you would find that nothing had changed. Why? Because there is a quality, or *factor*, missing from the equation. If you pitched a tent in that same desert spot, entered it, and didn't turn on your flashlight, it would be just as dark inside as when you stood outside. In one respect, you might not even realize you were in the tent. However, if you turned on the flashlight while inside, you'd find the entire space was illuminated. Why? Because the light would reflect off the material that formed the tent walls, much like a projection screen.

Without the substance or quality for reflection, there is no illumination. This is a critical aspect of knowing our true self. This quality of reflection is called *Lucifer,* the *Daystar* or *Morning Star.* Another Biblical name for this screen creating the state of reflection is מָסָךְ (masach), as in Exodus 26:36. What gives substance to fashioning the screen is "the resilience" to transform *receiving for oneself alone* into the *Desire to Receive and Give.* In other words, it transforms the Ego and transfigures it with its *complimentary quality.* We see this screen מסך (masach) described in the New Testament as *the garment of humility* (1 Peter 5:5; James 4:6).

The *Desire to Receive* had the choice to either receive and reflect, or receive for itself only. *Lucifer* (Isaiah 14:12), *the Morning Star,* is the quality or state of reflection. In other words, if a screen is erected to reflect it, "the Light" is clearly seen and revealed. To take this a step further, not only is the Light being reflected, but also the Divine Image contained within its ray. Think of a cinema where the projector behind the audience shines a light on the screen in front of them. Within that beam of light are living images, people, plants, trees, buildings, and more. If the screen, or the wall behind it, were not present, there wouldn't be an image. If there was a disfigured screen, the image would also be disfigured. Consider what this means. The Desire to Receive can either

33

receive the Divine pleasure *selfishly* or *selflessly*. If it is resilient to the temptation to receive egoistically and instead shares it, all Creation fills with the Light and the Divine Image is revealed. On the other hand, if it receives the pleasure for itself only, there is no reflection and the result is darkness. Another way to say this is that the Divine Image is not visible, only the Ego. Another way to say this would be that the true identity of the Creature is not realized. This is why the Apostle Peter says:

> *"...you do well to heed as a light that shines in a dark place, until the day dawns and the Morning Star rises in your hearts."*   *(2 Peter 1:19/NKJV)*

This is not about the Devil living in or arising from our hearts, but the spiritual status of הֵילֵל (helel), reflecting the Image and Likeness of Christ. When we choose to raise the anti-egoistic screen within our hearts, the illumination and revelation of Christ is unveiled within us and throughout Creation.

Because of this, the initial Creature was given the choice to receive for itself only or to receive and reflect. Because it was in the state of being called Lucifer, it was receiving and reflecting. The moment that changed, so did the state of being. The scriptures tell us that eventually it decided to receive for itself alone. What was once a "vessel," a reflective screen מסך (masach) of Light, shattered into fragments. Thus, the reflection or visibility of the fulness of the Light was extinguished, except for the tiny flashes each of the incomplete fragments exhibited. Paul writes in Colossians that Christ is the fullness of the Godhead, and we are complete in Him (Colossians 2:9-10). Fast forward to Jesus Christ. He is the example of us individually, each part fully reflecting the Light. Christ is also our completeness as the whole, the מסך (masach), the collective of humanity fully revealing the Godhead to all Creation. When the Lucifer shattered, the "Earth," ארץ (eretz) stopped reflecting, and the Desire to Receive and Reflect became what we know as the Ego, Selfish Desire, Pride, and so on. This gave birth to its Hebraic etymologies, רץ (ratz) *fragment(s)*, רצץ (ratzatz) *broken vessel* and *oppression,* רצח (ratzach) *manslayer* and *murder,* and מרצה (m'rootzah) *violence.* Thus, a fragmented desire and a broken view of reality, including lust, greed, and violence, came into being.

From a physics point of view, if there is no reflective element at all, that state is called *true black.* But, because there are fragments of the shattered screen/vessel, we don't see true black. Rather, we see a blend of the fragments, which physics calls *generic black,* meaning there is still an aspect of light being reflected, although limited, fragmented, and chaotic. In the same manner, theoretical physicist Steven Hawking points out that even a black hole, which seemingly absorbs all light, still emits radiation at the quantum level. In Moses's day, when he was growing up in the Egyptian education system, there was no physics department discussing the theoretical vocabulary of quantum mechanics, yet the concepts were still there. When Moses wrote the Torah, he described the changing of this state from light to darkness using his known vocabulary, coupled with its native block logic. In his description, what remained was the fiery residue of the Light shattered into ash-like embers. This shattered selfish state is called הׁשׂטן (ha'satan), the Satan. The Creature that once reflected the Light is now like a spiritual black hole, absorbing everything for its own egoistic, selfish pleasure. Hence, the Satan *is the ultimate egoist,* unlike Christ, who is the expression of the Infinite God of Love and holds all Creation in union (Hebrews 1:3). The Satan, on the other hand, is selfish, self-gratifying, contentious, and divided (James 3:14-15). It's the Ego that tells us that we are separated from God, that there's blame to be placed, and that we're all independent from each other. It even fabricates a "distinctive devil," also separate, who afflicts and gives us a reason to make war. Yet the real Satan hides unnoticed behind the proverbial curtain, like the wizard in the Wizard of Oz. Remember when Dorothy, Scarecrow, Tin Man, and Cowardly Lion did as the Wizard requested and obtained the Wicked Witch of the West's broomstick? They returned with it, hoping for the help he promised, but instead got a vehement wizard who loudly bellowed not to bother him! While the imposing image shouted from illusions of flames and smoke, Dorothy's little dog, Toto, noticed a curtained room off to the side. With his mouth, Toto pulled back the curtain to reveal a small, pudgy, white-haired man operating machinery that controlled the large, fiery, green mock wizard. When the small, white-haired man realized what happened, he shouted into the microphone, "Pay no attention to that man behind the curtain!" In the same way, whenever we discover an egoistic aspect of ourself, it quickly *redirects* and *deflects* us to focus on something else. "Pay no attention to those egoistic, selfish desires! The devil is over there! They are the problem! It's that person and those people! Make war in the heavenlies, you got the power and authority! Break the power of the devil," hisses the Serpent.

When we awaken to our true self, we can no longer say the devil is doing this or doing that. Nor can we simply say that the devil is attacking me. The fundamental attacks or activities of "The Satan" in our lives are when we're being egoistic: self-serving, self-centered, self-justifying, and self-aggrandizing. Compound that idea with Jesus's point that when two or more are gathered together He is in the midst (Matthew 18:20). The Egoistic self is no different, it gathers with other egoistic factions to seek affirmation and self-righteousness. It gathers to assert its correctness and power. Forces are in the midst of such gatherings as well, whether we realize or not. For example, the Tower of Babel was a manifestation of egoistic desire, and as the scripture says regarding the Babylonians, "...nothing was restrained from them," (Genesis 11:1-6).

On a personal scale, much of our spiritual warfare is a reflection of our egoistic self. What we claim as an attack from Satan is, in most cases, an apparition of our own selfishness, later intensely mirrored back at us, And yes, it's hideous, even demonic. Both the Old and New Testament describes this as the principle of "Sowing and Reaping" (Proverbs 22:8; Galatians 6:7). So the next time there seems to be a hideous, demonic force attacking our life, we may need to take a spiritual step back and realize that instead, it could very well be what our ego looks like when it bears fruit.

Refresher 4: The Creation of "The Adam"

The Satan, now described as hot, burning ash of egoistic desire, is also called *"the dust of the ground"* in the book of Genesis. In Hebrew, the word אדמה (adamah), *ground,* is spelled the same as Lucifer's defiant proclamation in Isaiah 14:14, *"I will be like..."* The word עפר (aphar), *dust,* is also *ash* (Numbers 19:7; 2 Kings 23:4). In self-aggrandizement "to be like God," the illusion of independence and separation occurred. In that moment, in self-serving reception of Divine pleasure, the Creature, Lucifer, shattered. Once a whole vessel of reflective Light, it became egoistic fragments of selfishness and separation. Nonetheless, God continued the creative process and didn't leave His Creation in that state. He reached into the burning desire, breathed into it the Breath of Life, and the Adam came forth as a *Living Soul.* From a binary point of view, this could seem like a bad choice and an undoing of God's intention. From the view of Divine Life, it simply became part of the process.

The Adam, created as the Image and Likeness of God, with its masculine and feminine attributes, was commissioned in that likeness to do two things: first, *be who they are* and reflect the Light, thus filling Creation with the Divine Nature; second, *subdue* the egoistic desire. Why subdue? The Hebrew רדה (radah) means *to subjugate* and *to prevail against* (Judges 14:9), most known as *rule over, dominate,* or *dominion*

(Genesis 1:26). The Adam was to subdue and transform any selfish desire into gentle meekness (Matthew 5:5). In other words, receive the Light, Life, and Love of the Creator, and rather than keep it for himself alone, reflect it and share it with Creation. The Adam was to rule over the egoistic desire, not by might and power, but by *humble service* עֲבֹד (avad) (Genesis 2:5). In other words, consciously fashion the reflective screen, מָסָךְ (masach), and illuminate Creation. For a timeless eon the Adam did this. However, while subduing the egoistic desire and reflecting the Light, every encounter was faced with the choice to do either. In other words, every act of humble service and giving, large or small, comes from a choice. In Genesis this choice is portrayed at the center of the Garden in the figure of the Tree of Life, and the Tree of the Knowledge of Good and Evil with its coiled Serpent.

Before we can discuss the Trees, we must return and explore the significance of the spiritual qualities of the masculine and feminine. In the Genesis drama, the Serpent didn't speak to the woman because she was the weaker of the two, as many misapply a statement made by the Apostle Peter in his epistle (1 Peter 3:7). It's because of the Hebraic meaning of *female* נְקֵבָה (n'qeva), which by letter definition means *the seed of the horizon* or *future house.* The feminine is a picture of *the womb of the future.* (Remember the first verse of Genesis depicting the masculine fattening or impregnating the feminine). What the Ego was attempting to do was change the focus of Creation by affecting, or seeding, the future. At this point, it's good to note that the nature of God is the *Eternal Present,* which spans both past and future, yet not linearly, as in the world of time and space. The Eternal Present is defined this way:

> *"Grace to you and peace, from Him who is and who was and who is to come..."* *(Revelation 1:4/NASU)*

When we live in the Eternal Present, which is, was, and is to come, we live in true grace and peace. However, the Serpent-Ego refocuses us from the present, where the Great I AM abides, to the future or the past in linear fashion. For example, in this linear world of time and space, when we regularly contemplate the future, which from that view hasn't come into existence yet, we forget our I AM-ness and live in a phantom world hoping for, or fearing, tomorrow. Whether we realize it or not, even if we are "hoping for a better future," if such doesn't emerge from our identity in the Eternal Present, we're still living in a phantom world of illusion. In egoistic thought, this is no longer reflection, but *replacement.* When the feminine and her male counterpart received the egoistic seed, the Adam focused on an illusion of another reality. By choice, their Likeness was changed from Divinity to self-centeredness and separation. Now they reflected the Serpent and, as a result, transformed the Serpent into another form as well. The Serpent went from an existence coiled in the Tree to being stretched out on its belly on the ground. Hence, to the Adam, time and space changed from an eternal present in the World Above, to an elongated, linear experience in the World Below.

With the importance of the feminine quality as the future, it's critical to note that the Hebrew word for male, זכר (zachar), means *to remember the past.* When the fruit of the Tree was received by the female and passed along to her male counterpart, not only did the focus of the future change, but so did the view of the past. Thus, an illusion (called the *Death Sleep* in the first volume) came into being in lieu of Divine Reality. The physical world as we now perceive it became our certainty. Consequently, when we remember any of the past, we don't just remember an event or occurrence, but the story we create around it. Such memories and the stories we tell ourselves about them, refocus us, clouding the vague remembrance of our true self. Therefore, we no longer remember that we are the Likeness of the Creator, but a fabricated story we tell ourselves.

At that moment, the masculine and feminine qualities were altered, plunging into a binary/linear cosmos of right and wrong, good and evil, past and future, life and death. Rather than Creation being complementary, now it became contrary to itself. From that point, animals ate each other and humans killed each other. Herein is a noteworthy linguistic commentary we should point out. The word *serpent* in Hebrew is נחש (nachash), which is the same as *copper* or *brass.* In Numbers 21:9 and 2 Kings 18:4, the phrase *bronze serpent,* נחש הנחשת (nechash hon'choseth), is used. This phrase is the same word repeated one after the other, but with a modification. The first use of נחש (nechash) is in the masculine gender. The second, הנחשת (hon'choseth), is the same word but in the feminine gender. The masculine and feminine are now the echo of the Serpent's qualities. To take

41

the phrase further, the feminine usage denotes the glistening of the serpent's scales. The glistening, fiery scale segments refer to the shattered vessel mentioned earlier.

This egoistic illusion of the shattered union between God and the Adam, as well as the masculine and feminine qualities, is typified when the masculine says, *"It was the woman YOU gave me..."* (Genesis 3:12). Here the egoistic nature is revealed in full force. The masculine does the unthinkable; he justifies himself by accusing God and his female counterpart. He selfishly proclaims that his dilemma is the result of the actions of the woman, and faults God for giving her to him. What were once the Divine qualities of a united reflecting vessel become a seriously fragmented one.

Until this point, the Adam had one name with two qualities. After the Fall, the masculine retains the name Adam, but the female is given a new name, "Eternal-Life-Giver" (Genesis 3:20). [In the Septuagint, her name is literally **Ζωή** (Zoé), Eternal Life; later it's mistranslated as *Eve*. (The name *Eve* doesn't appear till Genesis 4:1)]. It's proclaimed that through the feminine, a birthing of Divine Life will come. Why? Because unlike the masculine quality who justified himself and accused both God and his counterpart, the feminine is honest, telling the truth to all, even at the expense of exposing her failure. Thus, this Truth-Bearer can also be a Life-Giver who will bring forth the *Divine Seed*. This Seed will crush the egoistic Serpent, which materialized through them both, and undo the viral qualities of accusation and self-justification with compassion. What will be birthed through her is a version of the masculine, born from the glimmering Light that

42

remained (Genesis 3:15), the qualities of a Truth-Bearer and Life-Giver, the Christ, the Dayspring (Luke 1:76-79).

CHAPTER 1
MELCHIZEDEK "OUR GRACIOUS KING-PRIESTHOOD IN CHRIST"

"Joy, beautiful spark of Divinity,
Daughter from Elysium,
We enter, drunk with fire,
Heavenly One, thy sanctuary!
Your magic binds again
What custom strictly divided;
All people become brothers,
Where Your gentle wing abides."
An die Freude (Ode to Joy) Verse 1
Friedrich Schiller
(Symphony #9: Movement 4 "Recitative"
Ludwig van Beethoven)

How we perceive God determines how we perceive ourselves and reality. With that in mind, the stories we tell within ourselves about reality effect how we perceive and navigate this existence. In a dream-like illusion since the Fall, the Serpentine Ego has become part of the winding stream of our thoughts. It's ever telling us stories of our virtue and depravity, our worth and worthlessness. With equal intensity, it coils within our minds with a poised extended finger, or better said, serpent-like fang, with tail rattling toward others. With each sizzling rattle it sizes up the other and evaluates them, culminating with definitive judgments and verdicts. It guards our hidden, unacknowledged inner frailties, ready to lunge for our protection. More so, when the other is properly evaluated, it secures our illusion of superiority, temporarily easing our underlying dread. This winding and coiling of our thought life also makes up stories about what once happened rather than what actually happened. It reinterprets what is happening into what could happen, becoming our prospect of reality. Then we rename this view "the truth." This serpentine truth becomes our world, the source of our certainty and, in many cases, the definition of our god, or lack thereof.

In this acceptance of the surreal world, an occasional apparition appears. It doesn't fit the narrative, though it speaks. It's that distant sound or illusive figure in the mist. Quickly, we disregard it, saying our mind is playing tricks. In some occurrences, we try to grasp what we see and hear, only for it to fade into the swirl of our coiled illusion. Yet, this apparition is the most unchangeable truth, piercing through our contrived certainty. You could say these occurrences are a momentary awakening from our unconsciousness. In those moments we may hear a voice say:

> "The Amen, the witness who is faithful and true, the originator of God's creation, says this…"
>
> (Revelation 3:14/ISV)

Herein is the antidote of our Death Sleep. When we yield to, rather than attempt to grasp, this apparition, we will say as King David, *"My ears you have opened,"* (Psalms 40:6). The irony of these occurrences is that in most cases they are not external hauntings, but internal projections. As mentioned in the previous volume, we see this occur when Abram and Bera, the King of Sodom, were discussing what to do with the spoils of war. Seemingly out of nowhere, the King of Salem, Melchizedek, appears and speaks with Abram (Genesis 14:17-24). It's as if the entire discussion between Bera and Abram is interrupted. Abram communes with Melchizedek, then refocuses and continues to speak with Bera. What's odd is that Bera seems to have no awareness of Melchizedek's presence, nor is a participant in the conversation. It's as if Abram left the world of time and space and entered a world where there is no beginning of days nor end of life. To say this another way, it's as if Abram left the world of flesh and linear time, and entered the Eternal Now; the I AM. The result of this moment sets in motion a covenantal relationship with Abram and God Most High, which changes everything Mankind knew about God and how they relate to Him. For example, prior to this conversation the Torah said:

"The Lord had said to Abram..." (Genesis 12:1/NIV)

But immediately after Abram's encounter with Melchizedek it says:

"After this, the word of the Lord came to Abram in a vision..."   *(Genesis 15:1/NIV)*

Now it's not just a voice, it's *"the Word of the Lord"* and it *"came in a vision."* Something clearly changed. This apparition and his priesthood are the antitoxin of the dream world of illusion, and the awakening to true consciousness. Like Morpheus in the 1999 film *The Matrix*, this priesthood offers all a choice. *"You take the blue pill—the story ends, you wake up in your bed and believe whatever you want to believe. You take the red pill—you stay in Wonderland, and I show you how deep the rabbit hole goes. Remember: all I'm offering is the truth. Nothing more."* Like taking the red pill, the Melchizedekian priesthood unveils the Eternal Creator, the Tree of Life, and *our true self in Christ.* It's the remedy through which we unravel ourselves from the coiled egoistic stories we believed. It anoints our eyes with eye salve (Revelation 3:18) so we can see reality as it truly is.

For many in Christendom today, the Gospel is the story that's comprised of four books in the New Testament, with added epistles as revelatory commentary. We reenact those Gospels, we make films about them, perform musicals of them, write songs, and of course, tell more stories. While in and of itself the New Testament is a spiritual account of the Christ and has the qualities to guide us to awakening, we can still just simply "know the stories" and sleep in the dream world of religion. Similar to our waking in bed in the morning, we have the choice to rouse ourselves and get up, or simply turn over and go back to sleep. The alternative before us is another choice between the two Trees in the Garden. When we were conscious in the Garden, we had the option to choose Life, something we were experientially familiar with. In contrast, we also had the option of the Tree of the Knowledge of Good and Evil, which was something we had no awareness of, nor its consequence. One may say, "But God said to them, if they ate of it they would surely die." But what does death mean to someone who has never seen or experienced it? It's like trying to explain the color green to someone who has never seen it, or the sound of a Glockenspiel to someone who has never heard it. You can try to relate it to something. "Do you know the color blue or yellow? Yes? Well, if you put the two colors together... No, it has nothing to do with blue and yellow stripes." Or, "Do you know what a xylophone sounds like?" *Sigh...* "No, it has nothing to do with a telephone." The same is true with the Gospel of Christ. There is almost nothing in this world that one can relate it to. We can't point to the good in the Tree of the Knowledge of Good and Evil and say, "Christ is like that," since even Jesus made the point that He isn't "good" because He is not of that system of thinking (Matthew 19:17; Mark 10:18; Luke 18:19). For Jesus to point the way to the Good News (the Gospel), He first asks one who called Him good if he keeps the commandments. When the person responds with, "I keep them all," Jesus tells him, "Sell everything you have, give to the poor, and follow me," (Matthew 19:21; Mark 10:21; Luke 18:22). Wait...What? Sell our possessions, then give all the money away? That's not a commandment, that's not even mentioned in any of the 613! Which is the point. It isn't about doing good, which seemingly makes one good, but being empty of both good and evil and being a Life-Giver.

49

In the egoistic world of the knowledge of good and evil, we are faced with a similar choice. In our dream-like state, when the Gospel of Grace breaks through as a surreal apparition, we are faced with a choice once again. Either we turn over, continue our dream, and dismiss the moment, or a new desire is stirred and we rouse for a glimpse of consciousness. However, it's easy to simply dismiss the apparition and alter our dream. So we roll over and continue our illusion, now with added stories of a Jesus religion and its morality. We point to a savior who forgives our past moral failures yet enforces that we continue in good works of faith to keep our blessings and relationship. Sounds good! But it isn't Christ.

There is a positive aspect to all this. The momentary glimpse we had has pierced our dream world, and like an antibiotic taking effect little by little, it stirs us again and again. Sometimes, this stirring can occur in the most unsettling of ways. There are moments of consciousness that occur, which at first we may respond to adversely. Nonetheless, these moments rouse a sense of déjà vu. These distant memories can engender more questions than answers, seriously unsettling our sense of religious certainty, so we try to suppress them. Yet something significant has happened. A desire has arisen, not so much to know, but to be aware. Therein is the first real conflict. Because of our egoistic identity, we want "to know" rather than be "aware." Being *aware* requires sensors we are not accustomed to using. Nonetheless, they are stirring. It's like experiencing cognitive sight for the first time.

In the end, Life will have its way. When it comes to grasping our own awakening, you could say there are some who are more conscious than others. As we become conscious, this is where a type of real *spiritual warfare* abides, to borrow a phrase highly misused in Christendom. It's the inner struggle between the ego's desire to know, giving way to our true identity's resting in Divine awareness. The result is the transformation of how and why we begin to perceive reality differently. This is not about doing more right things than others or obeying the rules more perfectly. Nor is it about being more committed, more loyal, or more dedicated. Nor is it about praying longer in tongues, prophesying more frequently, or healing through the laying on of hands. It's about becoming conscious, becoming awake. All of humanity is in some stage of the process. Some are still primarily asleep. Others are tossing and turning, egoistically doing all they can not to open their eyes. Some are stirring with momentary glimpses of reality and then falling back asleep for a season. Some open their eyes, while still lying down, and groggily try to sort out what's happening and where they are. Some will sit up, and with fuzzy consciousness, accept the Divine world, even if they don't fully grasp what it affords them. Then there are the few who will actually stand and decide to walk in the unveiling awareness of Christ. When one truly starts to recognize this measure of consciousness, what comes along with it is another sense called *selfless compassion*. It's through this sense of compassion that an understanding emerges, an understanding that there are those who are yet to awaken, or are in some aspect of awakening. Here the ego's false identity, which once held its quantifying tool of evaluating others through *morality*, is replaced by our true Divine identity, which quantifies through *Divine compassion*. While those who are conscious give this compassion to all, the anomaly is that it's more overtly seen toward those who sleep or are early in their awakening. Looking to Jesus, we find this to be dynamically true. While He was stern with the Pharisaical (those who were asleep, yet egoistically claimed to be awake - John 9:41), it was born from a compassion that was resolved in giving its life for their transformation. Thus, rather than enter a moral conflict with religious values, Jesus allowed Himself to be crucified. While He had the supernatural power to stop the crucifixion, He yielded to the higher power of *compassion* for the sake of the ones who murdered Him. To the egoistic or religious mind, this is seen with horror. "How could they have murdered the one who loved them?" But the Divine mind sees this very differently. It's moved by compassion, aware that through this surrender of love can come redemption, transformation, and wholeness to the very ones that desired murder. In the economy of the spiritual world, such restoration could come no other way.

As a wonderful friend of mine once said, "Jesus is not an example for us, *He is an example of us.*" While those statements may sound repetitious, they are quite different and understanding the difference can aid the stirring of the Divine memory within us. When someone is an example *for us*, they show us who we can possibly be. By comparison, they become the standard by which we judge ourselves and others. They are the distinction of what we are not, and perhaps who we could or should be. Their exemplary illustration divulges our delinquency. Please note the words: standard, distinction, contrast, delinquency, and judge. None of these words are in the vocabulary of Jesus in the Gospels. Jesus never came to show us His perfection or point out our lack of it, either directly or indirectly. In God's reality, Jesus is an example *of us.* He shows us who we are, nothing else, irrespective of what stories we tell ourselves. For that matter, Jesus adds, "What I do even greater shall you do!" (John 14:12). Think of it, He doesn't just reveal who we are, He says we can even do and be greater! He becomes the agent through which our true selves are unveiled. He focuses on the opening of our hearts to who we are. In other words, it results in us unbecoming who we're not. Like the two trees in the Garden, the Tree of the Knowledge of Good and Evil forms contrasts, the Tree of Life displays empowering regard. You could say, the first shows *otherness,* while the second reveals *oneness.* Such oneness is the central aspect of the Gospel of Jesus. Yet, the violence of *otherness* is apparent. One may think that the revelation of Christ is met with joyous acceptance, but the serpentine ego within us is not that yielding. Rather, many times such Divinity is met with horrific violence (Matthew 11:12). Though we may have perceived that the writers of the New Testament intentionally used contrasts, we may want to reconsider what was actually being said. Because we live in a knowledge of good and evil system, it may appear that we begin with contrasts. However, eventually that view changes and becomes all encompassing, something we perceive with an appended set of eyes.

Part 1: The Melchizedekian Priesthood and Violent Response

In Classe, Italy (near Ravenna) is the Basilica of Sant'Apollinare Nuovo. It was built early in Christian history around 504 AD and was developed over 100 years. During those years, wonderful mosaics were fashioned in the Basilica. One key mosaic stands out which speaks to our topic. It's one of very few, and possibly the first, early Christian depictions of the high-priest, Melchizedek.

As with the art of that period, besides having the typical pictography of characters in a known story, there are additions suggesting a deeper or expanded meaning. On the left is Abel presenting the gift of a lamb to Melchizedek. In addition to the regular attire of his day, Abel is also wearing a priestly chasuble (something not mentioned in the biblical text). Based on the design, it depicts that he is giving the

54

offering as a priest himself under Melchizedekian authority. To the right is Abraham with Isaac. Knowing the biblical account of Abraham offering Isaac, what is not shown is a dagger prepared to strike or the ram from the thicket. In addition, Abraham is dressed as a Roman senator, bearing the senatorial shoulder-to-hem stripe. Of course, he was not a Roman, as Rome didn't exist in the days of Abraham. However, it's depicted in the iconography of the period to make a point to the culture of its time. In other words, it presents information in a way the observer would understand. Dressing Abraham as a ruler signified that this king-priesthood had great authority yet submitted to Melchizedek. At the top left, over Melchizedek's right shoulder, is the hand of God, symbolizing Divine participation. In the center is Melchizedek himself who, rather than receiving the blood of Abel's lamb or Abraham's sacrificial ram substitute, is breaking bread before a chalice of wine. Key point, there is no bloodshed in this mosaic. Why?

All this culminates around Bishop Sant'Apollinare, of whom the basilica is named. As Church history records it, he was made the bishop of Ravenna by the Apostle Peter himself. He walked in the power of the Holy Spirit with healing, signs, and wonders, evangelizing intently. The irony of his ministry is that one would expect he'd be wonderfully received by his contemporaries with his message of grace and healing. To the contrary, he was severely persecuted. He was beaten in the mouth with stones, cut with knives, and had scalding water poured over his wounds. Again, *why?*

Melchizedek isn't just a biblical character who ambiguously appears, meets with Abram (Abraham) in Genesis 14, then disappears and isn't heard from again. Rather, 1,000 years later, he is briefly mentioned by King David in Psalm 110. Then, another 1000 years later, he uncannily reappears in the New Testament book of Hebrews in chapters 5-7. In Judaism, some speculate that Melchizedek was probably Shem, the son of Noah, which wouldn't match the New Testament description, to say the least. We also find Melchizedek appearing in the recently discovered Dead Sea scrolls, the Nag Hammadi texts, the writings of Philo of Alexandria, and the Book of Enoch in a rather extraordinary way.

What is intriguing about the Book of Enoch's account (written approximately 300 BCE, hundreds of years before Jesus ever walked the earth), is that Noah's brother's wife, Sopanim, barren her whole life, gets *miraculously pregnant* in her old age. We see a parallel to the Gospel of Luke, which describes Elizabeth, wife of the priest Zechariah, miraculously pregnant in her old age. While it's not defined as an immaculate conception (like Mary) or that Nir (Noah's brother) is the father, it is miraculous in that it's unknown to the family as to how it happened. In fear and embarrassment, Sopanim hides herself from both family and community. When Nir finds out, he is disgraced, rebukes her sharply, and sends her into exile. When he does, she collapses and dies, apparently from the trauma and her age. They bury her in a black shroud and hide her in a secret grave to avoid public shame. Then, the most uncanny miracle occurs: the child within her womb doesn't die. Fully developed, the infant is born in the grave from its dead mother! In terror, both Noah and Nir realize this is the work of the Lord and name the child Melchizedek. They then prophetically proclaim that he is to be the head of the thirteen Divine priests in the Heavens and that later there will be another type of Melchizedek who will be archpriest over twelve more. (Sound familiar? Remember this was written several hundred years before the birth of Jesus.) Forty days after the birth, the child is taken up to heaven by Michael the archangel, while the Lord proclaims, "My child, Melchizedek."

So why in the basilica mosaic is there no blood sacrifice before Melchizedek? Why was the bishop whom after the basilica was named treated so horribly? Why, 300 years before Jesus ever walked the earth, does the strange tale of Melchizedek's birth have an apparently accurate prophetic view of the coming Christ and His twelve apostles? As we further discuss the order of Melchizedek from a Christ-centered vantage point, there will emerge a compelling, plausible answer. In the first volume we endeavored to expound on the theology of the Melchizedekian (Christ) priesthood, contrasting it to religion as exemplified in the Levitical priesthood. In this volume, as we continue with a similar idea, we intend to expound on it in broader terms and concentrate on its spirituality.

Part 2: The Priesthood From Forever

"And having been perfected, He became the author of eternal salvation to all who obey Him, called by God as High Priest 'according to the order of Melchizedek,' of whom we have much to say, and

57

hard to explain, since you have become dull of
hearing."   *(Hebrews 5:9-10/NKJV)*

Once again at the outset, we must take in the phrase, *"...of whom we have much to say, and hard to explain..."* This priesthood is as vast as the Eternal God it represents. Yet it's not easily explained because "the Ego" and "the Knowledge of Good and Evil" tend to veil its reality. This priesthood is more than just an iconic representation of a deity with temples, commandments, rituals, and symbolic garments. It's one adorned with the Eternal Itself, which is why Jesus didn't wear the formal attire of a priest; the Divine presence was and is His attire. Some would say His attire was the anointing, which would be correct, but the notion of pouring oil over someone or something still has more of a symbolic representation, where the true Melchizedekian garment doesn't abide in the symbolic. Its garment exists in spiritual reality, thus the statement, *"...He became the author of eternal salvation..."* The Christ became the author of eternal salvation because He was from the eternal.

As Jesus said:

"You are from beneath; I am from above. You are of
this world; I am not of this world." (John 8:23/NKJV)

He came from true reality, the eternal realm of forever, and manifested in this physical world. For that matter, He did not ascribe to this world in the same way the pagan, Greek, or Jewish religions did. Rather, He ascribed Himself to another system, even though He was in this physical world. Keep in mind, the notion of *the world* is not about a planet but the cosmos, or system of the Tree of the Knowledge of Good and Evil. The weightiest manifestation of the Ego and its Knowledge of Good and Evil system is the physical world as we know it. This is why the incarnation is so important. The central idea is that we can live in this world and not be subjected to its system, hence, the Melchizedekian priesthood. While the Levitical priesthood revealed only a shadow, a veiled reference to the existence or status of Divinity, Christ maintained complete connection with the upper realm. Therefore, even the crucifixion could not silence Him. The resurrection was the inevitable result! Our system of death could not silence, sacrifice, or kill such a Divine Life. Christ came from forever and continues forever.

> *"This hope we have as an anchor of the soul, both sure and steadfast, and which enters the Presence behind the veil, where the forerunner has entered for us, even Jesus, having become High Priest forever according to the order of Melchizedek."*
>
> *(Hebrews 6:19-20/NKJV)*

The Apostle continues with a powerful statement, *"This hope we have as an anchor of the soul..."* This hope, comprised of two immutable things: that God cannot lie and that Christ as high priest after the order of Melchizedek entered in beyond the veil as the forerunner of those who would follow of the same order. The veil is defined in the epistle as the flesh (Hebrews 10:20). This culminates in the idea that Christ, our

Melchizedekian high priest, anchors us so we are not drifting or tossed about with the egoistic desires of the system of the Knowledge of Good and Evil. By anchoring humanity in the system of Life, the serpentine egoistic illusions of separation and independence cannot prevail any more than the crucifixion could. Our eternal existence is forever anchored in Christ, not in our knowledge of right and wrong, good and evil. To say this in another fashion, it's not found in our performance of good and resistance of evil, nor in bloody sacrifices and ceremonial rituals, nor in laws redefined as Christianized rules.

> *"This Melchizedek was king of Salem and priest of God Most High. He met Abraham returning from the defeat of the kings and blessed him, and Abraham gave him a tenth of everything. First, his name means 'king of righteousness'; then also, 'king of Salem' means 'king of peace.' Without father or mother, without genealogy, without beginning of days or end of life, like the Son of God he remains a priest forever."*   *(Hebrews 7:1-3/NIV)*

Before we proceed there are two misnomers about these verses we should clear up. The first is, *"...Abraham returning from the defeat of the kings..."* The King James version has a closer translation rather than the word *defeat,* which is *slaughter.* The Greek word is **κοπῆς** (kopes), which literally means *carnage* or *to cut up in pieces.* The idea that Melchizedek, as the representative of יהוה God Most High, would approach Abraham with the bread and wine, sets the tone for the transformation happening in Abraham's life. Melchizedek comes as the "King of Peace," not a general of war. For that matter, in the future Abraham will never go to war again. Instead, he learns who God is and who he is in God. A few chapters later in Genesis, rather than taking pleasure in the destruction of a sinful people, we find Abraham interceding for Sodom and Gomorrah's preservation, which is the divine point and a lesson learned.

The second issue occurs in the actual account in Genesis:

> *"And he blessed him and said: 'Blessed be Abram of God Most High, possessor of heaven and earth; and blessed be God Most High, Who has delivered your enemies into your hand.' And he gave him a tithe of all."* (Genesis 14:19-20/NKJV)

The phrase *"...Who has delivered your enemies into your hand"* is another one of those Hebraic block logic roots and branches, double entendre declarations:

אשר מגן צריך בידך

(asher miggeen tzareyka b'yahdeka)

"...which to hand to another your tightness in your hand."

Abraham was a rich man. His family made lots of money selling idols in the land of the Chaldees, and when they departed, they left with abundance. Yet he is now a follower of יהוה who is very different in nature. God Most High was unveiling His character within Abraham. If we let the verses say what they say, the word we translate as *your enemies,* צריך (tzareyka), can also be translated *your tightness* (see Numbers 22:26 CJB; some translations use *narrow).* The next phrase of the verse is, *"And he gave him a tithe of all."* God really wasn't freeing Lot from the fallout of war with the King of Sodom. He was transforming Abraham from being a miser into a giver. The picture of the Hebrew letters and language paint a mural of a tightly closed hand, now willingly opened and giving from one to another, like the Creator. This undeniably points to the words of Jesus we mentioned earlier, *"Sell all you have, give to the poor, and follow Me."* Once again, the concept of roots and branches comes through. The REAL enemy foiled here was not an evil king that wanted to conquer the area, but the tightness of Abraham's hand. Listen to the thoughts in the next verse and see how it opens what we are saying in a much deeper way:

> *"Now the king of Sodom said to Abram, 'Give me the persons, and take the goods for yourself.' But Abram said to the king of Sodom, 'I have raised my hand to the Lord, God Most High, the Possessor of heaven and earth, that I will take nothing, from a thread to a sandal strap, and that I will not take anything that is yours, lest you should say, 'I have made Abram rich'."*   *(Genesis 14:21-23/NKJV)*

At this point, Abraham (Abram) is very clear; he has raised his OPEN hand to the Lord. He was not going to take (which is a closed, tight hand) from Sodom. Rather, he was willing to give all the people and their goods back. Why? Because something was changing. He was not going to allow the King of Sodom to say that war and victory made Abraham rich. Abraham was aligning himself with the nature of God Most High, the King of Peace, trusting יהוה as his source of supply. Why is this important? Because if we stay in the view of the branch form, we miss the point of what is really happening in the upper world. If we just stay in the purview of good guys winning and bad guys losing, we are veiled by the Tree of the Knowledge of Good and Evil. This is about the unveiling of God Most High within the heart of Abraham which, for all intents and purposes, is the garment of the Melchizedekian priesthood. Just like anyone who walks the journey with Christ, our minds are transformed (Romans 12:2). To make a final point, God never told Abraham to get involved and conquer the kings of war to liberate Lot and his family. As noble as it seemed, Abraham did this on his own. In the end, Lot and his family remained in liberated Sodom and things got worse. In one respect, winning the war didn't change anything in Sodom. Eventually Abraham learned a valuable lesson. He went from being a man of war and carnage, to finding himself under a tree with three supernatural beings and interceding for the preservation of Sodom, a place that, not so long ago, he was willing to devastate with war. The events surrounding Abraham were not as much about the deeds of God for judgment or blessing, but the unveiling of God in and through Abraham. Consider, Abraham was an idol maker who became a true worshipper. He was a man of war who became a man of peace. He was a miser who became a giver. He was a man of condemnation who became a man of mercy. He was a man of fleshly deeds who became a man of faith.

The words of Hebrews 7:3 makes it very clear. It changes any preconceived idea that the Melchizedekian priesthood is from any physical origin, any relationship to a particular bloodline, genealogy, and mortal birth or death. It unashamedly declares that this priesthood is of the eternal, upper worlds, or as Jesus declared, *"...from above."* It's made in the likeness of the Son of God, who remains a priest forever. The power of this declaration is also an invitation. It invites humanity to enter its original form of eternal Divine Likeness. It does not matter what physical lineage any man or woman has. It does not matter the religious origins of anyone who approaches. It does not matter, their gender, marital status, race, social class, sexual orientation, and on we could go. To summarize, it doesn't matter that we are from the egoistic, serpentine cosmos of the Tree of the Knowledge of Good and Evil and its multifaceted forms. What matters is that we are offered the choice to change our orientation from that system of Death and put on the eternal garment of Life, our true identity, which is the likeness of the Son of God.

> *"Now if perfection had been attainable through the Levitical priesthood (for under it the people received the law), what further need would there have been for another priest to arise after the order of Melchizedek, rather than one named after the order of Aaron? For when there is a change in the*

priesthood, there is necessarily a change in the law
as well."   *(Hebrews 7:11-12/ESV)*

The change in priesthood demands a change in its law. The phrase, *"Now if perfection had been attainable...what further need would there have been for another priest to arise..."* declares something so profound that if every person who claims Christ truly practiced what this means, it would change everything in the known evangelical world and beyond to radical proportions. The priesthood is what superimposes its practice over the law. Now that the priesthood has changed so has its practice. To put it in explicit terms, the Levitical priesthood, its Law with its 613 commandments, its temple, and its paganistic blood sacrifices, have nothing to do with the practice of the order of Melchizedek. The new, yet original priesthood of Melchizedek has a completely different commandment. What's mind boggling is that the new "so-called law" is not something that can be performed as a ritual, an attained achievement, or obedient practice; it has to originate from one's nature.

"A new commandment I give to you, that you love
one another; as I have loved you, that you also love
one another."   *(John 13:34/NKJV)*

That about says it. The commandment is surprisingly not a commandment. We cannot be commanded to love. If we love simply because we're told to, it's not really love at all, it's just following a ritual or being obedient to a rule. This so-called commandment is being turned inside out and on its ear. What

Jesus is telling us is something which is an emergence of one's nature or desire for others. Remember what Melchizedek said to Abraham, and Jesus said to the rich young ruler. Let's think this through. If we are commanded to give to the poor and do so, the underlying concern is not about the poor, but the necessity to obey, even if we've convinced our religious self that obeying is a way of loving God. A more base response is the egoistic desire resulting in the consequence from the fear of disobedience. This takes us right back to knowing good or evil in the simplest form, fear, and the very thing such knowing empowers (Genesis 3:10). On the contrary, love is an emanation of one's nature, and more so, an unveiling of the nature of God (1 John 4:16); it's the point to the entire Melchizedekian priesthood. Thus, you cannot "choose" to love. Love is something you are. God doesn't choose to love, He is Love. God gives because He is Love. What Jesus is telling us is, "Be love, as I AM Love. That being so, you will love one another." The writer of the epistle takes this notion even further, if one can imagine.

> *"And it is yet far more evident if, in the likeness of Melchizedek, there arises another priest who has come, not according to the law of a fleshly commandment, but according to the power of an endless life. For He testifies: 'You are a priest forever according to the order of Melchizedek.' For on the one hand there is an annulling of the former commandment because of its weakness and unprofitableness, for the law made nothing perfect; on the other hand, there is the bringing in of a better*

hope, through which we draw near to God."
(Hebrews 7:15-19/NKJV)

The above statement once again dismisses the notion of bloodlines and genealogies. It even translates the phrase quite accurately, **νόμον ἐντολῆς σαρκίνης** (nomon entoles sarkines), *a law commandment [of the] flesh.* Therefore, the law with its covenant is disannulled in its entirety (Hebrews 8:13). The new covenant of love, emanating from the world of forever through an endless life, makes the former obsolete, resulting in the transmigration from the cosmos of the Tree of the Knowledge of Good and Evil, from which the Law derives its power, to the cosmos of the Tree of Life, who is the Christ and from which the order of Melchizedek originates. The only recourse for the former is to be obsolete by it vanishing from the consciousness of our hearts. This, in the most literal sense, is the *annulling.*

In the Melchizedekian order, we *only* see bread and wine. It's a Life-Giving priesthood which came from *endless forever* and continues in *endless forever.* Therefore, there are no bloodlettings or sacrifices in its order. On the other hand, in the Levitical order (like pagan priesthoods), we have the blood of bulls, goats, and lambs, with the inevitable culmination in human sacrifice. Unlike the Melchizedekian priesthood, it comes from death and begets death. Herein then is the looming question: How did we depart from a view of God as the Creator of Life, the Eternal Father, later revealed through Christ (the Light) and empowered by the Holy Spirit, to a god or gods of blood sacrifice, condemnation, judgment, and eternal damnation?

CHAPTER 2
THE RECIPE OF DEATH: LOST IN THE FOREST THROUGH THE TREES (A FINAL REFRESHER)

"Men once we were, and now are changed to trees;
indeed, thy hand should be more pitiful,
even if the souls of serpents we had been."
The Divine Comedy, Inferno
Canto XIII, 37-39
Dante Alighieri

Having explored the refreshers in the prologue and the basic explanation of the Melchizedekian priesthood in the previous chapter, it makes sense to focus on this particular refresher as a chapter in itself. When we think of all that Christ has done through His appearance, life, death, burial, and resurrection, we cannot help but point to why. Why would the limitless, eternal Christ come in human form? The cause is as important as the manifestation itself. The one is the catalyst of the other. For all that follows in scripture, this timeless primordial event in the Garden of Eden sets the stage for all that unfolds. For all the rules, laws, rituals, and traditions that we in Christendom have fabricated, we've gotten lost in the forest of religion. Our propensity to describe the events in the Garden as we do presents a misfocus to the key realities at the center, the two Trees. More specifically, the Tree of the Knowledge of Good and Evil. It is imperative that we understand the origin of what caused the loss of Paradise. Without clarity and surety of this single, initial occurrence, all that follows in our discernment, perception, and logic becomes disfigured and skewed.

Part 1: The Primordial Slaughter

"All who dwell on the earth will worship him, whose names have not been written in the Book of Life of the Lamb slain from the foundation of the world."

(Revelation 13:8/NKJV)

John of Patmos states that the Lamb was slain from the foundation of the world. Literally, the Greek text states: *"...the Lamb murdered from the unseating of the authority of the cosmos."* Some interpret this verse as meaning that, before the Fall took place, God in His foreknowledge saw that it would occur and had the notion of sending His Son as a sacrificial solution. But the implication of God "in his foreknowledge" sending His Son as a sacrificial offering creates several problematic insinuations. The text speaks rather horrifically of what occurred, not just a fond notion of a Father sending His favorite Son to solve a serious problem at some future time. Remember, the **λόγος** (Logos), the Divine Thought, who is also called the Living Word, doesn't just ponder thoughts and then create. *His thought is Creation.* Unlike humanity in its current state, we may ponder many ways something can be done long before we act. Hence, we think the only thing that matters is what we do physically. Yet, it's different in spiritual reality, and for the Divine mind it's very different. *His thought is the action!* For example, Jesus tells us how the spiritual world functions when He states that if we lust after a person, we've already done the deed in our heart (Matthew 5:28). *Thoughts are actions in the spiritual world.* Thus, when the Trinity thinks, They create. For that matter, when we ponder all the ways we can do something in the physical, we have already done them many times in the spirit, though we only decided on one particular physical action. Harkening to what Jesus said, when we ponder all the ways we can engage in lustful interaction, we've done them all. Why? Because in the spiritual world, our intention is our action. We were created in the Image and Likeness of God, whether we realize it or not. Thus, like God, our thoughts are spiritual actions as well. This is not to make a moral judgment regarding our thoughts, it's simply an explanation to where spirituality emanates. Jesus was pointing out to "the lawfully moral" Pharisees that their *intentions* were vile in contrast to their external conduct. This is why love can never be achieved through selfish desire or peace through violence.

If in the Living Word there's a conception of violence and slaughter as a solution before it happens, then who is creating the violence and slaughter? The quick, religious answer is, "The Father and Christ looked into the future, saw how horrible our sin was, and devised a system of blood sacrifice to deal with it." Therein is the quandary of Christendom's religious tradition of the last 1000 years, and particularly the

71

last 500 in Calvinistic thinking, returning to what ancient pagan religions saw as a solution. Consider that if the Divine Thought conceived it, the Living Word would be as much the cause as the response. To add to that simplification, if the Divine Thought conceived it before it occurred, it also conceived something far more sinister. God would be the engineer of the violence, slaughter, and sacrifice. This is what evangelicals call, and include in their theology, as *the wrath of God,* which is a far departure from the Gospel of Jesus Christ and the description He lays forth of His Father. Modernity has taught that the sacrifice wasn't just to redeem Mankind, but because God's wrath had to be satisfied. Thus, God never forgave anyone, rather their blood satisfied a need for justice and gratified their sentence. That version of God is the Beast that rises out of the earth and the False Prophet who heralds his message (Revelation 13:11).

How does **τοῦ Λόγου τῆς ζωῆς** (tou Logou tes Zoes), the Absolute Eternal Word of Life, beget death? How does it murder? Or worse, how does Life Everlasting beget an eternal death, flaming eternally conscious torment, or an eradicating annihilation? If anything, the message and life of Jesus reveals the complete opposite. *"...it was impossible for death to keep its hold on him,"* (Acts 2:24/NIV). Why? **Because Absolute Life cannot be killed, and Absolute Love will not kill.** In the reality of God, Life begets life, and that which seems dead comes to life, not the other way around. Only a consciousness from *within* the Tree of the Knowledge of Good and Evil, the Tree of Death, could devise and proclaim a creation of blood sacrifice to satisfy wrathful justice. This is not how to

72

approach the scripture in Revelation, nor what Jesus Christ revealed about the Godhead.

First, the verse definitively speaks of *slaughter,* or more literally, *the cutting open of the throat.* The image of the Father pondering with the Holy Spirit that His Son's throat will need to be cut open for the sake of what we traditionally considered an ignorant, inexperienced, disobedient child, is truly disproportionate, even abusive. Yet for many, this is what the *religion* of Christendom has professed. It has preached that this is the *extreme* Love of the Father, coupled with the Father's need for *exacting justice* and *holiness.* This beastly trait isn't alone. It includes *a vengeful wrath* that had to be satisfied. "SIN HAD TO BE PUNISHED!" We don't deny there's a voice proclaiming such. But whose voice? The Father's? Think again.

Who, because of one act of ignorant disobedience, would be so outraged at the violation (traditionally called "original sin") that His only recourse is unyielding eternal damnation in everlasting flames or total eradicating annihilation? One theologian friend floored me with an explanation using scriptures to support these different ideas. He said that the unrepentant will go to eternal torment to pay for their sins and then be annihilated. He added that he believed in annihilation after the fiery punishment, because eternal conscious torment, which would go on forever, was too cruel. *Wait...What?* God torments people till the debt is paid, then annihilates them? That's even more cruel than simple annihilation! Even the ancient religions realized that quickly slaughtering a sacrificial victim was more merciful than torture.

The view of this religious tradition, redefined as so-called extreme love, divine justice, and appeasing righteous wrath, actually proclaims this: "I will love you forever, but you have to love me back! If not, I will let you be tortured forever, saying that it's your own fault because it was the path you chose." As if that's not enough, some add, "Keep in mind, once I've flung you into eternal torment, even if you beg for forgiveness, forget it. It's too little too late. You had your chance!"

Let's explore this version of the "not-so-good-news gospel" that parts of Christendom have been preaching for over half a millennium:

Consider little Billy who has never experienced what it means to hold and drink milk from his own glass. His father says as he pours it, "Now be very careful. Hold the glass with both hands and don't drop it. If you drop it, I'll beat you till you're unconscious, kick you out of the house, and banish you from the family forever. In other words, if you drop it, you shall surely die!"

One day, one of Billy's brothers tempts him to hold the glass with one hand. Wanting to be like his brother, Billy tries using only one hand and drops the glass. *Crash!* Milk and broken glass are everywhere around Billy. Then, for some dysfunctional reason, his outraged father takes his belt off and is about to whip the little guy senseless. However, Joshua, Billy's older brother, steps in and says, "Don't whip him Dad, he didn't realize what he was doing." The father shouts, "My wrath needs to be satisfied! Justice must be served! Someone has to pay for his disobedience!" He reaches for little Billy. All the children around the table shout, "No please!" The father repeats his declaration, adding, "If not him, then one of you must pay! My wrath over this disobedience must be satisfied! This is Divine Justice!" Grabbing the eldest son, Joshua, the father shouts, pointing to little Billy. "Let me show you, little sinner, spiller of milk, how much love I have for you! I am willing to have my favorite son take your beating!" He takes Joshua and says, "Let's show Billy what love really looks like!" So, in front of all the children, Joshua receives such a severe whipping that he dies. The father then rushes Joshua to the hospital. The doctors work on him for three days and manage to revive him. However, the marks of his beating will be with him the rest of his life. The father returns home with partially unconscious Joshua wrapped in bandages. The rest of his children are cowering in fear of their father's wrath, hiding in different places in the house. He sits Joshua in a very comfortable chair next to his in the living room and shouts, "See what you did! Because you sinned and dropped the milk, Joshua had to die! Now he's been revived, and he will have the marks of my wrath because of your sin on his body forever! From this point forward, when you see the scars on him, you will recall them not as the marks of my wrath, but the scars of your sin. You need to realize the love I have for you as a father! Joshua stepped up for your wickedness and paid the price. So, I took... No... *I gave* my favorite son to receive the punishment of my wrath, which you justly deserved! Now THAT'S what your Father's love looks like!"

What's wrong with this picture? Bad enough there's a shattered glass and milk all over the floor. Why does their father respond with such horrific violence? The sleight of hand, the misdirection, seemingly points to a compassionate older brother who takes the brunt of the beating for his younger one. Even if the older brother willfully took the beating, we must ask, "What in *Heaven's Name* is wrong with this father?" This is the craft, the sorcery of the Serpent, and the deception of the Tree of the Knowledge of Good and Evil. This is the root of religion. And yes, *our own inner-Christian-Pharisee loves this stuff.* While the older brother is very important, the real focus and question should be, why is the father in such a rage in the first place? Who in his right mind would want to be in a family with a parent like that? No wonder the world doesn't want to be part of this "Christian religion." We need to ask ourselves, why is this view of so-called "righteous-rage" even acceptable? How does this father's outrage and violent interaction with his son somehow get redefined as love? This is not to say that the Passion of the Christ doesn't reveal love; the challenge is our distorted and horrific portrayal of it and who is ultimately responsible. Where is the supposed Good News in this seriously bad attempt at a Stephen King horror film? Furthermore, we in evangelicalism take this horror story and try to pass it off as a deeply romantic, intellectual piece of literature.

Consider, now that we have the Lamb brutally slain, besides the definition of *the cutting open of the throat,* ἐσφαγμένου (esphagmenou), it also means *ritually butchered.* The next part of the verse speaks of a deposition, meaning the unseating or removal of an established authority. The unseated authority was the Adam, in whom the Image and Likeness of the Lamb/Christ was revealed. Thus, when the Adam received the fruit of the Serpent and its Tree, the point of authority changed. Consequently, both the Adam and everything associated with them shattered and fell. The fall was from Life to Death, from Grace to Works, from Love to Ego, from Sharing to Selfishness, from Union to Separation, and from Vitality to Murder. Not only was there a change of authority, but an alteration in Creation's arrangement. The Cosmos was rearranged from one of Divine Reality to one of dissimulation, impersonation, illusion, and delusion. In this realm of the Tree of the Knowledge of Good and Evil, the Creator became a destroyer, the Life-Giver became a life-taker, and the Garden of Pleasure became a dry desert with a mirage of a self-centered oasis. In that deposition, *the Lamb was brutally slain.* It wasn't a fond twinkle in the mind of the Father to correct a sinful wrong. Rather, it was the Christ, the revelation of the Father, slain when the Adam received the seed of the Serpent and his Tree. To say it another way, the Light was eclipsed in the Adam's perception as they began to emanate the nature of the Serpent, the Ego. To put it yet another way, as self-preservation, self-justification, and the intrinsic separation it causes and sustains, the veil of a fabricated world became reality. In this contrived world, this violent butchering would be religiously branded as holy. This would repeat over and over in different forms in various religions and governments. Consider all the animals and humans who were taken by clerics in such systems and cruelly sacrificed to their gods. Each were brutally murdered, their

77

lives taken in a system that redefined such gruesomeness as ceremoniously pure, holy, worthy, and divinely pleasurable.

Part 2: The Recipe of Death

"Then the serpent said to the woman, 'You will not surely die. For God knows that in the day you eat of it your eyes will be opened, and you will be like God, knowing good and evil.'"   *(Genesis 3:4-5/NKJV)*

Up to this point, the Adam was the Image and Likeness of God. There were no qualifying rules, laws, rituals, or traditions the Adam had to do or attain to reveal his Divine Likeness. All the man and the woman had to do was nothing, just be who they were created to be. Simply stated, they just had to be their true selves. They enjoyed and received Divine pleasure from every aspect of the Garden. They were told they could eat of all the trees in the Garden (Genesis 2:16), except the Tree of the Knowledge of Good and Evil, and if they ate of that one, they would die. Thus, the Biblical definition of "death" is first mentioned here, long before the physical world as we know it came into existence. Death, in summary, is simply not being who you were created to be. It's not being your true self. It's not being or revealing Divinity.

Herein is the key to everything. In the Biblical account, the Serpent, the representation of the egoistic nature, *the Desire to Receive for Oneself Only,* tells the Adam that they will *not die,* rather their purpose will be fulfilled and they will be like God. It adds that God knows when they eat of this special tree, their eyes will be opened. The subtlety of these words implied that at that moment, their eyes were not fully open, or possibly not open at all. The Serpent suggests he knows something about God that they don't, and that God knows something about this special tree that He never revealed. The Serpent plainly states that God knows if they eat of it, then and only then will they be fully like God. He insinuates that God has been holding out on them. He tells them that God led them to believe they were like Him, but they aren't fully; they're really incomplete. Pushing it further, the Serpent alludes that God knows if they eat of this *special tree,* then the process will be complete! The Serpent used their created purpose to manipulate them. In misdirecting their desire to emanate their Creator, they yielded and partook of the very thing they were supposed to subdue. Now the Adam became like the Serpent, self-centered and selfish. To that end, the knowing of good and evil is the source and sustenance of the Ego.

In that moment, several concurrent phenomena happened to the Adam. First, to believe that they *needed something more* to become God's Likeness, was to believe a lie. **This very thought was and still is THE FALL.** For the Adam to accept the impression that they needed something more was to also accept that they were not enough, they were insufficient. To put the final seal on the "death" of Creation, they were then told the way to attain Divine Likeness and find completeness was by the knowing of good and evil. **This is the incarcerating illusion that CONFINES AND IMPRISONS ALL to the present day.** Like the elusive fountain of youth, we, now a fragmented Adam, are forever chasing this knowledge, from religion to philosophy, and from sociology to science. We aspire to be at the center of our own universe with our ego telling us what we should or shouldn't be. With fond delusion, we believe the more good we do and evil we shun, the more we please God and gain His acceptance. But such beliefs, thoughts, and illusions only reinforce the dreamworld contrived by our ego as we slumber in the Death Sleep. It's a world of illusion whose grip never tires, and we are forever exhausted from trying to escape it. The paradox is, trying to be loosed from its grip is the very thing that tightens it. Just like a rodent caught in a serpent's coil, the more it struggles, the more space it yields so the coil can tighten. Hence, the more right or wrong we see in our knowledge, the more we yield to the illusion.

The consequence of this illusory world is that all the Adamic fragments—we call them people—exist with one of two basic mindsets. The first mindset is the delusion that a supreme being or divine source simply doesn't exist. It deduces that the only reality is *me,* the *I, the individual separate from the tribe.* When it asks itself, "What's my purpose?" the fundamental answer is, "To receive all the pleasure I can get." The Ego proclaims, "You only live once!" Hence, each individual devises their own system of right and wrong based on a sense of certainty and need for gratification. This outlook develops communities around others who have similar values. We commonly call this *culture.* Lastly, in this mindset, those who claim to believe in the existence of some supreme being or beings, are arrogantly regarded as either uninformed or unenlightened. They are marginalized as religious, those who trust in figments of their ignorant imaginations, only to calm their illiterate fears.

The other mindset is as far from its counterpart as the ocean is wide. It's comprised of those trapped in a nightmare with a monotheistic or polytheistic view of Sovereign Divinity. Their phantasm is comprised of a god or gods who reign with a plethora of necessary rules to placate any potential wrath or judgement they might unleash. Thus, the follower must ultimately be faultless. Their deities impose many rituals, usually culminating with some form of blood sacrifice to satiate their need for justice. Within this mindset, some believe they will never truly gratify their deity, and that their sheer existence is at their deity's mercy. With fearful, trembling gratitude, the worshipers thank their gods for being merciful and hope to stay in their favor. For others, attaining a hope of acceptance and blessing, not to mention the remote possibility of likeness or holiness, is to work very hard at living by the "specified religious code." In this landscape, those who don't claim a belief in a god or gods are piously regarded as uninformed and unenlightened. They are marginalized as secular, those who trust in what they ignorantly rationalize intellectually through the five senses. Many times, with one broad stroke they are considered evil, devilish, and the cause of the many woes in society and on the land.

Face to face with the Tree of the Knowledge of Good and Evil, in a flash like lightening that fell from Heaven, *religion with its congruent political systems was born!* The Adam found themselves dominated by a multiplicity of tyrannical gods and goddesses, conflicting forces, cravings, and warring notions of whether the Divine existed at all. They were subjected to whatever their contrived authoritarian and aggressive phantasmagorias were. Simultaneously, the Infinite Creator was now completely concealed from and by His Creation, much like when a curtain drops between the acts of a theatrical performance.

The Adam resembled a lovely crystal glass through which the glorious Light shined, revealing all its colors and brilliance. However, now it's as if it slipped from one's hand and plummeted to the ground, shattering into pieces. Each shard fell, entranced in the Death Sleep, fantasizing egoistic grandeur. Splintered, humanity lay in spiritual unconsciousness. However, the Creator still sustained them as if connected to a life-support system in a critical care unit because, in His reality, they never really shattered and were still very much His Image and Likeness. Nevertheless, it was the egoistic illusion of their choosing that told them differently. In the Heavenly ICU, the Divine Image remained intact yet unconscious, wrapped in a massive canopy, like an oxygen tent, as if creating an atmosphere. Within the sleeping illusion of separation, each fragment (now called individual people, tribes, and cultures) was attached to a life support system. In a spiritual coma and oblivious to Divine reality, each fragment dreams of living an existence separate and distinct. Their only connection to any sensation of life is the dreamy atmosphere and organic machines that sustain them. The tented atmosphere is what we call "Terra Firma" and the organic machines are physical bodies. There humanity dreams one dream with many parts and segments, some living together, lusting together, and warring together, oblivious of the Divine reality that cradles them.

SECTION II

MANKIND'S CREATION: RELIGION

CHAPTER 3
RELIEVING THE PAIN WITH SPIRITUAL HEROIN (HOW RELIGION WORKS)

> *"These are the bonds that bind me.*
> *I became ruler through treaties;*
> *by my treaties I am now enslaved."*
>
> *Die Walküre*, Wotan
> Act II, Scene 2
> Richard Wagner

The consequence of partaking of the Tree of the Knowledge of Good and Evil is not just that it set our world in motion; *it is the actual world we live in.* Thus, our world is not a depiction of reality, but a filter through which we see reality. Like visible light and the electromagnetic spectrum, our eyes only see one millionth of one percent of the entire spectrum. In other words, we don't see reality, we only see a small sliver of it compounded with self-centered stories and emotionally energized memories. This becomes our reality and our truth, neither of which is in their fullness. As we examine this restricting filter further, we find there's a programming construct which always defaults to the same conclusion, regardless of what's presented in the equation. Can you imagine having a computer that, regardless of what information it's given, always gives you the same result? You'd say there's something wrong with the operating system.

With serious drug addiction, regardless of how hard one tries to stop, the result is always the same: *relapse.* Without going through a true detox with the help of skilled professionals, along with the necessary psychological support, the conclusion is the same. Even with a good and successful rehabilitation program, there are those who go through it and still relapse.

When we discuss the topic of a person being a heroin addict, most of us feel a serious sense of uneasiness. Frequently, the uneducated observer says, "How could he? Doesn't he know he's destroying his family and his life? He should enroll in a drug program and stop destroying himself and those around him." Another adds, "I've tried to talk to him, but he doesn't want to listen. He'll tell you that he knows what he's doing is wrong and even go so far as to say he wants help. Then, just give him a few days and he's back shooting up. On top of it, if he doesn't have the money to score his dope, he won't think twice about stealing it from his 85-year-old grandmother."

How many of us at one time or another has met a person who's strung out on heroin or some similar drug? It's a horrible thing to see, but if you've never been addicted to a drug like it, you'll never really understand what's happening to the user. Listening to descriptions of their withdrawals are horrific.

This elixir is not like having one too many martinis on a night out with friends, then vomiting in the toilet the next day from a hangover. Nor is it like smoking a potent strand of marijuana at a party, passing out, and hours later waking up in a room with no knowledge of how you got there. Heroin is a euphoria of pleasure, followed by a living death in a syringe. It's as ferocious as a wounded fire-breathing dragon. The point of this chapter is ultimately to expound on the fact that all of us are addicted to an even more potent narcotic. In comparison, what we are addicted to makes heroin look like candy. I don't say this to be sensational, but in total seriousness. Before we can discuss our hideous addiction, let's take a moment and understand a few concepts about opioid addiction, because they are similar.

Like Codeine, Vicodin, Xanax, and OxyContin, heroin is known as an *analgesic*. In other words, it's a serious painkiller and does its job very well. While the first several drugs mentioned are not as powerful, they also do an efficient job. You can't just purchase them from a store. They must be prescribed for you by a doctor and filled at a pharmacy. Besides being really good painkillers, they also have something else in common: they are known as *iatrogenic* drugs.

To properly define what *iatrogenic* means, we must understand first what it is not. For example, if a person suffers from angina (severe chest pains resulting from inadequate blood flow to the heart), a physician might prescribe nitroglycerin tablets. The tablets temporarily open the blood vessels and allow more blood to flow to and from the heart. So far so good, but there's a *side effect* from using the tablets: severe headaches. In contrast, an *iatrogenic drug,* rather than having a side effect, has a *direct effect.* The direct effect of these analgesics, and heroin in particular, *is addiction!* When a physician prescribes an iatrogenic drug to a patient, he knows fully well that *he is creating a dependency.* To say it another way, addiction or dependency is the *direct effect,* while pain relief is the side effect. Codeine and Vicodin are not as potent, so their dependency is easier to break in comparison to OxyContin or heroin. Nonetheless, some patients cannot free themselves from the less potent drugs without additional medical help. For example, when a patient is weaned off Vicodin, they may feel their pain returning in serious measure, even radiating into other areas. It's common after a doctor has stopped refilling the prescription for a patient to ask for more. Their doctor will explain that they're experiencing withdrawals from the painkiller and eventually the discomfort will go away. Sadly, some feel their doctor doesn't understand their pain level, so they go to another doctor for "a second opinion" and further treatment. They deceive themselves, as well as their family and friends, that their pain is chronic, even though the original source of pain may have been resolved through surgery or some other treatment. They're relieving their withdrawal symptoms with more drugs; *they are addicts with a dependency on prescription drugs.*

Now enters the seriously more potent heroin. Once both the physical and emotional euphoria wears off, things may appear to go back to normal for a day or two, if that long. Then the iatrogenic properties begin. It may start with horrendous headaches and nausea followed by uncontrollable shaking. Minutes seem like never-ending hours, and you're unable to sleep. Just when you think it can't get worse, it does. As one former addict described, "The muscles in your arms and legs feel like they have razorblades in them. With every move you make, you feel like someone is under your skin, cutting you from the inside out." Then comes vomiting, uncontrollable shaking, stalling of time with sleeplessness, all augmented with thousands of tiny razorblades under your flesh, stabbing and cutting into your every moment. No wonder the addict would do anything, including stealing from their 85-year-old grandmother, to get another fix. This is the iatrogenic effect. Like the wonderful high it once brought, it brings the equally horrific suffering described. Because the withdrawals are so severe, the suffering addict has only one recourse for relief; the only painkiller that will really do the job is *more heroin!*

What if all humanity had a serious heroin addiction and there were dealers on every street corner offering good smack? Think of the constant manipulation and control of each other, the sexual abuse, the power struggles, the malnutrition, the lust for wealth, all to obtain more drugs. Over-extravagance, burglary, larceny, embezzlement, and terrible violence would all be endless. Sound familiar? It sounds like the daily broadcast on a 24-hour news network. The key is, we all have a deep inner reoccurring torment brought on by a spiritual iatrogenic drug called *religion.* The analgesics mentioned above are all opiates. They are derived from the opium plant, thus have similar results. The iatrogenic drug called *religion*

91

comes from the plant called *the Tree of the Knowledge of Good and Evil*. Thus, all religions, or the lack thereof, have similar results. Consider our definitions of ceremony, ritual, and superstition. When you add the egoistic roots of right and wrong, good and evil, us and them, I'm in and you're out, this is mine and that's yours, *religion* is not limited to the worship of some god or deity. It's much more. It's the religion of politics, the religion of secularism, the religion of philosophy, and on and on we can go. Some are as harmless and fun as team sports, while others can be as deadly as the abuse of political power.

To focus on how this spiritual iatrogenic identity-killer affects us on a more personal level, let's return to the Garden of Eden for the setup. Put yourself in The Adam's place for a moment. There is a very intentional, prosperous drug dealer in the neighborhood. He's known as *the Ego*, or by his street name, *the Serpent*. He's well-dressed and almost glistens as you approach. His beautiful eyes sparkle and his smile is radiant. You notice his neck and forearms, which are exposed through his expensive clothing. He apparently has a body tattoo that covers him completely. It's a lovely, paisley-like tree with artistic branches swirling all over his form. He manages to entice you to take a ride on his "white horse" named "Thunder" (street names for heroin) and he's willing to give it to you for free. He tells you how wonderful and fulfilling it will be. He reminds you that you were created to be the image and likeness of God and suggests that this will complete that process. As your desires are piqued, you're convinced that he knows what he's talking about. It's as if he and God have a special relationship because he seems to know something about God's thinking that you don't. He hands you the syringe and you think, "Now I will fulfill the will of God. I will be in God's Image!" So you inject yourself. The euphoria is unimaginable. You immediately turn and give some to your friends. We're all on a high that is beyond anything we've ever experienced. We don't just *feel* superior, we KNOW we are! And we don't just know we are, we are totally *right* in thinking so! The egoistic euphoria floods our minds and emotions. In the shade of our sense of rightness, reality is transfigured and we believe we can clearly evaluate the world around us. For some, the egoistic bliss forms a view where we don't need the crutch of some mindless belief in a supreme or an intelligent designer; we are the masters of our own destiny. For others, it's a view of a god or gods that are lofty and powerful, and we as mere humans are nothing more than pawns of their sovereign will. Yet others believe the reason we're lowly humans is because we are nothing but sinners in the sight of the god or gods, and our sin separates us from them. The only remedy to appease them is to realize our wrongness and to keep the gods' prescribed moral code along with the proper sacrifices.

What's hidden in the forest of our egoistic bliss and realization of sinfulness is an emerging sense of prideful piety. In recognizing our apparent unworthiness, we're still focused on ourselves with a seemingly inverted self-importance, which ratifies that we are not enough like God. Stripping away the religious piety, we seek the same gratification and self-centeredness as those who claim to deny the existence of a god or gods. It's just a different way of achieving the high. Superiority and unworthiness are opposite sides of the same egoistic coin, whether one believes in a god or not. Finally, we begin establishing our own kingdoms, heaping them with the multifaceted rules of politics and culture. What was once a spiritual, life-giving Garden has been malformed into an egoistic, fleshly world of illusion and delusion. The land, vegetation, and animals are now to serve our pleasures. We manipulate and even violate creation for our gratification. This raping and pillaging evolve to the highest level when we "religious-ize" such acts into holy ceremonies, immolation rites, blood rituals, animal and/or human sacrifice, and the conquering of other people groups, all in the name of a god's will and worship.

After hours of egoistic euphoria, we crash from our high and become aware of another sensation: *fear,* the other side of the self-important Ego. The iatrogenic effects begin to creep in. Maybe we're not good enough, smart enough, wise enough to be the rulers of our own kingdom, let alone our own universe. *Gasp!* "If I'm not good enough, the gods know I'm not worthy. Wait! What if one of my friends is better or more worthy than me? Then he will get what should be mine! No, wait! What if my own spouse is better or more worthy? Then they'll get my portion!" The feeling of vulnerability and exposure start causing emotional shakes. "I have to protect my possessions and myself from THOSE PEOPLE!" The spiritual nausea starts because of *the fear of death* (Hebrews 2:15), in other words, imaginations of loss of life, status, possessions, security, with the added dread of embezzlement, theft, and robbery. The constant fear becomes a driving, subconscious phobia, eating away at our awareness like razorblades under the surface of our soul. There's only one answer. We must have more of the knowledge of good and evil to feed our ailing ego. The more knowledge we have, the more power we have. The sense of inferiority fueled by our anxiety is unbearable. Fortunately, we don't have far to travel to get our fix. Our egoistic dealer is readily available. However, this time it's not free. Like with any dealer, the second time has a price.

The Ego/Serpent says, "If you let me take control, fear and dread will go away. I'm what makes you, YOU. I'll protect you, empower you, and make sure THEY won't take what's yours!" Its comforting tone hisses a minimal sense of relaxation as it offers a feeling of certainty and safety. So we wonder, "Is there a cost?" The Ego/Serpent quickly retorts, "Not really. Just think of what you get in return! You get the sensation of *knowing*. You'll know what to do in every situation. You'll know what's right and what's wrong. You'll know how to pursue pleasure for yourself and get it. If you believe in the gods, you'll know how to please them too. Think of it! Everyone will be happy, but most importantly, YOU will!" Then we ask the important question, "What's in it for you?" The iatrogenic fog in our mind is so sharp, it's polarizing. With a surge, a flood of realization occurs! Determination with relaxation floods our mind. "Wait! Why am I so concerned? I know better than those @%&! I'm going to take what's mine and they better worry if they get in my way!" As our mind starts to clear—meaning our mind is flipping the coin of fear for the other side, arrogance—the fully emptied, fang-like

95

syringe is now hanging from our forearm. We can feel the rush of knowing better than *those people.* With a pompous grin, we look to the sky and thank the gods. A wonderful sense of certainty overshadows us. We tell ourselves it's peace from the gods. We know we're right, and the gods are on our side because we're right. No, let's empower our religious narcissism with a dose of false humility; the gods are always right, we've simply chosen to side with the gods. We take the syringe out of our arm and put it in a safe place, just in case we need it again. Then somewhere in the back of our mind, we hear a distant voice, like a faint memory. "This is not you. This is not real. This is a fantasy world created by your selfishness." As quickly as the thought appears, it's gone, suppressed by our rightness and reason.

From pagan deities, to cults, and even mainstream religions, coupled with their entangled relationship to politics, they all end up with "an offer you can't refuse." The point is, the more we get high on our Ego, the more seriously dependent on it we become. From the moment the physical world was created, the Ego was our serpentine master. In that strange, addictive, codependent relationship, we are forever trying to be free from the iatrogenic effects, and yet, we keep running into its arms for relief. Whether we allow it to take on the form of political parties, religions, cults, or secularism, we will run to any one of them for consolation, even though when we do it we know deep down that something is rather twisted.

To amplify the dynamics of the Ego manifested in religion and politics, like fear and arrogance being two sides of the same egoistic coin, the same is true of religion and politics. The one always influences the other, even in the most presumed secular societies. For that matter, secularism is nothing more than a synonym for theocracy. The diversion is that the rule is not defined by a deity, but by an ideal. Either way, men and women will die in sacrifice for it. Thus, politics is nothing more than a type of palindrome for religion.

Let's put all the above in context. The notion of the word, *mainline,* meaning *to put the needle in the principal vein,* can now potentially refer to a *mainline* religion or political affiliation. Therefore, we flick the syringe with our finger, making sure that any air bubbles of Divine truth are removed because we wouldn't want to have a egoistic embolism, then with a small pinch... (A dramatic pause, then slowly...) *"Ooooh yeaaah, there's my Ego..."* What euphoria! There's nothing like the sensation of being right in our own eyes and being right with god as well.

CHAPTER 4
THE OTHER CREATION BEFORE GENESIS

"When the heaven above was not named,
And the ground beneath did not yet bear a name,
And the primeval Apsû, who begat them,
And chaos, Tiamat, the mother of them both,
Their waters were mingled together,
And no field was formed, no marsh was to be seen;
When of the gods none had been called into being.
Uncalled by name, their destinies undetermined,
Then it was that the gods were formed within
them."

Enûma Eliš
Babylonian Creation Story
Translated by James B. Pritchard

When we look to the Bible, opening its leather bound covers or pressing the icon on our tablets, we see it as the sole ancient document of faith, safely handed down through the ages. When that thought is combined with our favorite translation, we have God's personal love letter to us. If only such were true, but it isn't. There were many religious beliefs and documents written on parchment and stone, long before Moses looked to climb Sinai, or the Apostles were filled with the Spirit in the Upper Room.

Part 1: The Bible, Late in the Game

The immolation of animals and people as an act of worship to a deity occurred long before we see it recorded in the Bible. The notion of *blood sacrifice* existed effectively in all religions from both the East and West, dating back to primeval history. Consider that from the time of the Earth's reboot, meaning the events of Noah and the flood, to the time of Moses, who penned the story, there is approximately 1377 years. Historically, by the time Moses is writing Genesis, we have already passed through the Chalcolithic (Copper) Age and we're in the Bronze Age. The challenge for many contemporary Evangelicals is that we tend to see the Bible through a narrow lens, romanticizing our view as the only definition of God. We really don't peer into the cultures and religions surrounding the time it was written, or even the earlier times it spoke about. If we did, it was sadly only to support and confirm what we desire to believe, rather than to shape our perception.

From before the time of Noah and after the flood, diverse religions and governmental systems were well established and dominated the known world. When we read of Enoch, Noah, Abraham, and the succeeding Biblical characters, God was breaking into those religious-political systems for the purpose of liberating Humanity from their hideous aspects. This doesn't mean that messages of liberation weren't within those systems, the issue was that Egoistic Mankind consistently tainted any suggestion of them. Keep in mind, God never tried to move Humanity from one religion to follow another, nor migrate them from one political system to another. Rather, God was at work to liberate Humanity from their "less than Human" egoistic view of themselves, which defined how they saw their gods. Many of the gods and goddesses, whether polytheistic or monotheistic, were nothing more than projections of fallen Mankind's view of themselves. Nevertheless, while God was speaking in those systems, He was heavily overshadowed by their religion and politics. So He had to step outside of those systems and speak to those who would listen and walk in what they heard. This is no different than the revivals of Christendom. How many times has God had to step outside of the *mainline* Church and speak to the unconventional, like the "Jesus Movement" of the 1970s. The Bible wasn't written to a people who were the centerpiece of the one and only true global religion, but to a group of oppressed, marginalized people who had nothing else to do but to listen.

In addition to all the amazing aspects of Scripture, from the meanings of each Hebrew letter to the multifaceted spiritual connotations of each verse, there is yet another facet. It's no accident that Moses used the words and images he did as he was inspired to write the Torah. For example, the creature in the Garden of Eden who instigates the Fall is a *serpent.* Besides all the powerful truths we can extract from such imagery, consider what Moses was scribing to the children of Israel.

What was on the headdress of Pharaoh? Pharaoh wore what is called the "nemes." On it was Nekhbet, the vulture, and *Uraeus, the serpent.* At the time of war, Pharaoh would wear the *Khepresh,* which was a blue skull cap with a *shiny gold serpent* in the center. He would have worn this when he and the 600 chariots chased the children of Israel during their exodus. To Moses's audience, the serpent wasn't just spiritual symbology or a depiction of some spirit being, it was a clear representation of what they were delivered from, both politically and religiously: Egypt.

The imagery doesn't stop there. The tree where the glistening serpent is coiled is famously known as the Tree of the Knowledge of Good and Evil. It's no accident that the Hebrew word for evil is רע (Ra), which is also the name of the Egyptian sun god. The sun god, Ra, and the serpent, Apep, would fight in battle daily. Interestingly, Apep not only represented the darkness, which was the opposite quality of Ra, the sun, but he also embodied *chaos.* Hence, we have Egypt's sun god, which became the Hebrew name for evil, and the image of the serpent representing chaos. The Hebrew word for *waters* is מים (mayhim), which is the word we use in English to describe *chaos.* The very opening verses of Genesis not only give us the so-called "Creation Story" but are using terms and concepts that the children of Israel would distinctly understand. It contrasts the Egyptian world where they were in bondage, with the distant land of liberty to which they were called. God, through Moses, was bringing clarity to what his followers, as well as other nations, understood. Ra was at war fighting Apep. Thus, good conflicted with evil. Yet, in the Genesis story both are considered Death in comparison to the true Divine Life. In effect, they are the "good and evil" which is the *Tree of the Serpent* and far from the consciousness of *the Tree of Life.*

To make the point another way, the Hebrew word for Egypt is מצרים (mitsrayim), which means *to seize, squeeze,* or *press in.* Its root word, צור (tsor), is often translated as *adversary* (Exodus 23:22), *distress, vex, trouble,* and *lay siege* (Deuteronomy 2:9; 1 Kings 15:27). So consider the known symbolisms Moses was using. Let's have a look at Moses's opening phrases of a common translation of Genesis and then explore the Hebraic symbolism:

> *"The earth was without form, and void; and darkness was on the face of the deep. And the Spirit of God was hovering over the face of the waters. Then God said, 'Let there be light'; and there was light."*
>
> (Genesis 1:2-3/NKJV)

When we look at these verses from the standpoint of Moses's use of word and letter definition, we see the poetic drama unfolding.

> *"The earth sieged (Egypt) with the desire to receive for itself alone (Ego), was an indistinguishable ruin a wasteland [from the heat of the sun (Ra)], and darkness was on the face of the uproaring*

> *bottomless pit (Apep). And the Spirit of God was*
> *fluttering over the face of the chaos."*

Based on the known Egyptian religious system, by verse 3, God through Moses is saying, *"The ongoing fight between Ra, the god of the sun (good), and the darkness of Apep (evil), is put to an end when the Eternal Creator says, 'Light Be!'"*

The *good and evil* dynamic between Ra and Apep ends with the revelation of the Infinite Source, the Father of all Creation, declaring the Light, the Christ. This Source is of a different world, the world of the Tree of Life, not Death. The Serpent (Apep), lives in the Tree of Good and Evil, which sits on the skull cap (the place of Knowledge) of Pharaoh. Moses redefines both Ra and Apep (Good and Evil), as the Serpent. Fast-forward to Jesus's crucifixion at Golgotha, "the Place of the Skull." The knowledge of Good and Evil will always crucify the Christ, therefore in the book of Revelation it references Egypt, מצרים (mitsrayim), as the place where the crucifixion took place, *"...Egypt, where our Lord was crucified."* (Revelation 11:8/NKJV)

While the scripture is revealing Divine truths, it's also referencing and utilizing the known symbology of the day. Once again, it's a form of roots and branches. But by the time we read them thousands of years later, those branches lose their meaning, so our point of reference is lost. At the time Moses wrote Genesis, it was late in the third quarter of the Bronze Age with its world of religions. When the Torah was first penned, the ancient religions and civilizations of

Mesopotamia (Sumerian, Assyrian, Babylonian, etc.), as well as Egypt, India, and China already existed. When the first word of Genesis was scribed, the Mesopotamian religious systems had been around for over 2000 years and were in full force. Most importantly, the practice of blood covenant and sacrifice was prevalent in virtually all of them. These pagan religions did not get the practice of such bloodletting from the Eternal Life-Giver, the God who said, "Light Be!" Rather, they received it from the dealer of Death, the one who is *the god of this world* at the Fall, the Serpent (our dealer of iatrogenic, egoistic religions) in the Tree of the Knowledge of Good and Evil.

The challenge for the modern Bible reader is that we see acts of sacrifice in the Old Testament and God ostensibly participating for man's sake and deliverance. This is where we really miss the revelation of who God truly is. We infuse into our reading of scripture an assumption that God condoned, or even encouraged, this violent practice. But, as we will soon see, this was not the case at all. Rather, **the Eternal Creator entered into the violence of religion and became its victim to deliver humanity from its heinous grip!** The ultimate display of this culminates in the collision of the Divine Nature expressed in Christ, then to be executed at the hand of the supreme illustration of religion, the High Priest Caiaphas, with the collusion of the governing world power, Pontus Pilate. Add to them the adornment of the religious court, the Sanhedrin, and *the mob of people* who were incited by them, shouting, "Crucify Him!" But why?

105

Part 2: The "Other" Original Creation Story

In addition to the direct assertions of Moses's use of Egyptian imagery to speak to his followers, he was also addressing a prevailing "creation story." Dating back to before the time of Nimrod and Babylon, the known creation story was called the *"Enûma Eliš"* (the first nine lines of the first tablet are written above at the beginning of the chapter). This story, with some variations, was repeated throughout the known religions, up to and including the Greco-Roman world. We will discuss both the early Sumerian/Babylonian version and the latter Greek version to show continuity through the ages. In addition, being that the Babylonian version was written long before Moses wrote the Torah, and the Greek long thereafter, it makes the point of how profound aspects of Moses's writings are within their content.

The Sumer-Akkadian/Babylonian *Enûma Eliš* points back to creation prior to the time of the flood. The gods and goddesses mentioned also give us a hint of the preflood religious systems (more on this in the next chapter). You may be thinking, what does this have to do with *Melchizedek, the Tree of Life,* and *Jesus Christ?* Actually, everything! It will be Moses who scribes the story of Melchizedek and Abraham, which is set in the time of Nimrod and his rule. Thus, this "other" creation story was the prevailing religious/political world view. The following is a summary of that creation story:

Apsû (Fresh/Deep Water) and Tiamat (Salt/Oceanic Waters) are two organic deities that initiate creation. By the two

106

intermingling, Apsû impregnates Tiamat and in her womb their children (the lesser gods) are created and live. As the children grow within Tiamat, they make much chaos and noise. Their constant chattering and screaming upset Apsû to the point that he wants to kill the children. (This is the origin of the name Babel, *the mingling noise of the lesser gods.*) The principal son of the two is Ea, and is considered a member of their union, a "triad." Ea learns of his father's desire to kill his brothers and sisters to stop the chaotic noise, and devises a plan to kill his father. Ea gives Apsû an elixir that puts him into a coma-like sleep. While asleep, Ea removes his father's crown, places it on his own head as he claims he now rules the gods, then kills his father.

After seizing the throne, Ea takes the glorious Damkina as wife. Tiamat, the mother of Ea and the other gods, takes another husband, Kingnu. Over time, she becomes resentful over the death of her former husband, Apsû, and seeks revenge. Though dead, within Apsû's loins another son, Marduk, is slowly developing. Ea and Damkina take him and nurture him. However, Marduk, like his brothers and sisters before him, annoys the gods with all his frolicking. Tiamat is now plotting her revenge, especially after she is mocked by some of her sons and daughters for standing idly by while Apsû was murdered. She enlists them to form an army. She also makes serpent-monsters to use in battle. Marduk, learning of his pseudo-mother's plan to kill him and some of his brothers and sisters, approaches Ea and Damkina claiming he can lead them to victory. But he has a condition; he must be made the new ruler of the gods. Ea and Damkina agree to his demands. Marduk then kills Kingnu, Tiamat's second husband, and then kills Tiamat, ripping open her body and tearing her in two. From her torn body the skies, land, and waters are created. His brother and sister gods that were fighting on Tiamat's side are forced into slave labor. From the dead Kingnu's blood, mankind is created and also made to serve the ruling gods.

One of the key points of the Sumer-Akkadian/Babylonian *Enûma Eliš* is that humanity is born out of the bloody violence of the gods, the ripping open of Tiamat's womb, and the blood of Kingnu. This is how they justify that all humans are innately violent. In addition, in forming their (and our) religions, they are subordinate to their gods as servants and if they fail to obey the gods' code of conduct, disobedience must be paid for with a blood sacrifice. The use of the blood of animals and/or humans is a reminder as to why they exist. They were reenacting the murder of Tiamat and Kingnu, reminding them that the ruling gods slew "the parents of creation" and they were born from their blood. Thus, if they violate the blood of the sacrifice in some way, whether by accident or rebellion, the gods will inflict judgment, death, and torment on them.

The Greeks have a similar, if not identical creation story, thousands of years later. This is a summary of that creation story by *Hesiod's Theogony:*

The gods are created by two organic forces, Ouranos (the heavens) and Gaia (the earth). In some more ancient versions, Gaia created Ouranos first and together they created the

Titans, the twelve original gods. Among the twelve Titans was Cronos, their leader, and his wife, Rhea. Over time, Ouranos and Gaia gave birth to two horrendous giant beings, Hecatoncheires (the hundred-handers) and Cyclops. In fear of what they created, Ouranos chained them in the dark, hellish caverns of Tartarus. Gaia was outraged by this and tried to persuade her other Titan children to overthrow Ouranos, their father. None of them would do it except Cronos. Gaia and Cronos plotted an ambush for Ouranos. While Gaia spoke with Ouranos, Cronos attacked him with a stone sickle and castrated his father. Cronos threw his father's testicles into the ocean, from which emerged Aphrodite. As his father's groin bled, the blood fell to the earth, creating other beings.

Cronos became ruler and together with Rhea fathered the gods known as the Olympiads (there were also twelve of them). Cronos, learning that his sons were plotting against him because of what happened to Ouranos, swallowed them alive. Rhea, then pregnant with Zeus, the only god not swallowed, secretly gave birth to him on the isle of Crete. When Zeus grew, he learned of the fate of his brothers and sisters and conspired with his grandmother, Gaia, to liberate his siblings. Gaia gave Zeus an elixir, which he then gave to Cronos, that caused him to vomit up his brothers and sisters. Zeus sentenced the Titans to imprisonment in Tartarus, yet liberated Hecatoncheires and Cyclops. Prometheus (one of the Titans that didn't join Cronos in the rebellion) was not confined to Tartarus. Rather, he was given the task of creating mankind from the earth where Cronos's groin bled.

All the creatures of earth were given skills to serve the gods. But when it came time to give mankind their portion, there were no skills left. Thus, Prometheus stole fire from the gods and gave it to the humans. He created them upright like the gods, forming them with four arms, four legs, and two faces, joined at the spine. They had three genders, male, female, and androgynous. When Zeus heard that mankind was made upright like the gods, he was enraged. At first, Zeus wanted to destroy mankind, but then realized there would be no one to worship and pay tribute to him. So Zeus split each person in half as punishment and consequently doubled how many would sacrifice and pay tribute. Zeus also had a box created with plagues, illnesses, and misfortunes. It was sealed and given to a woman named Pandora (meaning *gifted*), instructing her never to open it. The subtle plan was that by telling her not to open it, it would create the curiosity and desire to open it. Additionally, when anyone was near the box they could hear the contents singing in a sweet voice. Needless to say, she opened the box, which meant that Zeus could never be accused of bringing the plagues upon humanity, but she was blamed for her arrogant curiosity and rebellion. Zeus manipulated her from a distance and she, unwittingly, did what he wanted all along. From that point forward, the only way for humanity to navigate through the plagues was to ask for the assistance of the gods through tribute and blood sacrifice. Thus, to secure humanity's worship, Zeus created the very plagues which afflicted them. He loosed the misfortunes through manipulating and blaming Pandora, so ultimately the gods would become the sole answer to troubled humanity through worship.

The Greeks tell us a similar story as the Sumer-Akkadian/Babylonians, but in much more detail. We find a similar theme through Vedas, Egyptian, and Medo-Persian mythologies. Their justification and reasoning are that humanity is born out of the gods' violence, which is why humans are essentially violent. Mankind was made to serve the gods, never with the thought of equality or likeness of them. Again, in forming their religions, the only way to remedy any mistake or disobedience was by tribute and blood sacrifice. If they didn't perform those in the proper manner, *the wrath of the gods* would be unleashed. Hence, Zeus throwing his lightning bolts, or sending further calamity, would strike both them and their respective society. Consequently, the political-religious ramifications were intense. Political betrayal and religious scapegoating were the underlying rule. The notions of such practices were reformed, retooled, and justified for the good of civilization in many different forms.

Part 3: Changing the Creation Story

The first inclination that there was another point of view to the creation and the origins of mankind, begins with Moses's telling of the story in Genesis. We discussed this at length in the previous volume in *Chapter 5: In ~~the~~ Beginning, Part 3*, but we will refresh our thinking in summary. The opening phrase in Genesis 1:1 is:

בראשית ברא אלהים את השמים ואת הארץ:

(b'reeshiyt bara eelohiym et hashamyim v'et ha'arets)

111

The opening three words of the verse are very telling. First, it doesn't really say, "In the beginning..." Rather, it's just, "In beginning..." The root word for *beginning* is ראש (resh), meaning *head*. In Hebraism, the head can also mean *origin*, like the head of a river. The next aspect is that the word בראשית is in the feminine gender, which means you can actually translate the verse as, "In her head..." or in the feminine idea, "In her womb..." meaning, *the place of origin.* The next word is ברא אלהים (bara eelohiym), which we commonly translate as *God created.* The word *create* is actually *fat,* so it really means *the Powers fattened* (see 1 Samuel 2:29). The famous word אלהים (eelohiym), which we translate *God,* is plural and can also be translated *gods,* or literally, *the powers.* It's also important to know that the word is in the masculine gender. So one way you could translate the verse is, *"In her womb (origin) the Powers fattened..."* So now we actually have a similar depiction as in all the other religious texts; the masculine and feminine qualities united together causing pregnancy (fattening in the womb) with all of creation, including heaven and earth. One reason heaven is included within the womb is to suggest that the heavens, in which all other gods and goddesses of other religions dwell, are subordinate to this Creator (Exodus 18:11). We then, in the following verse, have the feminine aspect, the Spirit, fluttering over the waters. As a reminder, the word *waters* in Hebrew is מים (mayim), which also means *chaos.*

This is a direct reference to the Enûma Eliš. The significant difference was that, in the pagan religions, the chaos was a result of both the masculine and feminine, parents and children, warring with each other. There was murder and revenge, with children castrating their fathers and splitting open their mothers, not to mention how the parents wanted to murder their children to protect themselves, and children who wanted to murder their parents to survive. In the pagan story, it ended in violent bloodshed, with Humanity as a result. In Moses's account, it's very different. Rather than fighting and bloodshed, it's a love story that continues with the creation of a beautiful garden of unending pleasure. For that matter, God (the masculine and feminine qualities in union) creates and brings lifegiving order to the chaos through their Light. Thus, the Garden of Pleasure is the home of Mankind. They were not fashioned as servants or slaves to obey the legal code of the gods, nor pawns in some Olympian plan. They were created in equality, as the very Image and Likeness of their Creator, with no Divine regrets.

Another important point about the Mosaic Genesis creation story is that many of us in Christendom read into it something that isn't there:

> *"In the beginning God created the heavens and the earth. The earth was without form, and void; and darkness was on the face of the deep. **And the Spirit of God created the waters** and was hovering over them."* (Genesis 1:1-2 NKJV w/Mastrogiovanni modification)

Did you notice the change? *"And the Spirit of God created the waters..."* It never said God created the waters! It's important to note that throughout Genesis Chapter 1, there is a distinction between the heavens, earth, and waters. Yet we always assume God created everything out of nothing. NO! The waters, the chaos, was there before hand. Genesis opens with existing waters or chaos; the rest is an indescribable ruin and wasteland (without form and void). This will become important later as we discuss Noah and the ark. In the pagan stories, the chaos is either the result of the gods interacting or warring. In the Genesis story, in the first verse we see the masculine and feminine aspects in intimate embrace, creating the heavens and the earth. But the next part is followed by bringing order to the chaos through this illumination. Loving intimacy gives order and light to the chaos. The result of the union is the Light, the Messiah, the Christ, which brings order or, far better said, *harmony to the chaos.*

Another aspect later discussed is that in the pagan stories, humans are slaves and must obey the religious-political code. But the God that Moses reveals gives His creation the right to choose to be in a relationship with Him or not. Without that choice, His creation would never be godlike, nor in a position to love genuinely and freely.

The contrasts between the two versions are stark. One is filled with ego, self-centeredness, violence, murder, and death. The other love, light, life, intimacy, and the freedom of choice. It's not until Mankind chooses to leave the liberty of the Garden and enter into, literally create, a universe pervaded with the milieu of the Egoistic-Serpent and its Tree of Death, do we see a resemblance to the pagan gods of violence immerge. This is the key point of the Melchizedekian priesthood, the Tree of Life and Jesus Christ; they all bring a very different view of the nature and character of God. The revelation and entrance of truth, Divine Light, comes when we realize that the gods of violence and their sacrifices are not a depiction of God the Father, the Source of Creation, nor the Son of His Love, and most definitely not the Holy Spirit, the Life-Giver. Yet, because we live in the realm of the Tree of the Knowledge of Good and Evil, we now see a sliver of Divine reality through its limiting filter. Its egoistic iatrogenic programming will always fixate on violence, scapegoating, and blood sacrifice. Thus, when we read the Bible with that programming, regardless of what truth abides in the text, we default to a god of the same qualities as the world we chose and created. We see a god who egoistically mandates regular worship, demands tribute to give blessing, total obedience to avoid judgment, and requires blood sacrifice to appease its wrath.

One could say that we, fallen Humanity, have rewritten the Creation story with this subconscious underlying thought: "In the beginning, Mankind created gods and goddesses in his own image, and in the image of Mankind created he them. Mankind walked over the face of the earth naming what is good and evil. And Mankind said, 'My will be done!' and it was done. And Mankind called the good, 'right,' and the evil, 'wrong.' But Mankind could not agree upon what was right and what was wrong, thus violence broke out and murder spread through the land. Then Mankind called upon the gods he had made to resolve their conflicts. And to resolve Mankind's struggle, the gods demanded all to be obedient to their laws and to offer blood sacrifice if one was violated. And Mankind couldn't agree upon which gods to worship, so the various tribes chose their own gods. Then from this time onward, in the name of his gods, Mankind killed his fellow man, both in war and in worship. This was the evening and the morning of the first day."

CHAPTER 5
THE BIRTH OF RELIGION, BLOOD COVENANT, SACRIFICE, AND THE GODS OF VIOLENCE

"In our perplexity, we asked Calchas, the seer,
and he answered that we should sacrifice
my own child Iphigenia to Artemis..."
Iphigenia in Aulis, Agamemnon
Lines 89-90
Euripides

Part 1: Rebooting Earth

Before Abraham, the man called *the friend of God* (2 Chronicles 20:7) and *the father of our faith* (Romans 4:16), there was Noah. Noah was the key transition point from what we call the pre-flood Adamic era to the post-flood era. Why discuss Noah in a book on Melchizedek? Because the Noah story has the building blocks of all things Melchizedek, and therefore all things Christ. In addition, everything in the known world of today began with Noah. While the Fall of the Adam may have set in motion creation as we know it, the world and nations in which we now live began with Noah. With a swift, superficial overview of the latter part of Genesis, Chapters 5-10, it appears that God *rebooted* the known world. He seemingly removed all living creatures, from man to animal, with a global flood, keeping only Noah, his family, and selected animals, bringing them into a renewed world. (At least, that's how we've traditionally viewed those events.) Unfortunately, after just a short time this "renewed world" started to resemble the previous one. Once again, the ritual slaughter of animals and humans were being practiced from the Babylonians to the Aztecs and beyond. Then there's the eye-popping scandal at the conclusion of Noah's life equal to any modern religious-political figure (Genesis 9:24).

A key point is that the human condition doesn't change without an internal revelatory emergence of its true identity first. Realistically, this can't happen unless we see God as He truly is, which is also seeing ourselves as we truly are; they are one in the same. Thus enters the story of Noah, which changes the known world in his day, bringing an end to one and the birth of another.

In the evangelical and religious world, we've used segments of scripture to validate so-called godly acts of violence against those who commit deeds deemed wicked, evil, or ungodly. To the contrary, Jesus makes the point, *"You do not know what manner of spirit you are of,"* (Luke 9:54-56). We have, in the name of God, Christ, and religion, decimated people groups, cultures, societies, and nations, thinking that if we just dealt with "those people" the evil and chaos would be gone and everything would be fine. This is the scapegoating referred to

118

at the end of the previous chapter. But "those people" were never the real source of our frustration. Rather, it was our internal darkness, which could only be addressed by a Divine revelatory opening of our inner eyes. Sadly, the spiritual currency of the Serpent and the Tree in which it divulges itself has limited offers. When something is amiss, rather than an honest, Life-giving introspection, it selfishly suggests that some outside evil or wickedness brought it about. If the Ego, with its iatrogenic self-centeredness doesn't offer, "Your sinfulness brought it upon yourself," the only other alternative is, "It was the sinfulness of others that brought it upon me or us." After all, that was the theme from the very beginning, *"The WOMAN whom YOU gave me!"* (Genesis 3:12).

To this day, people continue to search for physical proof of Noah's Ark, yet whenever some artifact is thought to be found, further investigation proves it's not authentic. Still, this fascination with the Ark has resulted in the creation of a theme park dedicated to the biblical event. Created in 2016, The Ark Encounter is located in Williamstown, Kentucky, USA. Along with a replica of Noah's Ark, it has all the amenities you'd expect to find in a recreational destination: dining spots, hotels, exhibits, a zoo, presentations, events, and, of course, the obligatory gift shop. If a location like this exists, in the absence of historical artifacts, can you imagine what would happen if an actual piece of the Ark was discovered one day? We might expect that scientific proof of a divine event would be nothing but positive, but could it instead have an adverse effect? Imagine how it might play out...

Welcome to Ark World! After paying the admission fee, there's a guided tour to the location of the artifact's resting place. Then we go on an animatronic-type walk-through experience. We pass life-sized mechanical animals that move, grunt, and growl. All around us, flashes of lightning, the rumble of thunder, the drumming sound of harsh rain, and the creaking of wood all provide ambiance. There are sections with sculpted wax figures of Noah and his family performing certain chores, like feeding the animals and patching small leaks. For comic relief, there's a scene where Noah and his wife look very pale, hanging their heads over nearby buckets, obviously seasick because of the large waves tossing their buoyant home. When we finally exit the Ark, we enter The Dove's Branch, a gift shop where we happily purchase T-shirts, books, DVDs, mugs, action figures, and cute plush animals. We feel uplifted, as if we lived the experience, not to mention our excitement when we think of showing up to church next Sunday wearing our new T-shirt with a picture of the Ark and the slogan, "I survived Noah's Ark!"

What impact would this type of experience really have? Would it be spiritually transformational? Or simply religiously confirmational? To a person humbly seeking a spiritual, Christ-centered transformation, of which the central feature is the heart's attitude, it could have a positive impact. For that matter, any work of art, such as a painting, statue, or music, can assist in that way. In another sense, to such a person the external totem wouldn't be the agent of transformation. Whether he or she stood in the real ark or a fabricated one, or read its account in scripture, the transformational encounter is inevitable because what's sought doesn't require the five senses to be comprehended. In contrast, the religious, as they relish in their discovery, might say, "See! Lost souls need to come see this! This would prove that the Bible is right and they'd believe and come to the truth!" But those touched by the Kingdom-engrafted Spirit are aware that it's not archeology or tangible relics that transform. Even if the real Noah's Ark was in an amusement park, it's no different than the sculptured spear point which supposedly pierced the side of Christ, believed to belong to the Roman centurion, Longinus. The spear point currently abides in Hofburg, Austria, with the claim that one of the actual nails that pierced Christ is embedded within it. Yet none of these relics have any power within themselves. To the contrary, there is no need for a relic, real or fabricated, to encourage spiritual reality. It's the ongoing unveiling of the Likeness of the Everlasting Christ within and among us that transforms us inside and out. As Jesus said, *"See! For the Kingdom of God is within you,"* (Luke 17:21). It's not about what information we acquire or artifacts we unearth. *It's about discovering and uncovering the revelation of the eternal world within.* This may sound vague to some and complex to others, but it's actually the simplest of all realities and begins with a mere *humble desire.*

Throughout my years of study, I have heard many rabbis in lectures and books discussing the fascination with those who seek Noah's ark. The consensus is quite interesting. Many would say things like, "Who cares if we find the Ark? It would only divert our attention." Divert our attention? Wait...What? Wouldn't it prove that we and our belief system are right?

That our holy book is faultless? That our team wins another theological debate? Let's not forget the real issue, "Man, it really feels good to be so right!" But that's just the point. Don't think for a moment that you can venerate both the artifact and the revelation. Spirituality just doesn't thrive that way. Even if the actual ark was dry docked at Disneyland, we would still have to let go of the egoistic importance of the tangible relic to attain the spiritual realities beyond its figure. This is not only apt regarding relics, but also in the way we venerate the scriptures. To embrace God's Written Word is important, yet we have to stop romanticizing its contents into something it's not.

Noah was not a good Christian or an orthodox Jew. He was a man in a pagan society with many gods, yet he perceived something a little differently than the status quo. He had an inkling of, though scarcely understood, the nature of the Eternal Creator. More so, he was very familiar with the religions of his day (as described in the previous chapter) and understood the world through their lens. Nonetheless, he knew within himself that there was something different, something more, something beyond. Finally, that *something more* was realized. Prior to God speaking to Noah regarding the ark, the book of Genesis gives us the backstory, culminating with:

> *"The earth also was corrupt before God, and the earth was filled with violence." (Genesis 6:11/NKJV)*

Part 2: Origins of Blood Covenant and Sacrifice

The earth was corrupt and full of violence. This is a description of Mankind's egoistic desire, fully dominating and driven with its sense of self-justification and self-preservation. Yet, as is the path of the ego, not only was there self-justification and self-preservation, but also *self-deception.* The Ego redefined its selfish desires, doing what was necessary *to care for itself.* While self-care is important, and even a way of loving oneself, when self-justification and self-deception are involved, it becomes a tribal, political, and religious experience. The best way to preserve oneself is to be among others like ourselves and for us to protect each other. From the beginning, one person killing another was wrong in most cultures. But when a society, tribe, or nation decides that killing someone, or a people group, is appropriate, then it's no longer wrong but politically and religiously acceptable, and at times even necessary. While this kind of corporate care sounds needed, even rather benevolent, it's actually an increase of the desire for self-preservation, which gives way to all manner of corporate violence.

Making the situation worse was the type of violence that pervaded. It was the violence of religion and its so-called practice of worship, framed within its governmental and political structures. It was the condoning of innumerable forms of brutal sacrifices, bloodlettings, and political wars. By making them "religiously" sanctioned acts, it didn't just make such acceptable, *they became mandatory.* Thus, a decreed punishment or act of war became the will of the gods and even a godly quest. Self-justification and self-preservation were redefined by self-deception as a divine penalty or a holy war.

The following, borrowing from the previous chapter, is a short summary of the development of religious and political violence from the Fall, ranging from Cain and Able, to the time of Noah, and beyond in the post-flood era. The names of people groups or nations have been omitted to present these traditions in universal terms. There's a wealth of archeological and anthropological material in libraries, bookstores, and on-line that address the following discourse of violent sacrificial political-religious development. In effect, this is the story of civilization from the fall to the present.

There is a tribe of people who lived in a valley on the south side of a large mountain. They worshipped their gods with fervor, celebrating the different seasons their deities brought to them. One year, the frost god came early and destroyed a good portion of their crops. There was much unrest in the tribe. The people were hungry, and their frustrations began to foster measures of aggression. Infighting began to erupt. The leaders of the tribe and religious clerics were concerned about the loss of crops, but more so the corporate unrest. They launched an investigation to inquire why the frost god was so upset and would do such a thing. "What were the gods trying to tell us?" they asked. They sent scouts throughout the land to inquire of the people, and visited the land just beyond their boarders.

After a few days, the scouts returned with a report. They had discovered an unknown tribe living on the far north side of the same mountain. "They don't look like us, they don't talk like us, they don't dress like us, they don't even smell like us. But most importantly, they don't worship the same gods as us!" Immediately, the cleric-leaders knew the problem: it was *those people,* who didn't talk, dress, smell, or, most importantly, didn't worship like them. THEY caused the problem! The frost god was probably enraged and destroyed the crops *because of those people* who worshipped other gods!

The cleric-leaders called all the men together for war, telling them that the Northerners worshipped rival gods. Worse, "They worship *false* gods!" The men put on warpaint, made shields with the insignia of their tribe and their gods, and prepared to annihilate *those people.* After a time of worship with bombastic drums and loud shouts, they went off to war. Soon, they returned with a great victory! They had destroyed the (totally unsuspecting) northern tribe and decimated their idols. They allowed the women and children to survive, not because they were merciful, but because it was economically profitable to enslave them. After all, it was *those people's* fault that *their tribe* suffered. When the warriors returned, they put their new slaves on display in a type of triumphant march. Then, in lieu of death as payment for their transgressions, they were made to serve in the same fields the frost god had destroyed.

They celebrated their victory over the Northerners and the defeat of the false gods with a great feast. The cleric-leaders

125

proclaimed that each year upon that day there would be a feast day, commemorating the victory the gods gave their tribe. They then chronicled the event in their holy writings so it would serve as a reminder of why the frost god's wrath had been aroused. The essential point was to make sure their tribe was separate from those who worshiped false gods. They augmented their entry by noting that foreign tribes who neared their holy mountain, the boarder of their tribal land, would be put to death or captured and made slaves. Even so, wanting to believe themselves a merciful society, they added that if a foreigner would renounce their origins and learn the true ways of worship of the frost god, they would be allowed to live and join the tribe, not with tribal blood rights, but as accepted outsiders.

Thereafter, the leaders of the tribe regularly sent scouts into the regions beyond, making sure their land remained pure and unthreatened by both foe and false god. Many times, scouts would return with news of a tribe they found beyond the boarder, and off to war the Southern tribe went. More victories gave them more slaves, and eventually they became an economically powerful tribal nation, feared throughout the land. Even their frost god was feared throughout the region because of their victories. As they expanded their way of life, they kept taking land from anyone they deemed as *those people* who didn't look like them, talk like them, dress like them, worship like them, and so on. The Southerners believed their way of life and their gods were the true way of living. Thus, by conquering others and spreading their way of life, they led themselves to believe they were actually blessing those they conquered, giving them an opportunity to know a better way of life.

Part 3: The Scapegoat and Immorality

For several years the crops were fruitful, the slaves were toiling, the warriors were winning, and the nation flourished. Then it happened...the crops were once again destroyed by the early arrival of an angry frost god. The expansion of the tribe into a great nation had its positives and negatives. One major negative was keeping the masses from uprising in times of serious distress. Once again, they were frustrated because of hunger and economic lack. They were agitated and confused about why the frost god was angry, especially since they'd been doing everything their holy book and political-religious leaders told them they should. The political-religious leaders quickly sought answers, not wanting the people to become violent or irrational. Again, they sent out scouts. This time, the report only affirmed what they knew; they'd already vanquished the surrounding tribes, and the land was filled with only images of their frost god and his fellow gods.

Much discussion ensued and the issue became apparent. This was no longer about *those people* on the outside, rather it had to be *someone* or *some sect* on the inside! Inquisitions and interrogations began, with a promise to the tribe-nation that they would find out why the frost god became enraged and destroyed the crops. Finally, a soldier who was second in command to the high commander who oversaw the slaves in the field, approached the leadership. He said that he saw his high commander fraternizing physically with one of the slave girls. The leaders immediately called the high-commander and interrogated him.

"You have been found guilty of treason to your people and in violation of the holy writings!"

The high commander protested. "I have done no such thing! I was only moving the female slave to a different part of the field."

The leaders retorted, "We have all the proof we need. If you were only moving the female, the frost god would not have been angered. Look, our crops have been destroyed under your watch! Therefore, YOU have been found guilty of sexual misconduct and commingling with those who are slaves and worship false gods!"

With a struggle, the palace guards shackled the commander and took him to the community square. The people were gathered and the high-priest made a public announcement. "The High-Commander Causius has been found guilty of the crime of commingling with those who are slaves and worship false gods! He is condemned to death along with his family, as well as the slave girl and her family. At sunrise tomorrow we will offer him as a sacrifice to the gods to appease their rage and offer the others as a testament of our sincerity!" The crowd, with a great shout, offered thanks to their leaders and their gods.

In the morning, Commander Causius was bound upon a large, raised table placed in the community square (later, this will become known as an "altar"). The ceremonial drums were beaten to the gods and the people swayed in worship. As the high priest emerged, he declared the place holy ground to the gods. He announced the name of the twisted, serpent-like image on the sacrificial knife as he unveiled it. The worshipping crowd, now elevated to a unified mind (you could say a mob-mentality) were rhythmically writhing and chanting, "Blood! Blood! Blood!" along with the name of their frost god. The high priest stuck the knife into the chest of their victim-sacrifice and cut out his heart. Still warm and dripping with blood, the priest raised it to the sky, shouting praises to the frost god. The mob cheered! With a wave of his hand, Causius's family, along with the slave girl and her family, were brought up the platform. Each were stabbed by the assisting priests with a newly fashioned sacrificial knife. The victims fell lifeless to the ground, growing puddles of blood filling the area around the bodies. The mob again cheered. The high priest proclaimed, "The gods have been satisfied! Their anger is abated! Fear no more, may your worries and frustrations be brought to rest! The ceremony has ended!" With great applause, the people praised their gods and leaders, and left the square.

The following day the priests announced to the tribe that they've chronicled in the holy writings that the people should not commingle, commit sexual acts, or eat with those who were slaves or worshipped false gods. As a remembrance, they dedicated the day as Saint Causius Day, because *he caused woe* to his people, but *through his sacrifice* the anger of the gods was abated. From that day the tribe continued to celebrate with their feasts of victory over tribes of false gods, but they added the Feast of Saint Causius to the holy chronicle. Animals would be sacrificed and their blood poured out each year in his remembrance because his death abated the wrath of the frost god and saved the people. So, life was good...*for a while.*

Commander Causius was the *scapegoat* for the Southern tribe. In simple terms, a scapegoat is usually someone (or sometimes a group) who is made to bear the blame for others. In many cultures and religious societies, the scapegoat is identified as the reason for the problems and trials that occur. Many times, nations have blamed immigrants or special interest groups for their woes. Many times, "those people" have been the reason for "God's judgment" or "plagues" which befell a land or a nation. For example, several years ago there was a major hurricane that came to South Florida. It devastated miles and miles of land, wildlife, homes, and businesses. One Christian religious leader, who had a major television network, proclaimed that the reason the hurricane struck was because of the large homosexual community in the region. Based on where the hurricane collided with the land, it was several miles off target from the homosexual community supposedly to blame, not to mention all the "appropriate heterosexuals" who lost homes and businesses due to such divine bad aim. Would a god who judges with such detailed precision in regard to sin have such an ambiguous, haphazard, inaccurate execution of his punishments? That would be like Zeus, who is so blindly enraged by a people, he just throws his lightning bolt in the general direction of the offenders, not caring if some of his faithful are collateral damage.

Herein is another important point of such *serpentine political religiosity.* The explanation given when God, or the gods, judge sin in a tribe or nation and the holy in the land fall victim to that same judgment, is usually because the faithful didn't do anything to correct the wicked. Therefore, it's important for the "righteous" to "coerce sinners" to repent. At least, that's what we're told. If the holy ones don't bring to bear upon the sinner their sinfulness, and they don't change their evil ways, then the whole land will be judged. However, it's not only judged because of sin, but because of the neglect of the faithful for not moving the sinner back to righteousness with the gods. So really, it's not just about saving the sinner, it's also about the holy saving their own skin. The holy may say, "But we don't want the sinner tormented in the afterlife." Yet, the sinner could also retort, "You don't want calamity in this present life because you didn't stop us sinners from sinning!" When it comes to tribes, lands, and nations, it's interesting how we justify the need for the local sinner to repent. Of course, if they don't, the other alternative may be a needed imprisonment with torture to gain the necessary repentance, or a resulting punishment by death.

Caiaphas, the High Priest in the time of Jesus, said:

"And one of them, Caiaphas, being high priest that year, said to them, 'You know nothing at all, nor do you consider that it is expedient for us that one man should die for the people, and not that the whole nation should perish.' Now this he did not say on his own authority; but being high priest that year he prophesied that Jesus would die for the nation, and not for that nation only, but also that He would gather together in one the children of God who were scattered abroad."   *(John 11:49-52/NKJV)*

In this moment, Caiaphas made Jesus the scapegoat for the nation. He, like our earlier examples, weighed what the tribe possessed against what he feared they would lose. At that time the Jewish people were occupied and ruled by the Romans. They didn't have dominion over what they considered their land since the time of their kings almost a millennia ago. They lost their preeminence, their independence, their land, their temple, and their freedom to the Persians, then the Greeks, then the Romans, on through to the recent Ottoman Empire. The central aspect of their identity in the land from the time of King Solomon revolved around their temple. In that temple was a chamber called the Holy of Holies, which housed the presence of God in an object called the Ark of the Covenant. Hundreds of years prior to Jesus's arrival, Solomon's temple was destroyed and the Ark stolen. In the name of good nature and good politics, the Roman government chose to rebuild the temple for the community. Consider, the temple was rebuilt by pagans, King Herod the Great to be exact, and there was no Ark to be found in the newly fashioned holy of holies. Think about what little they had remaining from their former days of the great King David. Now they were ruled by a pagan empire, and they feared losing what little of their former fragmented lives they had. Of course, they told themselves that they'd never had it so good for hundreds of years. Truly God must have favored them! The Temple was rebuilt, funded by Rome, which created thousands of jobs for the Jewish people. They had a flourishing economy and could worship freely. Surely God used Rome to bless them, right? Not according to God Himself through Jesus Christ. If anything, it was the reverse (John 8:39-47). To have such an economy and freedom of worship there had to be a compromise: make the deeds of Caesar the deeds of God when necessary, and pay your civil taxes in addition to the temple tax.

Then came Jesus! Jesus pointed out, in no uncertain terms, that the relationship between God and Caesar only works when we know the difference and clearly only serve one master. The problem was that the Pharisees and the Herodians were in bed together (Matthew 22:16; Mark 3:6; 12:13). Jesus came speaking truth to the people regarding the Eternal Creator, but His words were difficult to receive because He made a clear distinction between God and Caesar. Because of this, the religion of the day needed to silence Christ for fear of losing what "little they had been given" by Rome. Caiaphas was clear that if they didn't kill Jesus, they would perish and lose "the nation." Jesus had to die. He had to become the scapegoat! Then, when Caiaphas spoke, he didn't stand as a man, or political activist, rather he spoke with the authority of the office of high priest. This was no different than any pagan before him. Yet for him to do so, he violated one of the key mandates of that office: no human sacrifice (Leviticus 20:2-5)! In that moment, the stage was set to undo everything that imprisoned humanity by his egoistic Serpent. The embodied legalism of the 613 commandments, the priesthood, their temple with their blood sacrifices and covenants, were about to come to an end. The initial intention of God in Creation was about to be restored to its origins. The final unveiling of the contrast between Divine reality and the illusion of egoistic political religion had come to its fullness. In the same way it is said that in the *fullness of time God sent His Son,"*(Galatians 4:4), it was also true of the former custodians of the oracles of God, the Jewish religion and paganism were finally one in the same.

Part 4: The Blood Sacrifice of Blessing

There's just no telling what really upsets frost gods and how to make them happy. After all, mere humans don't have the lofty wisdom of the gods. After a few years, the inevitable occurred: the frost god visited earlier than expected and destroyed most of the crops. Again, there was unrest and anger among the tribal nation. Shouting to their cleric-leaders, the people asked, "How could this be? We vanquished those outside our tribe who worship false gods. We keep our holy mountain pure by not allowing the existence of any tribe that doesn't look like us, talk like us, sound like us, and dress like us. We've expanded our tribal nation to protect our way of life and offer the truth to others. We sacrifice to the gods those who violate the holy writings, especially those who

134

commingle with slaves, and we do our best to keep all the holy feasts!"

The cleric-leaders (also good politicians) proclaimed with religious rhetoric, "We are forming a committee and we'll get back to you on that." Well, not exactly. It probably sounded more like, "Do not question the ways of the frost god! We priests will seek the gods together along with the holy writings and tell you what they say."

Within a few days the cleric scribe mounted the community square and proclaimed, "Until now, we have sacrificed honorable gifts to our gods, particularly our holy frost god. When members of the community have violated the holy writings, we offered them in sacrifice to our gods. This has been well pleasing to them, but we have fallen short in our devotion to the most holy frost god. As of this day, we will prepare to offer the supreme sacrifice! Rather than sacrifice because of our evils, we will now offer in blood from our goodness and of our best. We will give out of our devotion, offering a sacrificial blessing to the frost god. We will find among us the most beautiful, pure woman in whom is no guile and sacrifice her as a blessing of devotion. This will please the frost god, thus he and all the other gods will favor us!"

After some mumbling, the crowd called out, "Hurray to our new high priestess who gives herself to the gods!"

The tribal search began for a lovely young girl. Her family was told that for the gift of their daughter they would be given food, land, and the status of nobility for the rest of their lives. Within weeks, families were volunteering their daughters, willing to give them up for the high honor. A glorious temple was built for the new holy priestesses to dwell. Then, commencing each year after the high feast of Saint Causius, when the new moon rose, the high priestess would be offered as a sacrifice of blessing, a gift to the frost god. All the priestesses were highly taken care of with food, riches, and every luxury they could desire. Each year, one would be selected from among them as high priestess and for that year she would have as much authority as a serving male cleric.

On the special day of her sacrificial bloodletting, she was dressed in ceremonial white (or whatever was the combination of bridal and priestess attire for the culture). She was brought to the community square where they erected a statue of the frost god. She was tied to the sacrificial table, just in case she had any last-minute second thoughts about this high honor when the sacrificial knife was unveiled. The drums beat in ceremonial rhythm, and all chanted with mob-like unity, "Blood! Blood! Blood!" followed by the name of the frost god. When the sacrificial knife was revealed, the priestess did scream, but it was hard to hear her over the noise of the "worship." Swiftly, the high priest plunged the knife into her chest. He reached in with his hand, ripped out her still pulsating heart, and raised it up to the sky. The people cheered as the high priest shook with ecstasy and the high priestess lay lifeless in a pool of blood. He pronounced some unintelligible prayer and then clearly proclaimed, "The high priestess is now wed to the frost god! Let us celebrate their union in a feast!" Animals were ritualistically slaughtered throughout the square, then cooked. The people feasted, celebrating with dancing and drinking. (In a few cases, the priestess's family was given a special table with lavish food and drink where the people would bring them celebratory flowers and give thanks.) All rejoiced! At the end of the feast, the high priest stood and proclaimed, "All is well for the tribe of the Southern Mountain region! We are accepted by the frost god for another year! Return to your homes and continue to be thankful."

Part 5: Giving Children Back to the Gods

Once again life was good. Feasts of victory prevailed, ritual sacrifices were in full swing, and memorial celebrations were held. The wrath of the gods was halted and the yearly bloodletting of the high priestess secured their world. Right? *Wrong!* For some reason, a year arrived when the frost god came much earlier than in the past, bringing great devastation. Fortunately, the leaders and clerics had storehouses with extra food in case of another visit from the enraged frost god. (The storehouses were not intended for the people, but for the leaders and clerics. Lowly peasants in the community or converted foreigners were not so fortunate.) The unrest and agitation were very high in the once small tribe, now a huge nation. The peasants were dying and the middle class was eroding. The political leaders, on the other hand, were okay for the moment; they had reserves. Nonetheless, the social turbulence was getting difficult to manage. Commerce was down and the peasant work force was dying out, both of which were important to the upper class and the economy.

The cleric-leaders gathered the people throughout their respective communities at the town square. The announcement was proclaimed, "We have convened and found that the frost god requires a greater sacrificial blessing in addition to the high priestess once a year. He requires the purist of sacrifices: a child!" (Full stop...what? Children?) "Those families who would be willing to give of their children will be rewarded by the nobles with food from their storehouses. If you do not have children, for a small fee you may purchase food from the nobles and clerics. If you don't have the money, you may work in the fields with the slaves during this time for a better crop next season."

For obvious reasons, we'll refrain from describing the immolation of children (2 Chronicles 28:3), but it's horrible. The strategy of the cleric-leaders was impactful. Rather than peasants fighting and killing each other for food, or dying from hunger, they were offering their children so they could eat. Those who didn't have children went to work in the fields. It was economically beneficial for those who owned the fields, providing free labor for the harvest. For those who had a little money, buying from the landowners and nobles was an excellent way to ensure the landowners riches, or to sound more benevolent, to help the general economy. This was the final political-religious solution that worked and resolved any potential ranting of the frost god. It's not to say he didn't get angry and destroy crops every so often, but now a system was in place that kept the *castes* in order.

The nation cheered as they kept their feasts, sacrifices, bloodlettings, and immolations. After all, it was one's national duty to serve the gods and the system. The leaders waved at the people as they ate in feast-like fashion daily. The clerics indirectly ruled the leaders and the people through religious manipulation. Wait, as honest and truthful as that is, it doesn't sound very nice, so let's rephrase it to sound spiritual and politically correct, the way we're used to thinking of it. *Through the wisdom of the national leaders, the country flourished as they heeded the minister's guidance through prayer and the holy books.*

Part 6: Blood Covenant Union

Throughout all the stages of development in such political-religious systems, there was another aspect that was instituted. In the world of justified sacrifice and ritual murder, the ceremony of *blood covenant* was instituted to ratify contracts and marriages, and to end family feuds and wars. Because of the ego and distrust between fellow human beings, something more than just a word of promise and a handshake became necessary. In other words, for us to cohabitate and feel safe with our agreements, we instituted a sharing in one another's blood, coupled with another ritual sacrifice to ratify it. There were many variances of rituals, but ultimately, after trading garments, weapons, tools, and other tribal symbols, there was the exchanging of blood. Some cut fingers, others their wrists or limbs. Many times, they bled themselves into a cup, horn, or chalice, then mingled their blood with wine or a strong drink. They did this with a pledge agreement and drank to the new union in front of their respective witnesses, families, or tribes. This process would unite the participants and witnesses, but not without one ominous feature: the blood sacrifice of a choice animal (or on extraordinary occasions, a human) to the gods. This did two things. First, it involved the invocation of the gods into the covenant as a partner. Second, because a life was sacrificed, this meant that if anyone violated the covenant they were, in effect, violating the sacrificial blood that was shed and the only restitution would be death. To expound, it also would involve two things. First, the death and blood shedding of the violator. In many cases this extended to the entire family or tribe. At times the "death warrant" extended to future generations if all the family members were not found and executed. Second, it also invoked the curse of the gods. When the covenant was first cut, this was part of the invocation ceremony. When the sacrifice or immolation occurred, the covenant demanded that the gods would bring judgment, curses, and calamity to the violator, as well as their family and tribe. If a family or tribe was not directly involved in the covenant, but served as witnesses, that condition would extend to them, finding and bringing the violators to "justice." Regarding the invocation of the gods, the thought was that if the violated couldn't extinguish the violators, the gods were asked to make the lives of the violators miserable until the violated party could finish the annihilation. Thus, people and people groups often made sacrifices in fear and ignorance in addition to their regular religious demands. While they themselves may not have violated any covenant, they would think something bad had happened because a past ancestor may have violated a covenant. While this may sound murderously crazy, it did keep people in fearful guard of their agreements with each other.

To make the heinous point, not only were they sacrificing people, animals, and children to make the gods happy or abate their anger, more blood and death was added to make sure they kept their contracts and relationships.

To summarize, we can return to the statement we started with:

> *"The earth also was corrupt before God, and the earth was filled with violence." (Genesis 6:11/NKJV)*

SECTION III

TRANSFORMATIONS

CHAPTER 6
NOAH RISING

My bounty is as boundless as the sea,
My love as deep; the more I give to thee
The more I have, for both are infinite.

Romeo and Juliet, Juliet
Act II, scene 2, line 133
William Shakespeare

The story of Noah has the building blocks that later frame the Melchizedekian priesthood. It begins after the scripture states that the thoughts of Mankind's heart were continually evil (Genesis 6:5). This is a clue to the spiritual root. This isn't just a historical account about an unhinged apocalyptic preacher running through the town claiming the sky is falling. Rather, this is a story about a Divine spiritual attribute, latent in each of us, called *Noah*. When we sense, though fallaciously through the ego, a separation from God, or determine that the Divine doesn't exist, the thoughts of our heart are, in effect, *evil*. Before we jump to conclusions thinking that evil is our propensity for wrong-doing or a bad attitude, if we look to the Hebrew word itself it will lead us to its definition. Evil, רע

(ra), is nothing more than what the letters of the word describe: ‏ר‏ (resh) which means the *head, origin,* or *mind,* and ‏ע‏ (ayin) which means *eyes* or *sight.* In short, *evil* is a description of a person who lives life by *what they see with the natural eye and how they rationalize it in their head.* From a Divine point of view, it really means to live in a dysfunctional manner. Why? Because the person who solely processes information through their natural senses is not functioning according to their designed potential. The only energizing faculty that functions in that scenario is the self, the Ego. The Human Creature is far more than just five senses and a brain, which are quite powerful in and of themselves. However, if that's all that's used, we're still in the Death Sleep, living in the dream world of self-absorbed illusion.

Noah was and is different. He had something occurring within him beyond the five senses and the religious expressions of his day. This "something" provoked him to look beyond the physical and perceive the unseen. The truth that Noah unveiled was in stark contrast to any religious system.

Part 1: Qualities of a Builder of a New World

> *"But Noah found grace in the eyes of the Lord. This is the genealogy of Noah. Noah was a just man, perfect in his generations. Noah walked with God. And Noah begot three sons: Shem, Ham, and Japheth."* *(Genesis 6:8-10/NKJV)*

Arguably, these four sentences can be very misleading. We've traditionally read them in a way which suggests that Noah was a man who did all the right things and because his lineage (reaching back to the time of Adam) was pure, God extended His grace toward him. Think of it, if the reason why God was gracious to Noah was because he did the right things and had a holy lineage, how is that different from any other pagan religion of his time, before or after the flood? But what the text is telling us is something quite different:

ונח מצא חן בעיני יהוה:

(v'noach matsah cheen b'eeiyneeiy yahweh)

"And Rest unveiled grace in Yahweh's eyes."

In Hebrew, **נח** Noah is the word for *rest.* For example, in the epistle to the Hebrews 4:3 (referring to Psalm 95:11) it says, *"For we who have believed do enter that rest..."* Because we believe we enter rest. The question is, what are we to believe to experience this Divine rest? After all, most religious beliefs cause anything but true rest, at best a sense of rightness, at worst a sense of unworthiness. In either case, there's no real inner peace, only the striving to be right so we don't feel unworthy or sinful. Once again, we find the definition in the word itself, however, not only in definition, but in its *reflection.* To start with a leading suggestion, to attain this Divine rest we must uncover its fraternal twin, *grace.* This finding doesn't occur because we *perform* what is *morally correct* or *achieve success* in some religious quest. If we did do

147

those things, we might feel a momentarily diminished fear of vengeance, or be inclined to beg for a blessing. But again, that would be no different than any of the religions in Noah's day, or in our day for that matter. Doing things that abate the wrath or judgment of the gods and pleading for their grace or blessing never was and will never be *true spiritual rest.* Such thinking and believing only offers a momentary lull from the fear of retribution.

Noah, when looking into the eyes of יהוה (Yahweh), discovered something dynamically different from all the other gods. What he beheld was nothing but *grace.* Think of it, nothing but grace! No judgment, vengeance, wrath, or conditional blessing! When Noah witnessed the Divine gaze, like twins separated at birth and now reunited as lovers, *Rest* and *Grace* found each other. Can you imagine? What would it be like if you and your truest love were torn apart and separated? What would it be like if every day throughout your life you sensed the void and longed to be in their passionate embrace? You might go to the place you were together last. You might walk its streets, longing and remembering what being together was like. Then the day arrives when you go to that familiar place and the seemingly impossible happens! There they stand, searching for you as well. Your eyes meet. In bewilderment you ask, "Is that...?" Many thoughts race through your mind. "It's impossible! How can this be?" Oh, but it is! For a moment you can't breathe. Then, with almost thoughtless excitement, you run to each other and passionately embrace, kissing, hugging, burning with desire and yet, with a measure of disbelief you think, "It's too good to be true." Yes...it is! This is what it's like when *grace* and *rest* come back together: longing lovers reunited in enflamed embrace.

In many mythologies, like the Egyptian, Greek, and Teutonic, we find twins who become lovers and beget a type of redemption through their union. In most cases, such stories are not about an inappropriate incestuous relationship, but a description of a Divine union, separated for some reason and, in passion, finding each other once again. After all, isn't that the story of the man and the woman in the Garden? They were one, then like twins became two. The consequence of the Fall separated them. Then the one gave birth to the other, the redeemer. Once again, the man (Christ) found the woman (the Bride, the Church) and the two were reunited as one.

Remember to whom Moses was writing; the notion of a God of Grace giving rest to one's soul was an astounding declaration! When we view Rest and Grace, you cannot have one without the other, like Romeo and Juliet, who still found each other amongst the factions and violence of the Montagues and the Capulets. They gazed into one another in an amorous embrace and created their own paradise. On the surface, their ending appears grim, but it may not be as tragic as it seems. Their conclusion speaks of "transcendent love." Despite the factions, prejudice, and violence of their families, their love transcended it all. Yet, such love couldn't thrive in an environment of egoistic hostility, which is another important point. Their deaths awoke the Montagues and the Capulets to their warring futility, and the families made peace.

This isn't far from the Gospel message. Despite the egoism of Mankind, God's Love through Christ was revealed with grace and rest. Our egoistic hostility refused to embrace what was shown before us. Thus, we crucified Christ, and by extension, God's expression of Love. Nonetheless, such love was and is transcendent and lives on perpetually to Mankind, making peace between our illusion of hostility with one another and God (Ephesians 2:14-16).

Looking at the surrounding gods in both Noah's and Moses's day, through all their warring factions with judgment and wrath, Grace and Rest (the two passionate lovers), found each other and set forth for a new world. Like the Trinitarian concept of *perichoresis* (the spinning dance-like relationship of each of its members), the spiritual qualities of Rest and Grace are forever united in passionate intimacy, preferring one another in Divine pleasure. The one giving to the other, that one receiving and giving back, and on and on they go in the joyous cycle of Eternal Life. Rest was enthralled by Grace, and Grace was entranced by Rest. The spiritual quality called נח (noach) is the *heart-felt inner Rest* which emerges from the intertwined awareness of *Grace* seen in the passionate eyes of the Eternal One. This intercourse is called *DIVINE PLEASURE...Eden!*

But why call them twin lovers? Because they truly are *reflections* of each other. The word for *rest* נח (noach) is literally the reflection of the word grace חן (cheen). If you were to hold up the word *rest,* נח (noach) in Hebrew, in front

150

of a mirror, it would reflect back the word *grace* חֵן (cheen). The first letter in *rest* is the last letter in *grace,* the נ (nun), though the letter case changes at the end of a word; in *grace,* it appears in its final form, ן (we'll discuss this in a moment). In the same manner, the last letter in *rest* is the first letter in the word *grace,* the ח (chet). On top of this mirroring effect, the reason the final ן (nun) is used for *grace* is because that is the final decree. There is no limit and no end to God's grace, and that's final. There is no qualification that can be compromised, nor another point of view. There is nothing other than *Divine pleasure* in the eyes of יהוה as He *beholds us!*

When we recognize there's nothing else but this view of us within God, all the fearful turmoil of displeasing Him, agitating His vengeance, or incurring retribution, *is gone.* These two little two-letter words once again affirm the largest of truths. The forthcoming reboot of Creation with the flood addresses the political-religious violence done in the name of the gods, from Cain, to the murder of Able, to the human and animal sacrifices that followed. Finally, with all this going on, someone allowed himself to see past the veil and see God as He truly is. This changed everything! With the spiritual realities of Rest and Grace once again united, the necessary ingredient for a new world and a rebirth of Creation was possible. You could say that this union was the Divine Seed that gave birth to a new era. For that matter, the letter נ (nun) speaks again; its meaning is *the perpetual Divine seed, the*

151

throne of Messiah. The Messiah is the Son of God, yes, but you can also say He is the Son of the intimate union of *Rest* and *Grace.*

Remember, the text does not say that Noah was offered grace, rather he *found grace* in the eyes of **יהוה**. The Hebrew word *found,* **מצא** (matsah), beyond the obvious meaning of finding what was lost or discovering what was unknown, is also translated *to be present* (Esther 1:5), and in more modern translations, *to rescue* (Zechariah 11:6). Think of what those subtleties mean. In a world with gods of violence and war, Noah found what was lost, *the God of Grace.* Contrary to the religions that held rituals of law and tribute, Noah uncovered the presence and reality of the true nature of God, the Creator. Then the ultimate dichotomy appears before us. When Noah found grace in the eyes of **יהוה**, who really rescued who first? Consider this: The true compassionate God, the Eternal Creator of Life, was lost among the created gods and goddesses of Mankind. The people of the earth didn't know Him, see Him, or hear Him. Thus, was His sorrow over humanity simply because they were bad and doing horrible things? Or was it also because the love of His life, His Creation, no longer acknowledged Him? Remember, this all started with God creating as a love story. God the Eternal Creator living in, with, and through His creation, together as one, was the Divine dream. But He didn't program His Creation to obey a set of rules for their relationship, nor did He threaten their choice with retribution if they didn't. Rather, in giving us a free will and choice, He risked all for true love. He allowed

Mankind to choose its own way. Yet, even as we chose to leave by desiring the path of the Serpent, He never left us, despite the fact that we forgot Him and fashioned "lovers" right in front of Him (Judges 2:17; Revelation 18:4). Nonetheless, because of His love, God allowed us to continue down that path, trusting that our distant memory of true paradise would prod our thinking and the day would come when we would yield to it. Finally, the day came, and Noah found our lost Divine Lover with Grace in His eyes! Dare to think of it! Among the gods and goddesses of blood sacrifice and vengeance, Noah rescued the God of Grace, as the God of Grace rescued him. Only the beauty of Divine logic can reveal this!

Most importantly, this is not about external gods and goddesses high up on a mountain and a supreme, unacknowledged God in a celestial city. Nor is it about an angry God who is about to flood the globe because no one worships Him. This is not just about a flood, a large wooden boat, and the animals within, both clean and unclean. This is about our inner world, the inner world of the Adam, which begins within our hearts. We live life externally, rarely ever looking inward, where the Kingdom of God abides. We live life, create false gods ranging from religion to politics and everything in between. Yet the Living God within us, who's quiet to our sleeping ears, is there. You could say He's trapped within our hearts, chained in our inner Tartarus, waiting for that moment when that distant memory causes us to take a glimpse into the eternal world within. Like Noah, in that moment, in that discovery, when we see the reality of Christ within us, we are rescued into our true selves because we found and, in effect, rescued Him! You see, finding Him is finding us and when we desire to find our true selves, we can't help but also find Him. In that moment the world that we once knew is flooded and we are carried through an inner ark to a new world.

Part 2: A Desire Created

The only way we desire something is if we've encountered it before, either in observation of another or by direct experience. *Desire is created from a longed-for memory.*

Even the Serpent in the Garden, when speaking to the woman, created a desire for the Tree of the Knowledge of Good and Evil by manipulating the central desire of her spiritual DNA. She was created as the Likeness of God, thus it was within her spiritual DNA to desire and emanate that. All the Serpent did was redirect her inner state from fulfillment into longing. The Serpent simply suggested that she needed something more than she had. He didn't need to convince her through some intellectual wrestling match, he only needed to "suggest" the idea. To say it in modern terms, you may have the perfect car for you, then a commercial comes on television saying, "This is the car you need!" (Because the purpose of advertising is to redirect our desires and create a longing.) When it's told to us enough over time, it can build a desire for whatever "it" is. For example, despite their motto, Budweiser is not really the "King of Beers." They really don't make the best quality beer. Rather, they invest more in marketing than most any other beer company. (See the 2009 documentary, *Beer Wars*.)

Because Budweiser promotes itself more than any other beer label in North America, they gross more sales and can proclaim they're the king of ~~beers~~, beer marketing. The way of this egoistic world is simple: tell everyone you're the king and keep telling them, then continually invest financially, over time telling everyone you're the king, and eventually the public will believe it. By the way, if you're not a beer drinker, don't worry, some other form of marketing has probably gotten you at least once. If not for material goods, let's not forget the ever popular cable news networks, confirming one's political bias. And yes, even prophets fall prey to this.

To find the *rest* we seek, and despite the marketing of the iatrogenic Tree of the Knowledge of Good and Evil, it's about seeing with a different set of eyes. Actually, it's not even different eyes, but our true eyes simply being open. From the beginning of this book and its predecessor, we keep stressing this thing called the Ego. Why? Because, like our view of God and His grace, it too is closer than the nose on our face. It is the illusion of the "I" we think we are, rather than "Who" we really are. All it takes is a measure of crucifying the Ego to begin to see and to find that what we were seeking was in plain sight all along.

Continuing with the verses from the beginning of this chapter:

> *"These are the generations of Noah. Noah was a just man and perfect in his generations, and Noah walked with God. And Noah begot three sons: Shem, Ham, and Japheth."*　　　*(Genesis 6:9-10/KJV)*

155

אלה תולדת נח נח איש צדיק תמים היה בדרתיו את האלהים התהלך נח:

(eeleh tol'dot noach noach ish tsadiq tamiym
hayah b'dorotaiyv eet-ha'elohiym hit'hallek-noach)

In the King James, American Standard, Douay-Rheims, and English Standard versions, the word *generations* is used twice. The first time appears to refer to Noah's lineage: *"These are the generations of Noah..."* The second, it describes the time and the group of people Noah was living among *"...perfect in his generations."* But the English words may mislead the reader. Other translations use words like *account, story, history,* and even add words like *"...blameless in his [evil] generation..."* (Amplified), which still creates a picture other than what the text is communicating. Another way to translate this could be:

> *"These are the births of Rest. Rest, a man who walked the path wholly, was in his revolutions with the Powers; (himself) walked (in a state of) Rest."*

The verb *walked,* **התהלך נח** (hit'hallek-noach), is in the *hitpael* mood, which means, *to put oneself in the state of.* Thus, Noah put "himself" into this state of *Rest.* By extension, we must realize that we "put ourselves" into that state as well. More traditionally speaking, in order to walk with God we must put ourselves in a state of Rest. The New Testament calls this the Rest of faith or trust (Hebrews 4:3-11). We cannot walk with God and be in fear of His judgment or hope that He'll bless us if we do the right things. We must, by choice, *rest* in the reality of His *loving grace.* We must allow ourselves to see the Father's gaze of compassionate grace and rest in that truth. Once again, this is *our choice.* It is completely up to us to choose the Rest of trusting in His graciousness. When we hold back in the slightest, we have a propensity to fall back into the violence of works and sacrifice. (We'll discuss this further, when we address the section from the book of Acts regarding the death of Ananias and Sapphira.)

When we behold true Grace, the natural reflection is Rest, and together they give birth to the ability to "walk the Divine path." *Recognizing habitual, unchanging grace in the eyes of God is our eternal Rest.* We rest as we twirl together in an amorous embrace, which is another aspect of *perichoresis.* In practical terms, we are to *reconcile within ourselves that we are in the state of Divine Rest because of Divine Grace.* The scripture continues:

ויולד נח שלשה בנים את שם את חם ואת יפת:

(vaiyioled noach she'losah baniym et-shem et-ham et-yapheth)

"And bore Rest, three sons, the Name, the Hot, and the Opening."

One of the powerful aspects of the word *son* (or *daughter)* is that it literally means *to build with.* By letter definition, *son,* בן (ben), means *the house seed that flows continually.* Thus, what we birth or emanate is the continual flow of what abides within us. Like the Adam who inhaled the Breath of God and became a living soul, similarly, Rest inhaled the breath of Grace and exhaled three Divine expressions. (Note the harkening to the *perichoresis,* the one manifesting three and the three in one.) The first is שֵׁם (shem), which refers directly to the *Divine Name* or *Essence*. Remember, in Hebrew a name is not simply a title or designation, but a description of a spiritual quality or essence of a person, place, or thing. The first emanation of intimacy from Rest and Grace is *the Essence,* שֵׁם (shem), of the Divine Nature itself. Hence, שֵׁם (shem) is the first branch from the root, נֹחַ Noah, that extends and from which its two siblings shoot forth.

> *"...His divine power has given to us all things that pertain to life and godliness...that through these you may be **partakers of the divine nature...**"*
>
> (2 Peter 1:3-4/NKJV)

The effect of our restful inner state results in a revelation of His essence or presence within. We are not trying to become His essence, or obtain His presence, rather this is who we are at the core. We are not trying to earn His Divine nature through a system of merit. Most certainly, we are not trying to experience some outpouring of Divine presence by doing correct rituals or worship services. Rather, it's resting in the reality of what Divine grace sees, the real us. When we cease trying to become His essence, or attain His presence, and realize we are an expression of both, we will rest in true faith.

Once again, *we are an expression of both Divine essence and presence,* nothing less! If each person is a revelation of both Divine essence and presence, then it stands to reason that all humanity is a collective expression of the Divine in its fullness.

When we rest in the gaze of His grace, we are united with that same gaze. This is both the Old and New Testament's ultimate definition of the word *peace.* The Apostle Paul tells us that Christ is our *peace.* Not just offering some form of calm and tranquility, rather He is the tranquility that results in His unconditional unity with us. He reunites us, both in God and in each other, in heart and mind, removing the self-imposed veil or wall that divided us (Ephesians 2:14-18). In other words, when we realize the Living Word, the Divine Thought filled with Divine Pleasure within us, we reflect that in every manner of our being. Consequently, we *leave* the lower worlds of religion and self-centered gratification and ascend to the higher cosmos of Christ-Oneness, our place of origin. This is the embracing of what Paul calls *the Mind of Christ,* and our Jewish brothers and sisters call *Messianic Consciousness.* This is not simply thinking about Christ or all the red-letter verses that Jesus spoke (which is a great start), but realizing that, through complete selflessness, we are of one Divine Mind or awareness. This *mind in us* (which is also Christ) is our true self. It climaxes by radiating the realities of the Tree of Life, with all its attributes, in us and through us.

The second manifestation is חם (ham), which means *hot* or *heat.* In addition to being a product of נח Noah/Rest, this

159

word also appears as part of the process *"...seedtime and harvest, cold and heat (or hot)..."* By letter definition it means *to separate the flow of water,* or more accurately, *to transform the flow of water.* Even without modern science, the people to whom Genesis was written understood that heat causes water to transform from liquid to vapor, from one state to another.

חם (ham) doesn't change the essence, but the form of something into another. In a similar manner, the warmth of the sun aids seeds to germinate. Without the proper heat, seeds lay dormant and will not transform into the plants they are intended to be. In other words, חם (ham) transforms essence from one *form* to another. If שם (shem) is the Divine Essence, then חם (ham) is *the agent which reveals its form.* This is another side of the same block described in Genesis 1. It's another characterization of the מסך (masach), the reflecting screen that causes the Image and Likeness to shine throughout Creation. Later in the חם Ham story, he *"uncovered his father's nakedness"* (Genesis 9:22). Consider what happened. When נח Noah (Rest) got drunk, Genesis 9:21 says that he *became uncovered in his tent.* The key phrase is ויתגל (vayitagal), which is also in the *hitpael* mood, just like when Noah *put himself in a state of rest.* This phrase can also be translated, *"And he put himself in a state of exile..."* The same word is translated in 2 Kings 24:14, 1 Chronicles 9:1, Ezra 2:1, Nehemiah 7:6, and in other places as *exile.* What happened from a root view is that when we lose sight of *Grace, Rest* is put in *exile.* On the positive side, we immediately see

שֵׁם Shem, the *Divine Essence,* and Japheth (which we will discuss shortly), taking a garment, walking backwards, and "covering" him. Note how the Divine Essence, the Nature of God, doesn't uncover or expose. Let's take a look at both Old and New Testament declarations:

> *"...But love covers all sins." (Proverbs 10:12/NKJV)*

> *"He who covers a transgression seeks love..."*
> *(Proverbs 17:9/NKJV)*

> *"And above all things have fervent love for one another, for 'love will cover a multitude of sins.'"*
> *(1 Peter 4:8/NKJV)*

In the first volume we discussed that God distinguished the Light from the Darkness, and to do so He gave the Creature *(the Desire to Receive)* a choice to reflect the Light. The choice is made to reflect the Light, and that state is called Lucifer. Another way to describe it is that we choose to resist the temptation *to receive for ourselves alone.* When we do this, we offer the necessary spiritual material to reflect the Light, which contains the Divine Image and Likeness. We could also say that this anti-egoistic state is the result of our choice to raise the Life-Giving screen, מָסָךְ (masach). In this state, not only is there a reflection of the Light, but it also illuminates all the Life that's in it. As mentioned before, it's like a movie screen which reflects the projected light, having within it all the images, performers, colors, terrains, actions, and events.

161

(Refer to "Refresher: In the Beginning Again - Refresher 3 - The Transformation of Lucifer.") At one point, Lucifer chose *to receive for himself only*. Thus, the Light was no longer reflected, revealing Creation as intended. The מסך (masach) screen shattered, חתת (chatat), and because of its self-centeredness, entered the delusion of separation. It's also interesting to point out that the word *shattered*, חתת (chatat), is also rendered in some translations as *broken in pieces* (Isaiah 8:9), *to be dismayed*, or *afraid*. This is what happens when we *receive for ourselves alone*, thus not keeping intact the מסך (masach), the anti-egoistic screen. In that shattered state of disconnected illusion, the immediate result is *to be afraid*. We also see this occur immediately after the Adam partook of the same egoistic fruit (Genesis 3:10). The Ego, in its sense of separation creates fear, then quickly compensates with covering itself in pride, including all its attributes of self-justification, self-preservation, and self-centeredness. From the attitude of self-concern, it endorses the ego as healthy, calling it *being one's own person*. The irony is that the so-called "healthy claim" of being a separate individual is actually contrary to what we long for. The illusion of being one's own individual is that we've replaced our true existence as an integration of the Divine nexus, with the delusion of narcissism. Nonetheless, we still long to be part of a whole, to belong, and to be connected. Yet our varying levels of narcissism get in the way. *The egoistic claim for being a healthy, separate individual creates the very emptiness we're forever longing to fill.*

Looking back to the selfish decision of Lucifer (now renamed *Satan*, the adversary), God fashioned the Adam by taking of that same substance, *the Desire to Receive for Oneself,* also called the dust of the ground, אדמה (adamah), and breathed into it the Breath of Life. Remember, אדמה is another way of describing Lucifer's satanic proclamation, *"I will be like the Most High"* אדמה לעליון (Isaiah 14:14). We can also call this the unholy trinity of *me, myself, and I.* Yet, when the breath of Life came, the Adam became a *Living Soul.* They were restored to the place of choice to raise the מסך (masach) and reflect Divine Life. However, we know what happened next. They too fell prey to the egoistic desires of the knowledge of good and evil and succumbed to an adversarial state.

We must reconcile what, within ourselves, may be perceived as a dichotomy, yet in the realm of Divine Life is really a similarity. God intentionally created us to *receive,* so you could say we were created with a type of *ego.* You could say that this ego, when properly placed in the upper world of Divine Life, receives all the Light that God has *and more.* However, it doesn't just receive for itself alone, but has more than enough to share with others. Like the human body when it receives nourishment, each cell doesn't only receive for itself, but receives more than enough to share and pass on to other cells. This process, called *diffusion,* is for the purpose of attaining equilibrium. We have been given the capacity to receive way more than we need, hence, pressed down, shaken together, and running over (Luke 6:38). If we receive for ourselves alone and don't share, our brother or sister isn't properly cared for and is *uncovered*. On the other hand, when we receive and share, we are being our brother's keeper and covering them accordingly. However, after the shattering, or the Fall, the screen was not functioning according to design, thus the Ego fell from the upper world to the lower, *Receiving for Itself Alone*. This is where the Christ comes into the theater of Creation. Through His life, death, and resurrection, He revealed the pathway to reconstitute the screen. Literally, He revealed that separation was only an illusion and He, We, and the Father are One. Like שם Shem, the Divine Essence, who "walked backwards and covered their father's nakedness," Christ too "walked backwards," meaning He *returned our perception back* to its original state. He returned and restored to our thinking that we had a choice. He reminded our awareness that we could choose between egoism with its delusions of right and wrong or embrace *Divine grace and truth* (John 1:14-16). As each one of us realize the reality of Christ within us, we become aware of our connection in the Divine and each other. It's as if the projectionist in the theater reached into the dust of the shredded screen and unveiled that they were always united. In such awakening, the fragments were reunited. As each piece rediscovered its innate connection as a collective whole, the Living Image reemerged, and Creation was restored.

> *"...that they all may be one, as You, Father, are in Me, and I in You; that they also may be one in Us, that the world may believe that You sent Me."*
>
> *(John 17:21/NKJV)*

When the second manifestation is functioning, חם (ham) gives *form* to the *essence* and transforms *individuality* back to *oneness.*

Part 3: Understanding the Screen as Form

In the previous volume, we saw that the first chapter of Genesis isn't a mere scientific discussion regarding how God created the physical earth in seven days. To the contrary, it's a spiritual account of how God created and developed the Soul, which is the focus of His Creation. You could say it's a systematic disclosure of the spiritual science of how the egoistic nature of the soul is developed into His Image and Likeness. This development had six phases which collectively form a seventh, commonly called the seventh day. After the first day, which we previously discussed in extensive detail, the next phase occurred on what's called *the second day:*

> *"Then God said, 'Let there be a firmament in the midst of the waters, and let it divide the waters from the waters.' Thus God made the firmament, and divided the waters which were under the firmament from the waters which were above the firmament; and it was so. And God called the firmament Heaven. So the evening and the morning were the second day."*   *(Genesis 1:6-8/NKJV)*

In verse 6 it says:

ויאמר אלהים יהי רקיע בתוך המים ויהי מבדיל בין מים למים:

(vayomer elohyim yehyi raqyia b'tok ha'mayim
viyihyi mav'dyil beyin mayim lamayim)

*"And said the Powers, BE SHEET (flat cloth) in midst
of the chaos (the waters)! And was causing from
[the] dividing an understanding, chaos (waters) to
chaos (waters)."*

Previously, the first phase began with "Light be." Now it's
"Firmament be!" The function of this *sheet,* which is the literal
definition of *firmament,* was to bring *understanding* and
reformation to the egoistic chaos, the *Desire to Receive for
Itself Alone,* and return it to its higher state. In other words, to
bring *essence* to *form* and go from a *fragmented form* back to
united essence.

בין (beeyin), the word we usually translate as *between,* is also
the word *to understand.* In the Hebraic mind, wisdom,
knowledge, and understanding are quite different than in
Western thinking. In the West, we simply define *knowledge* as
obtaining the facts, *understanding* as prioritizing knowledge,
and *wisdom* as the ability to use knowledge with
understanding. In Hebraic thinking, חכמה (chokmah),
wisdom is like a flowing river, a constant stream of
limitlessness that can take on any form. בינה (biynah) [or

166

בְּין (beeyin)], *understanding* is like reaching our hand into that river and scooping out a part of it. In doing this, we isolate a part of the river from its constant flow. Then, as we take the water in our hand and drink, we taste its flavors, experience its refreshment, and it becomes a part of us. This is called

דַעַת (da'at), *knowledge.* The point is that knowledge is momentary, a mere segment of the flow. Though necessary, in one respect, it is only an aspect of the infinite flow, not the conclusion of it. Nevertheless, spiritual life isn't about solidifying *the knowing,* but the constant process of grasping an *understanding* as we stay *in the flow of wisdom's eternal river.* Therefore, the scripture says:

> "...incline your ear to wisdom, and apply your heart to understanding..." (Proverbs 2:2/NKJV)

> "The heart of him who has understanding seeks knowledge..." (Proverbs 15:14/NKJV)

A Rabbi in a lecture I attended used this example: חכמה (chokmah), *wisdom* is like a blank piece of paper. There is the potential for an infinite arrangement of stories, books, paragraphs, sentences, and letters to be written upon it. Yet, when we write our first word and subsequent sentences, בינה (biynah) [or בְּין (beeyin)], *understanding* takes form. It's then we acquire the דַעַת (da'at), *knowledge* of what is there.

The blessing and the challenge before us is that דעת (da'at), *knowledge* is merely a fraction of the whole (the innate potential of the infinite, חכמה (chokmah) *wisdom*. Therefore, when we hold to דעת (da'at), *knowledge* we immediately limit the forms of בינה (biynah), *understanding* that we can have. Ultimately, we totally remove ourselves from חכמה (chokmah), *wisdom* with all its Divine, infinite possibilities. To return to our river example, you can say that to stay in spirituality we must stay in *the flow* and not hold onto *the know*, just enjoy it for the moment.

The firmament's entrance is the quality that brings a Divine understanding to the depths of the waters. It forms the מסך (masach), the sheet or screen, revealing the reflections and thoughts of God's Likeness and His Intentions. In the same manner it also reveals ours. If the firmament isn't there, we are revealing our egoism, the Serpent, along with right and wrong thinking, death. If the firmament is there, we are revealing the Divine Nature along with Life, Light, and Love.

> *"...for actively alive is the word of God, and energetic, and sharper than any two-edged sword, going through even to the **dividing of soul and spirit,** and of joints and marrow, and is **a sifter and analyzer of the reflections and conceptions of the heart."*** (Hebrews 4:9/WUEST)

This firmament or sheet, which causes a mirror-like reflection of His Image and Likeness, is referred to in the book of Job. Note what Elihu says to Job and his friends:

> *"...have you spread out the skies, strong as a cast metal mirror?"*   *(Job 37:18/NKJV)*

The firmament is now called a mirror! The מסך (masach), or רקיע (raqyia), the firmament, the sheet, the screen, or *the mirror,* is all about reflecting the Light, revealing the Likeness of the Creator to Creation. If you analyze the letter definitions of the word firmament, רקיע (raqyia), they summarize the function of the screen: *the head (or mind) facing the horizon toward the infinite point where creation began and is seen.* יהוה the origin of all Creation, revealed by the Light (Christ), can be seen because it's reflected within us. The firmament isn't simply a cloud layer above planet earth, *but a description of our inner spiritual reality.* It's the anti-egoistic screen within our hearts, reflecting the Source of all Creation!

As the second day, or *the second phase,* progresses, God gives the firmament a new name: Heaven Wait a minute, Heaven? Yes, think of it! Heaven is no longer a faraway, ethereal place. Rather, it's the place where the Likeness of God is revealed. To the point, Heaven is not a place we are going to in the future when we die, but a place we *live from now* as the egoistic false self, dies. It's *the mirror* upon which the *Desire to Receive for Itself* is transformed into the *Desire to Receive and Give.* It's the definition of what both Jesus and King Solomon described regarding the eternal Kingdom. Solomon proclaimed that God has put eternity (or the universe) in our hearts (Ecclesiastes 3:11) and Jesus declared the Kingdom of God is within us (Luke 17:21). The infinite, eternal worlds of the Heavens, where the Creator abides, *are within us!* It's there we find our oneness with each other, Creation, and Christ. When we perceive this, *and not just believe it,* reality is transformed from the inside out.

Part 4: From Form to Radiance

These are the "building blocks" (sons) of the emanation of Rest and Grace. Therefore, **חם** (ham) is a description of the transforming power of the screen, which by choice gives form to **שם** (shem), the Divine Essence. By this choice, it can unify the sheet, the covering, and reflect the Source or stay uncovered and egoistically fragmented. This brings us to the next son or emanation, **יפת** (yapheth), the *Opening*. The word **יפת** (yapheth) comes from the verb **פתה** (pathah), which means *to spread wide*. Consider, we have the Light shining forth, reflected on the firmament, which is now being spread out, broadcast throughout Creation. When you look at the letter definitions of the ancient Hebrew script it's amazing what you find; **פתה** (pathah) is

$$\text{🜊†⌒}$$

which means *mouth, cross (the mark of faith), expression.* It's the proclamation of the Cross expressed to all! It's the mouth, *the message* of the cross revealed! In the story of Noah, before we talk about floods, animals, and the ark, it has the message that echoes throughout the ages. It reveals the nature of the Infinite Creator in Christ. פתה (pathah), by definition, *spreads open* a humility and willingness to love selflessly.

In addition to the definition *to spread wide,* another word that comes from פתה (pathah) is פתח (pathach), which means *open door.* In view of the Divine Essence (The Name) being revealed through the Mirror (the anti-egoistic screen), now it's unrestricted like *an open door* to all Creation! It's like a bright light that shines and spreads out and fills a house. Think of Jesus's words:

> *"Here's another way to put it: You're here to be light, bringing out the God-colors in the world. God is not a secret to be kept. We're going public with this, as public as a city on a hill. If I make you light-bearers, you don't think I'm going to hide you under a bucket, do you? I'm putting you on a light stand. Now that I've put you there on a hilltop, on a light stand — shine! Keep open house; be generous with your lives. By opening up to others, you'll prompt people to open up with God, this generous Father in heaven."*
> *(Matthew 5:14-16/MESS)*

To summarize, *the state of inner Rest, in the embracing gaze of Grace, produces the revelation of the Divine Essence reflected through the mind and heart, spread out and expressed to all Creation in Christ's Selfless Love.* This one sentence says it all. Consequently, this is why the Melchizedekian priesthood is so

171

unique from all other priesthoods. The purpose of the Melchizedekian priest is to be the Image in the mirror of the Eternal Creator. Therefore, Melchizedek is often viewed *as Christ.* Why? In the economy of God, you can't tell the difference. After all, the Image in the mirror is Christ and Christ is the Likeness in the mirror. Thus, you and I, when we live in this state of *Rest embraced by Grace,* reflect the Image and Likeness of Christ, which is the Source (2 Corinthians 3:18). Ultimately, all Creation is filled with the revelation of the Light, Christ, because of us (Romans 8:19-21).

All of humanity is a revelation of Christ, the Divine Expression of essence and form. Whether there is a consciousness of that reality or not, it doesn't change the Creator's intention, nor divert the destination in Creation's origin.

CHAPTER 7
REBOOTING CREATION

*"There are two ways in which the human machine
goes wrong. One is when human individuals drift
apart from one another, Or else collide with one
another and do one another damage...
You can get the idea plain if you think of us as a
fleet of ships sailing in formation."*

Mere Christianity
Book 3: Christian Behavior
C. S. Lewis

This brings us to the actual creation of the ark. The Hebrew word for *ark* is תֵּבָה (teevah), meaning *a box, container, or a vessel.* One of the most important descriptions of the Adam was that it's a *Living Soul* (Genesis 2:7), or *vessel,* through which the Image and Likeness of Christ is revealed. Yet, the question arises, what is the soul made up of? In the simplest definition, the soul is *Desire.* While we have been taught that the soul is the *mind, will, and emotions,* this Greek/Platonic definition only describes some of the forms the soul manifests. It doesn't define what "substance" makes up the soul.

For example: We can say that water is a solid, liquid, or gas. Those are the *forms* in which water manifests, but it doesn't describe the substance from which water is made. When we endeavor to explain water's underlying substance, the conversation changes from its manifestation to its molecular structure, which is H_2O (two hydrogen atoms to one oxygen atom). The union of the appropriate ratios of hydrogen and oxygen is what makes water. In the same way, the soul may manifest as mind, will, and emotions, yet the *underlying substance* from which its spiritual matrix is made is *desire*, רצון (ratson). We could say, citing Descartes' famous quote, "I think, therefore I am" (*je pense, donc je suis*). From the root substance we can better say, *I desire, therefore I think, I choose, and I feel.* In reality we are not our thoughts, we have thoughts. Our choices are a calculation based on desire as well, whether egoistic or from the Divine Nature. The same applies to our feelings. This is why we've spent so much time discussing the "Desire to Receive." Desire gives form to our mind, will, and emotions, which in turn causes receptivity to the kind of thoughts, choices, and feelings we allow to flow through us.

Part 1: The Creation of the Vessel, the Ark

In the same manner of roots and branches, when we explored Noah/Rest finding its lover, Grace, and their union's result being the building blocks of Divine Essence revealed in diverse Forms, Spread Out through Creation, now we see the same story told in another way. Consider a short version: A guy named Noah lives in a land where the *thoughts* of

Mankind are *wicked*. He's told to build a *vessel* that can contain him, his family, and two sets of every kind of animal, both clean and unclean, and rise above that lower world. Not much is said of what will happen to all aboard after the flood, but eventually they will settle upon a new or rebooted world. If you think about it, the same story has been told and retold in the Judeo-Christian Bible and the texts of other religions, starting with the man and woman in the Garden who were created from the dust and who were told to fill the earth, all the way to Christ who tells us He is going to prepare a place for us, breathes the Spirit into us, and culminates in a New Heaven and New Earth. The story is constantly repeated over and over in different ways. In the case of Noah, we have some of the most profound descriptions of that process in the entire Old Testament.

> *"Make yourself an ark of gopherwood; make rooms in the ark, and cover it inside and outside with pitch."*   *(Genesis 6:14/NKJV)*

עשה לך תבת עצי גפר קנים תעשה

את התבה וכפרת אתה מבית ומחוץ בכפר:

(Aseeh l'ka teevat atsy-gopher qiniym ta'aseeh
et-hatteevah v'caphar,ta otah mabaiyt umichuts
bacopher)

For the most part, the English translation above is straight forward. However, there are words that are encrypted and revelatory. The first one is in the phrase **גפר עצי** (atsiy gophar), where we translate the word *gopherwood* (literally,

175

gopher-tree). There seems to be no lexicon or commentary that can conclusively say what gopherwood is, regardless of what suggestions are made. Primarily, this is the case because we are not talking about lumber. Some commentators connect it to the cypress tree, others to the pine or cedar tree, with few variances. Yet, as the 1906 version of the Jewish Encyclopedia states, we have nothing from the pre-flood era to substantiate any connection to any of the trees mentioned other than assumption or speculation. Far more important than determining what kind of tree or wood it was is obtaining the spiritual root from this physical branch. In our first volume we revealed that at the fall of Lucifer, the creature shattered into a burning, fiery, egoistic dust. God took of that substance and breathed into it the Breath of Life forming the Adam, the Living Soul.

So why does God tell Noah to make an ark out of gopherwood? In Hebrew the word גפר (gopher), the feminine gender, גפרית (gaph'riyth), means *sulfur* or *brimstone.* Such words must conger up all kinds of fiery thoughts, and you'd be correct. When we think of *brimstone*, we always connect it to the phrase *fire and brimstone,* creating pictures of judgment, Hell, or hideous fire raining from the Heavens, as in the destruction of Sodom and Gomorrah (Genesis 19:24, see also Psalms 11:6; Ezekiel 38:22). From Genesis to Revelation, that phrase (with all its variants) is repeated almost a dozen times. Here in the Noah story, God is describing something similar and also establishing a precedent. The creation of the ark from gopherwood is another description of the gaze of Grace empowering Rest to take from the burning brimstone of human existence and fashion a vessel that transports it above the chaos to a new life. The vessel, the ark, is a type of the Adam before any Mosaic tabernacle or Solomon's temple became a type and shadow (Exodus 26:30; Hebrews 8:5).

From the hellish brimstone, also known as *the Desire to Receive for Itself Alone,* Noah/Rest creates a vessel with chambers in it where he, his family, and the animals will live. But to hold it all together, Noah/Rest is told to seal it with *pitch,* כפר (kaphar). The difference between *pitch* and *gopher* is one exchanged letter, the כ (kaph) for the ג (gimmel). The ג (gimmel), which is the third letter of the Hebrew alphabet, commonly represents *the foot.* The famous Jewish philosopher and scholar Maimonides tells us that the ג (gimmel) also represents *choice,* which is fundamental to the Jewish faith. Remember, this is all about the *Desire to Receive's* **choice** to either *Receive and Reflect,* or *Receive for Itself Alone.* At this point, like with Lucifer and the Adam, the condition of the Vessel was a result of a choice to *Receive for Itself Alone* and its spiritual quality is equated with fiery *brimstone*, hence the burning ash of Genesis. Interestingly, the כ (kaph) has the meaning of the open hand. Yet, as Rabbi Howard Cohen points out in his essay on the כ (kaph), its key meaning is כתר (keter), the Divine crown, and symbolizes "...a crown on the head of a prostrating king." Notice the depiction of a prostrating king, which is one of humility and compassion. The transformation of the ג (gimmel) to the כ (kaph) is

177

reformation of the burning egoistic desire to compassion and humility, which gives form to a new word.

Like *brimstone,* the word *pitch,* כפר (kaphar), is significant in its feminine form, כפרת (kapporet), which is translated over twenty-six times as *mercy seat.* Yes, the horrid, fiery brimstone, the egoistic *Desire to Receive for Itself,* is going to be covered inside and out with the compassionate prostrating king of the *mercy seat!* The fact that this is repeated twenty-six times becomes significate as well. Twenty-six is the numerical equivalent of the letters in God's name, יהוה. But let's not stop there. If we take the word כפרת (kapporet), *mercy seat,* and simply put the last letter, ת (tav), at the beginning of the word, we have the phrase תכפר (t'kappeer) *"...you shall make atonement..."* The building of the ark is the revelation of the redemption for the Soul! Hence, we can rephrase this verse as follows: *"Make a vessel from the violent egoistic fiery brimstone and cover it inside and out with the compassionate atoning power of that which proceeds from the benevolent merciful King's throne!"*

It's important to point out at this juncture that the definition of *atonement* in English has changed so much from its original meaning, particularly over the last half millennia, that it's altered the Western view of the New Testament to some degree. Christian theology went through several changes over the last two millennia. Its foundation was the "Victorious Christ Doctrine" which existed through the first millennium, ranging from the time of the Apostles to roughly through the establishment of the Holy Roman Empire. What followed was the significant adjustment known as "The Satisfaction Doctrine" of Amsalem de Bec (also known as Amsalem of Acosta, who was the archbishop of Canterbury). He changed the focus of Christ's victory through the resurrection, which regained Mankind's divine identity, to one of sin consciousness, giving emphasis to the humiliation of Christ on the cross. This subtly reformed Christian thinking from being Christ-identity-centered, to sin-centered. In other words, our sinfulness shamed God and Christ had to die to build a bridge to redeem Mankind from the shame it caused. About 500 years later (as mentioned in the previous volume), came John Calvin's doctrine of "Penal Substitution," also known as "Vicarious Atonement." Here, the Trinity is broken up and put in juxtaposition to itself. The Father is now a wrathful God whose vengeance must be satisfied on the principle of some kind of Olympian sovereign justice. The injustice exists because of the shame and violation of Original Sin and subsequent breaking of the Law. This is no different than the blood sacrifices of the gods of violence we talked about previously, whether human or animal. The response is for His prize Son to come in human form and absorb His wrath through being a crucified sacrifice as a substitution for Mankind. Thus, crucifixion "pays" for the sin of Mankind (not "forgiving" Mankind), staying the wrathful judgment of God.

This skewing of the Apostolic doctrine of Christ's Victory caused *atonement* to become a payment for sin, rather than its original definition. This change first occurred when it appeared in the Tyndale edition of the Bible in 1522 by Desiderius Erasmus, matching the penal substitution theology of the day. In contrast, the word *atonement* comes from the older Latin translation of both Testaments. It's the word *adunamentum,* which we still see appearing in the Italian version of Ephesians 4:11, *"...per lo perfetto adunamento de' santi,"* meaning, *"...for the perfect gathering of the saints."* It means *to gather together,* literally AT-ONE-MENT. Hence, the scripture is clear:

> *"...which is that God in the Messiah was reconciling mankind to himself, not counting their sins against them..."*   *(2 Corinthians 5:19/CJB)*

The Aramaic Translation is quite profound in its approach to this same verse:

> *"For God is in the Messiah. With his greatness, He that shepherds the world never considered their sins to them. He set in us our own word that opens-doors."*   *(2 Corinthians 5:19/Werner)*

The Father (God) was never contrary to, or in juxtaposition with, Christ or Mankind. *"God in the Messiah...never considered their sins..."* It was humanity that was wicked and wrathful against Christ and God. While God never considered our sin, the Serpent mentality of the Tree of the Knowledge of Good and Evil in us did.

"The God of our fathers raised up Jesus whom you murdered by hanging on a tree. Him God has exalted to His right hand to be Prince and Savior, to give repentance to Israel and forgiveness of sins."

(Acts 5:29-32/NKJV)

The New Testament is clear, GOD WAS and IS IN CHRIST. The Father and Christ were never opposed to each other; they were *One,* reconciling Mankind. However, Christ was the victim of a wrathful murder by the hands of a demigod called Man. Nevertheless, in this horrific, murderous situation, God still forgave humanity (Romans 1:16).

Continuing with the Noah/Rest story, God then tells him to make rooms or chambers in the ark. The word for *chambers* is קנים (qinniym), which also means *nests.* By letter definition the word *nest* קן (qen) means ק (kuf) *horizon, the place where light gathers,* followed by a נ (nun) which means *seed, perpetuity, the Messiah, the heir to the throne.* When you put them together you have *the gathering of Light, the perpetual seed of Messiah, the heir to the throne.* To say it another way, the throne of the Messiah is the place where all Light gathers and emanates. You can expand that with כפרת (kapporet), *the mercy seat* and see that the chambers are specific qualities of the Messiah's throne. Each of these chambers are a gathering place of Divine Light, Life, and Love. Comprehensively, the multifaceted seeds of the Messiah are gathered, received, and planted in the soul, the Ark chambers, which reflect His Fullness. Therefore, each chamber represents aspects of *"corrected desire."* Each time we transform one of our desires from Egoism to Love, from Selfishness to Selfless Compassion, we are opening the window of that chamber to receive and reflect the Light. With each *transformed* or *corrected desire* we can receive and reflect more precisely. As we experience these transformations, or inner corrections, we unveil our true self and we send a transmuting, rippling effect throughout all Creation.

On the larger scale of the grand Soul, the Adam, each of us is likened to a chamber in the fullness of its vessel; as in the description of the Body of Christ, each having its parts, each of us are a part of the whole. While we egoistically perceive ourselves as "separate individuals" having desires, more so, each of us are a desire in the vast, grand, victorious Soul, the Last Adam, Christ. As each of us experiences an unveiling of our true self, the whole Vessel experiences another aspect of unveiling or transformation. It's this unveiling that elevates the Vessel from one state of being to another and, most importantly, *fashioned for a world to come* while at the same time *fashioning the world to come.*

Noah is then instructed to add a window. The Hebrew word for *window* is צֹהַר (tsohar), which literally means *glistening light.* This word is more commonly translated as *noonday,* and in one place (Job 24:11) as *pressed oil* (because of its *sheen).* In congruence with the קִנִּים (qinniym), the light gathering chambers, the צֹהַר (tsohar) is the entrance of the Divine Light itself.

A development of the word **צהר** (tsohar) is **זהר** (zohar), which the name of the famous Torah commentary advancing the definition from glistening light to *radiance* and *splendor.* The **זהר** (zohar) was written by Rabbi Simeon bar Yochai, also known as the Rashbi (derived from his name), in the second century after the destruction of the second temple. It was later rediscovered and published by the Spanish Rabbi Moses de León in the late twelfth century. Two of the most famous expositors of the **זהר** (zohar) were Isaac Luria, known as the Ari (the Lion), from 1534 Jerusalem, and just 160 years later, born in 1698 Poland, Rabbi Israel ben Eliezer, known as the Baal Shem Tov (Master of the Good Name), the founder of the prominent Hasidic Judaism.

Therefore, the ark is not a simple rectangular boat of wood to house a small group of humans and a considerable herd of animals. Rather, it's a branch to a spiritual root. It's graphically telling us the story of redemption, transformation, and advancement to the next development of Creation. It's the primordial Soul, the Vessel which was and is the embodiment of the Image and Likeness of Christ, the Light of Creation. It's filled with all kinds of chambers, or desires, and when these chambers are filled with Light, each reflect the Likeness of God. If you add the **י** (yud) to the beginning of **צהר** (tsohar) you have **יצהר** (yitshar), which means *oil,* and in one place (Zechariah 4:14) it's translated as *anointed.* Remembering that *Messiah* **משיח** (mashyiach) means *anointed one,* the representation of the ark is astounding! The ark is the replica of the Soul raised up from its fiery brimstone, burning egoistic condition, covered with the atoning redemption of the compassionate Messiah's Throne. Now the Light of the Christ, the benevolent King, enters, abides, reflects, and is filled throughout all its chambers of Creation!

Another powerful aspect of the ark is its dimensions: 300 cubits, 50 cubits, and 30 cubits (Genesis 6:14-15). In Hebrew, each letter has a numerical value, and these three dimensions add up to a very interesting word, לשׁון (lashown) 353, which means *tongue, language, or speech.* The Living Word, God through the Christ, spoke the upper worlds into existence and Creation is held together by that power. Another interesting fact is that the Hebrew phrase, *the anointed* המשׁח (ha'mashach), also has the numerical value of 353. Thus, the Christ, the Messiah, the Anointed, is the Living Word. The Baal Shem Tov said, "...another meaning of the Ark, is the *Word.*" In other words, the Ark is the container of the Living Word and, for that matter, words are the Divine Seed and containers of the Divine Breath. Note how the writer of the epistle of Hebrews penned all of these ideas together in one section: the Ark תבת (teevah), the Vessel or *Soul,* emanating the Divine Image, the צהר (tsohar) the *glistening bright light,* the קנים (qinniym) *the gathering of that Light in union with the Heir to the Throne* (the Son), and the power of לשׁון (lashown) the tongue, *the Anointed* Word:

> *"...has in these last days **spoken to us by His Son**, whom He has appointed **heir of all things**, through whom also He made the worlds; who being **the***

brightness of His glory and the express **image of His person,** and upholding all things by **the word of His power...”** *(Hebrews 1:2-3/NKJV)*

In the spiritual world, a word is thought and a thought is action. Therefore, *as a man thinks in his soul, so is he* (Proverbs 23:7) and as Jesus taught that whoever looks upon a person (or thing) with lust in his heart, he has already done the deed (Matthew 5:28). When God *thought,* “Likeness,” Creation with all its subtle nuances came into existence. Our thoughts, which are formed by desires, are our inner spiritual speech. When our inner conversation is consistent with our outer, nothing is impossible to us! Jesus said it plainly:

“...whosoever shall say unto this mountain, Be thou removed, and be thou cast into the sea; and shall not doubt in his heart, but shall believe that those things which he saith shall come to pass; he shall have whatsoever he saith. Therefore I say unto you, What things soever ye desire, when ye pray, believe that ye receive them, and ye shall have them.”
(Mark 11:23-24/KJV)

Doubt in the heart has several aspects we can discuss, but one of the most prevalent is that it’s a fruit of our perception of separation. This is why the Greek phrase *shall doubt* is διακριθῇ (diakrithee), which means *to separate, divide,* and have a *divergent opinion.* In the same way, when we perceive reality from the fallen or egoistic state, we see things as separate and divided. The product of this perception is what

185

we call *doubt*. Doubt is another way of saying *a sense of separation;* it doesn't see reality as it truly is. Hence, to our Ego, obstacles appear as mountains rather than in their true form. Consider the concept of a *mountain* as we first shared in the previous volume after a measure of exegesis:

> "...the scripture speaks of the mountains, which refers to a rising up. A form of the word **הר** (har) *mountain* is **יהיר** (yahiyr) which means *arrogant* or *proud*" (Melchizedek Volume 1, page 518).

Thus, to remove the mountains in our lives, before we can even speak to them, we must approach them from the view of Divine reality. Mountains are nothing more than the fabrication of our egoistic desires. They appear as mountains because the ego always presents itself, like Pharaoh, as *a larger-than-life monster.* Yet, when we humble ourselves and see creation around us as Christ sees it, as a collective whole, our perception of reality changes. The Holy Spirit recently spoke to me and said, "If you have the power to move mountains, who do you think put them there in the first place?" Most of the mountains in our lives which we wish to move are our own creations from the beginning. This is why they seem so difficult to move. So-called "mountains" appear before us because, deep down, we are convinced that they should be there. Maybe we've done something and feel we deserve the mountain. We may say that we know intellectually and theologically that God doesn't consider our sin, but so often, on a deeper level, we as demigods hold them against ourselves. Similarly, maybe we haven't forgiven another person for some reason, thus because of our sense of unworthiness within our inner condition, the mountain remains and even seems more obstinate. While the faint voice of our true self says it shouldn't be there, the ego says we deserve it! Most of us have experienced this in one form or another. Thus, the Serpentine egoistic dichotomy of good and evil almost unconsciously rules over our knowledge of God and the revelation of our true self. In one respect we want the uncomfortable "evil mountain" gone. Our theology may even say it shouldn't be there. Yet, it sits there and in effect says, "Jesus I know, and Paul I know, but who are you?" Why? Because on a deeper level we believe it should be there, because it is right and just. It should be there because we have done something and are unworthy and deserve it. So, we struggle in the quandary of the pagan penal substitution. "I am deserving of this mountain of judgement. Yet, Jesus died in my place, so even though I am unworthy, I should be free. But I still feel unworthy!" We can then add to it the recent ideas of spiritual warfare where we ponder, "I did something that opened the door to the devil. He has a right to do what he is doing. I have to repent, kick him out, and close the door." These vacillations between right and wrong, should and shouldn't, attack and victory, are as old as the gods of violence in Noah's day. It's hard to move mountains when we've justified their presence. Nonetheless, Jesus made it clear:

"...whosoever shall say unto this mountain, Be thou removed, and be thou cast into the sea; and shall not doubt in his heart, but shall believe that those things

> *which he saith shall come to pass; he shall have*
> *whatsoever he saith."*　　　　　*(Mark 11:23/KJV)*

When we change our egoistic point of view to a compassionate one, the mountains in our hearts which have been arrogantly and judgmentally anchored are brought down to size and removed. To add to the point, the size or strength of the mountains in our lives are determined by the measure of ego we are emitting. On the other hand, if we raise our *Desire to Receive "for Ourselves"* back up to the higher worlds of origin, *the Desire to Receive "and Reflect,"* mountains virtually disappear before our eyes. This doesn't mean we don't go through things, sometimes hard things; the key is we don't get stuck there.

This is what the Ark is all about. It's about our inner spiritual *Rest* recognizing the constant unchanging *Grace* in the eyes of the Father. It transforms our seeing whatever aspect of our lives appear to be unworthy or not (the egoistic attributes of fire and brimstone) and views them as the building materials for the higher worlds where Christ sits on His throne. As soon as we gaze into the eyes of grace, we are at-one-ment, כפר (kaphar), covered in our thinking and feelings with compassion (mercy), inside and out. We bask in the presence of the Source who gathers and emanates the Light, translating our consciousness from below, back to the world above.

Part 2: Creation Exhales and Lives Again

Once the building materials were in place and construction finished, the animals, both clean and unclean, began to arrive. Yet, before God informs Noah of the coming animals, He says:

"And behold, I Myself am bringing floodwaters on the earth, to destroy from under heaven all flesh in which is the breath of life; everything that is on the earth shall die."   *(Genesis 6:17/NKJV)*

In contrast to the 14th verse, this verse spirals us into another direction. It's as if God is going to kill everybody except those in the Ark. While that sounds straightforward, we read much into this verse that may not actually be there. Does God so abhor the violence of man that his response is to be just like him, equally violent in return? One may say that you reap what you sow, which is very true, but then it isn't God who is destroying or afflicting, it's us doing it to ourselves. Yet, the way it appears in this verse is that God is about to do something contrary to His own nature and destroy His own Creation. The quick answer may seem to be, "God is the Creator so He has the right to do what He wishes, including destroying His Creation!" That sounds logical and easy, but that's just the point. From the Serpent mentality, it makes total sense, so we're back to our former paganistic god with a schizophrenic-bipolar disorder. To the point, God, the Source of Life, is not trying to destroy Creation, but restore it to its original intent. The only thing He would be destroying (for lack of a better word at the moment) is that aspect which

189

hinders Creation from realizing true reality, yet preserves its Divine attribute of choice. More accurately, it's not destroying, but covering and transforming, based on the preceding text.

From a spiritual-root point of view, the story of Noah is about *"Finding grace in the eyes of God,"* along with the significance of rising above the lower egoistic chaotic violence and attaining a new world. It's not about a select few who were good enough to receive a saving blessing while the rest of humanity drowned in a miserable death. Unfortunately, most of us in the evangelical world would say the destruction of all in the flood is a deserved damnation for being evil. Of course, it follows that in the afterlife they could never find themselves in Heaven, but in a conscious torment of a fiery Hell. Then, trying to present this as God's rightful sovereignty and making sure He appears in a pseudo-loving light, we say, "After all, God didn't send them to their torment, their unrepentant sinful life did!" Explaining this version of God's actions as some form of divine justice, we add, "God is so just that if you want to go to Hell, He will let you." Regardless of one's religious folklore, the notion of Hell isn't even mentioned in the story at this point. But in our modern evangelical thought, it's in the back of our minds. We will discuss the notion of Hell again later, but it seems good to make the following mention.

We've mistranslated the Hebrew word שׁאוֹל (sheol) as Hell in several places. In the case of the book of Genesis, the word doesn't appear for another 31 chapters. Depending upon how one looks at Genesis, 31 chapters might be quite a while or, if you're a fast reader, not so much. But consider this, if you go by the תנ״ך (Tanak) timeline, from Noah's birth in 1056 (on the Jewish calendar) to that of Jacob's, who first uttered the word שאול (sheol) in the year 2108 BC, there's 1052 years in between. Think of it, ten centuries or a complete millennium! So the notion of Hell שאול (sheol) isn't even mentioned, and when it is mentioned, it means absolutely nothing remotely close to what we've interpreted it to mean. Not to mention that when Jacob used it (Genesis 37:35), *it had nothing to do with eternal torment or a fiery annihilation.* Rather, it's the place he would go to meet his son after he dies. You can rest assured that righteous Joseph and his father Jacob, who God proclaims He is *"the God of,"* along with Abraham and Isaac (Genesis 50:24; Exodus 3:6) are not burning in Hell or annihilated to a crisp! Jesus was quite clear in correcting such a notion:

> *"Now about the dead rising — have you not read in the book of Moses, in the account of the bush, how God said to him, 'I am the God of Abraham, the God of Isaac, and the God of Jacob'? He is not the God of the dead, but of the living. You are badly mistaken!"*
> *(Mark 12:26-27/NIV)*

Upon Jesus's declaration, שאול (sheol) would have to be a place of the living and not the dead. So how did we get from שאול (sheol) being a place where Jacob and Joseph are reunited, to being a place of burning torment? Glad you asked, but that will be for a later chapter. Nonetheless, if we are going to be honest in our interpretation of these passages, Hell, or

שאול (sheol), is just not in its thinking. This brings us to Genesis 6:17:

ואני הנני מביא את המבול מים על הארץ

לשחת כל בשר אשר בו רוח חיים מתחת

השמים כל אשר בארץ יגוע:

(va'ani hin'ni mevi et-hammabbuwl myim al-
ha'arets l'shacheet cal-basar asher-bo
ruwach hayyim mittahat hashamayim col asher-
ba'arets yig'va.)

"And I, behold I, bringing the deluge of chaos (waters) over the Desire to Receive (the earth) to ruin all showing forth ego (flesh) which in him [is the] Wind of Life from under the heavens, all which in the Desire to Receive (earth) shall exhale."

The last phrase of this verse should give us a clue as to what's being communicated, especially in light of the context we previously discussed. The final word in the verse is **יגוע** (yig'va), which means *to exhale,* or *to breathe out,* or *give up the ghost.* While we can understand the notion of "giving up the ghost" is like dying or death, we mustn't confuse it with the word **מות** (moot), which literally means *die* or *dead.* Yet even **מות** (moot) has a wonderful, encrypted meaning in the letter definition, which we will share later. The difference between the two words is significant: **מות** (moot) in simple terms describes the Death Sleep, spiritual unconsciousness, being in a temporary state of darkness, thus momentarily void of the revelation of our Divine Source. But **יגוע** (yig'va) is considerably more specific. It's not just describing a physical death but depicting Mankind exhaling and returning God's Breath to the Source. Just prior to the notion of exhaling, the phrase *Wind of Life* **רוח חיים** (ruwach chayyim), or by extension **נשמת חיים** (nishmat chayyim), the *Breath of Life,* is used to make the point clear. If God Breathed into the *dust of the earth* and the result was the Adam, a *Living Soul,* then when Adam exhales that same Breath it returns to the Source. This is standard in Hebrew teaching; the Breath of Life always returns to God (Ecclesiastes 12:7). The logic as to why it returns is that it's an intrinsic aspect of the Divine Himself. Therefore, when we live from an egoistic, serpentine mentality, it's truly an illusion of separation and self-will. The very fact that we are a living soul, a created Desire to Receive, is a direct result of God's Breath. To live unconscious, thus contrary in nature to that Source, is not understanding who we are and what reality truly is. While we may perceive that our illusions are vivid, when we discover our true self, a manifestation of the Breath of God, we awake and begin experiencing what Life is.

By letter definition we have an additional aspect that opens much of what's being said. (Having shared most of these letters before, we'll focus on the one of the four that's less frequent, and then we'll assemble them all.) The word *exhale,* **יגוע** (yig'va), features the **ג** (gimmel), the symbol of *the foot that is running,* after the **ד** dalet [the letter which follows the

ג (gimmel) in the alpeh-bet, symbolizing *the poor man bowed over,* also as *the open door.*] The ד (dalet) is a *humble man which is an open door.* The word גמל (gamal) means *to yield to* or *to return what was given.* In Hebraic thought the ג (gimmel) describes *a rich man chasing after a poor man to give him a blessing.* The intention of giving and returning is its true function. The fact that we freely received the Light, Life, and Love of the Father and give it to Him in return as Creator and His Creation, reveals both the Source and His resemblance. Sound familiar? It is once again *the Desire to Receive and to Give.* It's the simple revelation of the Image and Likeness of God. We see this reflected in Jesus's words:

> "Heal the sick, cleanse the lepers, raise the dead, cast out demons. **Freely you have received, freely give.**" (Matthew 10:8/NKJV)

If we put together all the letters in יגוע (yig'va) they tell us *the infinite point where all creation begins (Divine potential) yields the Light that comes down from above and illuminates the eyes.* You may ask, what does that have to do with exhaling? If you remember from our first volume, we described an aspect of spiritual intimacy. The picture of God breathing into the Adam also means that the Adam inhaled that breath. As one inhales, the other exhales, and vice versa. Together, in intense intimacy, the cycle of joyous Eternal Life perpetuates. Thus, the Adam was truly a Living Creature because he and the Creator's Breath were one. This is simply another side of the block that described the Divine Light and

194

Image being reflected back to the Creator through the screen מָסָךְ (masach).

The situation in the Noah story is that Creation is "exhaling" and God is receiving back His Breath of Life. However, rather than God instantly exhaling and filling Creation once again, there is a Divine pause. This Divine rest causes a reverting back to when God first uttered, *"Light Be."* If we look at the entire verbal picture on the surface (the פְּשָׁט *peshat* level), we see the waters flooding the earth, the rain falling from above, and waters rising from below. Consider that description. There is no "firmament" dividing the waters from above and below, nor a declaration of "Light be!" We are right back to Genesis 1:2-6. As we will see, once again the Spirit is hovering over the face of the waters, poised to create, but this time with a significant addition or progression. Upon the waters is the form of an Ark, a Divine Soul being filled with Light through Rest and Grace. Remember the chambers and the windows in the Ark? The glistening light? Now the Ark becomes the Light which hovers over the face of the deep, bringing a revelation of Rest and Grace, which in the previous creative dynamic wasn't as clear because of the Fall. Thus, earth reboot (the Desire to Receive) upgrade version 3.0.

Have you ever noticed that the Genesis 1 account never said that God created the waters or the deep? Why? In the first volume we had to assemble from other scriptural places what occurred that led to Genesis 1:2 (refer back to Chapter 1 - *In the Beginning Again*). On another side of the same block, we found that these occurrences were described as *the dust of the earth* and *the Breath of Life.* It was from the fiery ash (the serpentine ego) God elevated and created the Adam, *the Living Soul.* In the previous story, the waters (the chaos) were to swarm with *the Soul of Life,* שרץ נפש חיה [singular absolute state] (Genesis 1:20). Thus, we have a progression in each state.

The *first* was Lucifer, the Morning Star, who reflected the Light and egoistically chose to no longer be that, and consequently became who we commonly call Satan, the fiery cloud of ash, also known as the dust of the earth.

The *second* was the Adam, who was created from the same egoistic substance, the dust of the earth. God breathed into it the Breath of Life and it became *a Living Soul.* (Or we could say, in keeping with the previous Light explanation, God filled the Adam with His Light and They reflected His Image.) Yet like Lucifer, the Adam chose the way of the Serpent, the Ego, and ate of the Tree of the Knowledge of Good and Evil; thus the Adam fell into the Death Sleep. To say it yet another way, the Vessel once again shattered into fallen, fiery sparks in a cloud of ash.

Now we see the *third* in the progression. Despite the violent egoistic state of the shattered Vessel, God in His grace and mercy raises the Vessel above the chaos and establishes a new world. The difference and progression now compared to the previous Adamic world is that His grace will prevail over mankind's religious morality or immorality. Most importantly, His grace will prevail over fallen Mankind's

196

perception of their wrathful gods. Can you imagine that? Until this point, favor or grace from a god could only be attained if moral correctness and blood sacrifice were offered to appease their wrath. Of course, that isn't the true God's grace, but a serpentine redefining of His Nature by the Tree of the Knowledge of Good and Evil. But God, who is gracious regardless, and doesn't change (Ephesians 2:4), was establishing a revelation of His nature to Creation. Why? Because the only way to reveal Himself and His intention *within* Creation is to first reveal His nature *to* Creation. This is no small task, but God has been developing His Creation to discover their Divine Likeness by *a conscious choice,* not religious coercion.

When it comes to free will or the freedom to choose, most think that certain choices can change how God views us. But that's the furthest from the truth. We also think that our choices determine whether or not God decides to bless us, which is also far from the truth. God's gracious view and choice of blessing toward humanity is unchangeable. Though it sounded revolutionary when Jesus said this of the Father, it was God's nature from the very beginning:

> *"But I tell you: Love your enemies and pray for those who persecute you, that you may be sons of your Father in heaven. He causes his sun to rise on the evil and the good, and sends rain on the righteous and the unrighteous."*　　　*(Matthew 5:44-45/NIV)*

This was and is startling to the religious mind! The religious always thought calamity came because they angered God and He wrought vengeance upon them. The fact is, in general, humanity didn't understand the Eternal Creator and only saw God through the closed eyelids of the Death Sleep, the thorny branches of the Tree of the Knowledge of Good and Evil. Hence, God was blamed (and in many cases still is) for a lot of things. More distressing is that once the revelation of Christ appeared, many caught a glimpse of grace, if only for a moment. Then, as has happened many times, we quickly relapsed back to the deathly dream of the lower world. The Apostle Paul called it the *"...weak and beggarly elements..."* (Galatians 4:9). We mutated and mutilated our view of the person of Christ through the thorns of the Tree of the Knowledge of Good and Evil. The Apostle Paul again warned us against such relapses, saying:

> *"But I fear, lest somehow, as the serpent deceived Eve by his craftiness, so your minds may be corrupted from the simplicity that is in Christ."*
> *(2 Corinthians 11:3/NKJV)*

We didn't simply take the proverbial triune peg of God and try to put it into the square hole of the Tree of the Knowledge of Good and Evil, which of course would end in failure. Rather, we took the Divine triune peg and insistently filed it down, with shavings flying everywhere, until we could jam it into the square hole. Then we stepped back and said to ourselves, "There! That's the way it was always meant to be!" We displaced the nature of Christ, shaved off the revelation of His

Love, and shoved it into a serpent system of good and evil. This myth was advanced yet again by mingling the Divine Nature with something called the "anger of the Lord," which totally perverts the view of the Father, especially toward the so-called sinner.

This is no different than the *"False Lamb"* that the writer of the Book of Revelation warns us about (Revelation 13:11-14). It's fashioned to look like the real Lamb, even appearing to have been slain and made alive again, having a mortal wound that was healed. Inevitably, when the false lamb speaks it sounds like it proclaims Christ, even with miracles and prophetic declarations, but it speaks the ways of the dragon, the Serpent (Revelation 12:9; 13:11). This *false lamb* and its perversion of Christianity changes the revelational narrative of the Father sending blessings on the just and unjust, to blessing only those who proclaim allegiance and consequential calamity upon those who don't. Of course, the false lamb proclaims its god is a god of love, so the calamities that come aren't directly from god, but due to an opened door in one's life to the devil. Hence, beyond god's acceptable judgements, with "justified" violence, wrath, and condemnation upon the disobedient, it also adds to its hierological rationalizations that any unforeseen, unjustifiable aggression to the faithful must be an unwarranted attack from that same devil. After all, if you're attacked you must be doing something "right" because the devil hates the good believer or he attacks because something is "wrong." Remember that open door? So which is it? Clearly both, right? If we do something right, the devil attacks. If we do something wrong, the devil comes through an open door.

Doesn't this sound rather spiritually irreconcilable? Especially as we pray and intercede about such things, we find ourselves having to remind God, Satan, the demons, and ourselves that "the devil is a defeated foe and the victory was won." Evidently, if we don't remind God, who seems to forget, He won't do anything on our behalf, and if we don't remind the devil, who clearly refuses to remember, he will do anything to our hurt. Good thing for us we have good memories to help remind everyone!

The fabrication of a "good god who demands payment for sin" and an "evil devil who attacks the sinner" creates a perpetual nightmare containing a lofty, monotheistic deity with schizophrenic-manic-bipolar disorder, along with a spiritual enemy who is a schizophrenic, demented sociopath. The result of this Christianized folklore fashions a type of spiritual warfare which is ongoing and never ending, demanding the faithful to pick a side, resulting in distancing themselves from anyone or anything that seems to be on the "enemy's team." This warfare then takes on a political form where one must pick a political party or posture that such a god condones. Naturally, it's one that's clearly against those demonically inhabited unbelievers whose agenda is to suppress the godly. Add to that belief system an eschatology where an anti-Christ, which has little to do with the one the Apostles discussed, comes to destroy the Christian with secularism, socialism, and global domination. This misdirection of Christendom also finds such evils in religions other than itself, and in foreign governments other than ones the false lamb decrees safe. Thus, rather than live in true spiritual Rest, embracing the love emanated from the eyes of Divine Grace, we war against "Satanic enemies" who seemingly thwart us from our blessings and peace. Consider how we in Christendom say, the victory is won, the devil is defeated, the peace that passes understanding has been given, we've received the measure of faith, the Holy Spirit is within us, and we've been cleansed from our sins, past, present, and future, yet it's still necessary for us to wage war! Really? If that is the case, then maybe we don't yet understand the Divine realm. If we need to wage war, doesn't it seem like the victory wasn't fully won, the devil only momentarily defeated, the peace that passes understanding tends to pass us by, our measure of faith doesn't always measure up, the Holy Spirit seems to vacate the premises when answers are needed, and our sins are cleansed, but only if we remember to ask each and every time we fail? If we're not quick to appropriate our forgiveness, there's an open door in our life to the devil and a god who is poised to judge and withhold our blessings. Has it ever crossed our minds that, by such descriptions, they both may be the same guy? If so, who?

God has, through His gaze of grace, given *rest* to His Creation. The result was the re-assemblance of the Vessel (the Ark) from its brimstone state, covering it inside and out with a type of at-one-ment, filling its chambers with Divine *desires*. We point out animals as desires because each Hebrew word for an animal, especially in this case (as in Genesis, Chapter 1), has an emotional or mental definition as well. For example: The Hebrew phrase in Genesis 7:3, *"of the birds (or fowl),"* is

מֵעוֹף (me'oof), which also means *to be dim, gloomy, or dark*

(Isaiah 8:22). Without the Light and its reflection, the desire מְעוּף (me'oof) is dim, gloomy, and dark. But when we receive the Light's glistening splendor and it reflectively fills our inner chamber, what was once gloomy and dark is now uncovered as the מְעוּף (me'oof) that can fly in the skies above, soaring in the Heavenlies. These descriptions are emotional or mental states within the chambers that, when illuminated with the Light (through their respective windows),   reveal Divine Likeness.

> *"But I will establish My covenant with you; and you shall go into the ark — you, your sons, your wife, and your sons' wives with you. And of every living thing of all flesh you shall bring two of every sort into the ark, to keep them alive with you; they shall be male and female. Of the birds after their kind, of animals after their kind, and of every creeping thing of the earth after its kind, two of every kind will come to you to keep them alive. And you shall take for yourself of all food that is eaten, and you shall gather it to yourself; and it shall be food for you and for them.' Thus Noah did; according to all that God commanded him, so he did."*
>
> *(Genesis 6:18-22/NKJV)*

These verses have many aspects to them in Hebrew so we will highlight the key points. The first is in the phrase, *"But I will establish…"* וַהֲקִמֹתִי (vahaqimoti), which actually reads, *"And I shall cause to rise…"* This is the second time this phrase is used in Genesis. The first time was, *"...Cain rose up against Abel his brother..."* The word in this verse is in the Hiphil tense, which means it's in the active-causative mood. In other words, God is going to cause whatever we are speaking of *to rise;* its root is always *to rise.* In the future, whenever you see the word *establish* in the Old Testament, if the word קוּם (qoom) is used, or a form thereof, it always implies that something is *rising to the forefront* or *above other things.* God is saying that He will cause His Ark, His covenant, to rise with us in it. In other words, together we form the assemblance of the Vessel from brimstone, covered with His gracious at-one-ment, and rise above the chaos. Please note there is no mention of any animal sacrifice or bloodletting of any human, only a reference to what is later translated as *atonement.* For that matter, this is the first time the word atonement/pitch כפר (kaphar) is used in the entire Bible. It appears only one more time in the book of Genesis, when Jacob gives Esau a gift to restore their relationship. Nonetheless, no blood is shed nor anything slaughtered, animal or human (Genesis 32:20). The word doesn't appear again till Exodus 29:33, after the Law and the Aaronic priesthood is instituted. However, with the downgrade of the covenant from one of faith and grace to one of rules and works, it is now used in the pagan form of bloodletting. To give some perspective of how long it took for this degeneration to occur, from the time of Rest and Grace (Noah), until the time of the Law and Aaronic priesthood—or as the Apostle Paul calls it, "the ministry of death"—is approximately 1,000 years.

Part 3: God Enters Into Pagan Bloodletting Rituals With Abraham

At this point we should spend a moment discussing covenant. When most of us think of covenant, we think of an irrevocable contract, fortified by certain rituals, leading up to a blood sacrifice and the intermingling of that blood in some form with the covenant family representatives. This is predominantly true from a pagan standpoint. We discussed this in detail in the previous chapter, focusing on ritual sacrifice and how it developed. However, also incorporated in the violent pagan world of sacrifice was this ritual of blood covenant. Similar to the concept of ritual sacrifice to the gods was the ritual cutting of covenants to join together families or tribes. The climax of the covenant ritual was a bloodletting before the gods. Sometimes the covenant representatives would drink the sacrificial blood, which was the bonding agent, mingled with their own blood after cutting a part of their body with a ritual knife. The ritual concluded with a feast where all the key members (and in some cases, all the members) ate the sacrificial animal. At some point in the ritual, a proclamation would be made, "To violate this covenant would be to violate the life that was given and the blood that was shed to join our two tribes. Therefore, before our gods we swear that whosoever violates these oaths, shall be hunted down and their blood shed as this sacrifice today." Some would add, "If the violated cannot fulfill this obligation of vengeance, then their family, their children, and their children's children may seek vengeance until the debt is paid." Others didn't stop there, but continued, "We call upon the gods, who witness this covenant today, to also pursue the violator and their tribe, striking them with curses, sickness, poverty, and war, until the debt is satisfied."

As always with the egoism of the Tree of the Knowledge of Good and Evil, on the surface this is a celebration of two tribes becoming one. That's good, right? They feast after the ritual, reveling in whatever manner was agreed upon. But like any treaty, after the festivities, it's time to make good on the promises. With that comes the other side of blood covenant, the underlying apprehension of falling short of fulfillment. Thus, the covenant foundation was the fear of potential consequences of violation. Some may say, "Well, that just shows the measure of commitment that's necessary to enter into a covenant. We commit to the death!" In many religions we superimpose such feelings and beliefs onto the gods as well. We have even injected such into the person of Christ and the New Testament. Some add, "After all, God was the one who initiated blood covenant, and we know that He swore in covenant many times." Really? Think again! God never initiated the ritual of blood covenant or sacrifice. Rather, He entered into our deathly, guilt-based system to raise us away from it and bring us to a new Kingdom with a new way of thinking. This new Kingdom with its new way of thinking was the original and only Divine way, until we chose another direction that would bring death to all, even, in effect, death to God. He knew what was set before Him and what it would cost to restore us, and He did it anyway. To say this in a more Evangelically flavored vernacular, God submitted to the Satanic system of blood covenant to redeem humanity from it.

Rather than God joyously desiring such blood covenants and expiatory sacrifices, the scripture describes Him very differently, as one who is full of lovingkindness and wouldn't even break a bruised reed (Hosea 6:6; Isaiah 42:3).

For example: In Genesis 15, Abram asks God who shall be his heir, which was an especially important question for an aging man with wealth and a newly found mission. God explains that the heir will not be anyone other than a son that's born to him. Then the scripture says that Abram believed God and He was

ויחשבה (vayach'sh^e'behah), *intertwined in his thinking* as they walked the path together (Genesis 15:6). That was easy! So Abram thinks, "I can trust God that somewhere down the road, someday, in some way, I'll have a son." Isn't it interesting that it's always easier on our ego to claim belief for something down the path in the future, rather than in the here and now? Then God challenges Abram's ego and expands the promise. He can't just leave it with a child in the future, but has to add that the land in which Abram dwells as a foreigner is also his possession, NOW! "Wait what? The land I'm standing on is mine, now?" thinks Abram. "Hold on, there are people who live here and I'm a foreigner." So, rather than accepting in faith what God was saying this time, Abram asks, "Lord God, how shall I know that I will possess it?" (Genesis 15:8). Nope, no faith now. Gone! Poof, like cloud of smoke. Previously, *"...he believed God..."* Now the ego wants a sign. Now it wants some assurance. This is not the kind of "knowing" that comes from laying down our egoism and perceiving with the eyes of God within us, but the kind where the ego wants center stage with assurances. Our ego basically says, "I'm not believing anything until I know, and I'm not going to claim I know anything until You prove it to me. And You better prove it to me to my satisfaction!" Here, God responds in a manner like never before. At first, God was in union with Abram's thinking simply by his believing. Done deal, righteousness complete, next subject (Genesis 15:6). As it's translated in the Mirror Bible:

> *"Scripture is clear, 'Abraham believed what God believed about him and that concluded his righteousness'."*   *(Romans 4:3/MIRROR)*

But now, God is faced with something else. Abram doesn't believe what God says, rather, Abram wants tangible assurance. In other words, rather than saying, "I trust you and believe your promise," now he asks, "How shall I know?" Hold on! You just believed, why aren't you trusting now? The ego doesn't mind allowing us to trust for something when it's far off. It likes when we live in either the future or the past. Why? Because, when we live in the past, the ego becomes our source of comfort, with its narrow rationalizations and attitudes. Similarly, it can utilize our daydreams, visions, and musings of the future to misdirect our energies in the now. How many times have we been seriously discouraged, or even depressed, because what we hoped would occur didn't happen, or it didn't happen as we expected? So the negative self-reflection starts and our musings of the future vision becomes the pessimistic impediment of today. The last thing our ego wants is for us to have a vision born of the inner timeless world of Divine reality and perceive it as the promise of the NOW. Then the ego will have to step aside from its role as our identity, comforter, and friend, and yield to a higher purpose. Yet, what does God do for Abram, and us, in the long run? He doesn't rebuke Abram and He doesn't threaten him with some judgment for being rebellious or unbelieving (remember, He is the God with the gaze of Grace). Rather, God does something unprecedented! He enters a framework that Abram understands to help him move forward: God enters the world of pagan blood sacrifice and covenant. Like Christ, the Living Word who becomes flesh so we can grasp who we are by seeing it modeled by Him, God enters a pagan blood covenant ritual so Abram can grasp His commitment. He tells Abram to take several animals, split them down the middle, and place them side by side (Genesis 15:9-21). Abram knows exactly what God is doing. This is *not* something new to him. The "Blood Path Ritual" was a typical Middle Eastern rite that was practiced when marriage covenants were cut. (See James B. Pritchard, ed., *Ancient Near Eastern Texts Relating to the Old Testament*, 3rd ed. with supplement [Princeton, NJ: Princeton, 1969], xix.)

God humbled Himself to Abram's pagan understanding so He could elevate him to a higher spiritual awareness. God didn't need a blood sacrifice to ratify His covenant. Abram's faith would have been enough. For that matter, God didn't need a covenant to keep the integrity of a promise, or to stay committed to Abram or anyone else. God commits because that's His nature (Numbers 23:19; Isaiah 45:23; Hebrews 6:13, 13:8). Amusingly, there was a complication that God faced when entering this pagan covenant. As stated earlier, the climax of such covenants was a sworn oath to the god of the tribe. Who does *"God Most High"* swear to? In one sense, you can understand the absurdity of what God is about to do. *"He swore by Himself,"* (Hebrews 6:13). But isn't that what God already did? He took Abram outside, showed him the stars, and said, "So shall your offspring be," (Genesis 15:5). In other words, "You have My Word on it." As far as God was concerned, the issue wasn't His integrity, rather it was Abram's egoistic need for assurance. This is what the nature of Divine Love and Grace will do, repeatedly, until it registers with a small point in the heart! From God entering a pagan covenant and swearing by Himself, to coming in human form and being sacrificed by the hands of those He loves, God's graciousness to humble Himself for our sake was never-ending. His Love is evidently boundless-crazy, and clearly not very rational. In one respect it's all absurd! Whatever happened to the unbiased, impartial judge of the world? In one respect, God in Christ said, "To Hell with that guy! I'll do whatever I have to in order to show you My love." We are once again talking about eyes with the gaze of Grace.

God enters a pagan covenant ritual for the sake of Abram's need for assurance. However, now there is another issue to complicate the ritual. When it comes to swearing by one's god, who does Abram swear by? If his God is *"Yahweh, God Most High,"* this all becomes quite redundant, not to mention that, if this was a legal contract today, there would be a major conflict of interest. God Most High swears by Himself, who is God Most High, and the person He's making the covenant with also swears by Him, God Most High. Really? How does that add up? As far as covenants go, it doesn't. This is why the Abrahamic covenant is called a *Grant Covenant*, or a *Grace Covenant*. Abram's contribution to the ritual wasn't much of anything, except to slaughter some animals and lay them out, which is what every other pagan religion did. But that's where it ended. (While we could take some time and talk about the animals, what their Hebraic meanings are and what that tells us, it might only cloud the point at the moment.) Think of it, after Abram lays out the animals, the sun sets, and he falls asleep. As he sleeps, a nightmarish darkness comes over him and tells him of the coming bondage of his grandchildren in Egypt. Was this God, or something else? In the phrase, *horror, and great darkness,* **אימה חשכה גדלה** (yimah chasheecah gᵉdolah) the word *horror* is rooted in the word **ים** (yam), which is the root word for *roaring sea and chaos*. The following phrase, **חשכה גדלה** (chasheecah gedolah), is *a great obscurity of the light,* which came upon Abram. It's intriguing that, being they're using a pagan covenant ritual, this is what first appears. After the great darkness proclaims the coming bondage, a smoking furnace and burning torch appears, dispelling the darkness and passing between the animal pieces. According to the ancient sage known as *Rashi* (Rabbi Solomon ben Isaac) from 1040 AD:

> *"The furnace and fire symbolized that the Divine Presence was there to seal the covenant, and the smoking furnace also symbolized Gehinnom, into which the Four Monarchies would descend."*

Surely the *fiery lamp* represents the presence of אל עליון (El Elyion) *God Most High,* but with Him comes a *smoking oven or furnace,* which Rashi calls גי הנם *Gehinnom,* later in the Old Testament called *Topheth,* the place Christendom has deemed *Hell.* In that dream, the Fiery Lamp speaks His promises and walks through the ritual alley. Does Abram walk through the blood alley swearing promises to his new covenant partner? Does he call on his God to bring a curse on him, or on his new partner, if they should fail the covenant? Nope! He stays in his trance-like sleep the whole time (Genesis 15:9-20). Despite the usage of Gehenna as the infernal torment that non-Christians are supposed to be thrown into, or annihilated in, this is a non-issue for the Abrahamic covenant. First, God makes the covenant for the sake of Abram. He then dispels the darkness as a Fiery Lamp and with an eternal promise. Think of it, while the darkness proposed a time of forthcoming bondage, God follows with a clear declaration of His promise being fulfilled regardless. Then, as God Most High walks the bloody alley, along with Him is the smoking furnace, Gehenna, the burning garbage dump. Why? In pagan covenants there's always the proclamation of the blessing and the curse. These covenants are derived from the Tree from which they spawn: the knowledge of good and evil, right and wrong, blessing and cursing. God has proclaimed the blessing already, but what about the curse for failure? That's just the point; there is no declaration of a curse on Abram or his seed! Rather, it all begins and ends with God Most High. God enters the most absurd version of a covenant humanity has ever seen to that point, offers the promise of it, swears by Himself to fulfill it, and even takes on the curse of failure for both Himself and His partner. Therefore, God's covenant with Abram, which is further revealed in the New Covenant in Christ, is true grace upon grace (Zechariah 4:7; Ephesians 2:4-8). You can hear the hideous hissing of the Serpent-Ego in our flesh coiling back and saying, "That's impossible! You are saying there is no consequence of moral failure! No penalty for disobedience! No judgment of the sinner! No condemnation for rebellion! No future punishment! No Hell! No fear of God or death!" All of Heaven would have to respond, "Yes! That's what a grant covenant is! That's what God's loving grace is like!" Then there would be a squeezing sensation from the serpentine grip. What about all the talk of judgment in the Bible? Glad you asked!

To reinforce the point, we mentioned that Gehenna, גי הנם (Gehinnom), was also named Topheth תפת, which was a place of child sacrifice. Gehenna's development culminated with sacrificial burning of children to the god Molech. What is profound regarding this, is in the words of אל עליון (El Elyion) *God Most High:*

> *"They have built the high places of Tofet in the Ben-Hinnom Valley, to burn their sons and daughters in the fire, something I never ordered; in fact, such a thing never even entered my mind!"* (Jeremiah 7:31/CJB)

In beholding the practice of the paganization of Judah, where they burned their children in flames, God says that this was

212

something He never ordered nor commanded, then added, *"...in fact, such a thing never entered my mind!"* Literally, **ולא עלתה על לבי:** (v^elo al'tah al-libbiy) "...and no thing arose to My heart!" When we follow this logic, it's mind boggling that the God who never commanded or even conceived of such a thing has become a Father who sends His children, humanity, to an eternal burning torment. Even if we reduce such a place down to a devouring annihilation, it is no better than what the parents did in offering their children to Molech. The point is, we transformed the God of Grace and Rest into a pagan god of propitiation and retribution. Clearly it was NEVER in His heart, but sadly, and most assuredly, it was in our Serpentine-Ego. We projected our unconsciousness on the gods we created. In our egoistic superimposition, we put the God of Grace and Rest behind a veil of blood sacrifice. Within approximately 420 years, by the time Moses would reach Sinai, it's as if God woke up one morning and thought, "I have so many rebellious and perverse children, I'm beginning to like the idea of burning their little insubordinate selves. Gabriel! Stoke a fire! From now on, if anyone doesn't obey my rules or love Me in a way that gratifies Me, throw them in the flames and let them burn. I've been observing the pagan gods and they seem to get far better results with obedience through fear. Let's do it just like our pagan god-friend Molech." No! From the beginning of the Abrahamic covenant, though it was born of paganistic ritual, God took the total responsibility of swearing by Himself, walking the bloody path by Himself, and took the curse of Gehenna upon Himself, regardless of whether He or His covenant partner failed.

213

Nonetheless, this Grant-Grace Covenant, by demand of His covenant partner's great-grandchildren (the children of Israel), would degenerate into a Suzerian-Vassal Covenant with rules, a physical temple, a sacrificial priesthood, and blessing with cursing, hence, judgment upon good or evil. Not only did this affect their relationship, but it regressed the revelation of God *until the appearance of Jesus Christ.* Jesus brought a revelation of God to humanity that reverted it back to the Grant-Grace Covenant with Abraham. He brought an end to the violence of blood sacrifices and bloodletting covenants. This didn't mean that those who, through egoistic unconsciousness, couldn't grasp this "limitless grace" still didn't view God the Father as one of blessing and judgment. Thus, the Gospel message, along with the Apostolic epistles, are laced with speech the reader can grasp. But because of how it's communicated, it is intended to stir the heart to a higher consciousness of the true nature of God. It was the intent of the Father, through Jesus, to restore our existence back to its original intent, which is exemplified in Abraham's original covenant, but also in the transformational story of Noah. For humanity, with very broad strokes, we simply have the choice to awaken and accept His promise of grace and rest in His love, or we can continue along the way of works, rules, external temples, and murderous sacrifices. Of course, there is even a third option. We can choose the most divergent manifestation of the Serpentine nature, which is to deny the existence of any god, and make ourselves the god of our own universe.

In the case of Noah, the covenant vehicle of the Ark and the symbol of the Rainbow point in multiple directions to the Cross and Resurrection of Christ. Remember, we already established the meaning of *"...the Lamb slain from the foundation of the world"* (Revelation 13:8). In one respect, in the physical chronology of time and space, Christ hadn't yet been crucified. However, in the higher spiritual worlds, Christ died at the moment of Adam's fall. Thus, the Ark and the Rainbow are both forward and backward looking, which ultimately means it's an eternal quality living in timelessness. The Ark in the story is a branch describing the Vessel, which is the spiritual root. The Ark is an eternal quality that will always rise above the egoistic chaos to its rightful place in the higher worlds and form a new one. It's the transformational mouthpiece of Christ that brought salvation to all, even those who died outside the Ark, the Breath returned to the Source. The Apostle Peter penned:

> *"For Christ also died for sins once for all, the just for the unjust, so that He might bring us to God, having been put to death in the flesh, but made alive in the spirit; in which also* **He went and made proclamation to the spirits now in prison, who once were disobedient,** *when the patience of God kept waiting in the days of Noah, during the construction of the ark, in which a few, that is, eight persons, were brought safely through the water. Corresponding to that, baptism now saves you—not the removal of dirt from the flesh, but an appeal to God for a good conscience—through the*

> *resurrection of Jesus Christ...* **For the gospel has**
> **for this purpose been preached even to those**
> **who are dead, that though they are judged in**
> **the flesh as men, they may live in the spirit**
> **according to the will of God."**
>
> *(1 Peter 3:18-21; 4:6/NASU)*

The Ark and the flood story are symbolically used by Peter to describe our reconciliation through Christ, calling it *a figure of baptism.* Notice, he doesn't just say that only those who prayed the sinner's prayer heard and received, but even those who died outside the Ark, those who were disobedient long ago. Though they were judged and condemned by Mankind according to the flesh, through Christ the Gospel was proclaimed that they might live as they truly were to God in spiritual reality. As we develop what the Genesis scriptures are saying throughout Chapters 6 and 7, it's important to point out that it's congruent to what the Apostle Peter is writing. All live by the Spirit, both inside the Ark and those who seemly perished outside the Ark. However, those inside the Ark see and bring a revelation of the Father of Grace into the new world which the rest of humanity doesn't perceive. Thus, the progression of God's Creation into being His Image and Likeness continues by "choice" and not coercion.

Up until this point the word for *die* or *died* in the story was the verb יִגְוַע (yig'va), which means *to exhale.* However, when we reach Genesis 7:22 there's an intentional change in the word usage.

"All in whose nostrils was the breath of the spirit of life, all that was on the dry land, died."
(Genesis 7:22/NKJV)

כל אשר נשמת רוח חיים באפיו מכל אשר
בחרבה מתו:

(kol asher nismat-ruach hayyim b'appyv mikkol asher beharavah mituw)

"All whose breath-wind of Life is in his nostrils (passion) from all whose in dry [land] they died."

It's important to note that God's "Breath of Life" was in those who were outside the Ark as well as those inside. It wasn't that Noah and his family were the special ones who had the Spirit of Life and those outside the Ark didn't. The key was awareness. Noah became aware because of how he saw God and because of that it continued to awaken him. You could say that because Noah became conscious of the God of Grace, it formed the Ark of transformation, which took form in the time of transition and was able to transport him from a world of egoistic violence, through the storm of metamorphosis, to a world of peace. But like any transfiguration, there is a death and rebirth. There is the conclusion of the former and the bringing forth of the new. It isn't an annihilation of the former and the making of something new with all new materials. Rather, it's the metamorphosis of the former into the new. In one sense, *"Old things are passed away, and all things have become new,"* (2 Corinthians 5:17), and yet, it's a change in consciousness. In other words, the original substance, the

217

Divine "Breath of Life" which is the source of our true self, hasn't changed. Rather, it's becoming aware of that truth, as those *"with unveiled face, beholding in a mirror the glory of the Lord,"* (2 Corinthians 3:18). The unveiling and beholding in a mirror is what causes the perceived old to pass away and all things to become new. Thus, the final word in the above verse in Genesis, *died,* is no longer, *exhale,* יִגְוַע (yig'va), which returns the breath from where it came, but the word מִתוּ (mituw), from the root מוּת (moot), which basically means what it says: *die,* a ceasing to exist. However, within this word is a very special meaning. In ancient Hebrew, its cuneiform-type lettering tells us a profound story:

First the (מ) ᴧᴧ (mem), which means *that which flows, as in water and blood.* The second letter is (ו) Υ (vav), which is *the tent peg,* and *the light that descends from above.* Lastly is the (ת) Ϯ (tav), which means *the mark* or *sign of faith; the cross!* When you put this all together you have Ϯᴧᴧ, *that which flows with water and blood pegged to the Cross.* Or, *that which flows, the Light that descends from above at the Cross.* It's inescapable! Even those who exhale outside of the Ark have a connection with the Cross, which is exactly what the Apostle Peter pointed to. Even in death, the Cross and all that it entails prevails! The story of Noah and the Ark is truly a prophetic description of complete and total redemption for all Mankind as well as a progression in the revelation of God's Image and Likeness revealed. By extension, another side of the block that we can ascertain from this is from the origins of the word, water **מים** (mayim), *chaos*. You could also say, *all the chaos is pegged to the cross.*

The Noah's Ark story, whether real or an allegory, or both, is a Divine telling of God's unrelenting love and purpose for all of us. From the beginning, God created a Creature, The Adam, *all of us,* to be His Image and Likeness. He did so, not because He was so egoistic that He wanted to revel in how He looked to Himself—like the witch Grimhilde, peering into the mirror in the tale of Snow White—but because He sought intimacy with a being *equal to Himself.* The way to accomplish this was through giving that same Creature a choice to love and be loved, or to honestly choose another life apart from Him. True love is only love when it's chosen. Given that privilege of choice, the Creature took another path. Yet God tirelessly pursued that which He loved. While the Creature chose the way of a false and fabricated reality, creating gods of violence and damnation in their own image, the Eternal Creator still pursued the one He loved. Finally, a spiritual quality from within the Creature momentarily broke through the illusion and it caught a glimmer of itself in the mirror of reality. In that moment, when the Ego believed its preeminence was fully realized and proudly eased its constricting grip, the Creature unwittingly had a glance of real love in their Suitor's eyes. In the midst of a knowledge distorted with good and evil, the Creature spotted Grace and Rest in the reflection. That mirrored glimpse of "the Creator in the Creature" was so strong, it inspired the gathering of the shattered Vessel from its burning egoistic brimstone. The strength of its gaze neutralized the fallacious knowledge of good and evil, and overshadowed the Creature. It covered its self-imposed fears and condemnation with the reflection of the Creator's At-one-ment. Silencing the stormy chaos of false accusation and judgmental excuse, the Creator raised His lover above the flood of selfish desire. Together they transformed that world of mayhem into an olive branch of peace. On the surface, one can view the path the Creature first chose as sinful and wrong. Yet, in the Creator's wisdom, it became something further reaching. It became a path of self-discovery, a self-sustaining realization of our At-one-ment with the One within who loves us. From the Garden to the Fall, to generations of violence from Adam to Noah, to a rebooted world from Noah to Abraham, God continued to reflect His love for and in His Creation. It was then, at the time of Abraham, that a reflection arrived, transcendent, eternal, and otherworldly, called Melchizedek, whose timeless gaze with bread and wine raised everything to an even higher consciousness than the preceding flood, to one that was Most High.

CHAPTER 8
REALIZING "LIFE" FROM ABOVE

"Life will not be contained! Life breaks free, it expands to new territories and crashes through barriers, painfully, maybe even dangerously... BUT... Life finds a way!"

Dr. Ian Malcom
Jurassic Park
Michael Crichton

Once one grasps the idea of the Tree of the Knowledge of Good and Evil with its Serpent, it becomes easy for the Ego to point out legalism, religiosity, and ritualism. This reinforces another aspect of its self-righteousness, just on the other side of the same road. Simply put, egoistically pointing out the futility of religion is just another Pharisee wearing a different garment. More to the point, our Ego is very deceptive. Under pressure, it will acknowledge its own religious arrogance with its variants. It doesn't just surrender and ascend back to the status of the *Desire to Receive and Reflect*, embracing the realm of the Tree of Life. To the contrary, in its newfound "liberty" a pseudo-freedom can easily arise as it departs from its sanctimonious habits. Emancipated from striving to achieve unattainable moral codes, along with immunity from retribution for not achieving them, our ego may think it can do as it fancies.

Nevertheless, if our inner garden has some unraked leaves of the Tree of the Knowledge of Good and Evil, we may find what we're about to discuss regarding the realm of "Life" difficult to ingest. There's a truth regarding our ego doing as it fancies, especially if there is no fear of judgmental retribution. Of course, there is still the principle of reaping what we've sown, a principle of this world's system. Without reaping what we sow, the Serpent would have no venom in its bite. Yet, to embroil God in the reaping as some form of His judgment is a misunderstanding of His nature as revealed in Christ. God Most High will not wreak vengeance on the so-called sinner if he or she has chosen a path apart from Him (John 5:22; 8:15). If He did, then we're not truly divinely free to discover His Image and Likeness. On the contrary, we're still bound by just another form of religion's slavery (Galatians 5:1-5). What Christ has achieved and freely given to us is true spiritual liberty. His triumph over our mindset of good and evil has once again (metaphorically) placed us before the two Trees in innocence and given us the liberty to choose without fear of vengeance. We can unreservedly choose between the Tree of Death with its Egoism, the Serpent, Satan and so on, or we can choose Life, our true identity, which is equal in form to God Most High Himself. To be more emphatic, this isn't just another one-time choice, like when the man and the woman first partook of the Tree of the Knowledge of Good and Evil. Instead, it's a perpetual freedom to choose. If this wasn't a central aspect of the Gospel, then the famous phrase, *"For God so loved the world,"* along with the crucifixion and resurrection, would be futile. This is where we progress past the perception of "being saved from sin or a burning Hell" and unveil God's original intention. If we're going to love like God, then every moment of every reflection must be of the purest choice. Love only exists in the boundless world of freedom.

Religion says, "If you really love God, then you will obey the rules!" Yet God would say, "If you love, you won't have to." Religion would add, "Exactly! If you love God, you will by nature follow the rules." Again, God would say, "Rules? What rules? In the realm of the Tree of Life, we don't have such things." Then the Father would add, "That's like saying you must have the darkness to see how bright the light is. Only in a world of false contrasts, like the *knowledge of good and evil,* would one hold such a view. If you must use such words as rules and laws, then in the realm of Divine Life there is only one law: Love. Yet when Love is made into a law, it ceases to be Divine, falls from the realm of the gaze of Grace, and veils our true nature. Love has no rules or boundaries. Love just loves because that's What It is and Who We Are. Love isn't a reasonable calculation of doing good and feeling good about it. Love is the Light where there is no darkness. Love is born of a choice of being Who We Are, not a choice to do a good deed, despite how we feel." Religion could counter by saying, "Okay, fine! But in this fallen world of fleshly people, we need such limits. So here, love puts structure, boundaries, and necessary rules for the betterment of everyone." Lastly, the Father would say, "Really? Consider your reality from My

223

point of view. I sent the Son of *Our* Love into such a worldly system. Yet the structure wouldn't receive Him, the boundaries imprisoned Him, the rules beat Him, and the leaders mockingly crucified Him, believing it was for everyone's betterment. Clearly, we have a very different perception of Love."

Whether it's our religiosity or letting our egos run wild, both are from the same root. Whether we are egoistically religious or selfishly indulgent, the source is still the Serpentine-Ego and its Tree. It's in this framework that the Serpent will take on another form, which may be the greatest delusion of all. Knowing it shouldn't be seen as legalistic and shouldn't be self-indulgent, it needs to find a new illusion to survive. So it slithers down the path of *asceticism.* Asceticism, the notion of a self-discipline that results in the denial of pleasures, is just as egoistic as all the above. One of the reasons for the symbology of the serpent wasn't only to reference the headdress of Pharaoh, but also its ability to change configuration and slither into all kinds of nooks and crannies. Whether it's coiled or elongated, or aspects of both, it finds its way into almost any thought or imagination. The idea that asceticism addresses the removal of our religiosity and indulgences is nothing more than another configuration of a self-centered existence intoxicated with the Serpent's venom.

The Tree of Life finds itself in the cosmos of *the Garden of Eden.* Most importantly, Eden עֵדֶן means *pleasure* (in the most fulfilling sense). Notice how the same word is translated as Sarah thinks about the Lord's promise regarding her having a child:

> *"So Sarah laughed to herself as she thought, 'After I am worn out and my master is old, will I now have this **pleasure**?'"* (Genesis 18:12/NIV)

This is why living a life that denies pleasure is not living according to Divine design or intention. So what do we do with all of this? It can sound so spiritual to deny pleasure, yet our origin is from the Garden of it. To deny pleasure is to deny our Divine origins. When we try putting both of those thoughts together it's nothing more than an exhausting, self-centered negation, like a dog chasing its tail. No religiosity, no indulgences, no pleasure, yet I'm supposed to have the joy of the Lord? Wait...what? As we simply rearrange the leaves of the Tree of the Knowledge of Good and Evil in our yard, not really removing them, we may think, "If we're not supposed to be religious nor indulge ourselves, yet not deny pleasure, then how do we have it?" *We must awaken to a new world within ourselves.* The entire inner construct of how we view ourselves and reality needs to awaken to its original state, which by nature radically changes our view of ourselves and reality.

Part 1: Born From Above

Jesus said it best when He was speaking to the Pharisaical ruler, Nicodemus, in what's become the famous "Born Again" discourse. That discussion climaxes with one of the most famous verses in all the New Testament, John 3:16: *"For God*

225

so loved the world..." Yet, what we've done with that verse and its surrounding conversation is a grave departure from what Jesus ever intended. Consider how we've read the verse. More so, consider what we've read *into* the verse. Let's first see how the average English translation reads:

> *"For God so loved the world that He gave His only begotten Son, that whoever believes in Him should not perish but have everlasting life."*
>
> *(John 3:16/NKJV)*

Now let's have a look at what we've read *into* the verse:

> "For God so loved the *people who would potentially choose Him* that He gave His only begotten Son *to be crucified for their sins because of the Father's judgment and wrath,* that whoever believes in Him should not burn in Hell forever but live with Him in Heaven happily ever after."

We may find ourselves so programmed into the vicarious atonement doctrine, also known as the doctrine of penal substitution, that we may not even see the actual words of the text. Jesus was never informing us that if we don't believe properly, our destination will be burning in eternal conscious torment or being annihilated forever. Then again, He also wasn't implying that if we do believe properly, we'd live in a mansion with a large, grassy landscape, a golden driveway, a motorized, monogramed brass gate, and a heavenly address. He also wasn't suggesting that we would worship in some huge castle-throne-room, in which is a temple-like sanctuary

MELCHIZEDEK: Tree of Life Realities

where a giant white-haired being called "the father" sits on an elevated pinnacle so all can see him regardless of where they stand in the throng. No! Jesus wasn't speaking about avoiding fires, nor some comfy mansion, nor castle-like temple. The entire discourse is about *a place we are to live from,* not a place we will someday go to!

> *"This man came to Jesus by night and said to Him, 'Rabbi, we know that You are a teacher come from God; for no one can do these signs that You do unless God is with him.' Jesus answered and said to him, 'Most assuredly, I say to you, unless one is born again, he cannot see the kingdom of God.'"*
>
> *(John3:2-3/NKJV)*

In the Gospel of John, by the time Jesus and Nicodemus spoke, Jesus had done only one miracle: He turned water into wine at the wedding in Cana of Galilee. Prior to this meeting, the only other thing Jesus had done, after His baptism, was to drive the moneychangers from the Temple. At that point, when the Pharisees asked Him to validate His actions by showing them a sign, Jesus simply retorted, *"Destroy this Temple, and in three days I will raise it up."* (John 2:19) What, then, could Nicodemus be contemplating? We could surmise that he'd possibly heard of other miracles Jesus had done, or maybe had even seen a few which were not recorded in the text. But even if he did, think of what Nicodemus actually said: *"...we know You are a teacher come from God, for no one can do these signs..."* If the "signs" that Jesus did, like turning water into wine, were the symbols of His Divinity, then the sorcerer,

227

Simon of Samaria, of whom it was said "had the great power of God" (Acts 8:10), must have been from God as well, right? Or is that just the point? Jesus's response wasn't about signs or what Nicodemus thought he saw, rather it was about "...*seeing the Kingdom of God.*" In other words, Jesus was saying, "Nicodemus, what you think you see and what is really going on has nothing to do with signs and wonders, and that being the validation of Me being from God." To further make the point that, "Nicodemus, you really haven't seen anything!" Jesus explains:

Ἀμὴν ἀμὴν λέγω σοι, ἐὰν μή τις γεννηθῇ ἄνωθεν, οὐ δύναται ἰδεῖν τὴν βασιλείαν τοῦ θεοῦ.

(Ameén ameén légoo soi eán-meé tis genneetheé
ánoothen
ou dúnatai ideín teén basileían toú Theoú)

Perfectly firm I say to you, unless a person has his
origin from above, it is not possible to *knowingly-grasp* the Kingdom of God.

Then Nicodemus responds:

"...'How can a man be born when he is old? Can he enter a second time into his mother's womb and be born?'" (John 3:4/NKJV)

In our Christian colloquialisms of the 1970s, we took Nicodemus's statement to mean being born twice and

228

inferring that the second time meant being born differently, or spiritually. We presume that being "born again" means salvation with a destination of Heaven and a renewed relationship with God (with the insinuation of being saved from Hell). In an essay by the late Rabbi Aryeh Kaplan, he tells us that, during the time of the Roman occupation, when living in the Kingdom of God was referenced it was about living or being born in a different era. Many of us who reminisce about the "good ol' days" might say something like, "Can you imagine when the Temple was finished during the days of Solomon? It would've been wonderful to have been born during that time, when God's Kingdom was at hand." During any occupation of Israel it was common knowledge throughout the Hebrew community that the Kingdom wasn't present. For that matter, the last manifestation of "the Kingdom" was during the reign of King Solomon when a unified Israel existed. It would be later in Judaism that the idea of being *born again* would signify a convert. Its meaning had nothing to do with Heaven, Hell, or having a personal relationship with God, but that by becoming a Jew one had fully become a person. At the time of Jesus, Judaism hadn't yet gotten that far.

Nicodemus wasn't referencing spiritual rebirth, discovering a friendship with God, being saved from Hell, or going to Heaven. No, he was thinking of being born in a different era when Israel was unified under a proper King. Can you imagine if you added to our rhetoric of "having Jesus in your heart?" Not only would Nicodemus be trying to figure out how to crawl back into his mother's womb, but also what it would mean to have the guy standing in front of him inside his chest!

If we impose our modern theological interpretation on this and think of it from Nicodemus's point of view, it's just disturbing. Jesus then refocuses Nicodemus's thoughts:

"Jesus answered, 'Most assuredly, I say to you, unless one is born of water and the Spirit, he cannot enter the kingdom of God. That which is born of the flesh is flesh, and that which is born of the Spirit is spirit. Do not marvel that I said to you, 'You must be born again.'" (John 3:5-7/NKJV)

When I first entered Bible college well over 39 years ago, we were taught that being born of water and the spirit meant being first born physically, speaking of the waters that flow during childbirth, then being born of the Spirit, which was being born into salvation and saved from eternal damnation. But what did Jesus really say (John 3:5)?

γεννηθῇ ἐξ ὕδατος καὶ πνεύματος
(genneetheé ex húdatos kaí pneúmatos)

...[unless a person] originate from water and spirit...

A key word is **ὕδατος** (húdatos) *water.* While we can try to force it to mean amniotic fluid, Jesus never mentioned being born of a woman, Nicodemus did. When Jesus began His response to Nicodemus, He specifically said, *"has its origin from above,"* or *"born from above."* Jesus later points out, being that Nicodemus did mention physical birth, that which comes

230

from flesh is flesh and that which comes from the spirit is spirit, making a clear antithetical distinction. He wasn't saying you must be born of flesh and spirit; He was speaking about a completely different world, the world called *Above*. In the verse, Jesus uses the common word for *fresh water*, which comes from **ὑετός** (huetos), which means, *rain*. Think of all the scriptures that speak of the rain. Here are a few to refresh our memory:

> *"Rain down, you heavens, from above..."*
> *(Isaiah 45:8/NKJV)*

> *"For as the rain comes down... So shall My word be that goes forth from My mouth...*
> *(Isaiah 55:10-11/NKJV)*

Jesus hasn't changed topics just because Nicodemus couldn't see or grasp what He was talking about. Jesus was clear, we must have our *origin from above*. We must originate from where the rain water descends from above, which is the origin of the Living Word. Please note, Jesus did not say water *or* spirit. He said water **and** spirit. Later, both John the Baptist and Jesus make it unmistakably clear:

> *"The one who comes from above is above all; the one who is from the earth belongs to the earth, and speaks as one from the earth."*   *(John 3:31/NIV)*

> *"But he continued, 'You are from below; I am from above. You are of this world; I am not of this world.'*
>
> *(John 8:23/NIV)*

The Apostle Paul takes this thought even further:

> *"...for if you are living according to the flesh, you must die; but if by the Spirit you are putting to death the deeds of the body, you will live."*
>
> *(Romans 8:13/NASU)*

The following verse clarifies what Jesus was talking about, especially if we read it without our traditional filters. Here He addresses Nicodemus's concern regarding being reborn of a woman:

**τὸ γεγεννημένον ἐκ τῆς σαρκὸς σάρξ ἐστιν,
καὶ τὸ γεγεννημένον ἐκ τοῦ πνεύματος πνεῦμά ἐστιν.
μὴ θαυμάσῃς ὅτι εἶπόν σοι Δεῖ ὑμᾶς γεννηθῆναι ἄνωθεν.**

(Tó gegenneeménon ek teés sarkós sárx estin
kaí tó gegenneeménon ek toú Pneúmatos pneúmá estin
Meé thaumásees hóti eípón soi Deí humás genneetheénai ánoothen)

This origin of the (meat) flesh, flesh it is and this
origin of the spirit, spirit it is.
Don't be astonished that I affirm to you it's a
necessity to *originate from above.*

There's a stark contrast between being from below and what
is of the Spirit from above. What we need to grasp is that
which is truly from *Above* remains above, it never really
descends. The misnomer is that Christ "descended" and left
His origin and came to the lower world. While this can be a
metaphor to express the Incarnation, or manna, the Bread
from Above, it's not spiritual reality. Even though Christ was
in physical form, He was clear, *"I am from above...I am not of
this world."* He didn't say, "I was from above, and now I have
come down and descended below." If He actually descended,
He would not be able to say, *"Whoever has seen me, has seen
the Father,"* (John 14:9). He never stopped being from the
upper worlds, *Above.* He never lived from the fallen base
nature of this cosmos, *Below.* He was of the Tree of Life and
never ceased being from it, though He walked among us in a
physical form. This is the true Incarnation. However, when we
describe a descent to the lower world, that "who" was us, the
Adam. Not only did we descend as we partook of the Tree of
the Knowledge of Good and Evil, but live from its ethos.
Therefore, living from Below is a descent, thus living in a state
called "through the fall", which is the Greek definition of the
word **διάβολος** (diabolos), commonly translated, *devil.* We
need not look in dark corners, dimly lit caverns, horror
movies, or other places we've deemed demonic. We only need
to look in the mirror of our egoistic selves and there we will

find the **διάβολος** (diabolos). We proved it when we murdered the One Who walked among us. We impaled Him on the Serpent's Tree in the form of a cross. We accused Him of being a demon, Beelzebub. We shamed Him, stripped Him, and beat Him. Nonetheless, He allowed Himself to become what we deemed sin, though He never knew it (2 Corinthians 5:21). He gave Himself up to our religious accusations of wrongdoing and blasphemy. He yielded Himself to our legalistic and pseudo-political judgments defining Him as a criminal. Through our lens of the lower cosmos, the world Below, He was the devil. He was the perfect sinner based on the Knowledge of Good and Evil system. Yet, by allowing Himself to be accused, not retaliating nor attempting to justify Himself, He revealed the Image and Likeness of the Godhead in the truest sense. Through not indicting, judging, or condemning His accusers, His Divinity was unquenchable, His Life inextinguishable; hence, the resurrection was inevitable.

Jesus continues:

> *"You should not be surprised at my saying, 'You must be born again.' The wind blows wherever it pleases. You hear its sound, but you cannot tell where it comes from or where it is going. So it is with everyone born of the Spirit."*　　　(John 3:7-8/NIV)

μὴ θαυμάσῃς ὅτι εἶπόν σοι Δεῖ ὑμᾶς γεννηθῆναι ἄνωθεν.

τὸ πνεῦμα ὅπου θέλει πνεῖ, καὶ τὴν
φωνὴν αὐτοῦ ἀκούεις,
ἀλλ᾽ οὐκ οἶδας πόθεν ἔρχεται καὶ ποῦ
ὑπάγει·
οὕτως ἐστὶν πᾶς ὁ γεγεννημένος ἐκ
τοῦ πνεύματος.

(Meé thaumásees hóti eípón soi Deí humás
genneetheénai ánoothen
Tó pneúma hópou thélei pneí Kaí teén
fooneénautoú akoúeis
all ouk oídas póthen érchetai kaí poú hupágei
Hoútoos estín pás ho gegenneeménos ek toú
Pneúmatos)

Don't wonder that I said, 'You must originate
from above.'
The wind (breeze) blows where it desires and its
sound you hear,
but you cannot tell where it comes and where it
goes.
So, it is with all who originate [issue forth] from
the spirit.

Jesus is telling Nicodemus that unless you emanate from above and your perception of reality originates from there, you cannot see anything that relates to the Kingdom of God. In comparison, anyone born from above is like the wind: though we may feel it or hear it, we really haven't seen it. Jesus is telling him, you're thinking that miracles are a sign that I am from God, but you're only seeing the effects of the wind and hearing its sound. You haven't seen anything. If you did, you would grasp that the *Kingdom of God* is at hand. This is why Nicodemus responds:

> *"'How can this be?' Nicodemus asked. 'You are Israel's teacher,' said Jesus, 'and do you not understand these things? I tell you the truth, we speak of what we know, and we testify to what we have seen, but still you people do not accept our testimony. I have spoken to you of earthly things and you do not believe; how then will you believe if I speak of heavenly things?'"*   *(John 3:9-12/NIV)*

"How can this be?" Those words are the proof that Nicodemus, though a supreme leader of the people, couldn't see from Christ's vantage point. If this was a discussion about "receiving Jesus into one's heart" and that being the definition of being born again, Jesus never would have said what He did. *"You are Israel's teacher and you do not understand these things?"* Clearly, this was not about saying *the sinner's prayer*. It was something far deeper and greater.

Part 2: Returning the Serpent to "Above"

As Jesus continues explaining to Nicodemus what it means to be "born from Above," He relates the story from the book of Numbers of Moses raising the bronze serpent.

"No one has ever gone into heaven except the one who came from heaven — the Son of Man. Just as Moses lifted up the snake in the desert, so the Son of Man must be lifted up, that everyone who believes in him may have eternal life."   (John 3:13-15/NIV)

This becomes one of the pivotal moments in Jesus's and our discussion. This is the awakening to a new world, a new sight, a new life source, a new origin from the one we are familiar with, the sweet fragrance of the Tree of Life. Why would Jesus equate seeing or entering the Kingdom to Moses elevating the bronze serpent? To grasp this, we must return to the source text that Jesus was citing.

"Then the Lord said to Moses, 'Make a fiery ~~serpent~~*, and set it on a standard; and it shall come about, that everyone who is bitten, when he looks at it, he will live.' And Moses made a bronze serpent and set it on the standard; and it came about, that if a serpent bit any man, when he looked to the bronze serpent, he lived.   (Numbers 21:8-9/NASU)*

The common phrase many translations use, *"Make a fiery serpent,"* or some say, *"poisonous snake,"* is technically incorrect. While we can assume that Moses is referring to a serpent based on the rest of the context, the difference is its positioning and why a different, significant word is used at first. (This is why a line is drawn through the word *serpent* in the above verse, because the word isn't in the text at that point.) When יהוה speaks He says to make a שָׂרָף (saraph),

237

an angelic being of the highest order, not a **נחש** (nachash), a serpent. Moses seemed to understand the relevance. A **שרף** (saraph), according to Isaiah 6:2-3, is a fiery being in the upper worlds that continually proclaims, *"Holy, holy, holy is the Lord of hosts: the whole earth is full of His glory."* This would be congruent with the description of Lucifer (the Morning Star, using the King of Tyre as a metaphor) in Ezekiel 28:11-15, which we've previously discussed at length. Note that, prior to its fall, this creature was full of wisdom, very beautiful, lived in the Garden of Eden, was the anointed covering cherub, and walked among the *fiery* stones. This is the clear description of the *Desire to Receive Reflecting the Divine Image.* This is that state when the **מסך** (masach), the covering screen, is used to reflect the Light of God, which is a fire. Remember, in one of the multitude of descriptions for God, He too is a fiery being (Ezekiel 1:26-28). It may be difficult for us in present day to conceive of God in such a manner, but in the time of Moses, incandescent, fluorescent, light emitting diodes (LEDs), lasers, and other such light sources didn't exist. The torch, fireplace, along with different campfire configurations, were how light was emitted during that time. Thus, for God to be the source of Light, He would be as such, a blazing fire (Deuteronomy 4:24; Hebrews 12:29). However, as Ezekiel continues, we find that instead of *Receiving and Reflecting,* Lucifer (as in Isaiah 14) chose egoistically to *Receive for Himself* and fell, creating the substance of this egoistic world of illusion.

When we think of the physical world in which we live, we consider that which can be perceived by the five senses as real. Then, if we close our eyes, the picture created within our mind is just a thought, dream, or illusion. But as we stated earlier in our refresher chapters, the reverse is actually true. This is not to say that the physical world doesn't have merit, but if we were totally honest with ourselves, it isn't the total sum of reality. For that matter, the physical world is only a small sliver of reality and, because we don't sense the totality of reality, our point of view isn't capable of telling us what is actually right in front of us. Most importantly, how we experience the physical world is totally within ourselves, from our egoistic point of view. Everything we experience through the five senses is evaluated by our ego, which is the harbor of self-centered pleasure. Every encounter is quickly evaluated based on whether it will be good or bad, and how it relates to a memory of a good or bad experience. So, before we are present in the moment, we literally have already told ourselves a story about what is happening, which then becomes the inner projection of our reality. Therefore, though our abode was in the Garden of Eden, when we chose to partake of the Serpent and its Tree, the reality of our existence changed. We weren't just kicked out by an angry parent for being disobedient children. Consider the key point to all of this. Regardless of how we currently view ourselves, we are the Image and Likeness of God. Thus, we have a type of creative power just like our Creator. According to Jesus, we can move mountains (Mark 11:23), and that's in our current state where we can only perceive a sliver of reality. When the Adam, of which we are a part, named the different aspects of

Creation, he gave them definition. In simple terms, while God created a creature, a fox wasn't a fox until the Adam proclaimed it was. Literally, the famous part of the verse:

> *"...and whatever the man called each living creature, that was its name."*   *(Genesis 2:19/NIV)*

Translates from the Hebrew:

וכל אשר יקרא לו האדם נפש חיה הוא שמו:

(v'col asher yiq'ra lo ha'adam nephish chayah hoo sh'mo)

...and all which called to him, the Adam, a soul living, its character [name] him.

In other words, God brought "living souls" to the Adam and whatever the Adam called them, that became their identity and character, thus their name. When we, the Adam, partook of the Serpent and its Tree, we gave to ourselves and the world around us its identity and character from that point of view. Because we have chosen egoistically and veiled the perception of God from ourselves, we view ourselves and the world by that definition. Hence, the world we live in is no longer God's creation, but ours. Therefore, creation is in a state of corruption and it groans for the sons of God to be revealed (Romans 8:19-22). When we change our source perspective from Ego-centric back to Compassion, Divine Love born from Above, creation ceases to groan and returns to its original state of rest.

When Jesus utilized the Moses comparison of the bronze serpent, the key point was it being lifted. Just prior to Moses lifting it up, the focus was the bite of the Serpent, which is no different than its voice in the Garden, resulting in "death." Based on what we know as the Biblical definition of death, these passages are not referring to the mere death of the body. More importantly, from a root point of view, it's referring to the deathly egoistic poison of the Serpent. The serpents that bit the people were on the ground, which is the same *form* the Serpent took after the Adam partook of its poison. Remember, after the Adam partook of the Knowledge of Good and Evil, the Serpent's status was changed from being coiled in a higher state in the Tree, to a lower state on its belly, eating the dust of the ground. Some have the view that the Serpent once stood upright like a human, though at this point, most scholarly examination doesn't seem to affirm scriptural evidence that the Tanak viewed the Serpent in that manner. On the other hand, there is strong scientific thought that proposes most snakes have a remnant of limbs in their embryonic skeletal structure. It's through a development process of the embryo that "Zone Polarizing Activity Regulatory Sequences" occur so they never grow. Regardless, whether coiled in the Tree (as in Isaiah 27:1/NIV) or standing upright, the issue is that when the Serpent and Mankind united, both fell to a lower realm at the same egoistic level. Notice how God speaks of the people of Jerusalem:

> *"You shall be brought down, you shall speak out of the ground; your speech shall be low, out of the dust; your voice shall be like a medium's, out of the*

> *ground; and your speech shall whisper out of the*
> *dust."*   *(Isaiah 29:4/NKJV)*

What God says of the people is directly related to what He spoke of the Serpent in Genesis 3:14. Notice also how He relates that "speaking out of the ground" was like a medium's voice, or one who whispers out of the dust. Fast forward to the ministry of John the Baptist, when his disciples and some of the Jews were arguing over what purification was. He said:

> *"He who is of the earth is of earthly origin and*
> *nature,* **and from the earth as a source he**
> **speaks."**   *(John 3:31/Wuest)*

Speaking from the earth as a source, or one who speaks out of the ground, points to our union with the Serpentine-Ego in its densest form. It wasn't until the Adam merged with the Serpent that the physical world as we now know it came into being. Equally as important, we didn't just "fall" to a lower state and become unconscious of the greater reality. The form of the Serpent changed as well and together we gave that realm, that lower state, identity, and function. The Apostles called it both "this world" and "the flesh."

The fiery ash, the dust, the ground, this world, and whatever other descriptions are found throughout the Biblical text, is the densest form of Ego. Another way of wording this could be the Satanic realm, or the realm of the "prince" or "god of this world" (John 14:30; 2 Corinthians 4:4). Another New Testament way of wording this could be the heaviest state, weighing us down to the lower realm (Hebrews 12:1). However, when the serpent was raised up, thus returning it to its higher, original status as a שרף (saraph), it once again represented that which reflected the flame of Divine Light. Consequently, when the people looked at the elevated bronze serpent—toward the world *Above*—they were healed. Why? Because it was the resemblance of their (as well as our) origin, the genesis of Divine intention. It was raising our Egoistic self from the ground back to its place of equivalency of form with God. Now consider the words of the Apostle Paul:

> *"Therefore if you have been raised up with Christ, keep seeking the things above, where Christ is, seated at the right hand of God. Set your mind on the things above, not on the things that are on earth."*
> *(Colossians 3:1-2/NASU)*

When the bronze serpent was raised up, it was a type of the egoistic nature being elevated back to its original form, *the Desire to Receive and Reflect.* This is exactly who Jesus was and still is. He is the revelation of *the Desire to Receive and Reflect.* This is why He could say, *"If you've seen Me, you've seen the Father."* He didn't need to be crucified to be a revelation of that. He lived His life as that and, when He was crucified, He never stopped being that. He didn't mutate on the Cross from being "God in Christ" (2 Corinthians 5:19) to a hideous substitutionary sinner separated from God, as if He became a sacrificial sponge and soaked all of our filthy sin into Himself. Rather, He was still the Divine Reflection, loving and forgiving, despite the fact that we suffused our egoistic sin over Him, causing Him gruesome pain and temporary death (Hebrews 12:2-3).

In the Garden, however, the reverse occurred. Rather than being *the Desire to Receive and Reflect,* we chose the path of *the Desire to Receive for Ourself Alone.* We must understand that we were created as *the Desire to Receive* because our Loving Creator wanted to Give and Share. What was before us was the choice of how we were going to receive. The Serpent was the touching point of that choice, which is why both Serpent and Tree were present even before the point when God breathed into us the Breath of Life. You could say, metaphorically, that it was the Serpent and its Tree which gave us the necessary ingredient to live as the Divine Image. It's not found in partaking of the Tree but in our resistance of enjoining ourselves to it.

Taking this thought a step further, the Hebraic meaning of the word *knowledge,* דעת (da'at), is not simply an intellectual grasp of something. Rather, like in our previous example, when we separate a segment (understanding) from a river of flowing water (wisdom) and then drink it, we become one with it (knowledge). The challenge is that connecting with only a segment doesn't give us the full-flowing awareness. Hence, the physical world in which we currently exist is only a small sliver, or segment, of the full-flowing reality. The next time we see the word *know* appear after Genesis Chapter 3, we get more of a fullness of its meaning. The man, Adam, *knew* his woman, Eve, and the result is a child, a product of their union (Genesis 4:1). It was a merging or a uniting of the two. Thus, the word *to know,* means *to unite* or *merge.*

What the description of the Tree of the *Knowledge* of Good and Evil brings to us is a fruit that is a union of *good and evil.* Therefore, the fruit is a hybrid, which cannot be separated by an either/or approach. Some may think, "You're saying that before the Adam partook of the Tree, good and evil were separated, right? Because that's what we're trying to accomplish, to be good and shun evil." Actually no, outside of the Serpent's Tree, good and evil as we understand them don't exist. For that matter, there's a very different axiom in the realm of Life. In the upper world, "good and evil" is simply called, "Death." In other words, this hybrid fruit is "Death." It's not half good and half evil, or any other combination. As we will see, the measure of either doesn't matter, it's just Death. What exists outside of Death, which is what one might want to call *good,* could in one respect be close to the idea of Life, yet is still sitting on its compulsory contrast of evil. Therefore, we haven't yet left the Tree of the Serpent at all; we've just reassigned the labels. Nonetheless, in God's economy that which is functional is called *Life,* and its vibrance doesn't have, or require, a contrast such as evil. You could say, from the lower world's perspective, that the contrast of Life is Death, like the contrast of Light is Darkness. However, there are no such contrasts in the Tree of Life system, nor in the Divine Light proclaimed in Genesis. In the upper world, *the world Above,* there is only *Life* (which is also depicted as *Light* and *Love).* In the *world Below,* there is only the absence of Life. Hence, Life, Light, and Love are absorbed rather than reflected. We must grasp that the lower world is not a state of equal value or equal contrast. The *world Below* is an egoistic illusion where Divine Life, Light, and Love are received and not reflected, thus concealed and indiscernible. This is why Christ came in the flesh and appeared in the lower world. It was the Creator's way of trying to uncover and reveal what Divine Life, Light, and Love looked like in a world where such is indiscernible. Prior to that, the Creator and Creation were Laws depicting good, contrasted with the infamous, "Thou shalt nots..." pointing toward evil. The result was that if you did good you would be blessed and if you didn't you would be punished. In that world, the true Creator of all things is concealed behind a veil and indiscernible.

For example: If we were to return to the classic 1931 black and white movie, *Dracula*, starring Bela Lugosi, we find that Dracula doesn't have a reflection in a mirror. There's a disturbing scene where Count Dracula is in a living room speaking with Mina (played by Helen Chandler). John Harker (David Manners) opens a cigarette case which has a mirror in the cover. It inadvertently reflects the conversation of the Count and Mina. In that moment, Dr. Van Helsing (Edward van Sloan) looks into the mirror by chance and sees only Mina with no reflection of the Count, even though there's clearly a conversation happening between the two. Van Helsing looks at the two in front of him, Dracula and Mina, then looks at the mirror and sees only Mina. Why? Why can he see Dracula standing there, talking with Mina and yet, there's no reflection of him in the mirror? Was Mina talking with no one? Was Dracula able to absorb the light and, as a result, had no reflection? There are several aspects to understanding this moment in the movie, yet there is the obvious answer. In Bram Stoker's novel, published in 1897, the first time this happens is while John Harker is looking in a mirror while shaving, and simultaneously has a conversation with the Count. He notices that Dracula doesn't appear in the mirror. Thus, who is he having a conversation with? Of course, there are several literary meanings, yet the bottom-line is, what we call evil, sinister, or satanic is an apparition that has no real reflection in the realm of Light. In summary, the sinister Dracula to whom we speak is only another aspect of ourselves; the only person to whom we speak is the one in the mirror, ourself. We project the other persona in the lower reality, so we don't have to be accountable for our own base desires. Dracula, in the movie and the novel, is ultimately our egoistic, base desires which we personify in an attempt to justify ourselves. Dracula is nothing more than an apparition of our egoistic self. Yet it's far easier to create an evil vampire than face ourselves in the mirror.

In like manner, when Jesus spoke to a religious people who believed there was a morally correct "good" which was contrasted with an illegal "evil" (twice in the Gospel of Matthew and once in the Gospel of Luke) He utilized words that may not be as apparent in our average translation:

"Even so, every good [quality] tree bears good [beautiful] fruit, but a bad [rotting] tree bears bad [heavy labor] fruit. A good [quality] tree cannot bear bad [heavy labor] fruit, nor can a bad [rotting]

> tree bear good [beautiful] fruit. … Make a tree good
> [beautiful] and its fruit will be good [beautiful], or
> make a tree bad [rotten] and its fruit will be bad
> [rotten], for a tree is recognized by its fruit."
>
> (Matthew 7:17-18; 12:33/NIV,
> brackets added for Greek nuances)

While this may seem to be a simple *either/or* description, the
Greek text uses several different words to describe to the
legalistic mind the incompatibility of what it considers as
good and bad, or right and wrong. The eventual challenge
Jesus offers is that in the "Tree of Life" there isn't merely good
separated or contrasted from what is deemed evil, but
something quite different. The mental gymnastics that Jesus
was pressing on the religious mind had to do with an
awareness of true spirituality as *beautiful,* in contrast to
toiling, or working hard, which for the sake of the hearer's
understanding, He called *rotten.* The notion of using the Greek
word **καλοὺς** (kalous), *beautiful,* is a totally subjective
concept. The same is true in the Aramaic/Hebrew, which Jesus
most likely spoke at the time of the parable. The language uses
two words. First is תוב (tov), which generally means *good,*
but more so is rooted in the idea of being *functional.* Thus, the
tree that is *functional* produces the second word, שפיר
(shappeer), which means *radiant-beautiful* fruit. He uses the
idea of radiant-beautiful fruit as a contrast to רקב (racav)
rotten, which describes one who toils with being or doing
good. The context of the fruit tree parable is about the
doctrine of false prophets. In other words, it is false if you are

being told to obey the Law, make sure you are a moral person, and so on, which all add up to being "proper functioning good fruit." These are concrete ideas, something a religious literalist can easily embrace because they fuel the ego's knowledge of good and evil. But to call fruit radiant-beautiful and contrast it to toiling is a mind bender. To add to the idea that the fruit is beautiful, we must remember that at the time of the parable, the Platonic saying, *"Beauty lies in the eyes of the beholder,"* was already close to four hundred years old. Beauty is abstract, so who is to say what is beautiful? The religious mind would say, those who do good works based on the Law, in other words, the knowledge of good and evil. Yet Jesus says, those who toil, laboring to do good works, have eaten rotten fruit. What Jesus is trying to tell us is that, regardless of your works to obey the rules or your failure in trying to keep them, *you are still beautiful as far as the Father is concerned.*

This is what religion, moralism, and legalism has difficulty with. Unlike the Tree of the Knowledge of Good and Evil, in *Life* there is nothing else. Thus, in the Tree of Life there isn't a "good and evil," neither merged nor separated. Therefore, Rahab the harlot, clearly a sinner, and the Zoroastrian priests of the Mithra religion, to whom the Gospel writers refer to as "Magi" and are outside of Israel's covenant, are all part of the unveiling of Christ. In the upper world where the Father resides, *the world of Life,* there isn't an illusion of right and wrong, or good versus bad. Rather, in the world of Life, it perceives the inclusive oneness of all Creation. So a prostitute who is a sinner to the religious mind, or a group of pagan magicians who are outside of Israel's covenant, are just as important "and holy" parts of the Divine process as anyone else in the narrative.

A system with good and evil as a differentiation is a dysfunctional system from the start. The essential point is that it's impossible to view them as an either/or; sadly, each one *requires* the other. In other words, the one must exist to have the other, which is ultimately dysfunctional, especially when it's applied to our identity. As simple as this may sound, the following does make the point. To know our Divine identity is to function according to design, which is a manifestation of Life, Light, and Love. To embrace the knowledge of good and evil is to be something other than who you are. To be something other than your Divine identity is to deny your true self, though many times we do this unintentionally. This is why, when the Serpent said, *"If you eat of this Tree, you will be like God,"* the concerning internal question arose, "If I don't know this good and evil intimately, then I must not be fully like my Creator? And if I'm not like the Creator, then who am I?" Conclusion, "I'll become intimate with this awareness of good and evil, with the hope of becoming like God."

In the status of the Garden of Eden, *the world Above,* we are being who we are: *the Desire to Receive and Reflect.* To perceive anything other than that—like the belief that we're not enough like God so we need the intimacy of good and evil to be complete—is a dysfunctional view of ourselves and, subsequently, our reality. It creates *the world Below.* The whole proposition of function and dysfunction, good and evil, right and wrong, is a false premise. Nevertheless, as we will discover later, this unavoidable false premise will press us to awaken from the nightmare of our egoistic illusion to our true nature, Compassion.

[handwritten: LOVE? Yes — Compassion is from LOVE]

Here's an example: If we have one "good" egg and one "rotten" egg, and we scramble them together, what happens? The entire mixture tastes rotten. It doesn't matter how many good eggs we have in comparison to rotten ones. We can have a ratio of ten good eggs to one rotten egg. We can even multiply that ratio exponentially, and the result will still be the same; the entire batch will have the flavor of rottenness. This is why we can't separate good from evil any more than we can separate good eggs from rotten ones once they've been scrambled. Taking this thought further, the Tree was already a scrambled omelet of good and evil before we ever consumed it. What this ultimately means is that we entered a system which was a prefabricated scramble of good and evil. Trying to separate the good from the evil is like trying to separate the rotten eggs from the good ones after you put the scrambled omelet in your mouth. It just can't be done. Can you imagine trying to differentiate a good egg molecule from a rotten one? Again, it can't be done. Yet, in our religiousness, we actually think we can. Worse yet, we think we have! Can you imagine being a chef and thinking that your version of scrambled good and evil eggs, is unlike all other religions, actually tasting "good" and fully digestible? Sadly, most of us in Christendom think this is what we have attained. Yet, as the famous Master Chef, Gordon Ramsey, would say, "I can't serve this! The whole thing tastes terrible! What are you (colorful metaphor)

[handwritten margin notes: "The purpose of the Garden" / "to judge...is to judge...to disown; to judge great People" / "Ask to disown; their eyes could see" / "so the veil was lifted"]

thinking? Do you expect my guests to filter each crumb of scrambled eggs? Get out of my kitchen," as he throws the plate against the wall. Fortunately, God is far more gracious. But even then, if we put our scrambled eggs of good and evil in a jar and put Jesus's picture on it, it's still a rotten mess. Jesus gave us insight into this when He told the parable of the tares and wheat being mixed in a field:

> *"So the servants said to him, 'Then do you want us to go and gather them?' But he said, 'No, lest in gathering the weeds you root up the wheat along with them. Let both grow together until the harvest..."*   *(Matthew 13:28-30/ESV)*

It's important to understand that this parable isn't speaking about people being tares or wheat; it's speaking about Kingdom values and having them corrupted with incompatible concepts. The point is that you can't address one without addressing the other. To attempt to root out what one thinks is evil will also damage what we perceive as good, and vice versa. One of the key reasons for this is that, in partaking of the Tree of the Knowledge of good and evil, we were merged into the mixture as well. So how do we remove ourselves from the scramble? WE CAN'T! Therefore "God was in Christ" not only reconciling "us" to Himself, but the entire *world Below* (2 Corinthians 5:19). If one can imagine, God's path to unscramble us doesn't just involve us, but the entire system of good and evil as well. Why? Because if you're going to dissect the omelet to liberate one aspect, then it all needs to be dissected. In the end, God's way of unscrambling is to dismantle the entire system and liberate us into a completely different one. The result is a completely different way of seeing reality. This Divine reality is called "Life." In other words, we must die to the way of Death and awaken to the way of Life.

> *"He has rescued us from the domain of darkness and transferred us into the Kingdom of his dear Son."*
> *(Colossians 1:13/CJB)*

We are back to the liberty of choice. Do we really want to get out of the scramble of good and evil, or not? Though we claim we received Christ and have "eternal life," are we still living from a good and evil perspective? Why the question? Because to truly walk the path, both in and as a revelation of Christ, we must no longer be part of the scramble. This means we must surrender the knowledge of good and evil as we know it and no longer season our world view with the potent spice of serpentine ego.

The Apostle Paul said:

> *"Your boasting is not good. Do you not know that a little leaven leavens the whole lump?"*
> *(1 Corinthians 5:6/ESV)*

In other words, *"Your pride or ego is not good. Don't you know a little egoism spreads through the whole?"* We must realize that we've compounded our scrambled omelet of good and evil by mixing in our egoistic seasoning. Not only was the good

253

and evil scrambled together, that same Tree was rooted in Ego, which seasoned the entire mixture. In other words, even if you remotely think you can discern between the scrambled molecules of good and evil, they've also been seasoned through and through with our egoism. The moment we received nourishment from the omelet of good and evil seasoned with the serpentine ego, it became our world view. The entire Creation as we knew it became corrupt. In our view, it became seriously distorted. However, being that we have left the realm of Eden and embraced the egoistic Tree of knowing good and evil, how can we know our view is distorted? Consider the Ego, which always believes its view is correct. How does it come to realize otherwise? This brings us back to our Prologue, "The Kingdom We Can't Remember." Thus, our memory of Eden is a distant present, yet it escapes our egoistic view like a vapor. At the same time that we were scrambled into the Tree of the Knowledge of Good and Evil, God was concealed, or veiled from our view. As a result, so was our true identity. Weighed down by the egoistic union of good and evil, the result is that we see only a sliver of reality. Existing from the view of *the world Below,* we think we understand Heaven Above, only to reflect another image of *the world Below* and calling it the Heavens. To us, there's the spiritual battle of good versus evil in the Heavens with demonic beings flying around, fighting the good godly ones. More importantly, we must *take our so-called authority* and command the one to assault the other, because if we don't, the evil will overcome the good. Thus, the multiplicity of our religious mythologies was born.

Part 3: Realizing the Son of Man

The purpose of Christ being compared to the bronze serpent, elevated to *the world Above,* is a revelation of our true self. Ultimately, this occurs by letting go of our selfish desire and any understanding we think we know about good and evil, which will begin the uncovering of our identity. To further explain this process, let's consider again that when we partook of the Serpent and its Tree, not only did the Adam fall, but the Serpent changed form as well. Until this point, we've addressed that the dust of the ground represented the lowest aspect of the *Desire to Receive for Oneself,* the Ego, the Satanic source. Even so, in the moment of the Fall something transmuted even further. In the book of Ezekiel, the writer uses Egypt and the Tree of the Knowledge of Good and Evil as interchangeable metaphors for each other. Note how the Tree in the Garden of Eden becomes self-centered and falls. Then God says the following:

> *"To the end that none of all the trees by the mayim [water] exalt themselves for their height, neither shoot up their top above the thick boughs, and that no trees that drink mayim may reach up to them in height; for they are all delivered unto mavet [death], to the depths of ha'aretz [the earth], in the midst of the bnei adam [sons of Adam], with them that go down to the bor (pit)."*
>
> *(Ezekiel 31:14/Orthodox Jewish Bible, bracketed words added for clarity)*

The Serpent, the Adam, the Tree, are all brought down to *the earth* and go even farther than its surface, as if it were possible, into a pit *below the ground.* In other words, together we created something even lower than the earth (the Desire to Receive). We created this world, which Jesus calls *Below.* Therefore, when speaking to Nicodemus, Jesus is seemingly appalled that such a leader didn't know these truths. You could almost hear Jesus saying, "Come on! It's right there in the Torah I gave you!"

When Jesus said that He was to be lifted up like the bronze serpent, He was speaking of transmuting the state of Mankind back to its origins. In other words, Jesus was equating Himself to that same higher spiritual place, from the world Above, which is the status of reflecting the Father. In that state, He draws all of Mankind to His Likeness. He was not saying that He was to be raised up as a substitute for sin, or that the imagery of the bronze snake was a symbol of Satan or our sinfulness. This would be reading into the text something that's not there. However, since the recent advent of the penal substitution doctrine, we interpret those verses through that lens, skewing the context. While there may seem to be a double entendre of crucifixion, that's not what the writer intended. Nonetheless, Christ came to be an example of us.

> *"And as Moses lifted up the serpent in the wilderness, even so must the Son of Man be lifted up..."*　　　　　　(John 3:14/NKJV)

The phrase *lifted up* is **ὑψωθῆναι** (huposothenai). In virtually every other verse in the New Testament, **ὑψωθῆναι** (huposothenai) is translated as *exalted.* For example: *"Therefore being exalted to the right hand of God..."* (Acts 2:33/NKJV). It has nothing to do with being impaled on the Cross, though there is much to be gleaned from the crucifixion. It's about Christ's example of *us* being exalted to the place from whence we fell. Because the Christ view sees us as one in Him, when we lift Him, we also lift ourselves. When we recognize Christ as exalted above the egoistic fray of the lower world, we are compelled to look into the mirror of His face, and ours as well. To see Jesus from *the world Above* but still see ourselves from *the world Below* means the reality of who Christ is in us hasn't been truly lifted to its intended status. Jesus didn't come to reveal His preeminence above us. Rather, He came to elevate our consciousness back to our origin in the world Above with Him. Please note, He didn't say "...if the Son of God be exalted..." but the ***"Son of Man."*** The intentionality of that statement changes the entire concept. If it were just "Son of God" we would say, "I need to lift Him up because He is God, and God's Son, who is worthy of my worship." Yet, that's not what He said. He said, *"...the Son of Man be exalted..."* What does that mean regarding *the Son of Man?* What does that mean of *Mankind* from whom He's the Son? Wait...What? Is He the Son of God, or the Son of Man? Or are the Son of God and the Son of Man one in the same? Exactly! Within the question is the answer.

You could say, we are comfortable with our descent, the Fall, and life in *the world Below.* The moment a revelation or a

257

prophetic insight occurs, we may experience its bliss for that moment and then return to *the world Below.* Yet not only do we redescend, but our new revelation, or prophetic insight, gets seasoned with the egoism and scrambled into the good and evil mix. This was very much so in the dilemma with the bronze serpent. While Moses was revealing our true nature in the upper world, something happened with it down the road. As with any perceived revelation, depending upon the relationship of our consciousness of the upper world and the denseness of our ego, it can be fleeting. We may want to believe that when a revelation is unveiled, what we attain remains, but that's not so. Commonly, because of the subtlety of our ego, that same revelation can descend into the world of ritual and dogma. Many religions have been born out of a descended revelation. Therefore, the writer of the Book of Revelation warns us of our potential in becoming an anti-Christ in thought, and a harlot church in practice. As Christians, we are not exempt from turning the truth of Christ into being religiously right rather than emanating Life. Nevertheless, there must be another ingredient emanating from us to sustain the unveiled revelation. It has little to do with prayer, Bible study, spending time in worship, or having throne room experiences, though those can help in a minimal fashion. Rather, it has to do with the contrasts of our inner positioning and our inner awareness of them. It's the difference between a serpent on the ground or the שָׂרָף (saraph) above. Before we unpack our migration to the worlds Above in the Tree of Life, we need to consider why Jesus was pressing this point to Nicodemus. In the case of the children of Israel and the bronze serpent, we find something very concerning by the time we reach the era of King Hezekiah:

"He removed the high places and broke the sacred pillars, cut down the wooden image and broke in pieces the bronze serpent that Moses had made; for until those days the children of Israel burned incense to it, and called it Nehushtan."

(2 Kings 18:4/NKJV)

Hold on... What? *"He...broke in pieces the bronze serpent that Moses had made..."* Why? Because the children of Israel took what was intended to be a revelation of healing and their true identity from the worlds Above, and turned it into an egoistic religious idol. Yes, this happens more times than we realize, and it materializes because we're not always cognizant of where we live. As we've said before, our beliefs, our use of the gifts of the Spirit, and our sense of "rightness" with God can blind us from our truth in Christ (Matthew 7:22-23; Luke 13:27-30). We've now come to the point where the children of Israel were burning incense to the bronze serpent. You could say, what Moses lifted up, they brought back down. This is why many Christian movements, even supernatural ones, become something other than Christlike. Most of the time, the worst of these descents is when Christianity and Caesar comingle. The real challenge is that we never think we are involved in such developments. To that point, they even gave the bronze serpent a name, נחשתן (nechushtan), which can be translated *the serpent gives,* or *the giving serpent,* totally degrading Moses's point, and God's intention.

259

Jesus is using this reference to liken His purpose and who we are. Then comes the famous declaration we are all familiar with:

> *"For God so loved the world that he gave his only*
> *Son, so that everyone who believes in him may not*
> *perish but may have eternal life. Indeed, God did not*
> *send the Son into the world to condemn the world,*
> *but in order that the world might be saved through*
> *him.*   *(John 3:16-17/NRSV)*

Before we proceed, let's look at one other statement by Moses:

> *"Then you shall say to Pharaoh, 'Thus says the Lord:*
> *'Israel is My son, My firstborn. So I say to you, let My*
> *son go that he may serve Me...'"*
>   *(Exodus 4:22-23/NKJV)*

Although **ישראל** (yisrael) literally means **ישר** (yishar), *straight*, and **אל** (el), *God,* meaning *straight to God,* despite some lexicons that translate the word as *prevailing prince* or *he who struggles with God,* the actual idea is one whose aim is Godlikeness and unveiling that despite any obstacle. The word is not so much about prevailing or struggling, but a focused objective. It's no different when God said, *"Light Be!"* in the darkness. He didn't say, *"I come against you, foul darkness, with the power of light."* The first expresses spiritual reality, "Light be." The second, "I come against you foul darkness...," is a misfocus. The first is a view from living in *the world Above,* and the second from *the world Below.* For that matter, the notion of coming against the darkness actually empowers it. From the view below, you could also say that the demonic forces are as strong as they are because we keep fighting them. Fighting darkness from that space and labeling it light doesn't mean anything has been illuminated, any more than our jar of rotten scrambled eggs with a Jesus picture on it makes it Life-giving. (We address this further in Chapter 14.) The point is, he whose intention is to go straight to Godlikeness, is that Son; and there is only *One Son.* When God told Moses to speak and say, *"My Son,"* He was speaking of the entire nation of Israel as His Son. He could have said, "My people," or "My sons and daughters," but in this case He spoke from the upper world view. *His Son was the entire collective.* Because of the way we've read John 3:16, we think in a very linear way with the backdrop of Vicarious Atonement, assuming the Apostle John is only speaking of Jesus. Yet, right up to this point, he wrote referring to the *Son of Man.* His intention is **הָאָדָם** (ha'adam), the Adam, or in Greek, **ἄνθρωπος** (anthropos), *the collective of all humanity as one being.* When Jesus spoke to Nicodemus, He didn't say, "For God so loved the sinner that He gave Me, His only separate special Son, different from all of you..." Rather, Jesus says clearly, *"...but from Heaven He came down, the Son [which is] of* **ἄνθρωπος** *(anthropos) Mankind,"* (v13) and *"...even so He must be exalted, the Son [which is] of* **ἄνθρωπος** *(anthropos) Mankind,"* (v14). Christ identifies as *the Son of us,* **ἄνθρωπος** (anthropos), the collective of Mankind. To keep it in context, the famous phrase, *"For God so loved the world..."* must be consistent in the flow. God is not just loving us as

261

individuals, but the entire system in which His reconciliation is implemented, hence, the scrambled eggs of good and evil, the Serpent and Mankind. Let's reconsider the verses of John 3:16-17 (in mechanical fashion):

Οὕτως γὰρ ἠγάπησεν ὁ Θεὸς τὸν κόσμον, ὥστε τὸν Υἱὸν τὸν μονογενῆ ἔδωκεν, ἵνα πᾶς ὁ πιστεύων εἰς αὐτὸν μὴ ἀπόληται ἀλλ' ἔχῃ ζωὴν αἰώνιον. οὐ γὰρ ἀπέστειλεν ὁ θεὸς τὸν υἱὸν εἰς τὸν κόσμον ἵνα κρίνῃ τὸν κόσμον, ἀλλ' ἵνα σωθῇ ὁ κόσμος δι' αὐτοῦ.

Hoútoos gár eegápeesen ho Theós tón kósmon hoóste tón
Huión tón monogeneé édooken hína pás ho pisteúoon eis
autón meé apóleetai all échee zooeén aioónion.
Ou gár
apésteilen ho Theós tón Huión eis tón kósmon hína krínee
tón kósmon all hína sootheé ho kósmos di autoú.

In this way then, [selflessly] loved God the cosmos [entire system], therefore the unique Son He gifted in order that all trust in Him should not lose

[themselves], but have absolute life perpetually.
Not sent forth God, the Son, into the cosmos to
judge [separate by opinion] the cosmos, on the
contrary in order to save [safely return, restore]
the cosmos [entire system] through Him.

There is only *one Son,* and that Son is Mankind. Yet, through the uniqueness of Christ appearing in human form—born of Mankind, hence the Son of Man—the entire cosmos (world system) is being restored. This restoration isn't just about what we think of as separate people who have chosen to believe the right religion, and to Hell with the rest. Remember, *"God was in Christ reconciling the entire cosmos (world system) to Himself."* **God was reconciling to Himself the entire scrambled omelet, with its good eggs, evil eggs, egoistic seasoning, and us!** When the Adam received of the Tree of the Knowledge of Good and Evil, everything that was *the Adam,* the Serpent, and the Tree, scrambled together and fell to the lower worlds. Better said, it created this physical world as we know it. In keeping with the evangelical tradition, one would say that everything under Adam's authority fell as well. All fell from the status of *the world Above,* similar to the way the שׂרף (saraph) descended and became a snake slithering on the ground, *which is a description of the densest state of Ego.* More accurately stated, when the Adam united with the Serpent and the Tree of the Knowledge of Good and Evil, together they transmuted reality into the Cosmos we now know.

So what was Jesus telling Nicodemus by relating Moses's use of the שָׂרָף (saraph) and the Cosmos? Think about His point; God so loved *the entire system*, He gave His unique Son (of Mankind) that whosoever trusts in Him would not lose themselves. Interesting, how does *the Cosmos* become a *whosoever* that trusts? Because it's all scrambled together! This couldn't have been about salvation from an eternal burning Hell and instead going to a happy Heaven in the afterlife, at least not in the way we evangelicals have preached it for a millennia. What if this is about, as Jesus describes, elevating Creation *by choice* from the lower worlds back to its origin? This would mean, by elevating Creation (the entire system, the Cosmos), it's unscrambling all the eggs through a very unique process and unique result.

Speaking with Nicodemus, Jesus explains that as Moses lifted the שָׂרָף (saraph), so is the Son of Man to be lifted up. He didn't say, "Like Moses lifted up the serpent, so am I, *Me, the only guy, Jesus, I'm the only Son, who is the only Son of God,* who gets to be lifted up." Then adding, "And by lifted up, I mean through a hideous execution on a Roman cross." Rather, He referred to Himself as the Son of **ἄνθρωπος** (anthropos), *Mankind,* who is to be lifted up by that same Mankind to His rightful origin. Can we awaken to what was just said? The challenge for our thinking is, why does Jesus keep telling us throughout the Gospels that He is the Son of **ἄνθρωπος** (anthropos), *Mankind, the collective of humanity?*

If we recognize that Jesus is the Son of ἄνθρωπος (anthropos) [the Son of *Man*], in the manner He describes, it guides us to both a revelational unveiling as well as an inner, Life-giving awareness of who We are. Jesus is both from and is ἄνθρωπος (anthropos), *Man,* and that ἄνθρωπος (anthropos), *Man,* is from above (John 3:13). Man's origin is Above, and God never ceased seeing us from that vantage point. From God's view, Mankind is not trying to get to Heaven in lieu of Hell before we all physically die. Rather, Mankind was and will always be of *the worlds Above,* regardless of what we think Heaven is, or we assume ourselves to be or not be. We cannot have the "Son of Man" be from Above and also have that which He emerged from, Mankind, be of a different origin! Being that we've been immersed in the doctrine of "Penal Substitution" or "Vicarious Atonement" for the last 500 years or more, we've had difficulty seeing Jesus's words as they are.

The Son of God and the Son of ἄνθρωπος (anthropos), *Man,* are one in the same. What does this mean? You could say, if God is Jesus's Father, then Humanity is His Mother, which is the expanded aspect of ζωή (Zoe), Eve, and the virgin Mary. In the same way that Jesus represents ALL of God, He also represents ALL of Mankind. In other words, all of God and all of Humanity, the two, *are one in the same.*

> *"I in them, and You in Me; that they may be made perfect in one..."* (John 17:23/NKJV)

Notice He didn't say, *"...that they may be made, at some future time, as one...,"* rather, *"...that they may be made 'perfect' in* one..." This statement is not about *they,* or *we,* currently being separate due to disobedience and that He is praying that God draws us back to a union which doesn't exist at the moment. No, if we read the context, *we are one* with Him and are an expression of Him, though unaware, or at best, minimally aware of that reality. In other words, if the Father and the Son (of Mankind) are ONE, then so are ALL of Mankind one with God, whether aware of it or not. Being made *perfect in one* means to be *complete in oneness.* In other words, coming to complete awareness of that oneness. Our completeness is in knowing we and Christ are One, and He-We are One with the Father. With that realization, we also see the rest of Humanity—which is us, them, Him, and the Father—all as one, all at the same time.

Jesus was telling us that the Son of ἄνθρωπος (anthropos), *Mankind,* must be seen in His original state from Above, otherwise we'll stay in a mindset of losing our true self (which can mean lost, or perish). The key is, if we see the Son of Mankind as the One from Above, the implications are radically transforming. If the Son is the offspring of Mankind and He is from Above, then we can't help but recognize that Mankind is from Above as well, thus also the Son of God. This is no longer just seeing "Jesus" as the guy from Above, but seeing Jesus, the SON OF ALL OF US (MANKIND) as from Above! This is the mind-bending truth. When Jesus said He was from Above, He was saying, "I AM from Above, and I AM from YOU! I AM the Son of Mankind. WE are from Above." As you can see, this is further reaching than just "receiving Jesus" on a particular date and saying, "I got saved from that point forward." While that's a good start in one respect, receiving Jesus means, regardless of the date, that we've recognized He is God's ultimate expression of Us, Mankind. Jesus in this Cosmos (Entire System) is the incarnate representation of all of us (Romans 8:29; Colossians 1:15). You could say that elevated Mankind is the clothing of God, the mended Vessel Reflecting and Shining the Light. It's another way of saying Mankind is *"God Incarnate"* or an unveiling of *the Incarnation.*

CHAPTER 9
I AM THE AWAKENING

*"My dull gaze is fixed on the sacred vessel; the holy
blood flows:
the bliss of redemption, divinely mild, trembles
within every soul around:
only here, in my heart, will the pangs not be stilled.
The Savior's lament I hear there,
the lament, ah! the lamentation from His profaned
sanctuary:
'Redeem Me, rescue Me from hands defiled by sin!'
Thus rang the divine lament in terrible clarity in
my soul."*

Parsifal

Parsifal, Act II

Richard Wagner

Part 1: The Stirring

When we say, "I received Jesus," or "I accepted Christ as my personal Savior," then add, "Now I know the Truth," what does all that really mean? In the 1800s, Dwight L. Moody promoted those phrases with an understanding of what they meant in his context. Sadly, they've quickly became a Western, and most definitely a North American, cliché of Christendom. According to the Apostle John, being fully awake is living in the same Light that Christ emanates (1 John 1:7). What's interesting is that our religiosity tells us we must first study and "believe in God" to experience Him, which is contrary to the narrative of both Old and New Testaments. The father of our faith, Abraham, clearly embraced belief *after* there was a measure of awakening within him. God reached out to him and spoke, *then Abraham believed.* Yet, when belief is put before some form of awakening, in most cases it will only strengthen our slumber. The reason belief is so important to religion and politics is that believing something does not require any spiritual awareness or consciousness. Rather, many of our beliefs are nothing more than an egoistic construct. The result can be "the god" that we create, rather than "the Divine reality that exists." This is why the New Testament's definition of "faith" is not what we've interpreted it to mean. To the average person *faith* simply means to believe something. Therefore, the Apostles employ the Greek word **πίστις** (pistis) for what we translate *faith.* **πίστις** (pistis) is NOT believing in what we don't see, it's actually opening our inner eyes and seeing what is truly there! Waking up, or becoming conscious, is not believing Bible verses, although that's potentially a good start. Faith comes in different levels and ways of seeing. As a rabbi taught in a class I took, there is faith below reason, faith within reason, and faith above reason. If faith is supposed to be a form of

270

awakening the inner eyes, then consider how we use the idea in modernity in contrast to the New Testament writers.

Faith below reason is simply believing whatever is deemed true. Someone says, "This is what the Bible says," then a scripture is recited, and we simply believe it because we are told that's faith. We're also told that to not believe what the Bible says is to not trust God. However, as we have referenced many times, Jesus warned us about such approaches to scripture:

> "And Jesus answering said to them, 'Ye go astray, not knowing **εἰδότες** (eidotes) [properly, *to see*] the Writings, nor the power of God."
>
> *(Matthew 22:29/YLT)*

> "You search the Scriptures, for in them you think you have eternal life..."   *(John 5:39/NKJV)*

In Matthew and John, Jesus wasn't speaking to unlearned disciples, but leaders in the faith. In both those verses there are strong signposts to what we're addressing. "You go astray, not *seeing* the scripture..." The word **εἰδότες** (eidotes) doesn't mean *know,* like **γινώσκω** (ginosko), which means *to know from learning or an experience.* The **γινώσκω** (ginosko) type of *knowing* has its limitations based on how one applies their experience. **εἰδότες** (eidotes) means *to see,* with the implication of presence. This is a broader type of *knowing,* similar in thought to the word for *truth* **ἀλήθεια**

271

(alethia) which means *not concealed.* You could say the first type of knowing is comprehending what the words are saying, the second is *seeing* beyond the words and *perceiving* the *unveiled consciousness* of the writer. In other words, Jesus is telling the Sadducees, "You are in error because you haven't really seen anything." This is similar to what He said to Nicodemus. This is further amplified in the Gospel of John, when Jesus tells the Jewish leaders that they haven't seen anything, even though they've been searching through the scriptures. Why? Because to actually *see* the scripture, there has to be an inner characteristic within the observer that's of the same quality. It's no different than listening to a radio or watching a television program. It requires that the receiver be dialed into the same frequency as the transmitter. Legalism, right and wrong, moralism, substitutionary sacrifice, and, most importantly, egoism, are not the frequency of the writers of the Scripture, especially if we believe they were inspired by the Holy Spirit. Therefore, those who were given and held the "oracles of God" (Romans 3:1-2) were unsuccessful in their searching the Scriptures. The point is, we are no different than the religious leaders of Jesus's day. This is not meant to sound harsh, but honest in respect to not being of the same conscious quality from which the Scriptures originate. We may search and "believe" that we've found a truth, take a clear definitive stance regarding it, and, like the Pharisees, not actually see anything. This is why Jesus called them "blind guides" (Matthew 23:24).

The one thing about being a blind guide is that our egos have convinced us that we see. Believing a Bible verse has its merits, yet it doesn't mean we've awakened. In contrast to what St. Augustine of Hippo taught, Jesus directed us to something quite different. Augustine suggested that "believing in what we do not see will result with us seeing." He is correct! Yet, this is how atrocities have been committed by both religious and political leaders from before the time of Noah to the present. How many times have we believed in something, then saw evidence when there was no evidence at all? In other words, if believing creates what we see and what we see is what we *want* to believe, this is truly *faith below reason.* Awakening is not something that's merely believed and studied, it's a process that occurs over time as our consciousness awakens to our inner qualities in their original state, which is the same frequency as the Creator (more on this later).

Faith within reason is rationalizing what we believe, or better said, giving our beliefs a rational context based on our sense of security. It's like faith below reason, but on a different level. It isn't professing, "I believe therefore I see," nor, "believing helps us see," as Augustine suggested. Rather, it's a calculation filtered through our egoistic values. We make choices regarding what to believe in the shadow of our self-portrait of right and wrong, hence *faith within reason.* From a positive perspective, we may be tossing and turning in our spiritual slumber and occasionally opening our eyes because Divine reality is shining over the horizon. The good news is that we can no longer "just believe" what we want, now it must make sense, it has to add up. It can't just be blind belief, it must come from some form of *knowing.* Yet at this point, the only form of

273

knowing we're familiar with is the knowing of good and evil. So unfortunately, despite the positives in the process, like the morning dawn filtering through our windows, the ego doesn't allow us to yet awaken from sleep. Regardless how brightly the Light shines, we pull our spiritual covers over our head (like a veil) and turn in the opposite direction, trying to continue to sleep. To awaken to something other than our illusion can be disorienting and very unsettling, even traumatic. Rather than opening our eyes to see a quite different reality, we rationalize what's happening. This can be the most blaringly self-centered, self-regarding phase. It's the Ego's ultimate surge for supremacy with a sense that its end might be in sight. We get a glimpse of the Light, then try to sift it through the context of our illusion. Hence, moralism becomes the tool used to veil Divine reality, and self-regard takes form in religious terms of righteousness and sin. It's like we had a taste of something Divine and then force-filtered it through the context of the Knowledge of Good and Evil. No matter how it's evaluated, when any aspect of Divinity is filtered through the Knowledge of Good and Evil, it will always result in Death. This potentially fuels our arrogance which forms self-preservation, self-justification, and self-exultation tethered to our religion and politics. Yet, if one has had a taste of any small aspect of Divinity, there's also the potential to recognize that our egoism is the opposite quality of what we just tasted, and awakening to true consciousness can start to emerge.

Look at what the New Testament says about being awake:

"Then he said to them, 'I am deeply grieved, even to death; remain here, and stay awake with me.'"
(Matthew 26:38/NRSV)

"...So he said to Peter, 'Can't any of you stay awake with me for just one hour?'" (Matthew 26:40/CEV)

"Servants are fortunate if their master finds them awake and ready when he comes! I promise you that he will get ready and have his servants sit down so he can serve them." (Luke 12:37/CEV)

"These things He said, and after that He said to them, 'Our friend Lazarus sleeps, but I go that I may wake him up.'" (John 11:11/NKJV)

"An angel of the Lord stood over him, and a light shone in all the building; and he pricked his side, and awaked him, and said to him: Arise, instantly. And the chains fell from his hands." (Acts 12:7/Syriac NT)

"For this reason it says, 'Awake, sleeper, and arise from the dead, and Christ will shine on you.'"
(Ephesians 5:14/NASU)

When we read the New Testament from the פשט (peshat), the surface level, we see disciples falling asleep when Christ asked them to stay awake. Was their slumber to make a point about our spiritual state of affairs? Or were the boys just tired? In that situation, Jesus is clear, "The spirit indeed is willing, but the flesh is weak." We also see a figure of speech where Lazarus was dead for four days and Jesus calls him "one who sleeps." Surely Jesus must have been using a metaphor, or was Jesus really seeing from *the world Above?* To Him, was Lazarus just sleeping and was the finality of death as we see it nothing more than a minor concern? Either way, a dead/sleeping man comes forth from what we call the grave. Is there a deeper message that transcends a man hobbling about in grave clothes after being in a "Death Sleep" for four days? Of course! If not, we'd just be awestruck that Jesus, the Son of God, can raise people from the dead. Then there's the Apostle Luke in Acts, telling us of an interesting "chain" of events. When the light had shone *in the prison* where Peter was *sleeping,* the messenger of light struck him and *he awoke.* The moment he became conscious, his *"chains fell off."* Whether or not the event literally took place in a physical prison in Jerusalem, there is a truth represented that transcends the physical. The notion that Peter was chained in a prison in Jerusalem is also no minor metaphor being that the Apostle Paul states that the *"Jerusalem which now is,"* is a place of religious bondage (Galatians 4:25). Then in Ephesians we hear the Apostle Paul refer to those who are sleep in a metaphor similar to Jesus's.

The idea of awakening, or becoming conscious, is an expression for our inner unveiling and recognition of our true spiritual state. In other words, it's describing our transmigration from *the world Below* to *the world Above,* from spiritual death to spiritual life, from egoism to compassion,

276

from self-awareness to universal-awareness of our interwoven life in the Creator and Creation. This is not something we can simply study, read about, or gather information. Why? Because if we are existing in *faith below reason*, it will usually get in the way when presented with a possible awakening. *Faith below reason* requires a highly functional, self-centered view of the cosmos. In similar manner, if we are existing within *faith within reason*, it too will get in the way when presented with a possible awakening. *Faith within reason* requires a highly functional self-regard for the cosmos's definition of right and wrong.

Faith above reason doesn't negate the rational egoistic knowing of good and evil, it transcends it. It also doesn't believe simply because we need to quell our underlying fears with a spurious truth. It **εἰδότες** (eidotes) *sees* beyond with another set of eyes, our true eyes, rooted in humility. The greater the humility, the clearer the vision. You could say that *humility* is a type of progressive spiritual cataract surgery (Revelation 3:18). In *faith above reason*, we're aware of the egoic reality, though we no longer live from that cosmos. In finding ourselves aware, we are conscious of being engrafted into something far more transcendent. The notion of faith as we've known it (believing, trusting, and having confidence in something, or even someone), is no longer born from an effort to believe despite what we see, feel, or understand. It's born of a new *knowing*, not of good and evil, but of Divine Life. It takes shape from the inner awareness of the nature of God emanating in us. It's a trust that's born from *knowing* Divine Love. It's no longer purposely believing that God loves us, especially when things are not going the way we think they should. Many times, it's those challenges, whether we are in a state of *faith below* or *within reason,* where the question arises, "If God loves me, why am I going through this? I've been doing all the right things, so why is this happening? I've been believing what the Word says, I bet the devil is attacking me!" Rather, *faith above reason* is a *knowing* that we exist because Divine Love exists. Thus, regardless of what we face, God's Love, Life, and Light within and around us are never a question. Rather, that deep knowing is the definitive source, the starting point from which we take the next step on the journey.

Here's a simple example: *Faith below* and *within reason* is as if we were told there's a chair in the next room (the next room is like the spiritual world). Though we haven't literally seen what's in the next room, we're told that faith is believing a chair exists there. All we need to do is pray and believe for the chair to be brought to us in the room we're standing in (the physical world). If we believe and properly use our faith, the chair will materialize in the room we're currently in so we can sit. (After all, the true believer doesn't sit on floors, He's a child of the King!) So, we believe. We spend time reading stories about the holy chair, how it held up the patriarchs when they sat down, and how the Apostles used chairs as they were moved by the Holy Spirit. We go to celebrations where there are songs about the chair. We hear sermons about how strong the chair is and how it's ours if we believe. We spend time reading the manufacturer's specifications (promises) about the chair and make the quality decision to trust "the word" of the manufacturer. So far so good, right? Augustine said that, what I believe helps me see, so believing is receiving, or in this case, believing is sitting; that's what we call faith. Of course, there's also the stipulation of missing the mark. Thus, sinning against the moral code can hinder our faith and prevent the chair from materializing as quickly, or being as strong, as we need it to. Nonetheless, we study the manufacturer's word about the chair. We attempt to live according to the rules and make sure we are right with the manufacturer. As long as we believe and do good, we can rationalize that we are worthy of the chair. Sometimes, we see friends get weary and not get the chair when they need it. We reason, there must have been some sin in their life, or they didn't have enough faith, which prevented the chair from emerging out of the other room. On the other hand, we sometimes see friends sitting on the floor but saying they found the holy chair. When another friend points out they're just sitting on the floor, they rise, irritated, and say, "Well, I believe I'm sitting in the chair! By believing it, the chair will come!" Yet their friend says, "I know you believe that, but look where you're sitting. It's just the floor. Why don't you stand, believe, and wait for the chair to come?" The irritated friend then says, "Man! You make me so angry! Now I'm going to have to sit here and repent so my anger doesn't hinder my faith! Plus, if I stand, then I'm not in faith to sit." The other friend says, "Well, sorry about that, it just didn't make sense to me. Don't get me wrong, I do believe in the chair." Thus, the clash between *faith below reason,* the friend sitting on the floor, and *faith within reason,* the friend rationalizing the faith of the situation. Both have nuggets of truth, yet both are wrestling in different ways with trying to believe to receive. This situation is compounded when an unbelieving friend enters the discussion. After all, we have such friends because they need to be saved and believe for chairs too. We wouldn't want them to leave this room and go into the next without a chair! The unbelieving friend says, "I heard you guys talking, and honestly, if you look around the room, there is no chair. You're sitting on the floor, and you're standing. Yet neither of you are sitting on a chair." The friend sitting on the floor sharply responds, "That's because you won't read the manufacturer's manual! If you did, you'd believe!" The other standing friend says to the fellow sitting, rather confidently, "Don't listen to our unbelieving friend, he just spews fake news."

Faith above reason emerges from a different place. *Faith below reason* is a start in one sense, though it's based on the belief that if we do the right things, we are worthy of the chair. What we've chosen to believe is rarely wrong, because we're sure that what we believe is right. It's an egoistic paradox. *Faith within reason* is similar. It believes as well, though in addition to study and doing the right things, it struggles with the rationalization of how the chair can happen. We've chosen to rationalize our beliefs. Once we've properly rationalized our faith, we feel secure enough that the chair will manifest. *Faith above reason* is an awakening that moves us away from mere belief or evaluating our beliefs on the basis of being validated by what we understand. When this awakening occurs, there is an entire shift in *faith* and *knowing*. When we awake to Christ within (Colossians 3:3), there's a realization that we no longer need to believe in the manufacturer's promises, or that the chair, when it materializes, will hold us up. Why? Because when we've become conscious, *we realize we've been sitting in the chair all along.* In this awakening, our beliefs, or faith, transform into a further type of *knowing* (Colossians 3:10). From this Life-giving *knowing,* a new trust or faith arises, called *rest.* There's no need to intentionally "trust" or "believe" what is written, rather in *the discovery of humility* we "rest in the superimposed knowledge of His Image within us, which is also Our Image." It's not that the written gospels and epistles don't have value, it's just that our filter of the egoistic knowledge of good and evil has been removed, and our effort of belief has ceased through meekness. Now we rest in the inner knowing of the reality of Divine Life within us. From that Life comes all wisdom, knowledge, and understanding. The notion of the chair is simply a metaphor for our true Divine Identity as revealed in Christ. Thus, in the perspective of *faith below reason* we're using belief to reach for something we don't yet have, though we're promised we will. *Faith within reason* is rationalizing our belief's ability to accept on merit that our Divine Identity is attainable. Both are egoistic calculations. The first is about what we don't have, though if we believe hard enough, we'll get what's promised. The second is similar, we're evaluating our ability to believe through merit to attain what's promised. *Faith above reason* is awakening to the inner reality that our Divine Identity was always present within us. It's not about how hard we believe, nor evaluating our ability to attain. Rather, it's shedding such egoistic calculations through humility and awakening to what was always there.

Part 2: The Snooze Button

When Jesus arrived on the scene, the Pharisees and the people of Israel were looking for an external Kingdom. They had securely aligned themselves with the current pagan government in the name of religious freedom. Keep in mind, they had been in such relationships with pagans for close to 536 years prior to this. They were looking for their Savior/Deliverer to come, hoping he would overthrow Rome, replace their rule with a Davidic King, and wreak vengeance on their enemies. Think of all the scriptures that *seem* to promise that. Think of how many Christians today seem to think the same thing about the return of Christ. Yet Jesus totally changed the focus. He taught that the Kingdom was not external, but internal (Luke 17:20-21). This is echoed by the Apostle Luke in the book of Acts, the Apostle Paul in Romans, Colossians, and Hebrews, and the Apostle John in his gospel and epistles. If we add the book of Revelation (within the original context it was written) that's exactly what it tells us as well, with very poetic, dramatic imagery. The book of Revelation was never about a savior returning to bring judgment and destruction to the lost, though many view it that way. Rather, it's a message to "the Ekklesia" (translated, the Church) regarding its loss of focus in the true Gospel and returning to a religion of works and blood sacrifice, both of which are contrary to the Christ and His revelation of the Father. It's a warning to us of becoming an antichrist in mind and deed (the mark on the forehead and on the hand), proclaiming a false prophetic message with a subversive image, a beast rather than Christ, and becoming a harlot church whoring with the governments of the world. Nonetheless, the book reveals the Living Christ, who brings His reward of liberty, freedom, and wholeness irrespective of our failures (Revelation 22:12/CWS Zodhiates). A key challenge to the book is textual issues in both manuscript and translation, which have been massaged to redefine the Christ into the very beast it warns us of.

To give the reader a brief view of these many textual issues, we can't get past the first chapter without a concern. Note how the traditional Textus Receptus (used as the source for the King James and several other translations) phrases the following verse:

> *"Behold, He is coming with clouds, and every eye will see Him, even they who pierced Him. And all the tribes of the earth **will mourn** because of Him. Even so, Amen."*   *(Revelation 1:7/NKJV)*

It appears that the response of the unbeliever, especially those who pierced Him, will be mourning (literally, beating their breasts) because they'll realize how wrong they were. As a result, His coming is one of sorrow. Some may think, "Of course! They rejected Him as Messiah and now it's judgment day. He has returned, and judgement and retribution are here!" If Jesus, who offered salvation to humanity in whatever flavor of denominational teaching one ascribes, and recognizes the authority of the verse that proclaims, *"Jesus is the same, yesterday, today and forever"* (Hebrews 13:8), how do we come to such a conclusion? How does the Savior change

His name from **יֵשׁוּעַ** (yeshua), *liberator,* to **סָפַד** (saphad), *lamentation?* He doesn't! Notice how the Aramaic words this same verse:

> "Behold he comes with the clouds. All eyes will see him, even those that pierced him. And all the tribes of the land **will dance about** him. Yes and Amen!"
>
> *(ARAMAIC, Werner)*

All the tribes will dance about Him, even those that pierced Him! That's the effect He has on humanity when He returns. Christ doesn't suffer from a bipolar disorder where he's happy to liberate people one moment and punishes them the next. He IS the same *yesterday, today,* and *forever.* The point is, the message of the Kingdom is consistent, filled with revelation, liberation, and celebration for all!

The central aspect of this Kingdom is that it is within us (Luke 17:20-21). For us to see the Kingdom (John 3:3) we must first awaken to its reality within. It's not simply that we believe because the Bible says it's inside us (meaning inside our bodies), it's our actual awakening from within that its limitless expanse IS there. We can call this being "spiritually conscious."

When Paul speaks of rising from the dead in the verse in the previous section (Ephesians 5:14), he was not referring to a physical resurrection, he was impressing upon us to arise from a spiritual sleep. This is what the writer of Revelation calls *the First Resurrection* (Revelation 20:5-6). This first resurrection from spiritual slumber may be even more important than any physical resurrection in that, without it, another incarnation, while necessary, would also be repetitious. Why awake? As Paul says, so the Light of Christ can be realized.

Take a moment to ponder his words while considering the time in which he lived. In the ancient world, oil lamps were used after sunset (if you could afford one), yet they would burn out after a short time. If someone was well-off enough, they could keep replenishing the oil and stay up later. Hence, the old saying, "Burning the midnight oil." This wasn't just about staying up late, which was then uncommon, but also that it was expensive and required sufficient oil storage. It wasn't until 1792 in England, when the first gas lamp started burning, that things changed and cities were lit throughout most of the night. Eventually, gas lamps were replaced with electric ones, and then cities would be illuminated all night. This changed the sleep rhythm of the world. It changed how we worked and how we played. You can't help but think of the lyrics from *New York, New York*, sung by Frank Sinatra, "I want to wake up in a city that doesn't sleep. And find I'm king of the hill, top of the heap." While awakening in the Kingdom of God is becoming conscious of a place that doesn't sleep, it's quite a different awakening than what the Chairman of the Board was singing about. Within our context it's the reverse, where the Ego sings, "I don't want to awaken from my illusion! I like a place where I dream, I'm king of the hill, top of the heap!" Still, long before the gas lamp, most went to sleep shortly after sunset and commonly awoke at the light of dawn. The point is, the light of dawn is what would arouse the sleeper. Paul is again speaking in the Hebraic paradox of block logic. He is saying, "You Ephesians were stirred to Christ at one point. Now awake completely and let what once stirred you fully awaken you. Become completely conscious and live in the Light."

In the verses above regarding Peter in prison, it says that it was not until he awoke into the already existing light that his chains fell off. We seem to think, "If I can just shake off my chains, I'll awaken." But that's not so. Understand that the Light has been shining. It was, is, and will always shine. It required something else to stir us to the Light and cause the chains to fall off. Yet, when we read scripture from a *faith within reason* point of view, we seem to convince ourselves that the chains must first come off before we can emerge into the Light. With that view, we can say that once again the Serpentine Ego constricts around us and keeps us in the Death Sleep.

It says that the Light was shining through the whole building before the awakening happened. It wasn't until the angel focused on **πατάξας** (pataxas), *the beating of the heart* (Thayer's Lexicon), that Peter awoke. In other words, the Light was shining and kept shining until the beating of Peter's heart synchronized with it. What's profound about this segment is the phrase *"...pricked his side..."* **πατάξας δὲ τὴν πλευρὰν** (pataxas de ten pleuran), which in deeper meaning could be translated, *"the beating heart now from his rib."* In Genesis, the Adam in the Garden was put to sleep and from his "rib" came forth the fullness of the Divine expression,

286

the feminine. Their union together is the "Image (masculine) and Likeness (feminine)," the totality of the Divine revelation. Similarly, when Christ was on the Cross, His side was pierced and blood and water flowed, the foundational elements that brought forth His Bride, the Ekklesia. Our union together in Christ is the dwelling place and revelation of God (Ephesians 2:20-22). The same is true here, just another aspect of block logic story telling. In certain aspects, this story with Peter gives us insight into the process to fullness and how we can also get stuck along the way, hence the prayer group at Mary's house.

The fullness came when Peter's heart was ready from inner realization. Its becoming was a cognizance of what was always shining, the Light. It was an awakening through the inner synchronization of the Divine Nature. To say it another way, it's the adjustment of one's awareness to the inner frequency emanating the Light. In the story, in that moment when the awareness occurred, the egoistic chains released and fell off. Then the real journey of Divine Life began. He left the prison-like construct of the egoistic Knowledge of Good and Evil, and emerged into the realm of Light, Life, and Love, which is true freedom.

The writers of both Old and New Testaments were very deliberate in how they wrote what they did. In the book of Acts, Luke was purposeful when he told us the number of guards on each side of Peter and at his cell door. What's amazing is that it says the Light shined throughout the entire building, yet the guards were unaffected. Was it because they couldn't see the Light? If we read this solely from a literalist, branch point of view, even if the guards couldn't see the Light because it was something spiritual, there would still be the issue of those at Peter's side when the chains fell off. This is where we can lose sight of what the Spirit is saying from a root view. Unfortunately, to validate our literalist view, we tend to introduce ideas that are not in the text. For example, the guards were blinded by the light and couldn't see what was happening. Or all the guards were asleep, so they were unaware of what was going on. Of course, the text doesn't say anything like that. The point is, from a root view, though the guards were present they became irrelevant when Peter's heart was synchronized with the Light, the Divine Nature. The guards of egoism, legalism, right and wrong, are powerless in the Light of Divine Love (Colossians 2:14-15). After all, the only reason someone is in prison is, either they have "done something wrong," or they're being held for trial because of an "alleged wrong." Thus, the egoic knowledge of good and evil, right and wrong, are necessary to hold one as a prisoner. However, when there is no Law, hence no contrived knowledge of good and evil, there's no violation, which means there's no wrong, which more so means there's no prison, nor guard, nor power that can hold us (Romans 4:15-16). As Luke continues to write he tells us the number of guards, how many wards there were to the prison, and even specifies the kind of gates the prison had. One of the key elements in the text is that the gates were made of iron. This is no accident because of what it means in Hebraic thinking. Rav. Michael Laitman tells us the meaning of iron from a Torah point of view: "The iron wall [or gate] is inside our hearts, between its *egotistical intention* 'for ourselves' … and the *altruistic intention* 'for the Creator'." Making our point, when we are synchronized to the Divine Nature, we have migrated from the serpentine egoistic desire to the *Divine Desire to Receive and Reflect.*

There is a saying, **"When the student is ready, the teacher will come."** This is a profound spiritual truth. The angel came when Peter was ready, and not a moment sooner After all, this took place during the symbology of the Passover, which means Peter was in prison for several days. However, when Peter's heart was beating with synchronicity, he was ready to emerge. Another interesting aspect of this story is when Luke writes, *"Then Peter came to himself and said, 'Now I know…'"* (Acts 12:11). It was then he became aware that he was liberated from *the world Below,* which was held together by the unholy alliance of politics and religion. When one awakens to the Kingdom of God, it quickly becomes evident that they're united with something far greater and otherworldly (John 18:36). In the story, Peter realized a higher knowing. He changed residence from the knowledge of good and evil to the knowledge of Life. He saw a reality which was "governed" and "drew its source" from the *Eternal.* The *world Below* sees the necessity for political governance, influenced by religious moralism, usually dubbed spirituality, to make life better. Yet as Einstein said, "No problem can be solved from the same level of consciousness that created it." Trying to solve a problem in the world of the knowledge of good and evil only perpetuates the knowledge of good and evil in another form. What was good yesterday becomes today's evil. However, when we migrate to the *world Above,* because we've awakened to the Light, we release what we chained ourselves to *Below* and see reality with enlightened eyes.

Consider this (another chair analogy): If we try to move about in a room with our eyes closed, sleepwalking, we may stumble over a chair. Because we're in darkness, we've never seen a chair, nor understood how it's used. We may create stories about the chair, saying how it can hurt someone if we're not careful. We may tell our painful story to others who are also sleepwalking in the room. We may find they have similar stories, only confirming our beliefs about the evil chair. We may find ourselves in fear of the chair, or even angry because our toe was badly bruised. We may cuss at the chair, maybe even call it the devil! We may find ourselves rallying others to the cause of removing objects like the pain inflicting chair. After all, society would be so much better without such evils. Yet, when we humbly open our eyes and stir from sleep, nothing within the room changes, only the way we perceive it. Now the chair that once hurt our toe becomes a place in the light where we can rest and heal. Then the real challenge comes into view: trying to tell others who are still sleepwalking that the chair is not the devil, and it can actually help. (I think we know how that will turn out.) Hence, it's far better to approach others from another level of consciousness; when the student is ready to open their eyes, the teacher will come. In the meantime, rest in the chair and enjoy a drink, someone will stumble over it sooner or later. Then you can gently reach out, lift them up, give them a place to sit, and help them rest and heal. Maybe, if they're ready, you can even help open their eyes and see what the Light reveals.

Part 3: Awakening is a Process

There is another layer of truth that emerges and introduces an important paradox into the story of Peter, the prison, and the prayer warriors. When Peter was put in prison, we find that the Ekklesia earnestly prayed for him (Acts 12:5). However, when *"it dawned"* on Peter (Acts 12:12) to join himself to the very group that prayed for him, there was a problem. When Peter arrived at Mary's house and knocked on the door, Rhoda, a servant girl, responded. When she heard his voice she excitedly announced to everyone that Peter was at the door. What was the intercessory prayer group's response? *"You're out of your mind!"* (Acts 12:15). It didn't stop there. When she insisted, they said, *"It must be his angel."* However, Peter kept knocking! This sounds reminiscent of the famous section in the book of Revelation when Jesus arrived at the Laodicean church and knocked, saying:

> *"Behold, I stand at the door and knock; if anyone hears My voice and opens the door, I will come in to him and will dine with him, and he with Me. He who overcomes, I will grant to him to sit down with Me on My throne, as I also overcame and sat down with My Father on His throne."*
>
> *(Revelation 3:20-21/NASU)*

Here's an excellent example of how we are one Body in Christ, yet at the same time can be in very different states of awareness. How many times have people prayed for another's spiritual release yet, when it occurs, the liberated are left standing outside? Sounds strange, doesn't it? It's more common than one may think. How can Christians pray, or share what understanding of the Gospel they have, and yet shut out the very ones of focus? The answer begins with why Christ was left knocking outside the lukewarm church of Laodicea. The summary of Jesus's exhortation was that they believed they were spiritually rich, yet that very arrogance made them blind and naked. From the moment the Ekklesia emerged, it was easy to fall back into the egoistic veil of religion, hence, the purpose of the Book of Revelation with its warnings to the Church. The one who *overcomes* and is granted to sit with Christ on His throne is the one who opens the door through the Light of selfless humility born from Divine Compassion. This powerful imagery is consummated in the conclusion of Revelation, saying:

> *"On no day will its gates [door-ways] ever be shut,*
> *for there will be no night there."*
> *(Revelation 21:25/NIV)*

When one finds the synchronicity of Divine Compassion, you could figuratively say that the door is opened and the Love of Christ is allowed in. What defines synchronicity is not the deed, but the root of it, *the intention.* We can delude ourselves by doing good deeds for others and call what we do Divine Love, but that's not necessarily so. We can tell ourselves that we are doing something for another because "God told us" to, which can be no different than obeying a momentary command and calling it Divine Love. The secret to synchronicity is that our intention is as selfless as Christ.

When we find the intention of Divine Compassion, *we have found ourselves.* In that moment, in that awakening, Christ is unveiled within us and such a figurative door is never shut again. Rather, as the Light shines from within, it shines out with an open door to all. The irony is, though the door of our thinking was shut, when we open the door to His knock we find He was sitting in our inner living room all the while (Colossians 3:11). It's challenging to our egoic thinking to grasp that our Christianized belief system can leave Jesus, the Head of the Church, knocking outside the doors of both our hearts and our gatherings. It comes down to the religious façades we put in place which create the hindrance. You could say it's the walls and doors we build that put Christ outside, as if that's truly possible. It's like the notion that we have to be free from our chains to see the Light, when the reverse is the case (just ask Peter). Such things are like putting the proverbial cart before the horse. Sometimes, we don't even put the cart before the horse, we just keep the horse tied to the hitching post, put a Jesus sticker on his rear, and then claim he's spiritually free. Yet, neither horse nor cart has moved or been truly unfettered. Nay, nay! Sadly, because we see our spiritual gifts working, the prophetic flowing, the miracles happening, and so on, we assume all is well with our perception of God, ourselves, and reality. Nonetheless, Jesus told us that such things mean little to *the world Above* (Matthew 7:22-23). What matters is the *intention of selfless Compassion.* It's not about us accurately prophesying or praying for someone's liberty and feeling like we obeyed as we did so correctly. It's about laying our life down in selfless Compassion for another, whether sinner or saint (John 15:12).

In other words, "laying our life down" actually means laying down the egoistic façade we created of who we think we are and allowing our true self to emerge.

When Peter arrived at Mary's house, the group was so focused on their prayer meeting and the need to pray regarding his imprisonment, they couldn't fathom his liberty, especially when it was proclaimed from someone they least expected. It isn't to say they didn't have a love for Peter, or a desire for his freedom. The issue was their focus upon themselves and their criteria surrounding his freedom. This is evident by how they responded to Rhoda, a servant girl, or pre-teen youngster (which in that culture basically amounted to the same thing in status). Not only were they focused on their intercession, but they couldn't believe she just saw Peter, free and standing at the door. She was a "servant girl," or worse, an "immature youngster," not a mature intercessor as they were. Surely she was unable to understand what was happening in the spirit, maybe even *out of her mind.* More emphatically, there is only one Greek word used to describe their statement that she was *out of her mind,* **Μαίνη** which means, *Raving mad! Demon possessed!* (see John 10:20). Can you imagine? They put her excitement in the same class as someone who was raving mad or demon possessed! How horrible! In their eyes, she was of a lower class, just a lowly servant or immature youngster who didn't have the same spiritual insight or maturity as the rest of the group. At best they believed *she saw Peter's angel,* and unlike the rest of them, she would have been incapable of discerning the difference.

When Peter was finally allowed in the house they were ἐξέστησαν (exestesan), *astonished*, literally *put out of place*, which is the same Greek word as *bewitched* in Acts 8:9 & 11 (KJV, Tyndale). This wasn't that they were simply excited to see Peter. No, they were stunned in disbelief that he was actually there! While they were shouting, Peter (literally) *threw down* his hand, told them to be silent, and explained how his liberation occurred. However, there was no apology to the servant girl, no mention that she saw correctly, and no sense of regret that they belittled her. No sooner had Peter finished than he told them to share the news with James and the other believers and then *departed to another place* (Acts 12:17).

Within the Ekklesia there are different dynamics of consciousness. How many intercessory prayer groups, ministers' gatherings, and church eldership meetings have "unconsciously" hit the spiritual snooze button and fallen back asleep into the pattern of religious egoism? It didn't mean the person or people of focus weren't loved, it's just how our religious correctness sets a criterion for what liberty looks like or how it will come about. How many times have we said things like, "Well, they have been saved for two years now, they should be free from that vice." Really? Could we be assuming that the external vice that's bothering us is bothering God in the same way? Could it be that the Holy Spirit is addressing other areas of the person's life, and what bothers us isn't the priority in God's economy at the moment? Could it be that what we see as a problem is really a problem to our ego? How about the possibility that Christ has left the issue unaddressed because it reveals our arrogance and religious discomfort? How many times has God inspired *the least likely* to challenge the criteria of our view of freedom?

In the case of Rhoda, Peter, and the prayer group, this is the third time in the New Testament that *the least likely* proclaimed someone's freedom and wasn't believed. The first was Mary Magdalene (John 20:18) and then those who were on the road to Emmaus (Mark 16:12-14). When Jesus appeared to the apostles it wasn't a celebration at first, it was a rebuke because they didn't heed the proclamation sent through *the least likely*. On the other hand, this didn't deter their ultimate purpose; Jesus still gave them the Great Commission, but not until the issue was settled regarding how they viewed the least among them. You could say that, before Jesus issued the Great Commission, there had to be a level of clarity regarding the Great Commandment. In the same way, Peter told the group to tell the matter to James (Jesus's brother) and the other church members, meaning their level of awareness didn't deter their ultimate purpose either, but it did complicate it. Consider the prayer group at Mary's house; they didn't even open the door to Peter until he knocked so loudly, they finally heard him. In one sense this is similar to the angel that awoke Peter, however, there wasn't synchronicity here. Think of this regarding the group. The young girl is shouting that Peter is at the door, Peter is banging on it as well, and yet the girl is the one who's negatively defined and labeled. Again, this is reminiscent of the Laodicean church who thought they were spiritually rich but were blind. When Peter awoke in prison, his chains fell off and he left the prison. In this part of the story, the prayer group doesn't leave any door open and leave anything. Rather, they stay in the same consciousness at Peter's arrival. How many times have we been so "spiritually focused" that when the answer to our prayer came knocking, the inner volume of our self-focus was so loud we couldn't hear it? To put this another way, how many times have we been so taken by our religiosity that when enlightenment knocked on the door of our consciousness we just rolled over and hit the snooze button so we could continue in the comfort of our illusion? The text in Acts 12:16 says, *"But Peter kept on knocking, and when they opened the door and saw him..."* (NIV) What's interesting is that the Greek text says, *"Moreover, Peter remained knocking,* ἀνοίξαντες *(anoixantes), when they opened, moreover they saw..."* What's consequential in the wording is that the phrase *"opened the door"* isn't actually in the text. Rather, the same root word is used in Matthew 9:30, after Jesus touched the two blind men, saying, *"It shall be done to you according to your faith,"* it then says, ***"and their eyes were opened."*** (NASU)

Similar to Peter in prison, a measure of eye-opening was required to see. However, in the case of the prayer group, Peter couldn't stay with them very long. The message regarding his liberty was a message of liberty to them regarding their prison. When Peter was finally allowed in, the scripture says, *"they were put out of place"* (what we translate as *astonished).* From a positive perspective, you could say that these events jolted their inner state and they awoke to a measure. At the same time, Peter didn't stay once he shared, he moved on *to another place.* For him to stay would have been a hindrance to him and to them. Keep in mind that he told them to go and tell James. That would be the next phase of their possible increase of consciousness. Why not tell James himself? Because of what James represents in the story. If we refer to Galatians (2:11-15) and the events that happened there, we find that Peter, who received the message of grace and faith with Paul, reverted to religious legalism when "certain men" from James arrived. At this point there was clearly a spiritual difference between Paul, Peter, and James. Paul lived the message of grace and rest in Christ. Peter was grasping it as he spent time with Paul and the Galatians, but when the men from James arrived, he quickly reverted to legalism, *fearing them.* Another thing to consider regarding Paul, Peter, and James, is that Paul, who never met Christ in the flesh, seemingly had the most significant revelation of the Gospel among all three of them. Peter, who walked with Christ in person, seemed to struggle at first between the revelation of God's grace and the fears of religious moralism. It's as if when the men from James arrived, the rooster crowed once again. While James, the Lord's half-brother, had the loudest voice and most significant position (mainly because he was related), he also had the least understanding of the Nature of Christ at the time.

Once again, we are to reconsider the value of position, power, and visibility. Just because someone has a large following, a very visible ministry, a strong voice, and holds a position of power, doesn't mean their revelation of the Gospel is on solid footing. If anything, the Gospels, the book of Acts, and the Book of Revelation tell us its highly possible the opposite may be true. Unfortunately, the system of religion tells us if we have such things, we must be spiritually potent. On the other hand, Paul—formally Saul, who persecuted the Church—was *the least likely*, and yet he embodied a vast understanding. This isn't to say that someone with a small ministry has a great understanding of the Gospel either. It's simply saying that someone who seems to have a vast understanding isn't as motivated by all the above. Rather, *their interest is in what it is to emanate the nature of Christ as they love and serve their neighbor.*

Peter didn't just leave Mary's house and her prayer group to go down the street to another meeting. No, he left them with the responsibility to tell James, the church leadership, and the other believers. I have often wondered, based on the events with the men from James in Galatians and the events in Acts 12, what happened when Mary and her prayer group approached James and the leadership. Did James and the leaders respond like the prayer group did to Rhoda? There's evidence of a pattern based on the other scriptures referenced.

The next and last time we hear from Peter in the book of Acts is several years later in 49 AD at the Jerusalem council. The council felt it was necessary to come together to discuss what some Jewish believers wanted to impose on the Gentiles. What was the topic of discussion? "Inform the Gentiles that if they want to walk with God, they have to obey the Law." Luke is politely poetic when he writes about this discussion in the Book of Acts. If it had been me (and if they'd mobile phones at the time), I just would have texted, "SMH, you've got to be kidding me!" Peter was the most vocal, taking a stand that this shouldn't be a burden put on the Gentile believers. He called it *a yoke of bondage* (Acts 15:10). You have to love his typically brash, to-the-point logic! He would have tweeted, "Why test God, you devil? If we Jews knew the Law couldn't save us, but the grace of Christ, why put that bondage on their neck?" While addressing the council's religiosity, he also pointed to their overt classism and racism, stressing how God doesn't make such distinctions (Acts 15:6-11). It could be that Peter was emboldened to address these issues, being that Paul and Barnabas were present, who were of the same mind. Nevertheless, Peter was clearly in a different dynamic of consciousness than the rest were. In other words, Peter *was in another place.* In the end, James gets up and agrees with Peter to a point but adds that there are a few legalistic things that should be imposed on the Gentiles. The first on the list is not to eat food offered to idols, then abstain from sexual immorality (literally, *prostitution),* and then another two Law-based rules about food. Really? You would expect "no prostitution" to be the first on the list! Nope! Food offered to idols. While the council agreed to this, you can see Paul, Peter, and Barnabas acquiescing to avoid a prolonged argument. Why? Just a little later, Paul and Peter feel they need to address such things and explain God's grace a bit further:

> *"So then, about eating food sacrificed to idols: We know that an idol is nothing at all in the world and*

that there is no God but one. ... But not everyone knows this. Some people are still so accustomed to idols that when they eat such food they think of it as having been sacrificed to an idol, and since their conscience is weak, it is defiled. But food does not bring us near to God; we are no worse if we do not eat, and no better if we do. Be careful, however, that the exercise of your freedom does not become a stumbling block to the weak.

(1 Corinthians 8:4, 7-9/NIV)

Paul said that those who consider it a problem to eat food sacrificed to an idol are weak in conscience. Wait...what? Did Paul just insinuate that James and his injunction were coming from a place of weakness? Is he saying that James and his Apostolic Team thought that if the Gentile believers ate food sacrificed to idols their conscience would be defiled? Whose conscience is really defiled here? Is it the Gentiles having a happy meal at Idol Burgers, Wine, and Spirits? Or James and his team? Needless to say, it's not the Gentiles having a burger. Worse yet, what if James added the injunction just to placate the Jewish believers and make them feel good? If that were the case, then James, as an Apostle who is supposed to be a custodian of the revelation of Christ, just became a politician. The Corinthian verses also seem to imply why Paul, Peter, and Barnabas didn't argue their point; they didn't want to be a stumbling block to *the weak.* You can just see the three of them having a quiet discussion after the council was adjourned. "So, where do you want to go? Idol Burgers or Golden Calf Steak House?" There's a truth here which applies to all other religiously espoused views born of a good and evil conscience, whether we impose them on ourselves or others. When we continue to read, Paul's heart wasn't to belittle someone who is still bound by such thinking. Rather, that those of us who understand the grace and liberty of Christ should instead consider those weak in conscience and where they are in their journey. On the other hand, Paul does encourage those who understand such liberty to share the message with those who are weak (2 Corinthians 3). Also consider Peter, who's equally forceful but from another perspective:

> *"Now, since you are rebooted and redefined in this eternal conversation... Do away with everything associated with the old performance based mindsets! Anything perverse, all manner of guile and hypocrisies and spiteful jealousies as well as any kind of backbiting is to be shunned... Imagine how a newborn babe would crave nothing else but pure mother's milk; in just the same way, become addicted to the unmixed milk of the word. ... Once you've tasted pure grace, you are spoilt for life! Grace rules! The Lordship of Jesus is established upon the dynamic of his goodness."*
>
> *(1 Peter 2:1-3/MIRROR)*

One final thought on Rhoda hearing Peter at the door. Despite the religiosity of the group in the house, Rhoda was able to "hear beyond the barrier." In the same manner as being *the least likely*, immature, and of lower class, there is another aspect to the logic here:

"And he said: 'I tell you the truth, unless you change and become like little children, you will never enter the kingdom of heaven. Therefore, whoever humbles himself like this child is the greatest in the kingdom of heaven." (Matthew 18:3-4/NIV)

Rhoda, whether servant, or young immature girl, or both, it all comes down to the doorway itself. It is the doorway of intention, born of the Divine Nature and revealed in compassion, *a humble heart like a child.*

While this Grace in Christ is powerful and vast, there are some who fear that if we don't use a little law or have some rules, everything can still go sideways. So, like James and the prayer group at Mary's house, there is a gratefulness and sincerity of heart, yet there are still aspects of literalism, legalism, and classism. Consider the words of the Apostle Paul: *"...when the fullness of the time came, God sent forth His Son..." (Galatians 4:4/NASU).* God patiently waited until the right moment when humanity was ready for the first seeds of awakening in Christ. The challenge we have in Western Christendom is that we do not take such into account. You could say the modern evangelical's motto is not, "When the student is ready the teacher will come," but, "Ready or not! Here we come!" We go into the world not as physicians with a cure, but as soldiers armed with weapons. Rather than serve and empower, we run tactical operations to gain a winning advantage. We choose to whom we bring healing and with whom we make war. Of course, we make it a point to call this "spiritual warfare," but it never seems to just mean that in our outward practice.

Several years ago, I attended a ministers' lunch with my wife, Karen. The speaker was supposed to lecture on the topic, "How to Stay Encouraged When Negative Times Come to Your Ministry." He did speak on that for about 10 minutes, then for the remaining 20, he moved to the political topics of the day. What was most alarming was when he called the people of the democratic party, who according to his thinking needed to be helped to a Christianized world view, "Demon-crats!" (Wait! Retweet, "SMH! You got to be kidding me!") Admittedly, he didn't make that phrase up himself, he got it from the host of a popular conservative news program. That fact should give us pause in another way for a moment. Who really are the Apostles and Prophets of the hour? If we are influenced from hosts of conservative or liberal news programs, is it them? If our messages are tainted with theirs, and we bring it to our fellow ministers and congregations, isn't it them?

How many times has the Serpentine-Ego told us that we are the enlightened, we know the truth, we are right with God, and God knows we are right? We must save and heal those hellions because they are an enemy to God and society! This dulls, if not completely obscures, the revelation of Christ, making it more challenging for the so-called "unenlightened" to awaken. Surprisingly, this reveals that such a religious mindset is still deep in sleep. When the world hears a message of Christ laced with judgmentalism, criticism, and condemnation, yet in the next breath that God loves you, it only enforces why there would be an opposition to such a religion. You could say there is a type of spiritual warfare, the one us evangelicals create and then fight. Think of it, what does it look like when people

304

who claim they are awake are yet still asleep? To say it more pointedly, they are in part still spiritually dead, still eating the fruit of the Tree of the Knowledge of Good and Evil. Then they tell themselves what good people they are by trying to save the bad ones. They come treading through the community, trying to get those lost ones—the hellions, the others, those people—to assimilate into their religion. In parts of Christendom, we may call it evangelism, but to the rest of the world *it's a zombie apocalypse!* As we discussed in the previous chapter, who really is the Satan? For that matter, who is the zombie-lion walking about, and who are they trying to devour (1 Peter 5:8)? No wonder the so-called worldly ones run screaming, either hiding in dark corners, hoping one of the zombies won't see them, or adorning some form of antagonism, either in protest or political legislation, to stop the invasion. And how do the religious respond? "See! I told you they lurk in dark places! They try to pass laws under the political radar to stop us from preaching and teaching the truth! It's a war against Christianity!" Sadly, in many cases it's not a war against Christ, but a reaction to the Christianity we've portrayed.

Obviously, all Christians are NOT spiritual zombies! But we must take into account the real "spiritual warfare" if we are going to use that term. It isn't against the unenlightened. Rather, it's against our own egos telling us we are more enlightened or awake than we really are. **A momentary stirring of truth does not mean permanent consciousness.** Remember, in one moment Peter had a revelation of who the Christ was, then, within a few verses,

Jesus is rebuking the Satan which Peter was revealing. One moment Peter was stirring and seemingly enlightened. Yet, within a short time, he was misunderstanding that enlightenment and once again shrouded it with a religious, satanic, less than human point of view. He didn't forget what he saw, but it had "fallen" into a different context. Therefore, rather than empowering the revelation of Christ, he was now opposing it.

There is a process every person goes through to awaken. Consider again the ancient times. When a person awoke from sleep, the light was already shining; that's what woke them up. But it then becomes a decision to rise and become fully conscious and *live in the day* (1 Thessalonians 5:5). In the same way that Paul speaks of rising from the dead as an actual metaphor for awakening from sleep, we can say the same about what Jesus says in the Gospel of John, Chapter 11. To truly awaken someone from such a slumber, the Death Sleep, there is a process, and we should never assume because someone is stirring that they are awake. Many times, people stir in their sleep because they are dreaming. We know from the Gospels what that dream looks like. It's the dream of "the others" joining our religion and obeying all our perfect rules along with us. It's the dream of making a holy society with religion and politics working together to enforce those beliefs, making the world a wonderful place. (Smiling in that dream world, who needs to wake up when the dream is so perfect?)

Consider the Gospel of John's description of Lazarus coming out of the grave. It says he emerged "bound hand and foot with graveclothes" and "his face was wrapped" (John 11:43). What does that mean? First, he was not completely liberated into the Light of Day. To put it dramatically, he came hopping out of the grave, banging into the cave walls toward the entrance. On the positive side, because the opening had the light of day shining in it, through the wrapping on his face he was able to get a sense of where the opening was and stumbled toward it. How many of us Christians are like Lazarus? We glimpse an apparition of light and have a sense of direction, so we assume we see the light in clarity and now we're ready to liberate others. However, we are still bound hand, foot, and face. In other words, we see through the opaque lens of Good and Evil, Right and Wrong, not the Tree of Life. This is the danger of believing before fully seeing with our inner eyes. How wonderful! We have risen from the dead! But let's not stop there, let's go through the process of having our hands, feet, and face loosed. As Jesus clearly says, *"Unwrap him and so that he can move around freely."* (John 11:44b/MIRROR) This process involves our humility to allow others, who wear less grave clothes, to help unwrap us. Take a moment to pause and consider what this means. If what we commonly call "the Fall" is us egoistically partaking of the knowledge of good and evil, then the first aspect of being unwrapped of death's grave clothes is us humbling ourselves and letting go of what we know. One of the true earmarks of a spiritual leader in Christ's Kingdom is their measure of humility and awareness of Divine Life; everything else emanates from there.

This awakening can best be realized if we take a moment to explore our inner selves, our true eternal self. Death, or slumber, according to the conversation between God and the Adam, is the result of eating from the Tree of the Knowledge of Good and Evil. This tells us that the first aspect of awakening is opening our inner eyes to the awareness that knowing good and evil, in any form, is what kept us asleep (or dead). In that stirring, the second occurs and we begin to make sense of the Light (Christ). It's the realization that we've been existing "as the opposite quality" of the Light. To say this another way, we've been unconsciously in opposition to the Light. To be opposed to the Light is to simply not reflect it. For that matter, being unconscious is the state of fallen Lucifer, or what Jesus calls Peter, the Satan.

As we become conscious, we recognize that as we receive the Light, we can fully be its reflection. Hence, who we really are is its Image and Likeness. He is I AM and we are an expression of I AM. We and I AM are the SAME; the reflection is nothing less than the Source. Consider that when you look in a mirror and see your reflection, it is no more or less than the source. The Source and the Reflection are one in the same. There is a temptation to say, "Well, the reflection is not the same value as the Source, it's just a reflection," as if to demean what is seen, or to put it into "proper perspective" for the sake of the ego. This again would be the Serpent-Ego speaking. But Jesus and the Apostles never taught that. Jesus taught we are all ONE. For that matter, in John 17:21, when Jesus says we are *one* with Him and the Father, the Greek word used is ἓν (hén). According to the Theological Dictionary of The New Testament, edited by Kittel and Friedrich, "Only rarely is ἓν (hén) used as a digit in the New Testament. It usually means *single, once-for-all, unique* or *only,* or *unitary, unanimous...* Theologically, the most important feature is that God is one (Deuteronomy 6:4). There is none beside him (Mark 12:29), thus only Him. The origin and goal of the world are one in Him." The message is consistent: to believe we are separate, less than, or subservient to God, was never what God communicated or created. As a friend of mine, who is a monk, once said, when asked if he was saying that he was God, "No, I am not God, but every aspect of me is God." The reflection can say the same thing.

> *"Examine yourselves to see whether you are living in the faith. Test yourselves. Do you not realize that Jesus Christ is in you? — unless, indeed, you fail to meet the test!"*   *(2 Corinthians 13:5/NRSV)*

To awaken, we must realize our state and discover what's occurring internally. Failing the test could be believing a scriptural statement, or a doctrine that "Christ is in you." It's one thing to believe a doctrine and another thing to emanate it. So, we roll over, hit the snooze button, and continue to snore.

In the sleeping heart expressed through the mind, we exist with a "fabricated self." This is also assisted by our environment, community, and many times, our family. With the "fabricated self" (we will also call it "the egoistic self"), we learn of *the other:* those who are not like us according to our familiar environment. In an egoistic world, there is a lot of *us and them* to go around. This is where racism, culture, religion, nationalism, and the like comes from. None of these can exist without *the other.* We are taught this when we are very young, "There are those people, and then there's us. We are special because what makes us, *us,* is what makes us different from them." In this state, we really don't see the other person, or people, as they truly are. We only see through the lens of our perceived self, the egoistic construct we make of *them* in our minds. To reassure this egoistic security, we seek out others who agree. In practical terms, this is why subordinating one race over another, one gender over another, and so on, occurs. We can read the Bible with the same false-self construct and even use scriptures to validate our point of view, saying, "God showed me." As we seek out others to validate our egoistic self, we either yield to those that seemly have greater authority on the subject, or revel with those who see the world the way we do. When this happens, the conquest begins.

In contrast, if for some reason there isn't the infamous *other,* the egoistic self will create one. The egoistic self must have *the other!* There must be a devil, a demon, an enemy, sin, a contrast, a darkness, and so on. If there isn't, our egoistic-fabricated self cannot find an independent distinction. We can't be right, righteous, holy, true, moral, and good, without *the other.* In other words, I cannot create a *me* without a *them.* To validate the egoistic self, we seek out and find those who see the world as we do, which creates another anomaly. We validate one another to the point that we now have a superior US! This progression "falls" further to another level. Now, it's not just, "We know better than *they* do," but the view of *the other* devolves into, *"They* don't know because *they're* ignorant and uneducated. If we educate them, *they* will see and be like us." But, if *they* don't respond, this can degenerate into something worse, "The reason *they* refuse to know the truth like us is either because they're stupid or they're willfully ignorant." It doesn't stop there, though. This can even get worse. *"They* heard the truth, *they* aren't stupid, *they* aren't just being willfully ignorant, *they* really are evil and rebellious." Now *they* have become the enemy. Hence, "If *they* stay evil and rebellious, and don't join us righteous ones, *they're of the enemy* and must be dealt with if they don't change." Keep in mind, we did this all on our own, within our own tribe, within our own mind.

On the other hand, the egoistic self cannot survive in Divine Truth. It cannot exist when we recognize who *we* truly are and who *they* truly are. Hence, Jesus is called *the Prince of Peace.* There are no egoistic contrasts within Christ, there's only an awakening that sees fully the so-called us and them with what can seem like a new set of eyes. Actually, we're using the eyes we always had, yet without the egoic filter of sleep. The word for *peace* in the New Testament is **εἰρήνη** (iraynay), which means *to be one with.* In Christ—I don't mean in our agreed religious view of who Jesus is—there is no such reality of us and them. There is only Christ, who is the author and emanation of all Creation, which is another way of saying there's only one multifaceted expression of Creation and Creator. Saying this yet another way, there is only the Tree of Life, which, like all trees, is a multifaceted, mirrored expression of the root. Think of what a tree looks like. The branches look similar to the roots, and both give life to each other. The roots draw nutrients and moisture from the earth and the branches do the same from the atmosphere and the light in the heavens. There are no conflicts or adverse contrasts in it. In the Tree of Life, the roots uphold it and the leaves celebrate it; it's a multifaceted expression of Oneness. This is why it is said that its leaves are the healing of the nations (Revelation 22:2).

Let's take this a step further for inner reflection. When we think, "I love myself," or "I hate myself," (or anything in between) who is who? Who is doing the loving or hating? While it's seemingly a good thing to *love yourself*, the question arises, who is doing the loving of that self and who is the self that's being loved? You may be thinking, "Okay, now we're talking in circles." Are we? Or is that the point? The fact that we even think such things implies we still live in the world of duality, under the influence of the good and evil, serpentine egoistic-self. This is not Christ, Christlikeness, or the Tree of Life. In other words, there is the real me, which was created by and is an emanation of God, and the egoistic self, which was created by me. It is that egoistic, self-critical voice that says it either loves or hates, feels worthy or unworthy. To avoid the frightening notion of looking inward and figuring out that the egoistic self is a fabricated identity we claimed for ourselves, we look outward. It's a lot easier to calculate the loving or disliking of *the others,* which clearly validates *my-self.* Think of Jesus's words:

"You are from below, I'm from above. You are of this world, but I'm not of this world. That is why I told you that you will die in your sins, for unless you believe that I AM, you'll die in your sins." (John 8:23-24/ISV)

We can possibly grasp the idea of Him being from above and those of whom He speaks being from below, even though they are standing in front of each other on equal ground. However, the second part of Jesus's statement is the clincher. His words are deliberate: *"...unless you believe that I AM, you'll die in your sins."* Jesus didn't say, "Unless you believe in Me that I Am the Great I Am." Rather, He said, "Unless you believe that I AM." This is another one of those blasphemous statements from the same chapter. The challenge was, "If YOU believe that I, the 'Son of Man,' is I AM, then you cannot help but realize so are YOU! If you don't, then you will die in your sins, which is a fabricated reality that has nothing to do with the Father, Me, or who you really are."

The point where true awakening occurs, inner resurrection, Christlikeness, is when we realize that we have been identifying with the thoughts we have, thus egoistic images or forms. Thoughts are great and feelings are wonderful, but they are not the real us. Rather, the very aspect that we can observe thoughts and feelings tells us something about our true self. We are not our thoughts, rather, we are the ones who observe and choose which thoughts will have the right to exist within us. The Apostle Paul defines this in Romans 12:2, *"...do not be conformed to this world, but be transformed in the renewing of your mind..."* Wait...what? Until now we believed our thoughts were us. But Paul says we can renew them, literally **ἀνακαινώσει** (anakainōsei), which implies, *the continuous process of renovation.* Notwithstanding, our thoughts and feelings are the stream of either our egoistic-self or our true emanation of I AM. Paul is telling us that we are not what we think or feel, but that we have the privilege to create them. Then who are we? It all comes down to one "Jesus focused" answer: we are the creative emanation of I AM. We are not even a creation of THE I AM, because adding the definite article "the" still implies *otherness* and separation. Rather, we are in Christ, Christ is in I AM, We are all One. Therefore, We, like Christ, are an emanation of I AM.

SECTION IV

THE DIVINE REFLECTION

CHAPTER 10
I AM THAT I AM

"I'm Popeye the sailor man.
I'm Popeye the sailor man.
I yam what I yam
and that's all that I yam!"
"I Yam What I Yam"
Popeye, Cartoon Short
September 29, 1933
Max Fleischer

Having explored all we have up to this point—the refreshers, the story of Noah, the discussion between Jesus and Nicodemus, and Peter leaving prison *to another place*— we are ready to take the journey into *the world Above*; into the realm where *Tree of Life Realities* exist. Jesus told us that the Son of ἄνθρωπος (anthropos), *Mankind,* must be lifted up. Beyond being a reference to Christ dying on the Cross, which was not in the dialog at the time, it's the elevated awareness of how we see ourselves and reality, in Christ. In the Moses story of the שׂרף (saraph), we found that the people who were bitten by the venomous serpents, הנחשים

(nachashyim), would be healed if they gazed at the elevated **שָׂרָף** (saraph). Why were there serpents on the ground to begin with? When we united with the Tree of the Knowledge of Good and Evil and its serpentine egoism, everything changed form. The form that the cosmos (the entire system) is in now is the resulting mutation of that union. This story opens in Numbers 20:26-21:6, with an interesting set of branches for us to uncover in their root. The children of Israel were on Mount Hor, **הֹר הָהָר** (hor hahar), which is a depiction of the land rising up in arrogance, similar to the idea of the tower of Babel (see *Melchizedek*, Volume 1, Endnote #34). It was there Aaron was stripped of his priestly garments and they were given to Eleazar. When that happened, Aaron died.

It was then that Arad, the King of Canaan, **מֶלֶךְ־עֲרָד** (melek-arad), which means *the wild ass rules,* immediately went to war with Israel and took prisoners. The notion of a "wild ass" in most Hebraic circles is defined as *an unbridled ego.* It's no accident that Israel (those intended to go *straight to God)* where on a mountain of pride and then found themselves quickly losing in battle to an unbridled ego. When the Wild Ass won (in other words, Ruled), some of Israel was taken prisoner. Once again we find when the egoic nature is predominant, we're bound in prison, shackled and guarded like Peter. Then Israel made a promise, asking God to help them overcome the shackles of the Wild Ass and they would destroy its cities. Most translations say, *"...they utterly destroyed them and their cities,"* (Numbers 21:3). However, the word *destroy* isn't **בָּלַע** (bala) or **שָׁחַת** (shachath), which would imply destruction or ruin of some kind. Rather, it's the word חרם (charam). Why? Because this really isn't about destroying, rather *consecrating* or *devoting* something to God. For example: "*...I will consecrate* והחרמתי (v'ha'**charam**'tiy) *their gain to the Lord, and their substance to the Lord of the whole earth,*" (Micah 4:13/NKJV). It's a statement of *consecration* for transformation. Taking from one state, corrupt and unusable, and through consecration restoring its function as God intended. It's the Torah's way of saying, "*...a light shone in the prison...and the chains fell off his hands.*" It's taking the rule of the wild egoistic self and consecrating it back to God's original intention, *the Desire to Receive and Reflect.*

We have an insight into how this was done when God told Moses to create the bronze serpent and elevate it. The underlying thought is, complaining against Moses might have been part of the process of letting go of *the world Below* to elevate the inner self to *the world Above.* When we begin to be aware of the Serpentine-Ego as a "false Self," (which until that moment was what we understood as ourselves), it will start complaining, agonizing, and crying as we start loosening ourselves from its illusionary grip. Until this point, our egos still complained, agonized, and cried about things, even spiritual things; we just assumed that we were afflicted, inconvenienced, wronged, in a spiritual battle, and the like. This is the most crucial aspect of our spiritual lives. While this is an ongoing process, at the initial moment when we become aware that there's a true Divine Self, a wonderful, yet challenging conflict becomes evident. Grasping that we're an emanation of the Creator and Father of us all can be as wonderful as breaking through a thick, dark cloud and soaring above it, beholding a clear, sunny sky. At the same time, it's also evident that gravity is ever-present. This is to say that, at an opportune time, the Ego is quick to proclaim that it's the image of God and the definition of "right"-eousness.

When Israel began consecrating their Ego, they had to change their perception of it. The poisonous serpents were nothing more than an outward manifestation of the egoistic disposition complaining about their situation. In other words, just because we decree that we are consecrating or devoting something to God, doesn't make it Godlike. Like we said previously, our "knowing" that the Bible says we're the Image of God, doesn't mean we are an unveiled revelation of it. In many cases, the Ego will try to strengthen its grip saying, "That's right we are the Image!" It's no different than removing the legalistic garments of Aaron and putting them on Eleazar. Same script, different actor. It's like being in prison, chained to the guards, and affectionally embracing their way of thinking, much like Stockholm Syndrome. For many in Western Christendom, this is what we've done. We look into the New Testament with the eyes of a veiled priesthood, returning the recipient of the Gospel to forms of legalism, egoism, and toil. In Jesus's use of Moses example, the serpents were a depiction of their inner egoistic disposition, and their illness (being bitten by the serpent) was the fruit of that. Thus, we have to elevate our perception of ourselves and reality from *the world Below* to *the world Above,* where the *Tree of Life realities* abide. In doing this, not only are we changed, but the entire cosmos is impacted. This is *"God so loved the cosmos..."* in action. Prior to this elevation, we maintain our union with the serpent and its Tree, which is eating from the ground. Consider, Genesis tells us that the serpent will now go on its belly, eating the dust of the ground, while we toil and try to get the ground to produce something for us to eat, but all our blood, sweat, and tears produce are thorns and thistles (Genesis 3:14; 17-19; also see *Melchizedek,* Volume 1: Chapter 11 – "The Reign of Death and the Cross," Part 1: The Death Sleep Descent, middle of the section).

Think of it, both the Serpent in its form, eating the dust of the earth, and us toiling to eat what that same dusty ground produces, are all entwined. At this point, we could even ask who is who in the situation? Of course, this is the ultimate point: the Serpent, its Tree, and us, Humanity, are the intertwined *World, the Cosmos,* from which we perceive reality. Consider what Jesus said to Peter:

> *"Get behind me Satan...you are not mindful of the*
> *things of God, but the things of MEN."*
> *(Matthew 16:23/NKJV).*

If we look at this statement as an insult or a rebuke, who was being insulted? Jesus didn't say, "Get behind me, Peter! You are not mindful of the things of God, but the things of Satan (the Serpent)." If He did, traditionally speaking, we could say that Jesus rebuked Peter and told him that he was speaking like the devil. But not so, it's the other way around. Jesus spoke to Satan and said that he was acting like Man. Wait, did He just insult Satan? Did Christ just indict Satan, saying he was only mindful of the things of Mankind? It sounds like it!

321

Nonetheless, it wasn't so much an insult or rebuke, but an unveiling.

Part 1: The Genesis Effect

Having rehashed these events in the previous refreshers, we won't go into much detail, except to introduce the following. Though the Adam was seemingly the last on the list of creation in Genesis Chapter 1, it is important to recognize that though they were last in sequence, the intention reveals they were first in mind. We see this portrayed from Genesis Chapter 2 onward. In other words, Creation occurred with the Adam as the central figure, and all emerged from it. The intention was (if the reader can embrace this suggestion) that God, being who He is, the Creator, fashioned a Creature in His Image and Likeness to share love and intimacy. To achieve this, He created Them of equal status for such a union. However, to do this required the purest of intentions. Thus, He gave the Creature the choice to love and exist with Him in a relationship of total equality, or the choice to walk away and go another direction. Anything less than a true choice would not be an earnest Image or Likeness of the Divine, but an android, a גולם (golem), or possibly worse. If one can allow themselves in this moment to sense the higher worlds, *the world Above,* one can perceive such as God's intention. Not that the fall was His desire, but that the Creature would have *the choice.* He did not just create Eden; He was and IS Eden. He is the pleasure and the desire. He is the lover beholding His love, hoping they will choose Him, like a young prince who beholds the most beautiful lady from across the ballroom, hoping she will feel the same. They had to have the complete freedom to choose such a love! He took the risk of love. God fashioned a Creation—Us, the Adam—with that choice. If not, nothing about their relationship would be authentic and REAL.

God didn't create a planet with the intent to be the supreme ruler. Nor did He make children for the sake of being the ultimate perpetual parent. No! The union of the Father and Spirit, revealed in the Son, was to create something *greater.* To be the fullness of that greater expression there is, depicted first in branch form, a male and a female. Yet, once again, the scripture is not speaking of biology nor some form of physical gender identity, but of the spiritual root. That root is the union of *Giving and Receiving,* then *Giving in Return.* This is the eternal cycle, perichoresis, of Love, Light, and Life, perpetually creating and expanding. For the Son to be the full expression of who both the Father and Spirit are, they created a Creature *equal in status* for the Son. As from the side of the Adam came forth the union of the man and woman in the Garden, from the side of the Son came the union of Him and His Bride in the Kingdom of Heaven. To say it another way, it's the Christ and His Ekklesia. This is the brightness of the Light through the never-ending, ever-unfolding intimacy of Creation. In other words, He was creating a Bride, a Lover, an intimate Partner who would exist together in, as the Gospel of John calls it, ζωὴν αἰώνιον (zoen ainion), *Eternal Life.* Remember, *Eternal Life* in the Septuagint is the name the man gives to the woman after the Fall, "...*called his wife's name, Life,* **Ζωή** *Zoe...*" (Genesis 3:20). Entering Eternal Life is entering into the dynamic union of the Son and Bride. Therein is the paradox. To create seems to portray the making of children. Rather, it's the fashioning of a lover, a partner, a bride. In the same way, when we partook of the Tree of the Knowledge of Good and Evil with its Serpent, we entered a union, and both we and the Serpent and its Tree changed form. The same applies here. When we enter the wisdom of the Tree of Life, we enter into a completely different system, into a union, which also changes form.

This poses a difficult challenge to one's understanding in the binary world of good and evil. In that lower realm, each individual person sees themselves as separate. If we continue to think in binary terms, a child becoming their parent's betrothed sounds horrifically inappropriate. Yet, in the spiritual world, it's about the transmutation of form. Life does not beget away from its Source but exists in perpetual union with it. In one form, *the world Below* point of view, God, Spirit, and Son, are Father, Creator, and Lord. From *the world Above* view, there's a transmutation. Rather than God being Father, Creator, and Lord, He becomes united with us as Lover, Husband, and Father of "Our Creation." The notion of moving from one form of *cosmos* to the other is not that we are in or out, but of consciousness, or awareness. In other words, all Creation *is* the Kingdom of Heaven, the only thing pending is our dynamic of elevated awareness. Those who are awakening are becoming conscious of *the world Above,* we are one with our Lover, Husband, and Father of Our Kingdom Creation. Those who may be stirring and about to awaken may perceive God as Father, Creator, and Lord. But more commonly, before consciousness occurs, God is dreamt of as a taskmaster with rules, sacrifices, and judgment. If one is in a very deep sleep, God, gods, and goddesses may not exist at all. This is where the metaphor can appear in conflict with its reality. Thus, the observer is required to perceive in more than just an either/or way. It requires us to embrace the metaphors that existed all along in both Old and New Testaments and realize it's an issue of awareness. For example:

> *"Thus says Adonai, the Holy One of Isra'el, his Maker: 'You ask for signs concerning my children? You give orders concerning the work of my hands?'"*
> *(Isaiah 45:11/CJB)*

> *"I saw that even though backsliding Isra'el had committed adultery, so that I had sent her away and given her a divorce document..."*
> *(Jeremiah 3:8/CJB)*

In Isaiah, God calls Himself the *"Holy One of Israel,"* and refers to Israel as a male, *"his Maker,"* as well as *"my children."* In Jeremiah, God speaks of Israel as a *"her"* who committed adultery and says He gave *"her a divorce document,"* clearly implying she was His wife. Then of Jerusalem He says:

> *"You turn things upside down! Shall the potter be regarded as the clay? Shall the thing made say of its maker, 'He did not make me.'" (Isaiah 29:16/NRSV)*

> *"Yet you were not like a harlot, because you scorned*
> *payment. You are an adulterous wife, who takes*
> *strangers instead of her husband."*
> *(Ezekiel 16:31-32/NKJV)*

In Isaiah, God again speaks as the Creator and Maker of Jerusalem, the clay, addressing them as a parent would a child. But in Ezekiel, Jerusalem is called *"an adulterous wife."* Lastly, the Apostle Paul writes:

> *"...become blameless and pure, children of God*
> *without fault..."*   *(Philippians 2:15/NIV)*

> *"I promised you to one husband, to Christ, so that I*
> *might present you as a pure virgin to him."*
> *(2 Corinthians 11:2/NIV)*

Paul writes in Philippians that we are to be *"pure, children of God."* But then in Corinthians he tells us we are to be *"pure"* because we've been *"promised to one husband."* So we are God's children, who are promised as a wife. We can start pulling out our hair trying to fit this in a nice little binary box, saying, "Well, we're the Father's children, promised to Christ, His Son, who's also our brother. So, God is marrying a brother to his sister. Well, at least it's not as incestuous as if we were marrying our Father...Right?" Of course, we can always throw into the mess that Jesus said, *"If you've seen Me, you've seen the Father,"* and *"I and the Father are one."* On top of this, in the Kingdom of God there are no first, second, or third cousins. But let's not stop there:

"My dear children, for whom I am again in the pains
of childbirth until Christ is formed in you."
(Galatians 4:19/NIV)

We have now been called the children of God and bride to Christ, who is also God. Yet, He somehow is also our Husband and Brother. And our Husband and Brother are also the embodiment of the Father, who is being formed within us in spiritual childbirth. Wait! Who is the child? Is the Christ, who is our Husband, and is the expression of the Father, the Child being formed within us? Herein is the point: like *the Son of God,* who is also *the Son of Man,* who both clearly are from *the worlds Above,* are all branches, metaphors, to describe a spiritual reality for which there is no simple vocabulary in the lower world. Thus, it's time to awaken to another level of spiritual consciousness called *The Tree of Life.*

Part 2: "I AM" the Light in the Darkness

In Western Christianity, one base aspect which keeps us asleep is the most rudimentary of the ego: *fear.* Once we, the Adam, became *selfish-aware* from our union with our new egoistic, right and wrong reality, the first thing we did upon hearing the voice of God was to hide in fear (Genesis 3:8-11). In that moment our perception of reality became inside-out and the Life-Giver became someone to fear. From once being "inside aware" of the Creator, we made any form of God external. We made Heaven a place *we go to.* We veiled the Source of Life, God, *and concealed Him,* making Him invisible. Then we fashioned an external Hell, *the unavoidable destiny* if we don't do the right things and make the right choices. Such

327

beliefs are *the fig-leaf* we fashion to appease and answer these base fears. Yet, what we are being beckoned to do is to put away our binary thinking and be willing to awaken. In one respect, we must shelve what we think we know about God, Christ, and us, particularly any two-dimensional characters of Christian mythology, and give way to a Divine reality that's eternal and veracious. When God defined Himself to Moses as

אהיה אשר אהיה (ehyeh asher ehyeh), *"I AM that I AM"* (Exodus 3:14), it seemed simple enough on the surface, as if God was telling Moses His name. Nonetheless, that statement was, and is, far more reaching than a name, or Möbius designation, though the latter would be closer. God wasn't telling Moses what to call Him, but opening a reality in which He exists and showing that His reality is also our reality. Again, the notion of a "name" in Hebrew isn't a label, but a description of an essence. This wouldn't come to its confrontational fullness until Jesus said, *"...before Abraham was, I AM,"* (John 8:58), at which point those who heard Him picked up stones to kill Him. Why? Because Jesus equated Himself with God? Yes, but more so the *Son of Man* was equating Himself with that state of existence. Herein, the Son of Man was being lifted up.

It's not a very simple phrase to translate. While most suggest it should be, "I Am Who I Am," the middle word is what creates another level of challenge and clarity. אשר (asher) has many sides to its block. It's translated as *which* in Genesis 1:7 (the most common translation), then also as *who* (Ruth 2:3), *that* (1 Samuel 2:22), *whatsoever* (2 Samuel 15:15), and *because* (1 Kings 8:33). It's also translated as *happy* (Deut. 33:29), *blessed*

(Psalms 1:1), *step* (Job 23:11), *go* or *pursue* (Proverbs 9:6), and *guide* (Proverbs 23:19). Coupled with the first and last phrase, we have אהיה (ehyeh) I AM, which is the name, and יה (Yah), which means *IS* and *Shall Be,* as well as *Existing.* So the potential translation really is, "I Am (Existing Perpetually) blessed, happy, pursuing (on-going), because of that which I Am (Existing Perpetually)." Wow! It sounds like God is talking in circles, which may not be far from the point. A circle is a symbol of that which is perpetual, on-going, and eternal. The easy answer is that God simply says, *"I Am Who I Am,"* and we are supposed to say a rousing, "Amen!" This sounds so good, but why and what would that mean? The actual statement, *"I AM that I AM,"* is a description of existing in a state of *TOTAL REST.* Meaning there is no striving for identity or objective. This sounds crazy in *the World Below,* which believes not only in having objectives and goals, but that our lives need to be dedicated to striving for them in order to attain fulfillment. How many times have you been told that you need a vision for your ministry or business? Or that your goals are only as good as your plans? So we make decisive plans of how to attain our objectives. These are all true for our lives, ministries, and businesses, to a point, but not so with our spiritual lives. With a play on words, the writer of Hebrews says:

> *"Therefore, let us make every effort to enter into that rest..."*　　　　　　　*(Hebrews 4:11/LEX)*

The paradox is that, to make every effort to enter into rest means to make an effort to not make an effort, to just rest. The state of I AM grasps who He is, which is reality. There is no question about identity. In that state of being there's never a question that needs an answer or explanation. God is in a state of *total rest.* Consider the word we commonly translate from the Hebrew שאול (Sheol). It's been given the definition of the grave, or even Hell, but it actually means *Unknown.* It comes from the word שאל (sha'al), meaning *to inquire* or *ask a question.* In spiritual reality, when we strive externally for answers regarding our true self, inner identity, and being, we've not entered Divine Rest. Rather, we're in a state, or you could say a place, called שאול (Sheol). On the other hand, God is in the complete opposite state or quality of שאול (Sheol). He's in the state and quality of אהיה אשר אהיה (ehyeh asher ehyeh), I AM that I AM *TOTAL REST.*

When it comes to His connection to His Image and Likeness, there is only a state of rest when Mankind awakens to the same. Hence, on the seventh expression of the day, God rested. Why? Because the sixth was finished, the completion of His Image and Likeness. Another way to think about the verse above could be, *"Don't try to become, just Be."*

But why use the phrase "I AM" or "I Exist?" We've discussed that a Jewish person never pronounces God's name. Rather, they use two other phrases to avoid pronouncing it: השם (haspanshem), *the Name,* and אדני (adonay), *my Lord.* To pronounce the actual name, יה , or by extension יהוה , would be invoking the Creator and defining His essence in a matter. That which you label, you control and give identity to, which

330

is why God has so many names in the Bible. In the Garden as God created, we, the Adam, Mankind, gave identity and definition to that Creation; we named animated life. However, there's something quite profound in **יהוה** calling Himself **אהיה** (ehyeh), "I AM." He did that to have us bring definition and identity to ourselves! Think of it, if we've been given the privilege to bring definition and identity to Creation, and Creation is an expression of the Source, **אהיה** (ehyeh) I AM, then we need to look in the mirror and consider ourselves. Every day of our lives when we go to the store, go to work, open a book, turn on the television, we are unable to say we are doing any of those things without saying, "I AM..." We cannot go on vacation without saying, "I AM going on vacation." We cannot get married without saying, "I AM getting married," and so on. The point is, built into the very fabric of *our existence* as His Image and Likeness, is the identification and definition that we are, "I AM." The Great I AM, **אהיה** (ehyeh), made our identity synonymous with His. This is not to be taken as a parental gesture such as, "What you mean is that I am not Him, but similar to Him. Like my child is not me, but I created him, and he exists independently from me." To the contrary! This is where a paradox exists in the egoistic binary world of good and evil and is difficult to explain. As the writer of the Book of Hebrews says, *"We have much to say about this, but it is hard to explain..."* (Hebrews 5:11/NIV).

God is the Creator, the Source of all Creation. To Create, He takes of His own Life and fashions a replica, the Adam. We may call this a son or child, but as we pointed out earlier, it's actually an extension of Himself, as a bride, wife, or spouse. Paul suggests this on another level when redefining the relationship of husbands and wives to the Greco-Roman world:

> *"...he who loves his wife loves himself."*
> *(Ephesians 5:28/NKJV)*

This was not heard of in either the Western or Eastern world in the manner Paul was expounding. Keep in mind, Paul was relating these ideas to bring forth a revelation of Christ, rather than Greco-Roman hierarchy in male and female relationships. After referring to the Garden and citing the equal union of male and female, he concludes:

> *"This is a great mystery, but I speak concerning Christ and the church."*   *(Ephesians 5:32/NKJV)*

The notion of God creating a being of equal status and function for the purpose of being in united intimacy is hard to fathom with the intellect, but a lot easier with the inner self.

Part 3: The Great Mystery

If we look at the different sides of the logic of the Creature, the Adam, he is neither child nor wife, but an expression of the Creator in intimacy. The gender aspect is only describing a spiritual quality and function. This is difficult to grasp because we have nothing to really compare it with in *the World Below*, except the architypes of masculine and feminine, which in

God's economy are equal. This is why our Hebrew brothers and sisters call the fullest, or ultimate manifestation of God, אֵין סוֹף (eyn sof), usually translated *limitlessness* or *no end.* However, if we were to mechanically translate the phrase it would be *nothing end.* In other words, *endless nothing.* When we try to understand this with our intellect, we reject the notion, considering it a type of endless oblivion. The idea of using the word *nothing* is simply to say that there is *"no thing"* that we in the physical world can relate such an existence to. Hence, we use metaphors, or roots and branches. On the other hand, through prayer, meditation, and study, we can connect to our true self in the upper world and discover an awareness of who and what we, and God, are.

One way to explain it in metaphor is this: We see ourselves take a droplet of water from the ocean and put it on the tip of our finger. If we were able to perceive everything within that droplet, we would find all the aspects of the ocean contained within it, right down to the molecular structure. You could say that the droplet and the ocean are one in the same. This would be true! Yet, we can still say that both the ocean and the droplet are separate from each other if we perceive from a binary egoistic, us-and-them point of view. Thus, many in *the World Below* "believe" we're like God because we're told or read in the Bible that we are. So we loosely connect to יהוה through belief. Hence, *faith below reason.* Consequently, we egoistically assume that what we think, or how we feel about the world around us, must be "like God." Yet such assumptions only ratify the Serpent's claim, "I will be like the Most High." While the information is technically correct from a theological standpoint, we're not truly seeing with our spiritual eyes. What we know about the droplet is still in a form of dogma. In other words, because we checked off the correct boxes in our beliefs, we assume we've perceived spiritually. That being so, we assume if something angers us, it must anger God too. If something pleases us, we assume God must be pleased. We just relabeled our knowledge of good and evil into what pleases or displeases God. However, the moment we attain a perception of the upper world, we see beyond a droplet from the ocean and see the ocean itself within the droplet. For that matter, when we see the ocean, we also see the fullness of the droplet. In that moment we begin to sense a reality of no separation, as Zechariah 14:9 says, *"'The Lord is one,' and His name one."* It's like letting the droplet run off our finger and fall back into the ocean. Now where is the droplet in relation to the ocean? There is no separation, only the illusion there was one. The droplet is the ocean and the ocean is now a limitless droplet. This is the quality of *total rest.*

In a similar idea, consider a large (limitless, if you will) lake high up on a mountaintop. From the lake pours forth rivers cascading down the mountain's sides into large lakes around its base that find their way through the terrain to connect. Now consider Jesus's words:

> *"He who believes in Me, as the Scripture said, 'From his innermost being will flow rivers of living water.'"*
> *(John 7:38/NASU)*

A river is nothing less than the pouring forth of its Source. It's no more separate than a droplet returned to the ocean. For that matter, as the rivers merge into the lakes below, they are clearly one. Consider these words from Genesis:

> *"And a river went out of Eden, to water the garden; and from thence it was parted* **יפרד** *(yipareed, to scatter abroad), and became four main streams* **ראשים** *(rashiym, heads or minds)."*
>
> *(Genesis 2:10/Darby)*

While the rivers of Eden seemly part and go in four directions, they are still flowing from the same Source. Thus, they are the same, yet unique. In the same way, we are rivers of the Source. As we become conscious of our union, we merge in our awareness of reality and reveal "lakes," resembling that oneness from *Above.* We come back together as one, revealing the Source. Again, as Jesus says:

> *"For where two or three are gathered together in My name, I am there in the midst of them."*
>
> *(Matthew 18:20/NKJV)*

This is not a reference to everyone gathering in a building, singing the same songs, or listening to the same sermon. It's speaking of what the Hebrew word for *name,* **שם** (shem), means. Keep in mind it's a central word within a few other words, like **נשמה** (nashemah), which we translate as *spirit,* and **השמים** (hashamayim), which translates as *heavens.* In

335

Genesis 22:14, when Abraham ascends the mountain with Isaac to offer him as a sacrifice, he sees a ram in the thicket and offers it up instead, then he calls the place יהוה יראה (Yahweh Yireh, Yahweh Sees). In most translations we use the phrase Jehovah Jireh, calling it a name of God. While we ascribe it as a name, it was more so a description of what Abraham experienced regarding God's essence in that moment. Therefore, God has many names. Even *Jesus* in Hebrew, ישוע (yeshua), is more of a description than a label.

For that matter, like יהוה , it's an imperfect tense verb: ישוע (yeshua), means *crying (or shouting) freedom*. Therefore, we're named by Jesus, the ἐκκλησίαν (ekklēsian), the *called-out*. He's the cry of freedom and we are those who are responding to that cry.

The words and phrases regarding *the name, spirit,* and *heavens*, are regarding the very ethos and essence of something or someone. The essence of a person is their spiritual state which abides in the heavens. Remember, Jesus said, *"I AM from above..."* (John 8:23). Then a few verses later, *"...before Abraham was, I AM"* (John 8:58). With that in mind, it was just several verses before that He told us He was the Divine Source and we drink from Him, which are the same rivers of Living water that flow from us (John 7:37-38).

Consider, we are the rivers (emanation) of the Source (God), and when we become truly aware of this within ourselves, we can't help but become aware of the same in others. When we are aware of this together, the Divine Essence is in the midst, the Source (Christ), and is revealed through and among us.

This is a mystery: loving God and loving one another is loving ourselves. Again, Jesus speaks regarding the greatest of the commandments:

> *"And the second is like it: 'You shall love your neighbor as yourself.'"*   (Matthew 22:39/NKJV)

This was not a parabolic statement, that we should love others at the same level as ourselves, or simply treat others the way you want to be treated. That's a good start (Matthew 7:12), but the reality of the statement is that loving your neighbor *is loving yourself.* What's profound is that Jesus is quoting from Leviticus, which says:

ואהבת לרעך כמוך אני יהוה:

(v'ahav'ta l'reaka kamoca aniy Yahweh)
And you love to your neighbor like you I AM Yahweh.

Isn't it interesting how Moses, by inspiration, adds the phrase "I AM Yahweh" when it comes to loving another? We know from the Apostle John's epistle that he ratifies the essence of what makes God. God is Love (1 John 4:8, 16). John tells us when we love, we are abiding in God. Thus, we cannot be anything else than an expression of the Source. *The Source is Love, and we are an emanation of Love, streams of it, rivers of it, showers of it, lakes of it, oceans of it!* Loving another is drawing from, pouring forth in and upon His emanated essence. This is another way of saying, "the Desire to Receive and Reflect." It's receiving the Divine Source and returning it back to Him, which is in Mankind. This is Eternal Life; this is the revelation of the I AM.

CHAPTER 11
I AM ETERNAL NOW

"Oh, let the sun beat down upon my face,
with stars to fill my dream.
I am a traveler of both time and space
to be where I have been.
To sit with elders of a gentle race
this world has seldom seen.
Who talk of days for which they sit
and wait when all will be revealed."

Kashmir (Verse One)
Led Zeppelin
Written by Plant, Page & Bonham

The real "us" lives in the timeless reality of I AM. We can live from the world of time and space, *the World Below,* as Jesus terms it (John 8:23-24), or like Jesus, have physical form and emanate I AM from *the World Above.* Let's be clear, emanating from *the World Above* has little to do with spiritual gifts or five-fold ministry functions, but everything to do with love, humility, and selflessness. Rousing to that awareness is the first true appearance of resurrection in our lives. It's recentering where we live from, not a place we're going to. As we mentioned some time ago:

> *"And God raised us up with Christ and seated us with*
> *him in the heavenly realms in Christ Jesus."*
> *(Ephesians 2:6/NIV)*

The realm *Above* is not a place we are going to, but a place we live from. The same can be said of the Kingdom of God. This centers us, not in what happened in the past, or what will happen in the future, but in where we are *now.* What's interesting is that the Old Testament tells us this over and over. For example (the words in Hebrew are to the right of the translated English word):

> *"Yet regard the prayer* תפלה *(t'filah) of Your*
> *servant and his supplication, O Lord my God, and*
> *listen to the cry and the prayer* תפלה *(t'filah) which*
> *Your servant is praying* פלל *(palal) before You*
> *today."* *(1 Kings 8:28/NKJV)*

The word תפלה (t'filah) comes from the word פלל (palal) which specifically is the description of one praying, either to God or an idol. Literally, it means *to speak to one in authority.* תפלה (t'filah) appears approximately 77 times in the Old Testament, and פלל (palal) appears approximately 84 times. Since they mean virtually the same thing, we could say they

340

collectively appear 161 times. Now consider the following verses:

> *"And he said, O Lord God of my master Abraham, I pray* **נָא** *(na) thee, send me good speed this day, and shew kindness unto my master Abraham.*
> *(Genesis 24:12/KJV)*

> *"And Moses crieth unto Jehovah, saying, 'O God, I pray* **נָא** *(na) Thee, give, I pray* **נָא** *(na) Thee, healing to her.'"* *(Numbers 12:13/YLT)*

The word **נָא** (na), which many times is translated *pray* throughout the Old Testament, appears 405 times. In most cases it means *now*. It has the earnestness of a *plead*, a *beseeching*, and some translations will insert those words instead of *pray*. But ultimately it means *right now, this moment*, not referring to the past nor a time in the future. Think of how these verses can be read:

> *"...O Lord God of my master Abraham, bring about NOW to my face (before me) this day..."*
> *(Genesis 24:12/KJV*
> *Modified to better match the Hebrew)*

> *"And Moses cried to Yahweh, saying 'O God, NOW heal, NOW her!"* *(Exodus 12:13/YLT*
> *Modified to better match the Hebrew)*

The first word we mentioned depicting prayer, תפלה (t'filah), is a description of speaking. In *the World Below* we speak, or pray, to a deity with a sense of it being separate and external. From an observer's point of view, this was what Abraham and others did. Yet in most cases, the Old Testament prophets, Abraham, Moses, David, etc., didn't simply talk to a distant deity who they called יהוה. Rather, they entered that inner timeless space, *the World Above,* where I AM exists, called נא (na) *now.* In the physical *World Below,* time is a paramount issue. About fifteen years ago while I was speaking on a Wednesday night at church, right in the middle of my teaching, the Spirit spoke this phrase to me, "To the egoistic man, time is a prison. To the man who lives from *Above,* time is a tool." Our sensation of time gives us a picture of the past and the future. But the realm Jesus calls *Above,* (remember that He connected His identity to I AM) has no real past and future, because it encompasses time and space like a marble held in the hand. נא (na) *Now,* isn't in time; it's outside of it.

Before we open this further, there is another interesting aspect to נא (na) in its letter definitions. The נ (nun) is the fourteenth letter of the Hebrew aleph-bet and has a numerical value of fifty. In Hebrew it means *perpetual, the heir to the throne.* In Aramaic, like in the book of Daniel, the letter means *fish.* Let's not forget that the letter prior to the נ (nun) is the מ (mem), which means *water.* Several chapters ago we discussed Noah and the Ark. On the surface of the text, it seems that all life was destroyed and just Noah and his family survived in the ark. But if there was another set of survivors it was the fish that lived in the waters. They existed in both the past world and the future world. However, from their perspective, if a fish could have one, they existed in the נא (na) *Now*.

This brings us to the next letter in the word נא (na), the א (aleph), which is a silent consonant, meaning *unidentifiable strength, the unknowable*, and the intention of *that which is above reflected below*. The א (aleph) is made up of two letters, one repeated twice. The first (which appears both above and below the other letter) is the י (yud), which has a numerical value of ten. It means *the infinite point where all creation begins*. It's as if God's creative strength is in His closed hand about to open. The other letter which is between the two י (yud), is the ו (vav), which has the numerical value of six. It's an elongated י (yud), meaning *that which pegs (or joins) above to what is Below, the Light from the World Above that comes down to the world below*. Yet there is more. When we add up the three letters that make up the א (aleph), we have the number twenty-six, which is the same exact value of the ineffable name, יהוה. Putting all this together, you could define the word נא (na) as, *Now, the timeless, eternal existing reality*, יהוה. It's about living from *Above* and emanating that realm in this one and the world to come.

Part 1: We Are Out of Time

For many, the understanding of time and our existence in it is connected to some very simple road signs. We are born, thus we have a beginning, and we die, hence we have an end; the experience in between is how we gage the passage from one to the other. Because of our physical sense of beginning and ending, birth and death, we experience time. At least, that's how the egoic-self experiences it. This understanding is important, because we don't originate as beings of time and space, but as beings from *Above*. Remember, Jesus said that He was the Son of Man and then added that He was from *Above*. The message is uncomfortably clear, even to the ego: Mankind is originally from *Above* and not of this lower world. Consider, if God the Father, through Christ, is our Source, then our origins were never in this lower physical world. If we're going to be Christlike then we're compelled to understand the אנ (na) *now.* Yet, our perception is that we were here since the fall of Adam, and if we make the right choice of receiving Jesus as Savior, we'll go to Heaven when we die. But this is not the Gospel! Let's go back to the Garden and see how it all unravels.

In the book of Ezekiel, it says:

> *"Now it came to pass in the thirtieth year, in the fourth month, on the fifth day of the month, as I was among the captives by the River Chebar, that the heavens were opened and I saw visions of God."*
> *(Ezekiel 1:1/NKJV)*

ואני בתוך הגולה על נהר כבר

(va'ani b'tok haggola al nahar c'var)

*...And I in the center [of the] exiles over [the]
sparkling flow intertwined (like a wreath or net)...*

When Ezekiel is among the exiles in the sparkling flow intertwined like a wreath, he has "visions" מראות (mar'ot) of God. This word מראות (mar'ot) is not the word חזון (chazon), which is the common word for a *spiritual vision.* Rather, מראות (mar'ot) means *mirrors.* When I read this verse I couldn't help but think of two famous movies, James Bond's "The Man with the Golden Gun," and Bruce Lee's "Enter the Dragon." At the end of both movies, there's a fight scene with the villain in a room full of mirrors. In both cases, there are reflections of both the villain and the hero all over, some from behind, and from the right and the left. If we trace this word throughout the Old Testament, we find a similar situation. In other words, Ezekiel wasn't having a vision in the way we think. Rather, he was seeing manifold reflections of God. Think of Paul's phrase in Ephesians 3:10, *"...to the intent that now the manifold wisdom of God might be revealed..."* Yet, before Ezekiel transcended into the world of mirrors, he was in a sparkling flow that was intertwined like *a wreath.*

In the Old Testament, one of the words for *wreath* (sometimes translated *ornament)* is לויה (liv'yah), and its etymology is quite telling. Without the י (yud), it's the word לוה (lavah),

345

which means to *borrow* or be *joined*, like the *intertwining* of more than one. Hence the lender and the borrower are *joined* or *intertwined.* Without the letter ה (hey), we have the word לוי (levi), as in the priesthood, which also means *to be joined.* Yet when we change the ה (hey) to a ת (tav), making the word ליות (loiy'ot), it is also translated *wreath* (for example, 1 Kings 7:29-30, 36 in the NKJV, NIV, CJB, ISV, NASU, NRSV and ESV), usually *a wreath* worn on the head (Proverbs 1:9; 4:9). Why is all this important? Because there's another aspect of the word, which is לויתן (liv'ya'than). We usually translate this word *Leviathan, the wreathed serpent* of the sea (see Job 41:1, Psalms 74:14, 104:26, Isaiah 27:1).

When Ezekiel was with the exiles in the River of Chebar, *the sparkling flow intertwined like a wreath,* he was in the realm of Leviathan, the Serpent. He then transcended *the World Below,* into the higher worlds where he saw *reflections* of God. We mentioned earlier that when we were in the Garden of Eden, prior to partaking of the Tree of the Knowledge of Good and Evil, we communed with God, emanating the essence of the Tree of Life. There, both timelessness and the I AM, the Divine Present and the Divine Now, exist perpetually. However, the "coiled" serpent in the other Tree was also present. To us in that form, we were outside of time, as mentioned before, *like a round marble in the palm of our hand.* The coiled serpent, or circular serpent, is how that realm is represented, which is how the perpetuity of I AM perceives it. This is outside of time and space, and yet there is an acute awareness of its content. Nonetheless, when we chose to

346

partake of the Tree of the Knowledge of Good and Evil, we changed our awareness of *Receiving and Divine Reflection* to *Receiving for Ourselves Alone,* Egoism. It's as if we stopped existing outside of the marble, and we entered that marble. Perceptively, it became our world and we became entangled by it. *The wreath,* **לויה** (liv'yah), is worn around the head, and should be an *ornament of grace* (Proverbs 1:9). However, in that moment it became the constricting wreath of the Knowledge of Good and Evil. Rather than perceiving it outside of time and space, we entered it, and it strangled the Life from us. The result is what we commonly call, "The Fall." Why do I phrase it that way? Because in a later chapter we will observe this event from a completely different perspective. Remember, it wasn't only us that transformed, but the serpent as well.

From a coiled view in the Tree, it also changed form to an elongated view on the ground. In other words, it changed from a never-ending circle to a linear form with a beginning and an end, like birth and death. Consider further the imagery that Genesis offers. It specifically says that when we partook of the Tree, the serpent was to go on its belly and eat the dust. The serpent that was coiled *Above* in the Tree, is now *Below* on the ground and, for that matter, in the lowest possible form, *on its belly.* Another important point is that the Hebrew phrase in Genesis 3:14, "*...on your belly you shall go...*" is **גחנך** (g'honaka), and repeats itself in root form, **וגחי** (vagochi), which means *to be in labor* and *give birth.*

347

> *"Writhe in agony, O Daughter of Zion, **like a woman**
> **in labor**..."*   *(Micah 4:10/NIV)*

> *"Yet you **brought me out of the womb**..."*
>   *(Psalms 22:9/NIV)*

> *"Who shut up the sea behind doors when it **burst**
> **forth from the womb**...*   *(Job 38:8/NIV)*

Moses was specific in his choice of words. Rather than using the common word for *belly* or *womb*, which is used throughout the Old Testament, (for an example, see Genesis 25:23, בבטנך (b'bit'neek), *in your womb)*, he chose the word that signified giving birth. By using גחון (gachon), the implication is that when we partook of the Serpent and its Tree, together we gave birth to the perception of a physical, fleshly world of linear time and space. Thereafter, we no longer observe time as the wreathed, coiled, circular serpent from an eternal view, the view of I AM, but, from an internal linear view with the illusion of a beginning and an end. We now travel *through time,* rather than being outside of it. Thus, the way we sense time is through the Serpentine nature of Ego. Our experience of time and space isn't in wristwatches, clocks, and calendars; these are simply markers of where we are as the earth orbits the sun and the moon orbits the earth. Such time pieces, as we call them, are helpful in designating when we meet together, when we plant, harvest, and so on. However, the way we *experience time* is quite different.

Consider, standing in line at the Department of Motor Vehicles for over an hour to pay a driver's license fee. How many times have we made statements like, "Man, this is taking forever!" Then the serpentine fruit starts budding in the branches of our thinking. So, we say to ourselves, or to someone in line with us, "What's taking that girl so long? Doesn't she know what she's doing?" From this judgmental attitude arises the sentencing, "Damn! They should replace her with someone who knows what's going on. She's constantly asking for help. This is taking forever! I've got more important things to do than wait in line like an idiot, because of that idiot! When I get to the window, I'm going to ask for the manager and give them a piece of my mind. Bunch of jerks!" I guess we could say there was also *"...weeping and gnashing of teeth."* Now consider, how many times have we been at a party, thoroughly enjoying ourselves for several hours. Then we look at a clock and think, "Oh my gosh, it's late! How time flies. I've got to get up early for work. Where did the time go? It's like I just got here!" The point is, we experience time based on how our Ego self-interprets our sense of pleasure as we travel through it. The actual experience may not be physically painful at all, but the pain that occurs may come in forms of impatience, anger, and frustration, which can give way to forms of suffering like malice, envy, or some other judgment from our Tree of the Knowledge of Good and Evil. In the human experience everyone encounters pain of some kind. However, if we are not living in the moment from the I AM, the נא (na) *now*, and live from the Knowledge of Good and Evil, we suffer. In this context, suffering isn't a prolonged pain, but the tormenting bite of the Serpentine-Ego, like in the story of Moses, the people of Israel, and the brazen serpent. Hence, "Why is this happening to me? I don't deserve this! Why is God letting this happen? I'm not ungodly like those people! That's why, it's their fault! If they hadn't done what they did, I wouldn't be going through this!"

We created timepieces and calendars to measure what we think is time, but they only solidify our egoistic interpretation of the moment. Regardless of what our wristwatch may say, five minutes can either be sensed like a flash of lightening, or it can drag on forever and ever. Therefore, entering into the נָא (na) *now,* the realm of I AM, the place called *Above,* is seemingly so difficult. Our Egoistic-Self cannot be a part of that experience. Rather, it has to subjugate itself to our true inner identity, the one in the Image and Likeness of I AM. As the Apostle Paul tells us:

> *"...have stripped off the old self with its practices and have clothed yourselves with the new self, which is being renewed in knowledge according to the image of its creator."* (Colossians 3:9-10/NRSV)

In the New Testament *"the Sword"* is representative of the Divine Thought, or the Eternal Word, expressed by the Spirit (Ephesians 6:17; Hebrews 4:12; Revelation 1:16). Consider that imagery as we explore the following verse:

> *"At that time, with his fierce, mighty, and powerful sword, the Lord will punish the gliding serpent*

Leviathan—the coiling serpent Leviathan—and he will kill the dragon that's in the sea."

(Isaiah 27:1/ISV)

Notice that the Sword of the Spirit, the *timeless eternal expression of the Creator,* will *oversee* the Serpent. The word *punish,* though that's how it's translated in the International Standard Version, is better translated יִפְקֹד (yof'qod), meaning to *oversee, watch over* or *visit.* The Living Expression of the Father oversees Leviathan, the wreathed serpent of time and space, regardless of its form, whether coiled or gliding (on its belly). Why? Because the **λόγος** (Logos), the Living Word, the Divine Expression, the Christ, the Son of Mankind, remains outside of time and space. The Christ is *transcendent.* The notion of *"the Word became flesh"* was a selfless choice made through compassion. Thus, He can move through time and space and yet abide outside of it. Why? Because Christ is the expression of I AM. Thus, while standing in the physical world with the Scribes and Pharisees, He says, *"I AM from Above..."* and *"...before Abraham was, I AM."* In other words, though I AM appears in time and space, I AM also transcends beyond it. Equally important is that **ἄνθρωπος** (anthropos), the Adam, Mankind, of whom the Son of Man represents, can also be transcendent of it. When this occurs it's called *"the incarnation."* When the Serpent changed form, and time became a linear egoistic experience, we find in just a few verses the I AM telling the woman that *in pain she shall bring forth children,* (Genesis 3:16). It's in this transmutation of form that the "knowing" occurs in a self-centered sense. By partaking of this kind of knowledge, we egoistically know good and evil, time and space, and pain and pleasure. Mental and emotional pain are a calculation of good and evil, and suffering is its summation in comparison to what we experience as time. This is why living in the נָא (na) *now*, the realm of I AM, is so important. It lives from the Tree of Life. In that state, what we experience isn't evaluated based on good or evil, but an awareness of its temporality and our transcendent sense of the eternal (2 Corinthians 4:17-18). Thus, what we experience serves as a catalyst to emanate Divine Life. We are privileged with the choice between the two Trees once again, to shed *the World Below* and live from *the World Above.* Just like in childbearing, though pain is for a moment, it brings forth life that endures significantly longer.

When Paul tells us to *strip off the old self,* it's interesting to point out that the Greek phrase for *the old self* is **τὸν παλαιὸν ἄνθρωπον** (ton palaion anthropon), *the antiquated Mankind (the Adam),* and put on the *new,* **νέον** (neon, the accusative form of **νέος** neos), meaning, *belonging to the present.* He isn't telling us to shed bad behaviors of our past sinful selves prior to some form of introductory prayer. Rather, he's telling us to shed Mankind as we know it, changing our entire view of ourselves, others, and reality, and return to our origin. Paul is expounding on what Jesus proclaimed, that when we humbly lift up *the Son of Mankind* we also awaken to our true selves as sons and daughters of Mankind. We emanate that *which is created according to the Image of the Creator.* In shedding the egoistic self with all its Tree-like branches—good, evil, right, wrong, pain, pleasure, and time evaluation based on them—we unveil true Humanity, the Image of I AM, who exists *in the present,* the Eternal Now. This isn't about the crucifixion of Jesus, but the resurrection of our true self, who is also Christ (1 Corinthians 12:12). You could say, without awakening to the I AM within us, we continue to crucify the Christ over and over. We do this in the most subtle of ways, like when we egoistically focus on the stories we tell ourselves regarding our past. Or when we wish for a better or different future than anticipated. There we're imprisoned by the branches of Death and crucify the Living Christ within us on that same Tree. There we're chained to the prison guards of self-centered calculations regarding ourselves, others, and what we dream as reality. This doesn't mean we shouldn't plan for, or desire, a better future, or have clocks, or use calendars. What it does mean is that true metamorphosis cannot happen until we become fully conscious of our identity in the present. Our cognizance in the present defines our future. Paul continues to describe **νέον** (neon), *belonging to the present,* in this manner:

> *"So, as those who have been chosen of God, holy and beloved, put on a heart of compassion, kindness, humility, gentleness and patience; bearing with one another, and forgiving each other... Beyond all these things put on love, which is the perfect bond of unity. Let the peace of Christ rule in your hearts..."*
> *(Colossians 3:12-15/NASU)*

Another way to translate the first part of the first sentence can be:

Ἐνδύσασθε οὖν ὡς ἐκλεκτοὶ τοῦ θεοῦ...

(Endysasthe oun hos eklektoi tou Theou...)
Sink-down into the garment now as chosen of
God...

The implication isn't just that we are God's chosen, as if to suggest others are not, but that we are to sink-down into the garment chosen by God, the Eternal Now, the I AM. The thought of using the word **ἐνδύσασθε** (endysasthe), to *sink-down-into,* offers us a picture of *resting* and not striving. The further description of such a state is *Divine Compassion* with its attributes. Notice the words Paul uses to describe **νέον** (neon), *belonging to the present:* compassion, kindness, humility, gentleness, patience, and forbearing. None of these qualities calculate good or evil, right or wrong, pain or pleasure, or indicate how long we should express such, or tolerate the other. For that matter, if we do "feel" the pain of being wronged, which would imply we're not in a state of rest but egoistically evaluating, he says to *forgive.* Finally, he adds, superimpose *selfless-love* on all these things, binding everything together. This is how we experience true timeless peace. This is the peace that passes all understanding (Philippians 4:7), because any other form of understanding is an egoistic calculation. Paul then adds in Philippians that this peace will guard our hearts and minds, because we have centered our identity in Christ. At this point you can almost see the Apostle Paul, dressed in a Matrix-like long black coat, clipping sunglasses on his nose, and with a subtle grin, saying in a deep voice, "I'm trying to free your mind, Neo. But I can only show you the door. You're the one that has to walk through it."

Part 2: Now Is Eternal

For the most part, emanating from *Above* is not easily conceived with the intellect. Nonetheless, maybe we can grasp that we were once *outside of time and space* while in the Garden. With that in mind, we most likely can grasp that by partaking of the Serpent and its Tree, we created and entered this physical world in which we now feel limited and trapped. In this corporeal world of time and space, there isn't an obvious sense of existence prior to birth, nor beyond our impending death. To us, the higher eternal worlds seem concealed, or at best are very distant, if they're real at all. In other words, here we travel through time and experience distance or space. Yet, if we become aware of or sense what it is to be in the I AM, we can step out of the grip of time and into the Eternal Now. Consider again the words of the Apostle Paul:

> *"'For in him we live and move and have our being.'*
> *As some of your own poets have said, 'We are his*
> *offspring.'"*   *(Acts 17:28/NIV)*

We will discuss these occurrences further in Chapter 15, but here Paul quotes from Greek poetic mythology, citing Aratus's "Phaenomena," Cleanthes's "Hymn to Zeus," and Epimenides's "Cretica," which he quotes twice. In drawing from the truths of their own mythology, Paul tells his Greco-Roman audience that when we center ourselves in Christ, we awaken to living, moving, and having our being in I AM. This awakening, as we've been sharing, has little to do with "doctrinal information" that says we are His Image, and everything to do with a sentience of it from within. The doctrinal knowledge of this has two sides, the second being rather treacherous. It can create a desire for us to sense Divine reality from within and live from Divine Life. But it can also empower us egoistically to assume we're God's Image and what we think and do is approved and ordained by God. The first requires us to awaken to selfless Love and humility, expressed through *Compassion.* The second is a self-feeding delusion in doing what's right and feeling special because of it. It's then spiced with the illusion that we must win others to do the same so they too will be right and special like us. Therefore, we're right back where it all started, where the real choice is between the two Trees. Thus, the forthcoming question, "How do we awaken?"

First, let's make something clear: Our past religious or spiritual experiences are all part of the process, even the bad ones. Therefore, spirituality is a journey and not necessarily a destination. It's a letting go of the past and embracing the present as fresh and new, which opens a path to the future. Despite all the seemingly negative attributes egoism brings by living in a physical body, the body does offer an opportunity. In the spiritual world, the qualities of Light and Dark, Life and Death, Love and Selfishness, cannot dwell in the same place. However, in the physical world, both can meet face-to-face. As Jesus is quoted saying:

"Sacrifice and offering You did not desire, but a body
You have prepared for Me. ...to do your will, O God,"
(Hebrews 10:5-7/NKJV).

The hidden blessing within the physical world is that we can change focus from Darkness to Light, from Selfishness to Love, and Death to Life (Acts 26:18). In our physical state of affairs, most of us have difficulty focusing on any particular thought for a minimal amount of time, unless our ego is obsessed with it, through either fear or passion. Hence, we think, "If I can just change my thoughts from negative to positive, life will be much better." True, but changing one's thought-life requires first a change of inner focus. Egoistic thoughts and feelings, or to say it another way, desires we have, will only change from either bad to good, or good to bad, and the like. The inner focus and transmigration we are speaking of is unveiling the Tree of Life, our true nature in I AM. This is not just changing our thoughts from good or bad, or vice versa, but changing how we see reality.

For example, in the spiritual world there are a minimum of four key dimensions, or worlds, that our souls live in simultaneously beyond the physical. In the New Testament, the Apostle Paul speaks of the egoistic, or dark-side, of those worlds, in Ephesians 6:12: ἀρχάς (archas) *principalities* (the archons of the goddess Sophia, which we will discuss in Chapter 15), ἐξουσίας (exousias) *powers* (granted rights and privileges by court decree or law), κοσμοκράτορας τοῦ σκότους τούτου (kosmokratoras tou skotous toutou) *system-rulers of darkness of that power, referring to*

357

the previous realm and powers (a rare word used to define the controlling gods and goddesses as depicted in astrology; the planets and constellations in the darkness of the night), and their **πνευματικὰ τῆς πονηρίας ἐν τοῖς ἐπουρανίοις** (pneumatika tes ponerias en tois epouranios) *forces that stir the malice of the base nature from the heavens* (as believed by the Greco-Roman world, the gods and goddesses beyond the sky stir the nature of man to war and passion). Paul uses the language and mythology of the Ephesian people to explain how the base nature, the Serpentine-Ego, is really the controlling power depicted in the forces, rules, and laws decreed in the heavenly courts of the gods like Jupiter, Mars, and Vulcan of Rome (also known as Zeus, Ares, and Hephaestus of Greece).

It's interesting how we in Western Evangelical Christianity created a massive theology regarding "spiritual warfare" based on the Ephesian verses and a few others, while being unaware of how and why those descriptions exist apart from their Christ-centered counterpart. Those same verses, which seemingly suggest we war with an external spiritual enemy, eventually give way for us to war against, torture, and murder fellow human beings we've deemed threats because of their beliefs. Historically, this is evident both before and after Constantine conquered Rome. He claimed "...that about noon, when the day was already beginning to decline, he saw with his own eyes the trophy of a cross of light in the heavens, above the sun, and bearing the inscription, CONQUER BY THIS." Literally, "in hoc signo vinces," meaning, *in this sign thou shalt conquer.* This event supposedly took place on the

Milvian Bridge in 312 AD, according to Eusebius of Caesarea, as quoted. For a short season, Rome maintained its liberty for other religious systems to exist, except for the Jews, which was immediate: "Let us have nothing in common with the detestable Jewish crowd; for we have received from our Savior a different way..." and later with inclusions for the death penalty when necessary. (A segment of Constantine's edict from 325 AD. Sound familiar?) When one reads the edicts of Constantine from 325 AD after the Council of Nicaea, of Constantius of 339 AD, and of Theodosius of 439 AD, we see the notion of combating a "spiritual evil" morph into physical violence and persecution. Eventually, any non-Romanized Christian would have the same potential of torture and death because they were a possible threat to the "Christian State." By the 1400s, a famous document would be published by the Church, "Malleus Maleficarum" (The Witches' Hammer). It was used to torture and murder non-believers, and so-called Christians, who were judged as witches or as having some other demonic influence or disobedience to the Roman Church. It gave the Church the right to do these things in the name of Christ. Based on a sham religious trial, if deemed that a confession of some sin or evil was necessary, the laws of the Maleficarum were executed. This is just another reason why it's essential that through humility and compassion we awaken to the reality of the I AM, Christ within us, abiding in the Eternal Now. When we haven't awakened to our true identity, it's inevitable that our egoism will give rise to some form of Christian Nationalism in the name of fighting a demonic enemy. Which means that whatever relationship we thought we had with Christ has degenerated into the very "evils" it proclaimed should be eradicated. Of course, this will be done through our illusion of, "It's for the good of society and the faith." Hence, the demonic "rulers of darkness" are not external, unseen spiritual ones, but ones we've internally degenerated into. We've become the princes (the archons), the authorities of rights and wrongs, the dark system rulers, the stirrers of malice in both ourselves and in those deemed as the enemy, all done in the name of Christ in Heaven.

We've been taught and assumed that the Ephesians list was Paul disseminating a new revelatory theological description of our battle with the external demonic forces of Satan, which is not at all the case. Paul is expressing the known beliefs in the Greco-Roman world and expanding their mythological frame by putting them in a Christ-centered context. The list of the four barriers Paul mentions, in Hebraic thought, are called "veils of Light," hence *rulers of darkness.* Consider the veil of the Temple, the barrier between the inner court and the Divine Presence, with its כרבים (keruvyim), meaning *cherubim,* literally *imaginary figures* woven into them; in other words, the arrogant imaginations and thoughts of the mind (Luke 1:51; Ephesians 4:18). The denser, or thicker the Serpentine-Ego, the more obscure the reality of the I AM, the essence of Divine Love, Life, and *Light.* In Hebraic thinking, those worlds exist because of the veils. However, the barriers are not the focus but the upper worlds themselves. When we refocus our inner origins, the veils are removed progressively. Described in the Old Testament, beyond the מחסום (machsom), *the physical barrier,* which is also translated *muzzel* or *bridle* (Psalms 39:1), are the worlds of עשיה (asiyah) *action,* יצירה (yetzirah) *formation,* בריאה (briyah) *creation,* and finally, אצילות (atzilut) *absolute* or *nearness.* (These dynamics are spoken of in Isaiah 45, Ezekiel 1 & 10, Amos 4, as well as other areas.) The reason the word מחסום (machsom) *barrier* is also translated as *muzzle* or *bridle,* is because our false egoistic-self muzzles our true identity, or as the Greek in Ephesians states, σκότους (skotos), obscures it. In the same manner, our egoistic desires lead us about as if we wear a horse's bridle, which Ephesians describes as πνευματικὰ (pneumatika), forces that control. We think we're making choices out of free will, but being that we're still unconsciously *"ruled by the dark system,"* the Tree of the Knowledge of Good and Evil, our choices are nothing more than an egoistic calculation led by our bridle. When we live below the מחסום (machsom), the I AM within us is concealed. More emphatically, it's crucified as we sleep, veiling our true selves and led by the *Desire to Receive for Ourselves Alone.* This is an excellent depiction of the Greco-Roman god and goddess system, as well as "the veiled" Old Testament references to יהוה. They all behave more like egoistic humanity with their rules and laws, responding with unrestrained passion when violated, using their superpowers. Back in those days, when we'd just run someone through with a sword or take an army to war with spears and shields, we believed those principalities and powers, the gods, erupted volcanos, blew up mountains, destroyed lands, and caused tsunamis. Now consider what we said earlier. We've degenerated into *the rulers of darkness and* have accomplished what our Satanic Egos desired. We've ascended our thrones to the heavens and become the gods and goddesses of this world. Now WE have the power to kill, by blowing up mountains, destroying lands, causing tsunamis, and worse! Worse? Yes, not only in the measure of destruction to humanity, but that we do it in the name of tyranny and domination, or to advance and protect a belief in national Christian freedom. (Selah, pause for a moment and reflect.) However, when we ascend past the barrier and start to awake, everything begins to change.

To explain how we live in these four spiritual worlds, let's say we're going to pick up a glass of water and drink. Before we ever physically pick up the glass, we perform the עשיה (asiyah) *action* in our mind. This is the place we commonly experience our stream of thoughts and feelings. However, before we can perceive any action, it first must be יצירה (yetzirah) *formed*. To form a thought in a cognizant manner, it must be בריאה (briyah) *created*. We can probably grasp the idea of creating, forming, and visualizing an action in our mind before we do it, though this process seems to take place in milliseconds. This is not unknown to us, though utilizing the Hebrew and Greek phrases from the Old and New Testament makes it sound quite mystical. In one sense, it truly is, yet this is how Creation functions from the unseen to the seen, from the inner world to the perceived world around us. The world of sports has been aware of these realities and utilized them for a long time. Many great athletes use a type of meditative technique, creating, forming, and visualizing their actions to achieve their goals. Nonetheless, when we speak of being the Image and Likeness of God, it moves us into another arena of awareness. We may be able to fathom that our physical deeds are first actions in the mind and, before they appear as such, they're formed and created. However, beyond forming and creating, our inner veil seems to hang, dense and fortified. It's at that *barrier* where we seem to have little to no comprehension of what lies beyond its boarder, or from where and what "force" gives us the power to create our thoughts. Is the upper reality concealed from us because we're veiled with the knowledge of good and evil, right and wrong, pain and pleasure? Are our thoughts created from *the World Below,* from the Serpentine-Ego? Or are our thoughts created from the world of אצילות (atzilut), *absolute* or *nearness,* where the Father of Creation, the I AM dwells, emanating Christ? To assume the latter can be an indication of our inner serpent tightening its grip. However, with true humility and honest self-exploration, we can answer the question. Keep in mind, the goal of the Ego was to *"exalt itself above the Most High."* Thus, the world of the knowledge of good and evil becomes the god that rules, even though wearing a Jesus T-shirt and having a Bible in hand. This is why it's not only difficult to comprehend the realm of Life, but it's assumed that because we've done reasonable time in intense study, and in charismatic circles speak in tongues and prophesy, we must be aware of the world of אצילות (atzilut) *absolute* or *nearness.* But, as Jesus has shared with us over and over in both parable and straight talk, plus exemplified by His life, death, and resurrection, it's not the case. We simply have moved the sliding scale within the illusion of the Tree of the

Knowledge of Good and Evil, from what we as "sinners" once considered good to evil, and to what our religion, including Christendom, has now deemed right or wrong. In some cases, they become a direct flip.

It's virtually impossible to change our thoughts and feelings to emanate the mind of Christ if we haven't awakened to the source of their origins. Returning to the first chapter of this book, and the first chapter of Volume 1, "Exploring a Mystery," there are some clear realities of the Melchizedekian priesthood that send our Serpentine-Egos of *the World Below* into a panic. Consider the Mind of Christ:

> There are no commandments of good and evil, right and wrong.
> There are no special people ordained as priests.
> There are no natural lineages for their priesthood.
> There are no temple buildings.
> There are no blood sacrifices.
> There isn't a consciousness of sin.
>
> There is a Life of Love.
> There is an awareness of Oneness.
> There is a sentience of the Eternal.
> There is a realization of Christ in All.
> There is only the sacrifice of self.
> There is a consciousness of righteousness and peace; the Eternal Now.

Without piercing the מחסום (machsom), the barrier, the inner Egoistic veil, and tasting the world of אצילות (atzilut) *absolute* or *nearness,* the Mind of Christ, the first six items on the list would begin with the phrase "There must be..." The second set of six would then be redefined completely as conditional based on obedience of the first set of six. The question arises, how does one migrate from living in the illusion of the "first list" as "There must be..." as being real, with its commandments, right and wrong, consciousness of sin, and so on, to that same list being non-existent, and reality found in the second as a state of being and not a result of legalistic obedience? In other words, how do we migrate from *the World Below* to *the World Above?* Or how do we loosen the constricting grip of the Serpentine-Ego, and embrace the Mind of Christ? As we said earlier, this is a process of awakening as we journey through this life and becoming aware of the inner signposts when they occur. It's more like sitting in a dark room as the sun rises with its light shining through the window, rather than groping in the dark, searching for a light switch. There really isn't much of a "how," except a path and process of unveiling. Some may call this unveiling "revelation," which would be correct. Yet we mustn't confuse new information with revelation. When new information comes to our minds and hearts, it adds to our perception, which is great! When revelation comes, it doesn't add, it transforms the entire landscape. It doesn't add to our existing perception, rather it unveils reality beyond it, offering us a panoscopic view. When a sincere person humbly asks to see, which is a true prayer, it may very well be that a phase of awakening is upon them. You could say it's when the question transforms from, "How do I find the path?" to, "Unveil who I Am, I'll follow that path wherever it leads."

An entry exercise I use while teaching a beginner's prayer and meditation class is to first address the reality that we are often not as in control of our thoughts as we would like to believe. I have the attendees close their eyes and picture in their minds the first letter of the alphabet, "A", for 30 seconds without deviating. I tell them, "Just concentrate on the letter, see it in your mind, and don't allow other thoughts to overpower or alter it." Almost every time we do this, I shorten the focus time to 20 seconds without telling them. When the time is up, I ask if they were successful. Most everyone says they had different thoughts stream through their mind. Some have said things like, "After a few moments, the thought crossed my mind that I need to go to the grocery store for milk on the way home." Others have said, "As I concentrated, my letter started growing flowers, and would fade in and out with pretty designs." Some have said (with a subtle, lofty smile) that they were successful, and were able to focus on the letter, but it was hard. Then they realized that while they were focusing, they were thinking that "this is hard," which was as much an extraneous thought as those who realized they needed to go to the store on the way home or made pretty designs. Finally, there's a nervous chuckle when I tell them we didn't endure for the full 30 seconds, and that I shortened the time to 20. The key point is, what about those of us who believe we hear from God, or prophesy, or have a thought about a Bible verse believed to be inspired by the Holy Spirit? To begin with, sure, we can hear from God, or prophesy, or have a Holy Spirit inspired thought. However, how many of those inspired thoughts have extraneous thoughts and ideas added to them? Or how many of those inspired thoughts have subtractions because we cannot perceive them or we even reject them because they don't fit "our theology?"

The point of the exercise isn't only to show that we may add or subtract what we perceive is from God, but also to show that we constantly experience a torrent of thoughts. Many times, we suppose that "what we think" is who we are, in other words, our identity. We've been taught to believe that the stream of thoughts and feelings we have, are us. One might remember the famous statement by Descartes, "Cogito, ergo sum," meaning, "I think, therefore I am." This is a limited, egoistic view of oneself. If we were to understand how we were created, it's almost the inverse, "I AM, therefore I choose to think and what I think." The very fact that we can *observe* our thoughts and feelings tells us we are distinct from them. Consider, in truth, we can observe and *evaluate* both. This is where we can begin penetrating "the veils of Light." As we do, we begin to discover our true self apart from them, recognizing who we are, the Likeness of God. Think about this, before the Creator thought, *"Light Be,"* He still existed. The same is true regarding us. Before, during, and after any thought or feeling, our true self exists. For that matter, just saying, "think about this," puts us in a position to create and focus our thoughts by choice. Again, we are not our thoughts. However, because we energize them, we give them life, our thoughts become an animation of us in the spiritual world. Similar to the baseball pitcher or cricket bowler, we are not the ball but we give it animation, a type of life, when we throw it. Depending upon the intention of how the ball is thrown, it fulfills its purpose and accomplishes what it was sent out to do. Sound familiar?

> *"So is my word that goes out from my mouth: it will not return to me empty, but will accomplish what I desire and achieve the purpose for which I sent it."*
> *(Isaiah 55:11/NIV)*

Even when we exist from the egoistic *World Below*, we unconsciously function as the Image and Likeness of God and give the Ego an existence it doesn't have on its own. Remember the Tower of Babel? *"...nothing they plan to do will be impossible for them" (Genesis 11:6/NIV)*. Like throwing a ball, the same is true with our thoughts. The challenge is, because so many times we assume our thoughts are us, we don't ascend in our consciousness and see ourselves from *the World Above*. We simply yield to whatever sticks to us from the egoistic torrent. Thus, the Ego, the base nature, points to our thoughts with all the calculations mentioned previously and defines us. From this comes an egoistic façade personality, tethering us to certain religious and political views, as well as relationships that will feed the façade. This is why we watch cable news channels that confirm our bias, feeding our façade world view, using bits and pieces of fact to validate our illusion. As the story of the Tower of Babel continued, we found that because everyone "spoke the same language" they were able to unite in thought and create their egoistic edifice. The same is true with us in this very moment.

First, whether we are conscious of it or not, we are one, and we seek out others who are of a similar mind within our system of right and wrong, good and evil. Together we make tribes, towns, cities, countries, wars, religions, philosophies, cures, pleasures, and so on. Many times, the torrent of thoughts that stream through our mind are energized from the community we're egoistically connected to, whether large or small. These are in different levels and different strengths, hence the veils of Light. If we consider the power of media today in all its forms, we have done no differently than what the Babylonians did. We've once again used the power of our collective thoughts to figure out how to connect our language. Now it's binary, so we build towers, some of brick and concrete, others in the cyber world, even with its own crypto currency. Simultaneously, depending upon how we perceive reality, this is also a wonderful opportunity. We have additional tools to participate in rebuilding the Divine Vessel, the Body of Christ, on a global level. In one respect, with this unity we can manifest the Limitless Christ through the multiple dynamics of media in both the physical and cyber world (Matthew 18:20). Nonetheless, with this global network, the alternative also remains; we can unite, strengthen our egos, and veil Christ's Light. Once again, we are between the two Trees with a choice!

Second, consider that there's only ONE true reality: the one the Creator made. As the central part of that Creation, we were given by God's design the ability to define it (Genesis 2:19-20). We are co-creators with God. He would create life and we would define it. When we chose the Tree of the Knowledge of

Good and Evil, and transformed our *Desire to Receive and Reflect* to *the Desire to Receive for Ourselves Alone,* the Serpentine-Ego, we redefined the aspect of Creation that we had authority over. We know that God is Light (1 John 1:5), and such Light embodies Love and Life with all their definable attributes. So herein is how our egoistic veil functions, redefining and utilizing the Divine Light, Love, and Life He emanates. Both Old and New Testament writers understood that Darkness is nothing more than the absence of Light. The absence of Love isn't hate, but the sensation of being Alone (or Loneliness, Matthew 8:12, by Hebrew definition, אבדון *Abaddon,* Revelation 9:11, from the root אבד *abad* meaning, *to be alone* or *lose one's self).* We could say, that because God is Love, as His Image and Likeness, so are we. However, when we express ourselves from *the World Below,* we veil Divine Love and function as if we're alone. In our self-imposed aloneness, we pursue our desires for selfish pleasure. We wander around in our darkness claiming that we see, like a good Pharisee (John 9:41). Jesus asked a leading question, *"Do you bring in a lamp to put it under a bowl or a bed?" (Mark 4:21/NIV).* While the answer may seem obvious, He was pointing out that we do this with our Divine attributes repeatedly. We have this amazing lamp within us, yet we veil it. In light of our discussion regarding being unconscious or asleep, it's significant that He says, *"Do you bring in a lamp to put it under a...bed?"* Besides the fact that if we put a candle under a bed, we could potentially burn down the entire house, the implication is of us being "asleep in the light," which is exactly the point. I guess we could say that by veiling Divine Love, we did burn down the house, and here we are! If one believes in a fiery Hell, it wasn't God that lit the match, it was us (James 3:6).

Lastly, the absence of Life isn't death, as in a dead body, or non-existence, but Death as an existence in the egoistic, self-centered knowledge of good and evil (Genesis 2:17). In the figures of the two Trees planted in the Garden, both are in its soil, receiving nourishment. The issue illustrated is the difference in how each receives that nourishment, and utilizes the Life force provided. In simple terms, the Tree of Life is a transparent reflection and emanation of what it perpetually receives, thus it emanates Eternal Life. The Tree of the Knowledge of Good and Evil, in its current form, also perpetually receives that same Life force, but redefines it into selfish desire (Ezekiel 31:7-10), thus it's forever unsatisfied. Like in this example of the Trees, we are also constant recipients of the Life, Love, and Light of God. Such realities are constantly issuing forth to us, nothing is withheld from any one of us at any point. As tree-like recipients, we're nourished by the perpetual emanation of the Life of God. The issue is, how do we define it?

This brings us to the third point. God has designed us to experience Divine Light, Life, and Love, which is another way of saying the "pleasure" of His Likeness. When we reflect those same attributes, creation around us also experiences the pleasure of Divinity. Here is an example: Let's say we just found the love of our life. Being with that person is such a pleasure, it's amazing. It's not what they do or say, but who they are, and the beauty of their presence in our life. We want to kiss, caress, and serve them because we love them. Our pleasure is in pleasing them. The beauty of this kind of love is that we receive pleasure because we give it. This is a type of receiving and reflecting Divine Love. Please note, it was never said that they made us feel good because they had to do something. Rather, the pleasure we receive is in pleasing them. You could say that the only thing they're requested to do is to receive. It's even more spectacular when they feel the same way and there's a wonderful exchange of mutual giving and receiving pleasure. This is what many call "making love," and it is! Yet, it's not limited to physical contact alone, but in sharing Life together. But what happens when we enter into a relationship with the notion of the pleasure a person can give us? Many times, we call this falling in love as well. However, it's more so the idea that we're in love with the desire of experiencing pleasure from a person, whatever that may be. In some cases, by extension, we can call this lust. Perceive this, the pleasure we desire is the Love, Life, and Light of God, which is the "pleasure of His Likeness." Every pleasure we experience, whether it's food, sex, music, poetry, and so on, is rooted in the Life of God. The inner sensation of pleasure isn't so much about what wrapping the pleasure comes in, it's the awareness of pleasure itself. Thus, God says to us regarding Eden עֵדֶן (Pleasure), *"You may freely eat from every tree in the Garden..." (Genesis 2:16).* In other words, God is telling us to enjoy all the pleasure the Garden has to offer, in all the forms it takes. However, if we eat of the Serpentine Tree of the Knowledge of Good and Evil, it will change how we experience pleasure.

In continuing with our example: No sooner are we in a relationship with the supposed love of our life than we begin complaining that they're not meeting our needs. We may complain that we don't feel as loved as we should, that we feel distant or alone, and the relationship is too one-sided. What's happening? Believe it or not, we are still receiving the Light, Love, and Life of God in that moment, but we are redefining it egoistically and using it. Because we've veiled the Divine Nature within us, we interpret pleasure from a sense of selfishness. Now we find pleasure in complaining. In the perceived agony of our lovelessness, we accuse the other for not meeting our needs. This animates our ego to stronger levels, and we pleasure ourselves with self-centered love. "They're so wrong! I'm so right!" Think of it, cursing, conflict, anger, malice, even murder and the like, all become pleasures (Galatians 5:19-21). For that matter, when we do such, even killing, in the name of a "righteous" cause, the selfish pleasure is compounded. Think of the insanity of this statement from a Christ-centered, Divine Love, Light, and Life view. "As patriots, we killed them for a righteous cause. We won the war, the enemy was annihilated, God was with us!" (This is another one of those Selah moments.) We take pleasure from the egoistic wrapping of good and evil. If we don't receive "the good" we selfishly desire or if we feel threatened that we'll lose a pleasure we have, we then accuse, judge, condemn, and sentence the other. We *take* pleasure from all that effort, yet it's only a fleeting satisfaction. Before you know it, the relationship is in serious trouble; it's dying. How many times is the catalyst for the death of a relationship our egoistic need to be right, get our own way, and for the other to comply? In some cases, our behavior may coerce our partner to comply, possibly through fear or some sense of obligation, and we, reveling in our win, are clueless that there's a real problem. Of course, when we come home and find they left us, we are stunned. "We had a great relationship! How could there be a problem?" We've created a world system of knowing, simply put, of judging what's good and evil based on our assessment of the pleasure we receive in the moment. (This is not to say that we should allow ourselves to be abused or be in harmful relationships. But many times we may not realize that we are also causing the affliction.)

With each experience we receive the Light, Life, and Love that God emanates in the נא (na) *Eternal Now*. However, when we veil the נא (na) *Eternal Now* by redefining it to animate our self-centered desires, those redefining evaluations become the rulers of our darkness. On the other hand, when we penetrate the veils, dismantling the rulers of our darkness through *Compassion,* in that moment we embrace our Divine identity. We too, emanating Image and Likeness, receive pleasure by giving it. Thus, we reveal our I-AM-ness and Oneness. In that state, we've passed the rulers of the darkness, who Moses calls in Genesis Chapter 3, the כרבים (keruvyim), *cherubim,* the *imaginary figures* and the flaming dagger which goes back and forth (literally להט החרב המתהפכת, [lahat hᵃherev hᵃmit'hapahet] *the fiery enchantment of a dry sharp wasteland that changes form])* (Genesis 3:24). These egoistic imaginations that we create mutate and veil our perception of the Tree of Life. However, they are just an imagination in a form we create. Another way of saying this would be that they're just thoughts, validated by self-centered feelings, and not who we really are. Thus, we can walk through the fiery enchantment and not be burned (Isaiah 43:2). We can simply walk past them and enter Life. God is nurturing us from all forms of Eden's pleasures for our enjoyment. He wants us to experience them *consciously.* In our physical bodies, it doesn't mean that when we pass our egoistic imaginations we will be unaware of our *Desire to Receive for Ourselves Alone,* but we will have elevated that *Desire to Receive* to its Life-giving place, one that *Reflects and Gives.* In other words, when we are lifted up and live from *Above,* even though we may have egoistic desires and thoughts, we need not be condemned by them nor defined by them. The Apostle Paul was clear:

> *"But now it is no longer 'the real me' doing it, but the sin housed inside me."*   (Romans 7:17/CJB)

We can be cognizant of our true self in Christ, realizing that egoistic desires are just part of the journey, and even learn from them. Here's a simple meditative exercise that we can do, which can help us refocus and be נָא (na) *Eternal Now* centered:

Before you begin, it would be a good idea to get an alarm clock or timer that has the option to play music or nature sounds, rather than just a noisy buzzer or bell. This way when your time of meditation is concluded you're not startled, just gently nudged to finish. Set it for about 20 minutes so you can relax and not break your concentration by checking the clock. Take several minutes to get into a quiet, comfortable sitting position. Make up your mind that you're not going to move for the duration of the set time. Even if you feel like you need to scratch an itch, it will pass. Focus on your breathing. If extraneous thoughts enter your mind, don't concern yourself with them, gently push them aside; you haven't failed, it's just part of the process. The more you practice, the easier it will be to focus. From your breathing, move your focus to your head and do the same. Follow it by sensing your closed eyes, ears, nose, and mouth. When you've become very aware of them, travel down to your neck and shoulders. Once totally aware of them, travel to your favored arm and once aware of it, travel to the other arm. Then do the same with your chest and torso. Once fully aware of them, focus on your groin and buttocks. Then move on to one leg and then the other. Finally, concentrate on your feet in the same manner. Once fully aware of them, focus on every area of your body all at once, including your breathing. Try to sense your total body as one. Stay in that state of focus and concentration for the remainder of the time. If at any point you reduce focus or other thoughts move in, don't be concerned about them, it's normal. Continue to gently push them aside and return to concentrating on your body. You may ask, why concentrate on breathing and the vibrance of the body if the egoistic flesh is the thing that causes all the problems? Because, as stated earlier, there's a unique aspect of being in the body where we can change where we emanate our existence from *Below* to *Above*. When was the last time you consciously told your lungs to breathe, or your heart to beat, or your limbs to feel? You haven't. This is all done at a deeper, subconscious level, where the force of

Life animates the body. By focusing on what emanates from that deeper level, we can discover the place where the upper worlds of בריאה (briyah), *creation,* and אצילות (atzilut), *absolute* or *nearness,* meet. Remember, most of us grasp the notion of creating, forming, and seeing an action in our minds before we do it physically. However, perceiving beyond the realm of בריאה (briyah) *creation,* where our thoughts are created, is difficult because beyond it is the realm of Eternal Life. Most of the time we stay descended below the מחסום (machsom), *the barrier,* and allow our thoughts to be egoistically created. Doing this meditative exercise helps us become aware of that deeper subconscious place and move that awareness to a place of consciousness. This helps us be "present" in the נא (na) *Eternal Now,* the I AM. While doing this in a quiet place is very helpful, once we begin to sense that reality, we'll sense it anywhere—standing in line, riding on a train, and so on. It helps silence our inner noise of thoughts and feelings, regardless of the noise in the external world. Another phrase for this is יהוה שלום (Yahweh Shalom) *Yahweh is Peace* (Judges 6:24; 2 Thessalonians 3:16).

After doing the previous exercise for a week or so, try the next one: Start again by getting into a quiet, comfortable sitting position. Focus on your breathing till you become totally aware of it. This time, rather than thinking of the body, see yourself in a lovely field with a small, quaint house off in the distance. See it all as clearly as possible. Walk toward the house, then up the three steps to the porch and open the door. You will find there are three rooms in succession. The first room you step into is brightly lit with nothing in it except a mirror on the wall to your right. Stop and look at your reflection in the mirror. Observe how you look physically. Don't be critical of your appearance, just observe it from every aspect and take it in. Once you've fully gotten the picture, turn to your left and open the door to the next room. It's identical to the previous room, but it's somewhat darker. Look into the mirror on your right, but this time, observe your personality with all its attributes: your gifts and talents, your strengths and weaknesses, and so on. Don't be critical of what you see, just grasp what's there and take it in. Once you've done that, turn to your left and open the third and final door. Upon entering this room, you notice it's very dark, yet when you turn to the right and look toward the mirror, you sense the presence of God as you see your deeper, inner self. As you look, see with the eyes of Christ. Sense what you see through His eyes. Allow yourself to hear His thoughts of who you are and see yourself as He sees you. Take it all in, let it saturate you. When you sense that you've experienced all you can for this time, return to the previous room. As you enter the room where you viewed your personality, take an extra moment and embrace the Christ-centered awareness you just experienced. Turn to the mirror and observe yourself like before, but now with the added Christ-centered view. Once you've embraced it, turn, and open the door and enter the room where you started. Look in the mirror, view your physical self, but again with the added Christ-centered view. Once you've embraced it, open the door and leave the house, stepping into the lovely field. When in the field, focus on your breathing for a short while, then open your eyes.

The purpose of this meditation is to help us see with the Mind of Christ, the I AM, from within us. It's to help focus ourselves to sense that reality, *the World Above,* as we journey through our day. In many cases, I have found people's experience in the third room to vary from just being in awe, to perceiving God's love and acceptance in ways not grasped before. The point is, each time we practice going to that inner, Eternal place, we become more aware of the Kingdom Above on a moment-by-moment, "present sense" basis, a **נָא** (na) *Now* basis. Consequently, we no longer just live from the streaming thoughts and feelings we've known from our experience or allow into our mind from external sources. We're no longer just living in the past or wishing for the future. We're no longer evaluating a situation based on an egoistic sense of pain or pleasure. Rather, we are learning to embrace thoughts that emanate from the Mind of Christ, the I AM. Even time as we once experienced it transforms from something we travel through into a timeless reality of presence in God.

In light of the meditations and becoming aware of the I AM, consider Jesus's words to His disciples:

> *"Then he came to the disciples and found them sleeping; and he said to Peter, 'So, could you not stay awake with me one hour? Stay awake and pray that you may not come into the time of trial; the spirit indeed is willing, but the flesh is weak.'"*
>
> *(Matthew 26:40-41/NRSV)*

In the past, many of us have read this to mean that Jesus went off to pray, wanting his disciples to pray with him, but they fell asleep instead. Then, apparently frustrated, Jesus tells them that though the spirit is willing to pray, the flesh is too weak. We've been talking all along about being awake to the reality of Christ, the I AM. As we look at this section further, we find it really isn't about prayer as much as it's about *staying awake.* Putting this in the context of what we've been discussing, as Jesus entered the realm of prayer, the נא (na) the *Eternal Now,* His disciples fell asleep. Or, one could say, they weren't conscious enough to enter that realm with Him. While prayer is good, many of us still have a sense that we pray to a God distinct, and at times distant, from us. After what we just discussed, prayer is no longer about us trying to reach out to God, but reaching within.

Sometimes, in order to give ourselves a sense of closeness to God, we call Him Dad, Papa, or another term of endearment. Maybe we drop "the" from the phrase "the Holy Spirit" to make the connection more personable. While this is not at all wrong, and maybe even helpful to a degree, it doesn't necessarily mean we've awakened. When we're fully conscious, *staying awake,* we're not just close to God, or even aware of Him within, but we're an expression, an emergence of God. When we start to awaken, we realize He doesn't have thoughts about our situation that we need to figure out, but His thoughts are our thoughts. Rather, in our consciousness of being an emanation of God, we surface His Thoughts and Nature. It's about *being* in a state where Jesus says:

> *"...I tell you, the Son can do nothing from himself,
> except what he sees the Father doing; for whatever
> things that one does, these same things the Son
> likewise also does."'*   *(John 5:19/DBH)*

Notice the phrase, *"...the Son can do nothing FROM himself..."*
Most translations say, "...of himself..." but *from* is more
emphatic to the text. This is about being awakened to the
reality of *"I and the Father are One"* (John 10:30). This is living
from the deep inner-self where the Kingdom of God abides,
the realm of *Above,* the I AM. King Solomon said that *the spirit
of a man* will sustain, or nurture him, even in sickness
(Proverbs 18:14). Jesus was telling His disciples that when we
sleep, we're unconscious, our egoistic self prevails. Thus, self-
centeredness and trying to exist from a good and evil, pain and
pleasure sense of reality, is too weak to sustain us. It really
doesn't matter if, to quote Dickens, it's "the best of times" or
"the worst of times." When we're conscious, when we're
awake from the Death Sleep, we're sustained, producing as
the Tree of Life (Proverbs 11:30). True prayer, as one rabbi
said, "Is when your dialogue becomes a monologue." In other
words, we're hearing and seeing Christ in thought and action,
as ONE. When we've awakened to the present, the *Eternal
Now,* we see, hear, and do, because our thoughts are *created,*
emanating from the world of I AM. This is the place where
mountains are moved, hills are leveled, and valleys are filled
(Isaiah 40:4; Mark 11:23).We're no longer just wielding some
spiritual gift or superpower when a perceived obstacle is in
the way. It's no longer about making declarations or making a
command in Jesus's name. No, it's first seeing reality from a

completely different dimension. This is where we awaken to see with our real eyes, living from the reality of **אצילות** (atzilut), *absolute* or *nearness*. As Ezekiel puts it:

> *"And the Spirit lifted me up and brought me into the inner court; and behold, the glory of the Lord filled the house. Then I heard one speaking to me from the house, while a man was standing beside me.* **היה עמד אצלי:** *(haya omeed etzliy)"*
>
> *(Ezekiel 43:5-6/NASU)*

The last phrase can be translated, *"Ya standing joined to me."* The word **אצלי** (etzliy), *joined,* is the singular of the similar feminine plural, **אצילות** (atzilut), *absolute.* From this place of consciousness, mountains may not be mountains, valleys may not be valleys, the obvious direction isn't the wise one, and the wise direction may take us into the heart of the storm. Living in the **נא** (na), *Divine Eternal Now* is living from our Christ-centered identity, manifesting the Nature of the Father, and emanating the reality of the Spirit, all of which is, I AM.

CHAPTER 12
I AM COMPASSION AND REDEMPTION

Parzival, weeping, asked which way the Grail lay,
saying: 'If, this day, "God's goodness shall triumph
in me this company shall know, and see!' In that
direction, he bowed the knee, three times, to honor
the glory of the Trinity, the while he prayed, that
the ills of this man be stayed..."

Parzival
Book XVI: *The Grail King*
Wolfram von Eschenbach

In the previous chapter we said that rousing to consciousness is the first real phase of resurrection. With that truth, it's only the beginning. Being conscious is connected to the most Christlike attribute, *Compassion*.

> *"Then Jesus, moved with compassion, stretched out*
> *His hand and touched him, and said to him, 'I am*
> *willing; be cleansed'."*   *(Mark 1:41/NKJV)*

The continuing development of a resurrected mind and life is primarily the awareness of, followed by the demonstration of, *Compassion.* The physical resurrection of Christ wasn't based on a display of sheer sovereign power as much as it was the result of fully realized *Compassion.* The power of God that raises the dead is the Love of God revealed. God created because He loved. God came in human form because He loved. God allowed Himself to be crucified because He loved. Thus, because of that love, He came forth from the grave. The resurrection is a culmination of *Compassion's* expression. Anything else without that reality as the central theme may be a misunderstanding.

To be the Image and Likeness of God is to be *Compassion* expressed in every form. Compassion doesn't see "the other" as a problem, or as different, or even as an object to be pitied, rather it sees an extension of itself.

John of Patmos wrote something profound in the Book of Revelation:

> *"And they sang a new song saying, 'We proclaim your excellent worth! You are the only one in the universe entitled to open the scroll and break its seals, since you were slaughtered in sacrifice and in your blood redeemed mankind's authentic identity in God...'"* (Revelation 5:9/MIRROR)

When we spoke earlier of seeing through the lens of the divergent doctrines of Penal Substitution or Vicarious

Atonement, we see God in opposition to Mankind because of sin. Of course, we redefine that thinking by saying that Mankind is in opposition to God. Such a view sees God wanting vengeance and retributive justice as payment. At the same time, it's as if God has a type of divine schizophrenic disorder, displaying moments of disconnect from that need for justice when He claims a love for His Creation. In the end, the only way to resolve the antithetical dilemma is to try and coerce a connection. So, for God to love and forgive, justice must be satisfied. Simply stated, a type of celestial justice governs whether forgiveness is implemented. Considering all we've discussed, this is an excellent description of the Serpent's Tree and not the Throne of God. Thus, the message of Christ consistently speaks quite differently, including the Book of Revelation. When Revelation is read with the same lens of those divergent doctrines, we see a refocusing of Christ's resurrection to a warlike victory over sin, waiting for a time when He'll return, bringing violent damnation on those who didn't believe. This is completely to the contrary of what is opened to us in the Book of Revelation!

Christ on the Cross isn't about Him being our substitution, nor us vicariously dying when He died. Rather, it's the ultimate demonstration of the nature of God through a human being! More so, it displays God in Christ compassionately forgiving, despite Mankind's violence, or "sin," toward Him. Keep in mind, it's Christ's violent accusers that make Jesus "the other." In the mind of God, Mankind is never "the other," regardless of how lost we seem to behave. On the other hand, in the mind of Mankind, a compassionate God is very much "the other." In many respects, such a God is so much a distant "other" that He doesn't exist. The God that demands payment for sin, or a substitutionary, vicarious sacrifice, is so much easier for us to grasp, because it's one we've created in our own image. The crucifixion wasn't God's creation. The crucifixion was the display of our choice in the Garden. When we chose the way of the Serpent, we crucified Godlikeness in our mind, hence Golgotha, the place of the skull. Despite that, it didn't change the reality in God's Mind that we were His Image and Likeness.

What Christ redeemed wasn't our salvation from eternal damnation, but the reconciliation of our true identity as the Image and Likeness of God. In the Greek text, the phrase used to describe, *"...your blood redeemed mankind's authentic identity in God..."* is **ἠγόρασας τῷ θεῷ ἐν τῷ αἵματί** (egorasas too Theoo too haimati). This is what is known as the "Sacral Manumission of Slaves," according to *The Theological Dictionary of the New Testament* by Kittle and Friedrich. This was a Delphic legal inscription that was well known at the time the Book of Revelation was written. It was a decree that a slave *could use his own currency* to purchase his own freedom. Sounds crazy, doesn't it? Think of the paradox: a slave can purchase his own freedom. However, it was possible. In the dark history of American slavery, this was done on several rare occasions. The challenge was that a slave would have to find a way to make money after working all day for his master, which meant little sleep. In addition, there was a major risk in asking a master to purchase their freedom. If the master didn't agree, there was a high probability that the slave would be treated more severely for asking. On the other hand, if the master agreed, it was the master that set the price and the slave had little choice in the matter. In the cases of young James Bradley and Samuel Johnson, two names not heard of much, they managed to be successful in purchasing their freedom a few decades prior to the American Civil War. This was late in the slave trade era, and when they purchased their freedom they had to leave the area in which they lived in order to not be confused with a runaway slave. It's difficult to imagine that once a slave purchased his freedom, he then had to have enough money to move from the area. In some cases, he had to travel hundreds and hundreds of miles to a northern state that would be a bit more accommodating. Of course, there was an added complication if he had family. Their freedom also had to be purchased, and when it came time to move, even more money was involved. This is why the practice wasn't heard of much. The amount of money involved, along with the risk, made it virtually impossible.

In light of the troubling 500-year-old Penal Substitution doctrine, it sets a similar standard as the Sacral Manumission of Slaves, but with a few deviating caveats. In this case we're slaves to sin, and there is a hefty price to be paid if we're to be forgiven and loosed from its grip. Indeed, the price is so high, we can't afford it. This is where the sacrifice of Jesus comes into the picture. The doctrine says that He "paid the price" for our forgiveness, resulting in our freedom. The first deviating caveat is the misuse of the word "forgiveness." Forgiveness cannot be bought or sold. This notion is antinomic. Forgiveness is a willful choice to release someone from any wrong or obligation. Payment is irrelevant. On the other hand, if we were to properly state the doctrine without the façade of forgiveness and say that Jesus was the payment for our freedom, then forgiveness becomes irrelevant. A life for a life. However, because of our status of sin, our life wasn't worthy enough. His ransom was more valuable because He was sinless. Bottom line, His life was worth more than ours. The reasoning continues that God provided and paid for our freedom from His own spiritual account because we couldn't afford the debt. This masquerades as God's love, but it's simply a refocusing back to the Serpent's Tree and its values. The question to be asked is, "Who's getting paid?" If it's God, then this is not at all about love, but a good, legal business transaction. From the view of the Tree of the Knowledge of Good and Evil, this makes total sense. But, to ask the question again, who required the payment? Who established the price? Why couldn't it just be forgiven? If it couldn't simply be forgiven and had to be paid, then from whose account is the payment withdrawn, and into whose account is it deposited? Think of it. If the penalty of a person's sin is $1000 and that person's father decides to pay the debt, to whom does he pay it? If their father has a bank account with $2000, and he pays their debt, his account is depleted by $1000. Where did the money go? Who received the penalty payment? In that scenario, it clearly isn't the Father, who paid from his personal account. Nor is it his child, because he or she wasn't owed the $1000, they were the ones in debt. So who is this phantom to whom the debt is owed and paid? We mask all this by saying, this is what God's love looks like, He was willing to pay their penalty at His expense. Really? But once again, to WHOM?

This non-New-Testament, non-Christ-centered logic, begs the question: Who was the master that established the price and demanded payment? Was it some external devil, living on the other side of the spiritual world in a place we named Hell, or some other dark place in the heavenlies on planet Earth? If so, why would God pay the devil? Instead, God being God, why didn't He just demand Mankind's freedom? Technically, the Israelites were slaves of Pharaoh for almost 400 years since the death of Joseph to the time of Moses. (They weren't enslaved during the first 30 years of their time in Egypt.) Yet, when the time came for their liberation, Moses didn't pay a huge sum of money or give Pharaoh some other ransom. Rather, it was clearly the opposite. God didn't see the slavery of the children of Israel to Egypt as a valid contract, obligation, or liability. Hence, with God's decree they just left! When Pharaoh came after them, there was no negotiating or brokering a transaction, the Egyptians were drowned! God has done this repeatedly when it came to some form of prison or slavery. If we approach the Bible only from a literal point of view, we still see Peter escape from jail in the example from Chapter 9. No ransom was paid, no negotiation was brokered. It was a jailbreak, and the angel was a lot like Rambo in *First Blood Part 2*. On and on we could go with example after example. The notion that a "created external devil" had to be paid because our sin gave him the power to hold us in bondage, couldn't be the case. Surely he wasn't equal in power or authority to make such a demand? Did our sin give him that much power? Was he now equal to an omnipotent God? The issue in such a doctrine isn't about power, it's about "legal rights." God had the power to set us free; He didn't have the

389

legal right without proper payment. Really? Think of all the nations, the Egyptians, Babylonians, Assyrians, Philistines, and so on, who took the children of Israel into bondage. Most of the time, it happened because of their choices. Yet, once in bondage, we don't see God sending a prophet to negotiate a payment for their freedom. When Israel had enough and called out to God, He sent a liberator into the situation with long hair, no shirt, a red bandana around his head, and freed them. While it again sounds a lot like Rambo, it could've been Samson (Judges 13:5). Nonetheless, from the Serpent's Tree point of view, we say their captivity was God's judgment for their sin. In other words, they were in debt to God, not the other nations. God used the nations to afflict them because of their sins! Wait...really? In that system, such a God has a fondness for legalities, and upholds the rules, even unknown ones like before the Commandments were engraved in stone. It didn't matter that no one knew what they were, rules are rules. Then Jesus showed up, the guy who's the incarnation of God, and despite a key "known" commandment about working on the Sabbath, He healed people on that day (Matthew 12:10). Let's not stop there, his disciples pick grain on the Sabbath right in front of Him! As an act of labor, surely that was a transgression. Yet Jesus totally ignored it (Mark 2:24).

A quick answer for some who think that way is that a sovereign justice had to be satisfied by payment for sin. Then who created the justice system and why? If we're still holding onto the notion that the devil has us in legal bondage, then we have to figure that God created the legal system which He's capitalizing on. If it was the devil that created it, then it would be no more valid than Pharaoh claiming ownership of the Israelites. Even if the devil had rules, God clearly wouldn't be obligated to follow any of them. In the last 1000 years of Christendom's doctrine of the devil, when was he ever interested in justice? "The human race is the devil's fruit tree, his own property, from which he may pick his fruit. It is a plaything of demons." (Augustine of Hippo, *The City of God*, published 426 AD). Most of these ideas about the devil came from Augustine and later Dante, which influenced Christendom, Anselm, and Calvin, which are far from the Gospel, though all would claim they took their thoughts right out of scripture. In the last millennia, Christendom's view of the devil fits well with autocrats and corrupt politicians. Basically, go rogue, break any rules for personal advantage, tell your followers it's necessary because the other guy is using them to gain influence and power. Yet, make everyone else abide by the law, even ones newly created through which his rule oppresses anyone in opposition. On the other hand, if God created the legal system, we're back to the old riddle, "Can God make a rock so big that He, Himself, can't lift it?" The answer in the Penal Substitution doctrine is, "Yes! Someone has to pay, even if it means God!"

The challenge is looking at the spiritual dynamics of Mankind's dilemma through the eyes of the Serpent's Tree. It's the fruit we ingested, and the system we entered. We've forgotten the realm of Life beyond it. It's like we're a worm living in a radish, believing the radish is our entire world. It's only when we've eaten enough of the radish that we pierce its outer skin and realize there's an entire world beyond it. The conundrum with the Good and Evil system is that, rather than an outer skin you can eat your way through, it's a dream we must awaken from. Hence, trying to understand our dilemma from within the radish, *the World Below,* the Serpentine-Ego, is futile. The result of that thinking will be some form of Penal Substitution, Vicarious Atonement, and their foundational doctrine, "Satisfaction." Penned just after the first millennia by Anselmo d'Aosta, in *Cur Deus Homo,* "Why the God Man," he asserts that our sin defrauded, or shamed, God. So Jesus was sent to die to regain God's honor through His obedience. The reason for all this being so troublesome, is that such doctrines redefine the Nature of God revealed in the Gospel. "The god" it describes is an egoistic, human-like deity who necessitates a fee for our debt, rather than an exoneration of it. This is built on the notion of that "same god" being shamed by our failure, and apparently, his ego needing to be satisfied by legalistic obedience, even to the death. Yet, in New Testament truth, *WE always had the currency,* we just didn't believe we did! Why? Because the Tree of the Knowledge of Good and Evil system requires a settling of accounts when evil is done. In that Egoistic system there's the constant necessity for legalistic balance. Hence, an eye for an eye, and a wound for a wound (Exodus 21:23; Leviticus 24:20). Consider the horrific depiction of that system revealed by God in the following verses:

> *"Show no mercy. A life must be paid for a life, an eye for an eye, a tooth for a tooth, a hand for a hand, a foot for a foot."*   *(Deuteronomy 19:21/NCV)*

The phrase, *"Show no mercy..."* ולא תחוס עינך (v'lo tahose eyneka) can be better translated, *"And have no compassion in your eye..."* what evil was *done by them,* must be *done to them.* Now listen to the stark contrast in the words of Jesus, and the Apostles Paul and Peter:

> *"You have heard that it was said, 'An eye for an eye and a tooth for a tooth.' But I tell you not to resist an evil person. But whoever slaps you on your right cheek, turn the other to him also."*
>
> *(Matthew 5:38-39/NKJV)*

> *"Make sure that nobody pays back wrong for wrong, but always try to be kind to each other and to everyone else."*
>
> *(1 Thessalonians 5:15; Romans 12:17/NIV)*

> *"...not returning evil for evil or reviling for reviling, but on the contrary blessing..."* *(1 Peter 3:9/NKJV)*

Sound like heresy? It would if you believed in the divergent doctrines we've been speaking of. The Church didn't believe in such things for the first 400 years of its existence, though there would be a few writers who would emerge and attempt such thoughts. Eventually, Augustine seemed to be a key to starting the pivot. If there is a measure of cognitive dissonance at the moment, then blame Jesus and the Apostles for the dissent. We could imply that Deuteronomy is God's Law, so God set the price and the demand for payment. But that really isn't true! In the Torah story, as we explained before, we changed the terms of the covenant from a Grant Covenant to a Vassal Covenant. It was us! When we partook of the Tree of the Knowledge of Good and Evil, we established the penal substitution, satisfaction, sacrificial system. We created the gods who demanded the sacrifices in our egoistic image. We established the laws by which the bloodlettings would be necessary to satisfy any political or religious debt. We became, or better said, *are* the devil, and for that matter, the gods and goddesses who demand satisfaction and payment! In modern times, when a murderer receives the dues of capital punishment, we call it "closure." While murder of any kind is horrific and we can call its penalty whatever we wish— closure, satisfaction, an eye for an eye, a life for a life—it's still the Serpentine System we created. While we can argue the validity of us "being in this world and such laws and penalties are necessary," it's still dramatically inappropriate to see the Father, Son, and Spirit, the Tree of Life, from that point of view. Jesus was very clear to the Pharisees, who had in their possession the "oracles of God":

> *"You are of your father the devil, and the desires of your father you want to do. He was a murderer from the beginning, and does not stand in the truth, because there is no truth in him..."*
> *(John 8:44/NKJV)*

Remember, the word *devil*, **διαβόλου** (diabolou), means, *through the fall*. When we partook of the Egoistic Tree, we united with it and we became the adversary of grace and truth. How? By expounding on the Good and Evil system with law and sacrifice. Worse yet, we left God's initial Abrahamic Covenant of Faith and refashioned it into a Vassal Covenant, converting God into *our image* with vengeance and condemnation. Remember John's words from the beginning of his Gospel, *"For the law was given by Moses, but grace and truth came by Jesus Christ,"* *(John 1:17/WSB).* The Law, when read with the Serpentine Eyes of the Tree of the Knowledge of Good and Evil, obscures the Nature of God and becomes a penal substitution, sacrificial system. It sees the Bible, the Old Testament heroes of faith, God the Father, the story of Jesus, statements in the letters of the Apostles, all through the lens of rules and injunctions based on Good and Evil, culminating in bloodlettings and sacrifices, all of which veil the grace and truth of God. There may occasionally be glimpses of what could seem like grace and truth, but they're debased with blood and murder, both redefined as worship. However, when the Torah, as well as the New Testament, is read with the Christlike Eyes of the Tree of Life, it's a whole new world revealed, *the World Above.*

Part 1: Being Compassion

The Compassion revealed through Jesus on the Cross is a revelation of what God (Father, Son, and Spirit), actually looks like. Christ crucified is not at odds with a wrathful Father, nor the Father at odds with Humanity. Nor is Christ paying off the Father, or some external Satan, for a bounty to liberate Mankind from a cavernous debt. To the contrary, **Christ on the Cross displays what the Image and Likeness of God in Humanity looks like!** In that moment, Christ redeemed, purchased back with His own blood, *at His own cost,* what the Likeness of God looks like in Mankind. From whom did He redeem it? A wrathful Father? A dark, evil spirit called Satan? No! As Jesus told His disciples privately regarding the Kingdom of God:

> *"Again, the kingdom of heaven is like a merchant looking for fine pearls. When he found one of great value, he went away and sold everything he had and bought it* **ἠγόρασεν αὐτόν** *(ēgorasen auton)."*
>
> *(Matthew 13:45-46/NIV)*

And again, in the parable of the ten virgins:

> *"Then all the virgins woke up and trimmed their lamps. The foolish ones said to the wise, 'Give us some of your oil; our lamps are going out.' No,' they replied, 'there may not be enough for both us and you. Instead, go to those who sell oil and buy some for yourselves* **ἀγοράσατε ἑαυταῖς** *(agorasate heautais).'"*
>
> *(Matthew 25:7-9/NIV)*

In these parables, Jesus uses the same word for *redeem* as in Revelation 5:9, but notice the context. As the word describes, we see the manumission of slavery, and the slave using *his own currency* for freedom with God overseeing the transaction. For the one who "found the Kingdom," it was likened to one who "found a pearl of great price." He left where he was, sold (literally, exchanged) what he had, and bought the pearl with *his own money*. In other words, his portion in the Kingdom of God. It didn't say, a devil was paid-off, or a wrathful God, or some other being. Rather, *the person himself* left the world he was living in, sold, literally exchanged, all that he gained while living there, and acquired for "himself" the Kingdom of God. In other words, the person left the system of *the World Below.* He traded his false egoistic persona, along with all it gained for him, and in that moment, acquired the Kingdom of God. The man who left the system of the Serpentine-Tree, *redeemed* his portion of the Kingdom within himself.

In the parable of the ten virgins, the same word is used, but it's more emphatic. It begins with, *"Then all the virgins woke up..."* This is very similar to our example of stirring from sleep because of the dawning Light. Here we see two kinds of stirring. The first virgins arise and trim their lamps. How? It's clear by the parable's implication, they "bought for themselves" sufficient oil to stay awake in the World of the Bridegroom. The second group momentarily stir, but in effect roll over and go back to sleep. They didn't have enough "for themselves" to stay awake in the World of the Bridegroom. When they asked the first group of virgins for some oil, the wise ones responded, *"...buy some for yourselves."* Or, if we use the translation as in Revelation, *"...redeem some for yourselves."* The first group of wise virgins weren't being nasty or unwilling to share, but were letting us know how to stay conscious in the Light. Staying awake to Divine reality, the Mind of Christ, a consciousness in *the World Above,* isn't something you can simply give to another, like a book, a video, or even a Bible. This is about when the awakening occurs, humbling oneself away from *the World Below,* letting go of our fabricated beliefs about ourselves, God, and reality, and allowing ourselves to stay consistently in that mindset, or better said, "heart-set." By leaving the world of egoism, and embracing our true self through Compassion, we will always have enough oil to sustain the Divine Light. Our true nature, *the Desire to Receive and Reflect,* is the figurative oil that keeps Divine Love and Life sustained. As Jesus said, both of Himself and of those who allow themselves to be enlightened, *"You are the light of the world,"* (Matthew 5:14). No one "other than ourselves" can *redeem* what's necessary to be that. The Cross and Resurrection is God in Christ showing us the way of that redemption (Matthew 10:38; 16:24; Mark 8:34; 10:21; Luke 9:23).

An important point about awakening and arising to the Tree of Life is that preachers, teachers, and mentors can only assist a person in their awakening, they can't force or demand someone to awake. Like a nurse who helps a patient to their feet as they rise from bed, they may only assist to the level the patient can sustain standing. However, like a nurse, such preachers, teachers, and mentors need to be standing themselves before they can affectively assist another. They need to be truly conscious as well. As we've said many times now, reciting Bible verses, knowing Church history, and utilizing the gifts of the Spirit are not indications of consciousness. More readily, boundless humility and *Compassion* are. In the end, we need to *redeem* our own oil, resulting in a sustaining consciousness in the World of the Bridegroom, *the World Above,* the Kingdom of God, hence the

Tree of Life. The irony of Jesus teaching in these parables is that all the virgins had a lit lamp, and all of humanity is the Light of the World, or by extension, Creation. The issue is, are we conscious of it from a humble, compassionate, life-giving sentience? Or are we believing it from an egoistic posture, still viewing ourselves, others, God, and reality, from the Tree of the Knowledge of Good and Evil system? If it's the latter, we will find that, in the Divine economy, we have insufficient oil to keep the enlightenment, or worse, we just put it under a basket.

At the Cross and in the Resurrection, Jesus showed us how to redeem our portion of the Kingdom of God. He wasn't paying Satan, or some huge debt that roused God's vengeance. More accurately, He redeemed it from a demi-god, a ruler of Hell, an egoistic demon of sorts, made in His own Likeness, called Mankind. He restored and revealed who we were created to be, who we are in Divine reality, and in whose Image and Likeness we were fashioned. This is the *manumission* of our slavery, as truly described. While on the Cross, Jesus showed us a mirror, reflecting what we looked like in two forms. In one reflection, we see our egoistic satanic cruelty, how we're the demonic forces, the devils of torment and affliction. We see how we imposed violence upon Divine innocence, making the revelation of God in Christ our scapegoat, and finding joy in our wrath as we did. However, another greater reflection! What the non-shattered, uncompromised Likeness of God looks like in Human form. Jesus, as the Divine Image, didn't trade it to survive the crucifixion, or broker a transaction to avoid what we, the Satan, had in store for Him. He preserved

His Divine Identity, which is also the Divine paradigm of Ours. Despite the torture, beatings, a violent death, and the darkness of the grave, followed by a resurrective reemergence from it, He showed us who we are in Divine form. Jesus didn't redeem us through pagan penal substitution, or through us vicariously imagining His death as ours. He preserved our true identity, which was and is always within us. In other words, He revealed to us *that we always had the currency within* to be liberated. Just like Abraham, who believed what God said about him and it was accounted, intertwined in his thinking that He was walking the path in union with God, we too can open our inner eyes through humility and *Compassion,* cognizant of what God has said about us from the beginning. We can take that to the proverbial bank, accounting it and intertwining it with our thinking, revealing the path of the Tree of Life. No longer are there Cherubim with fiery daggers, false imaginations of moralism and sin, barring our way to Life. We've transmigrated from *the World Below* to *the World Above,* resting in the grace and truth revealed through Christ.

When we chose a world fashioned by the Tree of the Knowledge of Good and Evil, we sold our true self. We didn't sell it to an external being called Satan, but to a false self "we created." A self whom we can call, as Jesus did Peter, Satan, one who's mindful of the base nature of men. A false egoistic self that strives to be a god through the pride of knowing good and evil. A self whose failures or accomplishments ratify either our unworthy godlessness or our attainment as gods in our own eyes. This false self demands God to sacrifice Himself and pay for our unworthiness, calling it Love. Yet this same false self also demands God to simultaneously judge the sinner, coercing them through fear to accept the substitutionary sacrifice, or be condemned for a fiery eternity. On the other hand, Divine grace and truth is revealed by God through Christ in the incarnation, showing us we always had the Divine currency within us. The incarnation is an example OF US! We were always the Likeness of God. Jesus proved it through *Compassion* exemplified on the Cross, and that such *Compassion* couldn't remain in the grave, the prison system of the Knowledge of Good and Evil, hence, the Tree of Death. Rather, Christ showed us that everything we, the Satan, crucified Him over was completely undone! All the reasons why Jesus should die, politically, religiously, socially, and morally, were undone. Any of our rationalizations, personal or corporate, are all undone. Like the strong religious rationalizations personified in Caiaphas the High Priest, who attempted to preserve what was left of his nation and the illusion of freedom by condemning Jesus, all were undone. Or like in Pilate, who tried to govern by keeping the peace, trying to satisfy everyone, and giving the people what they wanted, washing his hands of the liability, saying, *"You see to it,"* all were undone. Or like in Simon of Cyrene who, through fear and complacency of all the above, carried the cross, the instrument of Christ's death, to the place of execution, all were undone. It's important to point out that in every account where Simon of Cyrene is mentioned, it says he brought the cross to *Golgotha,* the *Place of the Skull.* In other words, all these rationalizations, in their many justifications, images, and forms, have the propensity in our minds to crucify our

Divine identity as revealed in Christ. Yet, through humility and *Compassion* which passes all rationalizations, all are undone! **Christ embodied what God in Mankind looks like in life, death, and resurrection.** Hence, *it is finished!*

In the eyes of God, we always were His Image and Likeness. It was us that chose to believe something different, and that belief is what enslaved us. Consequently, the only thing that stands in our way of realizing this truth is that same delusional, egoistic belief that tells us we are not enough like God and must do the right things to attain it. God reconciled us to Himself by telling us, "You are forgiven for the crucifixion!" and "Peace to you in My resurrection." In other words, "My Compassion, displayed at the crucifixion, undoes everything that anyone did to put me there." Followed by, "My resurrection brings total peace, not vengeance for injustice." Thus, "I AM not at war with you, regardless of how you feel, or felt, about Me." The ultimate point of it all, "I AM showing you who YOU are. YOU are just like ME! You are Compassion, an incarnation of the Nature of God. You may now uncover, release yourself from the prison of the Serpentine-Tree, and live in your identity from *the World Above*. The subsequent verse in Revelation Chapter 5, where the manumission of slaves is mentioned, says:

> *"And you have made them unto God a realm of royalty to reign upon the earth as priests!"*
> *(Revelation 5:10/MIRROR)*

In other words, just like Christ Jesus, we can live from our identity in *the World Above,* while we are here in *the World Below.* From our perspective, it's God's intention that we're His Likeness. From God's perspective, it's His intention that He's the Likeness of Mankind. Christ's incarnation is the union of those intentions as ONE. We are now that Christlike incarnation, the union of those intentions. God in Man, Man in God, the Living Temple of God complete.

Part 2: But What About?

In saying these things, we often hear the questions, "What about this scripture? What about that scripture?" Well, for a few paragraphs it seemed to be a good idea before we proceed to address a few of those, *what about* moments.

> *"And are justified freely by his grace through the redemption that came by Christ Jesus. God presented him as a sacrifice of atonement, through faith in his blood. He did this to demonstrate his justice, because in his forbearance he had left the sins committed beforehand unpunished— he did it to demonstrate his justice at the present time, so as to be just and the one who justifies those who have faith in Jesus."* (Romans 3:24-26/NIV)

What about God giving Jesus as a sacrifice? The phrase, *"God presented him as a sacrifice of atonement, through faith in his blood,"* makes the point that a translation can refocus the meaning and change the context. The primary idea put forth is stated in the previous verse. It declares that we have been *"justified freely by His grace."* Please note the word *freely*, in Greek **δωρεὰν** (dorean), which means *"for nothing"* and *"without cause."* The same word in Romans, translated that we've been *justified freely by His grace,* is the same word in the following verses, for example (the bold words are for focus):

> *"Heal the sick, cleanse the lepers... **Freely** you have received, **freely** give."*   *(Matthew 10:8/NKJV)*

> *"Was it a sin for me to lower myself... by preaching the gospel of God to you **free of charge?**"*
>   *(2 Corinthians 11:7/NIV)*

> *"I will give of the fountain of the water of life **freely** to him who thirsts."*   *(Revelation 21:6/NKJV)*

The emphasis is not at all on a payment, but on something *freely* offered by His grace. It's free, as in *freely give* and *free of charge. Free* means no payment required, or with no necessary cause. One may think, "He freely offers salvation because He paid the price for it. He isn't charging us because He was charged big time!" Again, context is everything:

> *"But if our unrighteousness brings out God's righteousness more clearly, what shall we say? That God is unjust in bringing his wrath on us? (I am using a human argument.)"*   *(Romans 3:5/NIV)*

The whole notion of the "wrath of God" and Him bringing vengeance upon Mankind is a *human argument.* In other words, *it's a man-made line of reasoning!* What's to follow is a revealing of God in Christ, in contrast to that thinking. Paul was challenging the religious argument of pagan substitution and addressing that mindset. He does the same thing regarding the application of law versus faith in Romans 7:1, *"(for I speak to those who know the law), that the law has dominion over a man as long as he lives?"* Paul wasn't advocating legalism, but how Christ liberated us from that mindset as well. In both cases, Paul concludes that wrath and law go together (Romans 4:15), and that Christ brings us something completely different. The entire discussion Paul proposes in Romans is resolving the human, man-made arguments about the veiled God of Judaism and the pagan gods of the Gentiles, in contrast to Grace and Truth. He puts the caricatures of law and wrath in their proper place:

> *"What happens now to human pride of achievement? There is no more room for it. Why, because failure to keep the Law has killed it? Not at all, but because the whole matter is now on a different plane - believing instead of achieving. We see now that a man is justified before God by the fact of his faith in God's appointed Savior and not by what he has managed to achieve under the Law. And God is God of both Jews and Gentiles, let us be quite clear about that! The same God is ready to justify the circumcised by faith and the uncircumcised by faith also. Are we then*

> *undermining the Law by this insistence on faith?*
> *Not a bit of it! We put the Law in its proper place."*
> *(Romans 3:27-31/Phillips)*

Yet, in the earlier verses in Romans Chapter 3, something seems to go sideways, imposing the idea that God's grace could only be extended because Jesus was the sacrificial payment, or *atonement.* The first challenge is that such wording implies that God's graciousness was only available when a debt was paid. Hence, if we hadn't talked about what we did in the previous section, we'd be right back to asking the questions, "Who required our sin to be punished?" and "Who demanded payment for our forgiveness?"

The problem begins with the misuse of the word *atonement* in both translation and definition. The Greek word, **ἱλαστήριον** (hilasterion) is the word we translate *atonement,* or possibly better, *propitiation.* The English words *atonement* and *propitiation* mean two very different things. Propitiation means, *to appease* or *a pacification of a god.* It's a picture of an offended, wrathful deity that is being consoled by a bloodletting sacrifice. How does this measure up to the Father depicted by Jesus in the parable of the Prodigal Son, for example? How does it measure up to His conversation with the woman at the well? *It doesn't!* Which is Paul's point. This is the Serpentine-Egoistic mindset of Mankind, who personifies the offended, wrathful deity. Most of Paul's epistles address this confusion at one point or another. The problem is, if we don't see his writings from a Tree of Life vantage point, *the World Above,* an awakened, corrected view, we will see them from the Ego's corrupted view. But let's indulge ourselves.

(Before we open and read the pages of the New Testament, it would be a good idea to not only ask the Holy Spirit to show us what a verse or section means, but we should also pray, "Holy Spirit, give me the heart-set and mindset of the person who wrote this. May I see with their eyes as you gave it to them. Then show me its spiritual truth and how it applies in this moment." Why *this* moment? Because as we awaken and become more conscious, what we see will change as we receive greater clarity.)

It is important to understand that the word "atonement" was introduced into both Old and New Testaments in the Tyndale edition of 1522 AD. It then spread into other editions such as the King James version of 1611, then Webster's, the Revised Standard, the New International, the English Standard, the New Living Translation, and so on. Prior to that point, the word *atonement* meant something very different than how it was applied by the translators in the stated texts. While the intention might have been good, it painted a disfigured picture. According to the Oxford Dictionary of the English Language, the origin of *atonement* is "AT-ONE-MENT," meaning, *"one in nature and likeness."* It comes from the Latin, *adunamentum,* meaning *oneness* or *complete unity.* That's a very different usage than pacifying an angry god. While the word doesn't appear in the Latin Vulgate, it does appear in the Italian Translation of 1607 in Ephesians 4:12, and 2 Thessalonians 2:1. In both cases it has nothing to do with sin, its payment, a substitutionary sacrifice, a bloodletting, or ritual killing. Rather, it just meant the *union* of the saints. *Atonement* was never meant to appease a deity with an anger management problem, nor to *reunite* an offended god with his human underlings. The redefinition came later as the word was continually used in its reapplied form. It was introduced into the Biblical text, in both the Greek and Hebrew translations, for the pagan concept of *propitiation.* It was applied to the notion of a sacrificial payment that was necessary to reunite us after being separated from God (or the gods). In addition, it *appeased* a demand of sovereign justice and *satisfied* it. With that usage of *atonement,* it literally "covered over" the Greek word that was used to describe what was happening. With the introduction of the doctrines of Penal Substitution and Vicarious Atonement, which occurred at the same time of the Tyndale translation, the word replaced the pagan emphasis of the text. Since then, and to this day, many define *atonement* as *a covering over of sin, a sacrificial payment for our disobedience,* so our legal right-standing with God can be restored. You could say that the use of the word was to justify the doctrine that was being introduced at the same time.

On the other hand, *propitiation,* which is a far better translation, creates another problem. The challenge of seeing atonement as *a covering over* of sin also implies that the sin condition is still present but it's masked over so God can interact with us. It's like saying God wears special glasses while looking at humanity. Through them, He only sees Jesus's blood payment, despite our sinful behaviors. Worse yet, sometimes our sinfulness breaks through the glasses and we still must ask Him for forgiveness, because if we don't, bad things will happen.

The problem with *propitiation* is that it has everything to do with appeasing an angry God over our sinfulness through the intentional murder of an innocent animal or human. The word *propitiation* appears three times in the King James and four times in the New American Standard. Even if we include ten other English translations to our search, we would still have only five total occurrences of the phrase. Why all the mathematical and linguistic gymnastics? Because, in defining these words, the Greek scholar Kenneth S. Wuest tells us that ἱλαστήριον (hilasteron), *propitiation,* ἱλάσκεσθαι (hilaskesthai) *reconciliation,* and ἱλασμός (hilasmos) *propitiate, "...these words are used in Greek pagan religions."* Paul was addressing the man-made argument seen in paganism, not attributing those qualities to the Father God, the Source of all Creation. Making the point again from another source, in W. E. Vine's Expository Dictionary, he states regarding these same words, *"...in profane Greek meant 'to conciliate, appease, propitiate, cause the gods to be reconciled'; their goodwill was not regarded as their natural condition, but as something to be earned."*

That last part bears repeating *"...**their goodwill was not regarded as their natural condition, but something to be earned."***

This is most definitely not the picture Jesus (nor the Apostles) presented of the Father, Son, and Spirit. So you may ask, "Why use such words?" Two specific reasons: the Apostles were speaking to a paganistic world, and the Levitical sacrificial system, both of which they and the rest of their Christ-followers were no longer a part. In the paganistic and Levitical mindsets, the gods did not simply forgive, retribution was at the center. In blatant terms, both Jew and Gentile only knew of forgiveness through retributive sacrifice. You couldn't just go to Ra, Marduk, Zeus, Jupiter, or even יהוה (as He was understood by the Levitical priesthood), and ask for forgiveness and find them mercifully forgiving. Nope, something had to die first! Blood had to be shed. Keep in mind that, in between the sin sacrifices (when sin was not the problem), there was the bringing of offerings to keep the gods happy. Evidently, all-powerful, eternal beings don't have the wherewithal to have a positive attitude on their own, they require murderous sacrifices and offerings to encourage them. Note again, *"their goodwill was not regarded as their natural condition..."* Basically, the gods listed, and the multitude of others not on the list, are in an eternally bad mood! Unless, of course, mankind does something to make them happy. Not to mention that if you violate one of their rules or rituals, their already dreadful mood goes from bad to worse. It's as if God, or the gods, are basically unhappy with their playthings until one of them intentionally does something to make them happy. If one of their toys doesn't properly function, they stomp around their heavenly realm with thunder, lightning, and earthquakes, threatening to trash the entire toy box. In other words, trash the nation, city, or tribe they're upset with. However, if one of their toys voluntarily breaks themselves, or offers another toy as payment to appease their anger, the threats of destruction will cease, at least temporarily, until the next plaything messes up. (Who wants to go to heaven now? Sounds like, at times, it could be Hell up there!)

The notion of *propitiation* introduces a significant challenge. The Father of Jesus, the God of all Creation, does not exist in a state of ill-will as His natural condition, nor must any goodwill He has *be earned.* Rather, the summation of the Gospel is that God is LOVE, hence, perpetual goodwill. Remember the words of the angels at the birth of Jesus? *"Glory to God in the highest, and on earth peace, goodwill toward men!"* (Luke 2:14/NKJV) Jesus hadn't even had his diaper changed and God was already proclaiming goodwill! In other words, Jesus is not a pagan, Egyptian, Greco-Roman, Jewish (religious), sacrifice to appease a wrathful Father, though that's how we've read those verses after centuries of reconditioning. What does God Himself say about all this? Note the power of Isaiah's prophecy (the bold and capitalized print is to draw our attention):

> *"In fact, it was our diseases he bore, our pains from which he suffered;* **yet WE REGARDED HIM AS PUNISHED, stricken and afflicted BY GOD."**
> *(Isaiah 53:4/CJB)*

Here's a major look in humanity's eye, with a hearty, "Get behind me Satan!" *WE regarded Him as punished by God.* That

411

was *our* point of view. What Isaiah was telling us, prophetically warning us, was that when we see the Messiah crucified, we'll assume God was behind it, but He wasn't! The Father never sent Christ to be beaten, separated, and punished by His same Self. In other words, the Father didn't take a ransom from His own account and pay Himself. (That statement alone is a contradiction and negation.) Why all the divine fuss? Just investigate the heavenly bank account and say, "Yep! I AM lacking nothing, it's all there." No, it was, and is, our egoistic self that sees God needing to punish someone. Back in Chapter 5, we spoke of pagans offering innocent young, virgin girls (and later, babies) to the gods to keep them happy. The only difference in this scenario is that Jesus was an innocent young Jewish virgin fellow. When it comes to sacrificial systems, there is no race, religion, gender, or age discrimination; all are equal opportunity employers.

In truth, Christ was punished by us thinking we were doing God, or the gods, a favor. What punished, struck, and afflicted Jesus was our egoistic moral dysfunction. It was our Satanic expression that brought about His suffering. He presented a God of *Compassion,* who forgives and is always in union with us. A God of peace, without the mandate of retribution, drives our egoistic-self crazy! The "god" that demands retribution for the debt of sin isn't the man-made idol found in temples with priesthoods and alters of sacrifice. No! For one last time let's remind ourselves, the god that demands sacrificial retribution is called *Man.*

In the verses above, Paul is addressing that pagan mindset. It begins with *"we are justified freely by His grace,"* and then connects paganized religious thinking, which demands retributive justice to make a point. The good news is, Jesus is that reconciliation, not to His Father, or Himself--He didn't need it--nor to an external devil, or evil, that we contrived, but to that good and evil, egoistic pagan mindset we created. In essence, Paul said, "You false gods demanded payment! So you sacrificed an innocent God-Man, Jesus, and He, being who He is, Loved you anyway! He allowed Himself to go to the Cross as a universal religious sacrifice, upholding the integrity of God revealed in Man. He's the beginning and ending of all of it, including the demand for it, and the argument of it. Now there's no excuse! All our fabricated, broken covenants, laws, and ritual violations, born by our religious moral standards, are over. With that in mind, Jesus, along with His Eternal Father, by the Holy Spirit, forgives all of us for not knowing what in the religious world we were doing!"

In the verses in Romans there is a key that should give us a clue. It's in the phrase *"...because in his forbearance he had left the sins committed beforehand unpunished..."* Wait! What? If the sins beforehand were *unpunished,* what were all the human and animal sacrifices for in both the pagan and Jewish religious systems? A good penal substitutionalist would say, "Well, we know that all the bloodshed of animals couldn't satisfy the debt, so God had to send His Son." Really? From that same mindset comes the argument that God gave the Levitical system, with the Tabernacle, then later the Temple, the 613 commandments, and all the sacrificial variations, to satisfy

413

any violation. If God gave an insufficient system, what was He thinking? Why authorize the killing of all those innocents? Why wait 4,000 years (depending upon whose Biblical timeline you use) for Jesus to show up? Why not stop the murdering and subsequent sacrifices after Cain killed Abel? Rather, He gave us what we wanted, showing us its futility. From our father of faith, Abraham, to Isaac, Jacob, and Joseph, God never requested or demanded a payment for sin. He didn't need to, because He was full of Grace and Truth, which, when combined, are called *Compassion.*

This is what happens when we perceive God through a transactional, good and evil, sin and sacrifice mentality. However, the Apostle Paul tells us to put on the Mind of Christ (1 Corinthians 2:16), allowing us to see with eyes from the realm *Above.* Here's a translation, with inserted paraphrase of the same verses in Romans, that may help it make better sense:

> *"Jesus exhibits God's mercy. In his blood conciliation* ***God's faith persuades mankind of his righteousness*** *and the fact that he has brought closure to the historic record of their sins. (Not by demanding a sacrifice but providing the sacrifice of himself.) Jesus is the unveiling of the Father's heart towards us."*
>
> *(Romans 3:25/MIRROR*
> *Bold added for emphasis)*

414

God's faith persuades us! We see this same sentiment in the verses of Galatians 2:19-21 that tell us it was the *Son of God's faith and trust* that contrasted our proud egos toward God's gracious gift:

> *"For it was through letting the Torah speak for itself that I died to its traditional legalistic misinterpretation, so that I might live in direct relationship with God. When the Messiah was executed on the stake as a criminal, I was too; so that my proud ego no longer lives. But the Messiah lives in me, and the life I now live in my body I live by the same trusting faithfulness that the Son of God had, who loved me and gave himself up for me. I do not reject God's gracious gift; for if the way in which one attains righteousness is through legalism, then the Messiah's death was pointless.*
>
> *(Galatians 2:19-21/CJB)*

The pagan word, *propitiation,* is what should be present in both Old and New Testaments, not *atonement.* In those translations that happen to use the word *propitiation,* it should be viewed from its Greek roots, as a pagan, transactional sacrifice, and not as the desire of the Father revealed in Christ. To emphasize the point, Jesus died because of the egoistic thirst of Mankind. God in Christ became a pagan, ritualistic sacrifice, not because the Father needed to satisfy Himself, but because we would have it no other way. If God didn't enter our sacrificial system to liberate us from it, our condition would never have been undone. The Father, in

Christ, forgave us and offered us peace through the resurrection. God believed in us, despite us. He had *Compassionate* forgiveness toward us, and always stayed in union with us. At the time of the crucifixion, we, Mankind, saw Jesus as the enemy. But Christ looked at us with the loving joy of what was ahead (Hebrews 2:2), the undoing of it all through the Good News. Regarding the time beforehand, God in Christ, knowing we would see through the egoistic eyes of religious law and proclaim Mankind as guilty, he says"...*sins committed beforehand unpunished...*" Or better translated, "...*passing over of the bygone sins...*" *(YLT)*. God in Christ kept silent until the Cross and Resurrection (Isaiah 53:7; Matthew 26:62-65; Acts 8:32). He surrendered to our violence in silence for our sake, never compromising what God in Human Form looked like. To say it another way, there was no pending punishment from the bygone past (pagan or otherwise), because that's who God is. Revealed in Christ, there's only the realization of Love, *Compassion,* and release from any sin we can legalize and contrive, with the focus on us being His Image and Likeness. Mankind may attempt to condemn himself through religion, politics, rules, laws, and rituals, yet in the *mind of Christ* such doesn't exist. The notion of "What about this?" or "What about that?" must first be addressed by the *Jesus hermeneutic,* or through the Eyes and Nature of God from an awakened consciousness in *the World Above.* When we come across a translation or a textual variance that implies the Father demanded payment for sin, or some external devil did, or it was all Adam's fault 6,000 years ago, not to mention us poor humans being the victims of original sin, think again. In our egoism, we changed the terms of the Old Testament covenant and, in many ways, we try to change the New Testament covenant, but thankfully to no avail. The "wrath of God" is nothing more than "the wrath of a fabricated God" we created. Remember, in the beginning, we gave definition to Creation, and through the "Fall" we redefined it. Christ came as Man, redefining God to us and in us. His declaration was the final one worthy to be repeated, *"It is finished!"*

Reread those verses, and the New Testament for that matter, with a "heart-set" from *Above.* The Father wasn't paying Himself for sins committed, nor paying some demon for a debt. For what it's worth, though we made the demand, He wasn't paying us off, either. Rather, He forgave us for attempting to destroy His Image and Likeness, first in ourselves, and then exemplified in Jesus. But neither could be destroyed. In the same way that we crucified Jesus and put Him in the grave, only for Him to rise undeterred, we can't destroy who we are either! Regardless of how many times we rationalize it, legalize it, deny it, sacrifice it, or flat-out try to kill it, we were, are, and will always be the Image and Likeness of God. God has faith in us that we will come to ourselves realizing that, whether it takes all this life to figure it out, or a New Heaven and New Earth to realize it. Remember, Jesus said to His disciples, including those of us like Peter who denied Him, *"Peace to you."* Followed by the directive for us to discover who we are, and that as the Father sent Him, He was now sending us. He then breathed on us and said, *"Receive the Spirit,"* (John 20:19-22). From the egoistic Death Sleep of the Knowledge of Good and Evil, we can again awake with just a "breath" to the consciousness of the Tree of Life, and be the Adam again. This time, for the last time (1 Corinthians 15:45).

CHAPTER 13
I AM ETERNAL GRACE

"I do not like Christians.
They shake the tree of life,
forbidding it to bear fruit,
and they scatter to the wind its fragrant blossoms."

Lazarus
Leonid Andreyev

Blame, judgment, accusation, condemnation, war, law, order, right, wrong, good, evil, heaven, hell, angels, and demons, all exist because we egoistically believe we know better, we have the facts, we are right, and obviously God agrees with us, yet we miss the point despite our certainty. But what if we put all that aside? What if we lay down such thinking in the same manner that we are admonished to lay down our lives for the Gospel and Christ (John 15:13)? What if we actually did what Jesus asked of us? What if we took up our cross and followed, embodying Christ? According to Jesus, we would discover who we are, who God is in us, and unearth a peace that passes all understanding (Philippians 4:7). A minister friend of mine,

Will Wheat, once said, "When I gave up judging (the Tree of the Knowledge of Good and Evil), the peace I found was wonderful. I didn't have to judge others or myself, I could just rest in the Love of God."

It begins with a major, yet seemingly subtle, paradigm shift. What if the "saved people" were not the ones who just said the right prayer and got their heavenly salvation ticket? What if we saw with the eyes of Christ? What would that be like?

> *"This saying is trustworthy, and worthy of all acceptance. For we labor and struggle to this end, because we have hoped in* **a living God who is the savior of all human beings,** *especially those who have faith."*   *(1 Timothy 4:9-11/DBH)*

He is the Savior of *all human beings,* not just those who managed to figure out the spiritual riddle and pray the right incantation—like a frustrated Gandalf from *The Lord of the Rings*, who at the Doors of Durin tried for hours to figure out the right incantation to no avail. Of course, the correct incantation was right above the door in plain sight for all to see. It wasn't until the little Hobbit, Merry Brandybuck, looked up and asked, "What does it mean, 'Speak *friend* and enter'?" Gandalf then sprang up and said, "Friend!" and the doors opened. We're not much different. Awakening to our identity in Christ is that simple, but we make it complicated. *God in Christ* reconciled the entire Greco-Roman, Jewish worlds and beyond to Himself. In other words, He universally reconciled all religious and non-religious people to Himself. He is the

Savior of *all human beings,* from the far east to the deepest west! Whether one trusts in Him or not, that's their choice for the moment, but it doesn't change God's point of view. Those of us who trust may have recognized who Christ is and who we are in Him, but that doesn't mean we are better or preferred by Him. Rather, to a measure we've awakened to Divine reality. In so doing, we realize that others will follow at some point. The beauty of being conscious in Christ is that, in that view, whether we observe one who's awake or sleep, all are seen from a Tree of Life dynamic. In other words, without judgement, just with loving, patient, life-giving observation. We may be aware of who's awake and who sleeps, but from within the Mind of Christ, they're just in different stages of the process. Hence, those who are asleep and awake are one in Christ. To say it yet another way, "*...a living God who is the savior of all human beings, especially those who,*" have awakened to faith and realize that. Then the Apostle Luke says this:

> "*Repent therefore, and turn to God so that your sins may be wiped out, **so that times of refreshing may come** from the presence of the Lord, and that he may send the Messiah appointed for you, that is, Jesus, who must remain in heaven until **the time of universal restoration** that God announced long ago through his holy prophets.*"
>
> *(Acts 3:19-21/NRSV)*

Think of those words, "*...the time of universal restoration...*" This is probably the best way to translate that segment. When

421

we think with the knowledge of good and evil, we think in a very binary way. Yet God in Christ expressed thought in a multifaceted way. We think that to pray the sinner's prayer (usually the one derived by Dwight L. Moody) is what it means to be saved and go to Heaven. Still, that way of thinking isn't about complete universal restoration. While in one respect, salvation is a positive part of it, it still has the connotation of saying the right incantation to open the doors of Durin. If we just leave our understanding there, it still has the notion of who's saved and who isn't, who's in and who's out. The Apostles taught with another emphasis:

> *"This is a good and acceptable thing before our savior God,* **Who intends all human beings to be saved** *and to come to a full knowledge of truth."*
> *(1 Timothy 2:3-4/DBH)*

In Greek, the phrase **θέλει σωθῆναι** (thelei sothenai) isn't a hope that people will make the right choice and if they don't, it's sad but too bad. Rather, there are two verbs in that statement. The first is an active indicative and the second is an aorist infinitive. In other words, He fully intends that all will be restored to the former state of *well-being* with no exceptions.

How can this be done? How can all be saved, past, present, and future? How can all things be restored? We discussed how everything starts and ends with *choice*. We proposed that choice is what makes us the Image and Likeness of God. Choice is what makes Love genuine in nature and form. Yet, the ability to choose another direction, Egoism, which is opposite in nature, had to be a real option. Such a choice was in the Garden, and still is now every moment of every day. So, how does one have the complete freedom to choose, yet how does God in Christ save all and restore all things? This poses a real dilemma in modern day Christendom, based on the triad of our afterlife theologies. Here are the big three:

- *Eternal Conscious Torment* - being in Hellfire, burning in torment forever.
- *Annihilationism* - Being burned in Hellfire until one is completely destroyed.
- *Universalism* - There's no Hellfire, and all go to Heaven when they die.

The challenge is, when we currently read translations of the New Testament, we can basically prove all three points of view. Some of this is influenced by the paradigm of the translators, as well as the origin of *our axis of thought.* Nonetheless, despite the Hellfire notion, we are forced to deal with the New Testament writers who propose that God is a God of Selfless Love. Yet, two-thirds of Christendom offers the doom of a fiery judgment when the penal substitution of Christ is rejected. Of course, we are told this is a choice, but from a Christ-centered, Gospel view, it really isn't. Trying to make it sound choosy, one preacher said, "God doesn't send you to Hell, you paddle your own canoe." Not to mention, each person only gets this choice once during their physical life, then it's either bliss or flames forever. The other third poses that whether one chooses Christ or not, when they die physically they will appear before God, realizing all is well. This doesn't suggest much of a choice either, while it's an honest attempt to move God's behavior away from the "Hellfire Hellion." It's interesting, regardless of how we try to understand the eschatology, meaning how it ends both personally and corporately, WE have a propensity to create one with no choice. Once you're dead, you're done! We can recognize this started in the Garden with a choice and even a warning, but then somehow forget that's the central aspect of how this all began. Some portray God as sovereign, like the list of gods we mentioned in the previous chapter, who does what He wants while ignoring the original offering of choice, and the choices we make thereafter. To make matters a bit theologically worse, the same sources from which came the divergent penal substitution doctrine also introduced the teachings of *predestination* and *the sovereignty of God.* Predestination basically teaches that everyone is already fore-ordained by God, who is sovereign, to either Heaven or Hell. As some of us in Christendom later tried to reconcile those ideas, we've created a God who behaves more like a Mafia boss. You know the type, one who does some serious arm twisting through fear and intimidation for us to "choose rightly." Imagine Marlon Brando as Don Corleone, from the movie *The Godfather*, showing up at your front door with a few thug-like angels. With his raspy voice he says, "I'll make you an offer you can't refuse. Either join my family, or I'll burn your house down with you in it." Can't you just feel the warmth of God's love in that encounter? No wait, that's the heat from the flame of a lit cloth stuck in a gas can behind you!. It's held by an impatient, jittery angel known as Gab "the

Gaspipe" Gabriello, who's waiting for you to make your choice. He shrugs his shoulders, muttering, "Hey boss, this guy's takin' too long! What's he tink, he gots eternity? How 'bout I dowse him with gasoline 'n' have him light my cigar?" As amusing as the example is, it's alarmingly accurate. Rather than trying to mask this view of God as one of love and justice, or His all-powerful sovereignty, it's really the axis of our egoistic view. The God who created us not only gives us "choice," but also the right to totally misconstrue who He is, and even create Him in our image. Yet, He patiently waits, gently sustaining us in our unconsciousness, so that when we're ready, a true awakening can occur. Thus, it's not just about having a choice, but the total freedom to awake to one we haven't even perceived yet.

Part 1: The Axis of Noah

The reason we spent an extended time in Chapters 4 and 5 discussing the "other" creation stories—how religion, blood covenant, sacrifice, and the gods of violence came into being—was to address our point of axis. As we look at Jesus Christ and the Melchizedekian king-priesthood, we find a very different axis of thought. To quote Hebrews 5:11 once again:

> *"There is a great deal that we should like to say about this high priesthood, but it is not easy to explain to you since you seem so slow to grasp spiritual truth."*   *(Hebrews 5:11/PHILLIPS)*

The phrase, *slow to grasp spiritual truth,* isn't meant to be an insult, but to address the fulcrum point of the entire epistle. **νωθροὶ γεγόνατε** (nothroi gagonate), is translated *slow,* and also rendered *to be dull* (of hearing). In the entire Bible, this phrase is only used in Hebrews 5:11 and 6:12, , though it does appear in the Septuagint in Proverbs 22:29, translated as *obscure.* The key is the word's origin. Like its sparse usage in the earlier chapters of Hebrews, it reappears in root form in Hebrews 12:8, **νόθοι** (nothoi), and translated, *bastard.* To the point, the word's definition is about being *illegitimate.* The notion of animals or humans as blood sacrifices, especially deemed so by the Creator and performed day after day and year after year, is spiritually *illegitimate.* The challenge is, when addressed, the writer says we are *sluggish, slow,* and *dull* to grasp the idea, that this was never God's intention. The point is that the Melchizedekian priesthood has no part in such practices in any form, except when confronted with the blood ridden religions of men. But then His participation is not as one who slaughters, but the one who is slaughtered. This is why the context of Hebrews 12 is:

> *"Let us fix our eyes on Jesus, the author and perfecter of our faith, who for the joy set before him endured the cross, scorning its shame, and sat down at the right hand of the throne of God. Consider him who endured such opposition from sinful men, so that you will not grow weary and lose heart. In your struggle against sin, you have not yet resisted to the point of shedding your blood."*
>
> *(Hebrews 12:2-4/NIV)*

This is not about resisting some "sin" based on religious legalism or morality, but the opposition of *sinful men.* In this context, the sinful men are the illegitimate aspects of the Levitical order, which was born out of anger and a resistant heart (See Exodus 4:14 and *Melchizedek* Volume 1, Chapter 1: "Exploring a Mystery" - Part 1: Comparisons). As the egoistic progression occurred, from its founding till the time of Jesus, this order would degenerate further into allegiance with pagan rule. Eventually, in the name of freely being able to worship and live in its homeland, it aligned itself with the pagan King Cyrus all the way through to the Roman Empire. In similar fashion, as the family of Israel went to Egypt during the time of famine, what appeared as a blessing eventually ended in severe bondage. At that point, the Jewish religious system had gotten so far from its roots that it was no better than the pagan religions of Noah's day. As we clearly laid out, the Levitical system came to the forefront, *obscuring* the Melchizedekian. Thus, from the grant based grace covenant of Abraham, when we reach Moses and the captivity of Israel, the covenant that is ratified at Sinai is degenerated into a vassal covenant. This changed the view of the Creator, יהוה, to a binary, right and wrong, legalistic, bloodletting God who demands sacrifice, just like all the other gods. However, the redemptive aspect encrypted in that same vassal covenant, in the Torah, was the message of a Messiah. It puts forth that He would come and restore our view of God, like that of Noah and Abraham, terminating the vassal covenant and restoring the original covenant of grace. Consider the words of Matthew and Luke:

> *"For just as the days of Noah, thus shall it be at the time of the advent of the Son of Man. For as in those days before the deluge they were eating and drinking, marrying and giving in marriage, until the day Noah entered the ark, and they did not know until the deluge came and snatched them all away. Thus shall it also be at the time of the advent of the Son of Man. Then there shall be two in the field. One shall be taken and one shall be left. Two women shall be grinding at the mill. One shall be taken and one shall be left. Therefore, be constantly on the watch, because you do not know on what sort of a day your Lord is coming.*
>
> *(Matthew 24:37-42/Wuest)*

These verses, depending upon one's approach, either have a conclusive eschatological view, or more so, a prophetic and parabolic view. The statement, *"For just as the days of Noah..."* is very important, especially from what we learned. In the days of Noah, humanity was eating and drinking, marrying, and so on. The notion of marrying and giving in marriage is a covenantal statement. The pagan religious system of Noah's day was doing what it did, including blood covenant (marriage), along with all the other rituals of animal and human sacrifice. *"But Noah, found grace in the eyes of the Creator יהוה,"* which was the ultimate transformational aspect, causing the construction of a vessel to initiate a new world. For our time to be just as it was in the days of Noah, we must find *grace in the eyes of Jesus,* not bloodletting. *"Let us fix our eyes on Jesus, the author and perfecter of our faith."* Why?

428

Because like Noah (Divine Rest), when we look into Jesus's eyes, we see only the Divine Grace of the Father reflected to us. When we think of living a life of faith, we are really speaking of living a life of *Resting* in *Grace*. It's not about faith in the glorified murder of Jesus, but the love and grace of the Father and Spirit which He exemplified, despite it. It's there we find the birthplace of resurrection power.

"...Who for the joy set before him endured the cross, scorning its shame..." Let's finalize any thoughts regarding the use of a scapegoat so we can put it into perspective and embrace what it means to find *Grace* and *Rest* in the eyes of God. While stirring to consciousness, we see an innocent Jesus impaled on the cross by those "sinful men" and realize He's their scapegoat. So far so good, yet in modernity, we added a few things to the narrative. If we're honest with ourselves, we have several more scapegoats than just Jesus. As we stir from sleep, we're beginning to realize that in Satisfaction, Penal Substitution, and Vicarious Atonement type teachings, something is also distorted beyond just Jesus on the cross. Hence, not only did Jesus receive the Father's wrathful judgment and become our substitute, we now make "the person of Satan" a joint player behind it. We move the focus to an external devil, who used the Pharisees and the Romans to accomplish the violence. We imply that because the Pharisees were of their father the devil (John 8:44), Satan was the motivation behind all that happened. That being so, here are the added scapegoat anomalies. If we listen to much of our teaching today, we tend to bounce from one view to the other almost thoughtlessly, and assume our thinking sees this devil

and God as separate opposing forces. But in the end, it doesn't add up that way. In one sentence, we say that Christ on the cross depicts the wrath and judgment of God that was due us. Yet, it was Satan and our sin that brought this upon the crucified Jesus. Without Jesus's intervention, Satan would have free reign to do to us what he did to Jesus, and condemn us to Hell forever. When we merge the two thoughts, God's judgment allows Satan to do what he does. Let's not forget the ever popular thought that when we sin, we open the door to the devil and allow him to enter our lives, which can also be a form of judgment. At the same time, Satan is God's enemy and tries to attack us with the same afflictions that would be seen as the judgment of God: sickness, disease, poverty, torment, and so on. However, we specify that God and Satan aren't working together, they're enemies. We create lavish pictures of a courtroom where we stand with Satan, the accuser, and Christ, our advocate, who are having legal arguments over the events of our lives and the world's. The questioning arises as we pray, "Does the devil have the legal right to do what he's doing?" Or, "Can I activate the angelic realm by standing on the Word?" The caveat of the courtroom is that we must pray the right prayer, stand on the right promise, make the right confession, or Satan will continue to have the legal right to afflict us, especially if sin is involved. The Father, Jesus, the Holy Spirit, the angels, all rely on our "getting it right" and using "our authority." When we do, they can stop the devil from doing what he's doing. This is just another version of "Spiritual Warfare." Not only are we the victim of sin and Satan, but now we must empower God to liberate us. After all, we've been given His victorious authority over the devil. If it doesn't work, either we didn't use the authority correctly or Satan has the legal right to do what he's doing. Remember, the last thing we want is to be on God's judgment side of the equation, because He won't, or even can't, stop the legal right of Satan. We're getting what we deserve because of sin. So, is Satan accomplishing God's judgment? Is he then Heaven's executioner? We insist, "Never! God is not in a relationship with Satan. He's just allowing what the devil does." (Has this thinking come to light yet?) We rationalize that God is Love, He's not malevolent, He just uses someone else's malevolence to accomplish His acts of judgment. So which is it, especially if we buy into the sovereignty-of-God theology? If God commands it in the name of justice, isn't He directly responsible for what's happening and affirming the actions of this kind of devil? If God doesn't command it, but "allows it" for justice's sake, He's still giving permission if He's ultimately the one in charge. We usually see the Father as the judge and Jesus as the advocate. Regardless of what rationalization we use or what language we choose to use, the word *allow*, in Greek, **συνευδοκεῖτε** (suneudokeo), **ἐπιτρέψῃ** (epitrespse), or Latin, *consentitis, indulgentiam*, adds up to the same: *to give permission.* According to Webster's dictionary, giving permission means, "*Formal consent. Authorization.*" What's interesting is there's no such word as *allow* in Biblical Hebrew. Either you נתן (natan), actively give your consent, or you don't. There's no middle ground. In addition, there's no such thing as a "permissive tense" in Biblical Hebrew, despite what some of us charismatic ministers have taken from Young's Analytical Concordance in the Preface, item #70(b). Young mentions there may be a type of permissive tense in *six* *specific* Old Testament verses. We've taken that statement and made it a blanket doctrine so that in every instance when it appears God did something negative, it was a permissive thing, not a direct action. This is not linguistically accurate. Young was clear that he was only offering his opinion on those *six specific verses,* not the entirety of Biblical Hebrew. However, in those verses the Qal/Paal, Piel, Paul, Niphal, and Hiphal moods are used, none of which are permissive. This is why it's important to understand that the Bible was written in the form of roots and branches, and some of the other aspects of interpretation we mentioned at the beginning of this book.

We have introduced an additional *scapegoat,* the devil. We've pitted him against God, removing the severity of the focus from us. To say this another way, while we admit we are sinners and Jesus, *scapegoat #1,* died as our substitute, we're also implying we're really not that bad. It was our sin that crucified Him, not us. We wouldn't have directly participated in the beating, nailing, and crucifying Jesus, we were only there vicariously. It was the inspiration of the Pharisees and those horrible Romans who crucified Him! They were a vicarious representation of our sinfulness; it doesn't mean we would've actually done the hammering. We're probably more like our traditional view of Simon of Cyrene. We intend to help Jesus, not wanting Him to carry the burden of the Cross alone. On the other hand, maybe we would be like Mary, his mother, or Mary Magdalene, or the young Apostle John, who stayed with Him during the crucifixion, offering moral support. At the end of the day, it was the devil, *scapegoat #2,* using "really sinful people" to do his wiles. Yes, it was the devil, *scapegoat*

#2, manipulating those who are vulnerable to fulfill the Father's wrath and kill Jesus, *scapegoat #1.* If we take this to its conclusion, the wrath of the Father is *scapegoat #3.* Think of it, Jesus is the *real scapegoat* that humanity afflicted. But then, to distance ourselves from the reality of what all such implies, we *scapegoat* the Father too. It was "His wrath" that had to be satisfied. Then we *scapegoat* the devil, who manipulates sinfully deceived people to fulfill his bidding and implement the Father's wrath. It's not that *scapegoat #3,* the Father, really uses *scapegoat #2,* the devil, after all we can't claim that the devil does the Father's bidding. The Father just knew what *scapegoat #2* was capable of, and that he had legal right to bring such calamity. Plus, *scapegoat #3,* the Father, knew that *scapegoat #2,* the devil, wanted to destroy *scapegoat #1,* Jesus the Savior, since the Garden when he heard that the Savior was going to crush his head. This was after our "distant ancestors" Adam and Eve ate the forbidden fruit, and God, *scapegoat #3,* cursed everybody. For that matter, Adam and Eve, those more than 6,000-year-old super-great-great-grandparents are *scapegoats #4* and *#5.* If it wasn't for Grandma Eve, *scapegoat #4,* falling into temptation, believing the devil, *scapegoat #2,* our poor grandpa Adam, *scapegoat #5,* would have never eaten the forbidden fruit and we wouldn't be in this situation! Hence, we "innocent sinners" are victims of *scapegoats #2, #4,* and *#5,* because of what they all did thousands of years ago in Eden. By our subsequent naïve disobedience, following in the footprints of our super-old-great-grandparents, we ignorantly unleashed the omnipotent wrath of *scapegoat #3,* the Father. Luckily for us, mere pawns in this massive spiritual battle, *scapegoat #1,*

Jesus, stepped in for us. In the end, we're mere spectators watching a three-way scapegoat fight! The last two scapegoats, our super-old-great-grandparents, are dead because of their sin. We're not sure if they're saved or doing time in Hell, but God, *scapegoat #3,* has all that figured out. More importantly, Jesus, *scapegoat #1,* came in the name of our salvation to deliver us "innocent sinners" from all those other nasty scapegoats!

That was exhausting. But it takes a lot of mental gymnastics to make sense of where we are in the common theology of our day. In short, it makes us victims of the entire situation, and our sinfulness a product of our great-great-grandparents, Adam and Eve. This is what both Catholics and Protestants call "Original Sin." Thus, if it wasn't for the devil's temptations and our great-great-grandparents' disobedience, we wouldn't be in this mess. It's really all their fault! We're mere victims of their sin. Thus, we're born in sin because of our spiritual ancestors! In other words, the reason Jesus steps in and stops His Father's serious wrath problem is because we're really innocent sinners. After all, Jesus did say, *"Father forgive them, they don't know what they are doing."* (Once again, another misapplication of scripture.) Then we add, "Only the Pharisees and the Romans are the bad sinners, not us! We just got caught up in the moment!" Then we find ourselves subtly changing from being innocent sinners, to teaming up with that version Jesus and His wrathful Father. "If it wasn't for those Pharisees and those pagan Romans, our society and nation would be in much better shape. If we could just rid our land of those people, we would have heaven on earth! So get your

Bible and tell them of the wrath of God and His pending judgment. If they repent, receive God's sacrifice, and become like us, it will be good for everyone. On the other hand, if they don't repent, grab your sword, axe, bow and arrow, or if you have one, a firearm, and make them submit. If they get out of line, you know what to do. Unleash the wrath of God on them." Now we're right back to the days of Noah prior to the flood. Same violence in the name of religious morality and a god who would approve of it. The only difference is that this religious warrior wears a Jesus T-shirt and has an ichthys on the back of his chariot, or tank. Let's remember that this mindset also believes that when Jesus returns, He's coming with a state-of-the-art military to destroy all His enemies.

But what if both Matthew and Luke, who bring into view that the coming of the Son of Man will be as in the days of Noah, saw those scriptures about Noah with considerably more depth? For example, they include, *"One shall be taken and one shall be left."* What does that mean? We've probably heard both views. One says, *the one taken* is like Noah and his family (caught up and carried away in the ark), like a type of pretribulation rapture. *The one left behind* (who died in the flood) is the ungodly sinner. On the other hand, *the one taken* is the sinner (swept up in the flood) and *the one left* is the righteous (like Noah and his family who survived). Either way, one can see the very binary, good and bad approach in both those views. Is that really what the context of Noah's story implies? In this case, the Aramaic may shed a bit more light on the subject:

435

> *"Then two will be on the property: One will-be guided and one left. And two will be grinding with the millstone: This-one is guided and this-one left."*
> *(Matthew 24:40-41/ARAMAIC)*

Think of the phrase, *"One will-be guided..."* The Aramaic word for *guided* is **דבר** (davar), which is identical to the Hebrew word meaning *to speak of the matter, the matter of things themselves,* and *to arrange the matter.* When we speak to someone about a matter and thoughtfully arrange it so it can be understood, that's a type of guidance. The whole point of Noah and the Ark was about being *guided* by *rest* and *grace* to build a vessel that will bring him, his family, and the members of Creation on the Ark to a new world. Remember, the vessel was built from the lowest substance, brimstone. Yet, when it was seen with the eyes of *rest* and *grace,* the result was *"at-one-ment"* and it rose above the chaos. The Ark didn't have to be forced to rise above the waters, it was effortlessly doing what it was designed to do.

But what of the flood? What about the "exhale" of Mankind, and the breath returning to God? According to most lexicons, the Greek word used for *flood* or *deluge* in both Matthew and Luke is **κατακλυσμὸς** (kataklusmos); it's where we get the word *cataclysm.* Webster's Dictionary says it is *"a severe upheaval that brings about fundamental change."* The revelation of *at-one-ment* is a tremendous, intense, fundamental change to the way we of the *World Below* see our reality. Being that we're an emanation of I AM by Divine design, *at-one-ment* shakes the very core of the Serpentine-

Ego's framework. At best, the Ego will accept being a Creation of God as long as there's a distinct separation and difference between us. However, to be an emanation of Christ, the One who Loves and was willing to lay down His Life for Love's sake? Hold on. The One who's in a state of *at-one-ment* with all Creation, both sinner and saint alike? Oh, no, the Ego finds that a severe problem! "How can 'I' be *at-one* with wrong doers, when 'I' am a right doer?" As we know, the Ego is in complete contrast to our true Divine Nature. However, once we're elevated to our original consciousness, the *Desire to Receive* becomes the *Desire to Reflect,* and the Ego is transformed into a humble gift *Receiving and Giving grace* and *rest* to all.

Like the Ark, when we apply the awareness of *at-one-ment* to the egoistic brimstone, we seal all the cracks where mayhem and chaos would leak in. If we're not conscious of our *at-one-ment,* we remain sunk in *the World Below.* Think of this picture for a moment: there lies the Ark, fitted together with עֲצֵי גֹפֶר

(atziy gophar) *gopher wood,* but without כֹפֶר (kaphar) *pitch* applied. Noah *et al* board the Ark and close the door. The rains descend, the waters rise, the ark shifts, makes loud creaking sounds, and it's leaking everywhere! In just a short time, the waters fill the ark and all within it perish, no differently than anyone outside. What was intended to be a vessel of deliverance has now become a vessel of death, a tomb.

On the other hand, if we apply the revelation of כֹפֶר (kaphar) *at-one-ment,* the egoistic mayhem and chaos cannot enter, even though it's swirling around us. While the chaos was intended to keep us in a state of death in *the World Below*, the reverse occurs. We rise up to *the World Above* as the windows fill with the brightness of the Light, revealing שם (shem) the Divine Essence within, חם (ham), giving it form, filling and, יפת (yapheth) spreading wide the unveiled Image and Likeness of the Creator in us!

When the revelation of *at-one-ment* succumbs to a pagan approach of a wrathful God demanding sacrificial payment for broken laws, it is no longer *at-one-ment*. Instead, regardless of the word we use, the meaning becomes penal substitution, or as the Apostle Paul calls it, *"the ministry of death"* (2 Corinthians 3:7). This is not to say that the teaching of religious penal substitution or vicarious sacrifice was not mentioned in the Bible. Rather, it was practiced by most all religious and political systems, dating as far back as the Fall. However, this is not the revelation that Jesus, nor the Apostles, offer us of the true living God. This doesn't mean that they dismiss the language of those who understood such bloodletting. But this is where we seem to have a problem and get confused. The people to whom the Gospel was preached, both Jew and Gentile, only knew of these systems in various forms. The idea of God forgiving rather than requiring a blood sacrifice, as well as all Creation being a united emanation of Him, was a foreign notion to those of *the World Below.* So, to bring the message of a Messiah, who reveals a forgiving God *at-one* with all, to an audience who can't fathom such things, is why He winds up crucified. It would be like trying to explain that the earth is a large ball which spins on its axis at 1,037.6

mph (1,669.8 km/h), which is way faster than any chariot conceivable. Then try adding that it orbits the sun at 67,000 mph (107,000 km/h), and our entire solar system travels around with the stars in a thing called the Milky Way Galaxy at a speed of 515,000 mph (828,000 km/h). Saying such things 2000 years ago would get you more than just a raised eyebrow and a look like you were deluded by demons. After all, from their point of view, the earth was flat and motionless; it was the sun, moon, and stars that moved around us. Then add that the earth and solar system will completely revolve around the galaxy every 230 million years. You can imagine the response, shouts of "Demonic Heresy!" as they pick up stones and throw them at the maniacal, demonized messenger, who just became a real menace to society! Therefore, it's not only important to remember that the New Testament, and the encrypted Tanak (Old Testament), was written to a people that didn't understand the language of Divine Reality, but *neither do we in our egoistic selves.* It's the awakened, new set of eyes, when fixed on an unfiltered Jesus, the *gracious* author and completeness of our *restful* faith, that stirs us to awareness. Like Noah's view, Christ is rooted in the fullness of *grace* which gives us *rest.* This will awaken us to consciousness, transforming how we look at God, ourselves, reality around us, and importantly, the apostolic writings.

Part 2: The Axis of Pagan Sacrifice

The Apostles wrote in a manner explaining the revelation of Christ in humanity, with a hybrid vocabulary. This is not just an issue of understanding Hebrew, Aramaic, Greek, and Latin, although it's fine if we do. In the similar way we discussed hermeneutics and the Hebraic principle of Roots and Branches, there was now another logic presented: the mind of Christ. While the writers used a way of thinking and a vocabulary that the listener could grasp, at the same time they were presenting a new logic. Please carefully note the following words:

> *"The cup of the blessing that we bless — is it not the fellowship of the blood of the Christ? the bread that we break — is it not the fellowship of the body of the Christ? because one bread, one body, are we the many — for we all of the one bread do partake. See Israel according to the flesh! are not those eating the sacrifices in the fellowship of the altar?*
> *(1 Corinthians 10:16-18/YLT)*

This is a very good, almost verbatim translation of the text. Note that Paul is speaking to the Corinthians. This church had all kinds of problems in their development, some of which we mentioned in the previous volume. Corinth historically, according to the Encyclopedia Britannica, was occupied as far back as 3000 BC. Most Biblical commentaries refer to what we know from the 7th century BC. However, through more recent findings we unearthed their religious origins beyond that. The most rudimental findings were that the inhabitants who would become Corinth, practiced human sacrifice. While the religion's name is currently unknown, we do know that it was practiced all the way to Crete. The occupants were known as the Minoan people. They wore bull masks with horns, similar to that of Nimrod of Babylon, and their principal deity was female. Their practices gave rise to the later Greek myths of Theseus and the Minotaur. The minotaur was a human-like creature with a head similar to a bull with large horns and a tail. This was adapted later into the Christian religion as Satan and the devil. However, 1st and 2nd century Christianity did not make such a connection, or view Satan in that way. Another significant aspect was, though the principle deity was female, the human sacrifices offered to the minotaur were girls and youthful women. Moving forward, one of the Minoan celebrations was the chasing of bulls, mounting them, and then slaying them, like what we know today as bullfighting. Then they would eat its meat during a feast of celebration. When we overlay this with what we know from Greece and later Rome, we find that Paul's words are quite crafted and make sense in a broader light.

When Paul speaks of the fellowship of Christ's cup and bread, he's clear that it's the fellowship of our union with Him, as one body and blood: *at-one-ment.* Remember, at that point, this was a foreign idea to both Gentiles and religious Jews. The notion of being one in body and blood with a god identifies the partaker with that god, making them equal to and a representation of that god. To be emphatic, at the time Paul was writing, if you were the body and blood of God, you were God! When Jesus said this of Himself, making Himself the Messiah, Son of the Most High, saying, *"I AM,"* the Pharisees tore their clothes in protest and condemned Him (Mark 14:61-64). Until Paul's writing, sacrifices were either given as a scapegoat for sin, or as a gift to the deities to appease them.

Paul draws a clear distinction by being specific regarding the pagan substitutionary component, starting with Israel, to help the Corinthians understand what he was saying, *"See Israel according to the flesh!"* While all Greek texts read this way, it's important to point out that most modern translations leave out, or reinterpret the phrase, *"...according to the flesh."* Some say, *"Consider the people of Israel..."* (NIV), or *"Look at the nation of Israel..."* (NASV), or *"Look at physical Israel..."* (CJB), or *"Think about the Israelites..."* (NCV), or *"Think about the people of Israel..."* (NLT). That convenient omission is based on the modern adaptation of penal substitution and vicarious sacrifice.

(Note: I will no longer use the phrase "vicarious atonement" though that was one of the key names the doctrine had at the turn of the previous century, being that we've returned the word "atonement" back to its original definition.)

In other words, if we were going to redefine the Apostolic definition of the sacrifice of Christ to pagan penal substitution, it would behoove us to omit or change the phrase, *"...according to the flesh"* to focus on something else. What we've done for hundreds of years is redefine the sacrifices of the Aaronic Priesthood and place them as a valid, acceptable, even desired sacrifice of the Father. Though the Apostles say otherwise, if we are going to redefine the sacrifice of Christ to the level of paganism or Levitical temple worship, we can't look at the practices of the high priests as "fleshly." Nonetheless, Paul was clear that we're to see them as *fleshly.* He didn't say to see the spiritual significance, or that what they were doing was God's spiritual answer to sin's dilemma. No! He was clear, this is what the flesh, the base nature, or what the Ego does. He uses the same word when he says, *"For to be **carnally** minded is death..."* (Romans 8:6/NKJV). He then adds, *"...are not those eating the sacrifices in the fellowship with the altar?"* It's important to mention again that the word for altar in Hebrew is מזבח (mitsbeach), which means *the place of slaughter.* The first time מזבח (mitsbeach) is used is immediately after the cessation of the flood when Noah, not by the command or desire of God, chose to slaughter the animals as an offering. God quickly responded, correcting him by pointing to the rainbow as a sign of the covenant, and not blood sacrifice. Noah did this because that was all he knew from the violent pagan world from which he came. Sadly, the revelation of *Grace* and *Rest* which he brought to the new world remained incomplete because the altar of slaughter was still present. As the old saying goes, "Noah took two steps forward, and one step back." There's progress, but not completion. The good news is, since Christ, the revelation of *Grace* and *Rest* is now complete. Appealing to the Corinthian people in a language they understood, Paul was saying that from a carnal mind's standpoint, when you eat the meat of a particular sacrifice, you are identifying with its meaning and with the altar of the deity that demanded it. Using that imagery, Paul is attempting to reposition their entire view of themselves as the Likeness of God, and the person of God Himself. He continues:

> *"What then do I say? that an idol is anything? or that a sacrifice offered to an idol is anything? — [no,] but*

> *that the things that the nations sacrifice — they*
> *sacrifice to demons and not to God; and I do not wish*
> *you to come into the fellowship of the demons. Ye*
> *are not able the cup of the Lord to drink, and the cup*
> *of demons; ye are not able of the table of the Lord to*
> *partake, and of the table of demons;"*
>
> *(1 Corinthians 10:19-21/YLT)*

Notice he connects the sacrifices of Israel with that of the nations and clearly proclaims, *"They sacrifice to demons and not to God!"* He does not stop there, but adds, *"I do not wish you to come into the fellowship of the demons."* He was not just saying don't eat at the table of the Lord Jesus and then go down the block and eat at the table of pagan sacrifices. No! If he simply meant that, He would have never prefaced with:

> *"Therefore concerning the eating of things offered*
> *to idols, we know that an idol is nothing in the*
> *world, and that there is no other God but one...*
> *However, there is not in everyone that knowledge;*
> *for some, with consciousness of the idol, until now*
> *eat it as a thing offered to an idol; and their*
> *conscience, being weak, is defiled. But food does not*
> *commend us to God; for neither if we eat are we the*
> *better, nor if we do not eat are we the worse."*
>
> *(1 Corinthians 8:4, 7-8/NKJV)*

The issue was combining the murder of Jesus with ritual sacrifice. Paul points out that both Levitical, hence *Israel after the flesh,* and pagan ritual sacrifice are the same. We're not to combine those concepts and practices with the Lord's table. He goes as far as to call them demonic, the rituals of demi-gods. He later calls this the preaching of another Jesus (2 Corinthians 11:4). It's the notion that we're partaking of an altar of sacrificial slaughter, appeasing an angry god for a violation of its laws, and requiring a bloodletting to stay its forthcoming wrath. This was never the Father's intention, nor His Nature, on any level. The idea that God is a God of *Grace* has nothing to do with the presence of commandments and rituals being violated. The idea that God is a God of *Rest* has nothing to do with keeping those commandments, or offering ritual substitutionary sacrifices. The sole purpose in the Father sending the Son was to once and for all stop the violence! The intention was for humanity, both pagan and Levitical, to hear the message of *Grace* and *Rest*. Yet, God in Christ also knew this wasn't Mankind's egoistic mindset. He knew He would have to endure this demi-god's violence to undo it once and for all. Let's revisit this from Jesus's own words in all three synoptic Gospels:

> *"...A man planted a vineyard and set a hedge around it, dug a place for the wine vat and built a tower. And he leased it to vinedressers and went into a far country. Now at vintage-time he sent a servant to the vinedressers, that he might receive some of the fruit of the vineyard from the vinedressers. And they took him and beat him and sent him away empty-handed. Again he sent them another servant, and at him they threw stones, wounded him in the head, and sent him away shamefully treated. And again*

he sent another, and him they killed; and many others, beating some and killing some. Therefore still having one son, his beloved, he also sent him to them last, saying, 'They will respect my son.' But those vinedressers said among themselves, 'This is the heir. Come, let us kill him, and the inheritance will be ours.' So they took him and killed him and cast him out of the vineyard."

(Mark 12:1-8/NKJV)

Despite the myth that proclaims a wrathful Father had to send His Son as payment for sin, Jesus tells us something different. *"Therefore still having one son, his beloved, he also sent him to them last, saying, 'They will respect my son.'"* The Father's intention was that His Son be received and respected. Needless to say, the vinedressers didn't. Rather, they took Him, killed Him, and cast Him out of the vineyard. The issue wasn't whether or not the Trinity knew in Their foreknowledge what both the Sanhedrin and Rome would do. We know They knew, based on other New Testament scriptures. However, what was foreknown did not change Divine intention. To the contrary, even with that foreknowledge, Christ came with the hope set before Him (Hebrews 12:2) for something greater. While the vinedressers did what was anticipated, Divine intention affected 120 people who would find themselves in an upper room, knowing they could not return to the life they had. What's more compelling is the statement Jesus makes in the Matthew account:

> *"'Therefore, when the owner of the vineyard comes,*
> *what will he do to those vinedressers?' They said to*
> *Him, 'He will destroy those wicked men miserably,*
> *and lease his vineyard to other vinedressers who*
> *will render to him the fruits in their seasons.'"*
> *(Matthew 21:40-41/NKJV)*

Jesus asks what will the owner do to those who murdered the Son? The reply of the chief priests and elders, *"He will destroy those wicked men miserably..."* While it stands to reason, considering their religion, this would be the reply of the chief priests and elders, it wasn't the reply of the vineyard owner, the Father. This is the difference between the Gospel and the sacrificial rituals of the time, both pagan and *fleshly Israel.* Jesus continues:

> *"Jesus said to them, 'Have you never read in the*
> *Scriptures: The stone which the builders rejected*
> *has become the chief cornerstone. This was the*
> *Lord's doing, and it is marvelous in our eyes'*
> *Therefore I say to you, the kingdom of God will be*
> *taken from you and given to a nation bearing the*
> *fruits of it.* And whoever falls on this stone will be
> broken; but on whomever it falls, it will grind him to
> powder.*"*   *(Matthew 21:41-44/NKJV)*

Jesus directly quotes Psalm 118:22-23, which is attributed to King David. We will add the 24th verse to help make the point:

"The stone which the builders refused is become the head stone of the corner. This is the Lord's doing; it is marvelous in our eyes. This is the day which the Lord hath made; we will rejoice and be glad in it."
(Psalms 118:22-24/CWSB)

There's no argument that Jesus was proclaiming He's the rejected cornerstone and is the revelational foundation stone of the Divine Nation and Kingdom. However, we find that the notion of grinding someone to powder, as in Matthew verse 44, was added by a scribe. Many modern translations add a footnote telling us this verse did not exist in older manuscripts (Examples: NIV, CJB, ISV, NRSV).

"There is considerable degree of doubt concerning the presence of this verse in the text. Several scholars believe it to have been introduced early into Matthew's text on the basis of Luke 20:18. However, as TC-GNT indicates, the wording is not the same, and a scribe would more appropriately have introduced it after verse 42."
(United Bible Society, 1961-1997)

Why so? There's a similar saying in Luke 20:18, from which some scholars think it was borrowed and inserted in Matthew. It's also possible that the same scribe, or an earlier one, added it to Luke's Gospel as well. What we do know is that the verse is totally out of character with the preceding parables. We know this has been the case in other portions of the New Testament as well, as intensive study has been done.

Most importantly, it doesn't exist in any of the referenced verses. While there's a similar verse in Isaiah 8:14-15, never did Isaiah, or the writer of Psalms, speak of a rock falling on people and them being ground to powder. More so, since the New Testament writers inscribed their inspired ideas, the addition seems to occur much later referencing a Talmudic Midrash, according to the Jewish New Testament Commentary:

> *"'And they stood under the mount' (Exodus 19:17). Rabbi Abdimi ben-Chama said: This teaches that the Holy One, blessed be He, turned the mountain upside down over them like an inverted cask, and said to them, 'If you accept the Torah, it will be good. But if not, this will be your burial place!'" (Shabbat 88 a)*

Many other Jewish rabbis see this reference to Exodus differently, but the point is, what was truly *"marvelous in our eyes"?* The marvel was that the least likely, the one who the Father hoped they would respect and didn't, was the true foundation stone. What we can suggest based on the scriptural continuity is the follow-up verse from Psalms, *"This is the day which the Lord hath made; we will rejoice and be glad in it."* The day of the Lord is marvelous, and at His resurrection, no rock ground anyone to powder, rather it was rolled away! Jesus didn't condemn His enemies. God in Christ forgave them and reconciled the world to Himself. This doesn't mean that the world's system stopped working. The principle of reaping what one sowed still applied, but not as a judgment from God or a raging Father. Rather, the Good News is that we can ascend from *the World Below,* where death, the knowledge of good and evil, the Serpentine-Ego, the *Desire to Receive for Oneself Alone,* all exist, and be lifted to *the World Above.* This is the marvel! The foundation stone, the Christ, brings all to a full and final redemptive conclusion.

Jesus and Paul have no desire for us to merge the thinking of the vinedressers—in other words pagan, fleshly Israel, or demi-god like blood sacrifice—with the murder of Jesus. Rather, they would have us, *"Fix our eyes on Jesus,"* like Noah, and find grace, compassion, and forgiveness. They would not have us drink a cup of His blood as payment for sin, which is just another way of saying idol sacrifice, but as a *"cup of blessing"* in union with, and as one blood with, the Eternal Father and Creator in Christ. They would have us drink a *cup of "at-one-ment."* Notice Paul's conclusion:

> *"Grace sets the pace in my conscience, not people's suspicious scrutiny. Every meal to me is a celebration of what grace reveals. Live your life overwhelmed by God's opinion of you! Your eating and drinking is certainly a constant reminder that you are his glory. Every meal proclaims the fact that the life of your design is redeemed again in Christ; salute life! So live your life in freedom and wisdom. Thus the Jews, the Gentiles and the church will all witness the attraction of your life without taking any offence. I am so persuaded about every person's inclusion in Christ that I desire to be everything I need to be in order to win everyone's understanding*

of their union with Christ; my mission is to be exactly
what is required of me in every possible situation to
awaken every kind of person, whoever they are, to
own their salvation! I have no other agenda"
(1 Corinthians 10:30-33/MIRROR)

Part 3: The Axis of Grace

The Father, Son, and Spirit had no other agenda but to create us for relationship, to be a revelation of the union of the triune bond, and ultimately be an emanation of the Creator as His Creation. The Father didn't send His Son because He demanded a blood payment for sin. Rather, He sent His Son to reveal our union with Him, in the face of our Serpentine-Egoism. Nonetheless, God knew that for humanity to realize our oneness with Him, He would pay the ultimate price. He would have to face what our egoistic, fleshly, bloodthirsty, religious desires demanded. God isn't just the Savior of those who figured out some encrypted puzzle of salvation, but the Savior of ALL humanity. Through the process of the Tree of Life, through death and rebirth, we are given the opportunity to awaken to our true identity, even if it takes a New Heaven and Earth (Revelation 21:1) to awaken to it. God's love and compassion transcends time and space, including this heaven and earth, even to the creation of another. While God forever gives us the choice to Love, He never stops choosing to Love us from eternity to eternity.

God is *Grace* and *Rest.* Grace is not something that overlooks our moral failures or our breaking of commandments, or is merciful when we're contrary to the Divine Nature. This is a misunderstanding of the Apostles' usage of the words χάρις (charis) *grace,* and ἔλεος (eleos) *mercy.* When we think of these words, we think of *Grace* as meaning *getting something from God we don't deserve* (like His favor), and *mercy* as meaning *not getting what we do deserve* (like His condemnation). But neither is true, as we've stated before. In Koine Greek, taking its roots from classical Greek, outside of reformed and modernized New Testament lexicons, χάρις (charis) meant *pleasure,* and ἔλεος (eleos) meant *compassion.* Think of these verses from the standpoint of their original meanings (words changed to their original meanings have been bolded):

> *"To Timothy, my true child in the faith: [Divine]* **Pleasure, compassion** *and peace from God the Father and Christ Jesus our Lord."*
>
> *(1 Timothy 1:2/NASU)*

> *"To Titus, my true child in a common faith: [Divine]* **Pleasure** *and peace from God the Father and Christ Jesus our Savior." (Titus 1:4/NASU)*

> *"[Divine]* **Pleasure, compassion** *and peace will be with us, from God the Father and from Jesus Christ, the Son of the Father, in truth and love."*
>
> *(2 John 3/NASU)*

> *"Therefore let us draw near with confidence to the throne of [her]* **pleasure,** *so that we may receive*

> **compassion** *and find* **'pleasure** *to help' in time of*
> *need.* (Hebrews 4:16/NASU)

In the name of Divine Love from the very beginning, consider the following thought. If there was a distortion, a victim, a casualty, it wasn't just Mankind when he partook of the Tree of the Knowledge of Good and Evil, but God as well. This was the necessary risk that God as Love, Life, and Light was more than willing to take. You could say, He bet His Life on it. The call to awakening is that God never changed. Rather, through our choice we changed how we saw Divinity. The Creator of the Universe was, and still is, an emanation of Life-Giving *Compassion,* offering us pleasure and union in peace. It was us that changed how we saw reality, and we didn't do it as mere victims of temptation. We did it as Creatures, The Adam, who in egoistic ignorance made a valid choice to walk a different path. Yet God was still the same, nothing changed in His character or approach to us. He was still the Creator of the "Garden of Pleasure," and as *Compassion,* offered to let us discover who we were, who He was, and by our own choice. After all, how does one have an honest relationship with someone without first knowing themselves? How does one give themselves to someone in heartfelt intimacy if they really don't know what they're giving? It wasn't that we were just disobedient children who were punished by being kicked out of the playground and sent to their room with the door locked on an extended timeout. No, we were the Image and Likeness of God, and ignorant of what that meant. One may say, "They could have learned what they needed to without choosing the Tree they were warned about." While that might be true, we really don't know that. All we do know is that what happened, happened, and to hypothesize otherwise is to suggest that the Father should've created another, or better, scenario. On the other hand, this may be another aspect of our faith and trust. In other words, trust that God created the best possible scenario that would yield the best possible results. God, from His *Graciousness,* gave us the choice to learn our meaning, knowing full well that we had to discover it ourselves and then, again by choice, humbly inter-submit ourselves to intimacy. Whether we chose Life or the Knowing of Good and Evil, that was the best possible framework to fulfill and yield the ultimate result, Divine Likeness. The issue is not just the choice, but the winding journey of choices that would follow and how they create the atmosphere for our awakening to who we are, who God is, and our inseparable intimate union. (We'll discuss more on this in a later chapter.)

The Love, *Grace,* and risk this required of the Creator was to literally give of His all, and give us the choice to leave it all. We can see this personified in our relationship with God in Christ. Jesus, who the Apostle Paul calls, *"the Image of the invisible God"* (Colossians 1:15), came to humanity revealing Divine benevolence, healing, provision, and empowerment. All of which is just another way of saying, He came full of *Compassion* with *the pleasure to help* in our time of need. You could say, that while we're admonished to draw near with confidence to the throne of *Grace,* God in Christ was the throne of *Grace* drawing near to us.

As in the Garden, where we chose to leave and go the direction we did, we see this revisited in Jesus's parable of the prodigal sons, who demanded their inheritance and left (more on this later). God in His Graciousness gave us all we asked and allowed us to leave for a distant country of our own making. To Him, we had to go and learn who we were not, in order to realize who we might be. Even if it meant self-discovery through hunger in a pigsty or toiling in a field. By asking for our inheritance, something we would receive if our Father had died, we deemed Him as dead and in our egoistic ignorance our self-centered arrogance emerged. What is arrogance? We could say it's the contrived definition of one's self without truly knowing who we are. What's attractive to such arrogance is the pathway of the knowledge of good and evil. It's the path of learning through comparisons. In arrogance, we compare what's good and evil to give ourselves, and others, identification. Eventually, we will find this is of no more value than pig slop. Even with that realization, we still desire to eat it for a season. The younger prodigal son arrogantly spent all his egoistic desire, seeing whatever desire he had as good, and any unfulfilled desire as evil. We build entire cultures on that premise. At the end of the day, he found himself in a serious contrast to where he started. After spending such arrogance on every desired whim, he found he was still hungry and unfulfilled. It's interesting that in the parable, Jesus points out that the *famine in the land* only occurred after the young son spent all he had (Luke 15:14). In other words, abundance and famine are determined by our inner awareness of who we are. Regardless of how much we have externally, when we've awakened to who we are, we will always uncover life in abundance. In his famine he began to seek for identity, but he did so by trying to find himself through someone else. When we realize that our identity isn't in arrogant self-indulgence, we begin to look in other places. In the case of the younger son, he tried to find himself in another person who was in the same inner conscious state he was. Remember, both were in the same *distant country,* and the person he attached himself to was considered an established *citizen.* Looking for our identity in another is a developmental start. However, when we do it through seeking it in someone who's at the same level of unconsciousness as we are, it's premature. When we've awakened to Divine consciousness, we'll see ourselves and God in others, whether they're awake or not. Nonetheless, if that's not the origin of our seeing, it's still egoistic and premature. This is no different than feeding swine. We could say, he started looking for the path home, he just hadn't awakened to it yet. Eventually, that too left him hungry and unfulfilled. Another interesting point that Jesus makes is that the citizen of that country gave him the job of feeding his swine. Yet again, Jesus tells us, *"He longed to fill his stomach with the pods that the pigs were eating, but no one gave him anything,"* (Luke 15:16/NIV). Consider, he was the one with the pig food and he was the one who had complete access to feeding the pigs. Yet, he was still looking for "someone else" to give him what he had access to. The truth is, he had what he desired all along, even though at the time he perceived it in the form of pig slop, and unavailable. The false sense of self, the egoistic fabrication, doesn't see good and evil for what it is, but sees it as the source of its sustenance. Eating from that Tree is unfulfilling because there isn't anything in its fruit that can sustain our true selves. To the contrary, it fuels the comparisons of self-satisfying good and evil desire, and such desires result in more of the same: arrogance.

The older son, just like his younger brother, wasn't abiding in the Father's house either. Rather, he was in a field, a place of his own arrogant making, telling himself that he was doing all the right things. He too was feeding on comparisons, just another aspect or form of the knowledge of good and evil. Remember, once we've eaten of this Tree, there's a shapeshifting cherub, literally our egoistic imaginations, which takes on different forms of the same. Regardless of these egoistic mutations, the result is our blindness to the Tree of Life. This form like all the others, produces serious self-binging indulgences, just different ones. In this field, the older son's false self was fabricated not by attaching to someone, as the younger son did, but by being contrary to someone; the one he fixated on was his brother. The delusion here, brother or not, is that we'll never find our identity by pointing the finger at another and saying, "I'm not like them. They do that, I don't do that. I do this. What I do is different than what they do. That's what makes me, me." It's even more of a concerning comparison when we add, "What they do is evil, and I don't do evil. What I do is the opposite, which is good. My identity is not being evil like them, which means I'm really good!" It's very easy to forget that not doing someone else's evil, and doing the opposite, the so-called good, is still the same fruit of the same Tree. The older brother created his false identity by indulging his ego meticulously. He knew every predetermined evil his brother did, and intentionally did the opposite. He had the complete list of his brother's committed evils, which is important to justify how good we are. Not only does it mean we can pridefully say we know right from wrong, but in knowing that, it makes us the ones who are right! Stunned at his father's weak, compromising ways, the older brother declares himself a keeper of the good commandments! He's very clear, accusing his younger brother of spending his inheritance on harlots. What he didn't realize was that his religious creation was just as much a harlot, possibly the most expensive and diseased of all (Revelation 17). Like his younger brother, he had what he desired all along, and was just as unaware of it. In an ultimate display of arrogance, the older son accused his Father of not giving him anything, not even a goat. Yet, from the beginning, the entire inheritance was given to him as well.

While we leave both brothers in their respective fields for the moment, the question arises, where was the Christ? We see a father standing at the porch looking for his sons in the distance, but where is Christ in the parable? In the case of both sons, they'll eventually approach the father's house, though for very different reasons. The moment they started in that direction, the father left his house and quickly approached them. This leaving and coming to both brothers is the manifestation of the Father in Christ. Hence, as Jesus said to Philip, *"If you've seen me, you've seen the Father."* God in Christ comes to us full of joyous *Pleasure, Compassion,* and celebration, just like the father in the parable. He's the throne of *Grace* coming to us with open arms! The father leaving home and throwing his arms around his seemingly estranged son is God in Christ revealed to us. The younger son came to himself in the pigsty and realized the proper comparison, if any, wasn't in the indulgences of his ego. Rather, it was what existed in the father's house compared to where he was, so he started the journey home. The comparison in his consciousness began to change from one of good and evil to what Divine Life appears like compared to its absence. However, though stirring to something greater, he was still groggy with the knowing of good and evil, right and wrong. How many times do we get a glimpse of what Divine Life is like, but then repackage it as being good versus evil? While he realized fulfillment was in his father's house, he was still repackaging that truth through the lens of his egoistic understanding: *"Father, I have sinned against heaven and against you. I am no longer worthy to be called your son,"* (Luke 15:21/NIV). He even rehearsed what he was going to say to make sure it was "right." Of course, if his older brother heard him, it would only fuel his egoism, and being full of himself he would add, "Yes you did do horrible sins. Because of them, you're right, you're not worthy to be called his son, or to be my brother. But I served faithfully, doing all the right things, so I'm definitely worthy to be my father's son and be blessed of Heaven!" He continues with a gentle, condescending voice, "But being that I'm a merciful person and won't give you what you really do deserve, you're welcome to come to my home and be my servant."

We know that God in Christ ignored the younger son's admission of guilt. He doesn't acknowledge it or even say, "I forgive you." There's a Divine truth here, telling us that we've no need to forgive when we don't take offense. This is a lot easier to do when we've regained consciousness to the Tree of Life and allow the Tree of the Knowledge of Good and Evil to be redefined as the absence of Life. It was the father's good *pleasure* to completely restore his son's identity and have a major celebration. On the other hand, God in Christ also approaches the older son, and rather than throwing his arms around him, though we can be sure He desired to, He's now compassionately, fervently pleading. But the older son, in a self-righteous rage, wasn't hearing any of that. In Jesus's story of the prodigals, when the younger son approached the father's house, we don't see the father run into it, grab another son, maybe even a favorite son, and beat him to death to pay for his brother's sins, like in the pagan substitution model. We do see him do something else: kill a fatted calf. The killing of the fatted calf and the non-acknowledgement of the younger son's sins are connected. Remember, when we look to the sacrifice of Jesus, He's always identified as a Lamb, never a calf. As we said previously, the fatted calf was a type of the fabricated golden calf in the valley of Sinai. There's a direct correlation between the people rejecting God's voice from the mountain, and demanding Moses to go and hear from God in their behalf (Exodus 20:19). Sadly, this is a type and shadow. It depicts what's meant to be inspired by the Spirit in pliable human hearts, instead being legalized in stone, a symbol of the egoistic congealed heart, with the added institution of the slaughtered Lamb. While that was going on up the mountain, the people were forming a golden calf down in the valley under the direction of the High Priest, Aaron. The egoistic desire to reject the inner reality of God's Spirit and veiling it with stony commandments so the ego can know what's right and wrong, is most definitely a golden calf! Let's not forget this golden calf was defined as **יהוה**, and to whom a feast was made. But something drastically changes in the prodigal parable. This calf is killed by the father in celebration! This is the complete reverse of what happened at Sinai. There they celebrated the fabricated, legalistic idol of the golden calf. Here, the calf is destroyed, and all celebrate. In other words, sin consciousness is finally put to death by *Gracious Compassion,* and that's a perpetual celebration in the Father's house!

But what of the crucifixion? We know the older son's story ends with the Father in Christ compassionately pleading for him to rid himself of his anger and come into the celebration. If the parable ended with this son giving up his rage and entering the house, he would've been just as celebrated. However, what we see later is the older son in his rage murder the One who left his home to plead. In other words, the older son who kept the commandments, who did all the religiously correct things and did not live a sinful life by such standards, finds himself at odds with his father. By the preceding parables in Luke 15 and the subsequent ones in the following chapter, Jesus identifies the older son as the Pharisees. Now when the Father in Christ comes to plead with the older son, not only does the older son refuse to enter into the house, but something more sinister happens. The older son plots the death of the One who is pleading. Remember Jesus's words, "If you've seen me, you've seen the Father." In the parable the

Father slayed the fatted calf of religion, the older son of that religion, slayed the Father in Christ, the innocent Lamb. The older son said in his rage, *"...you never gave me even a young goat so I could celebrate with my friends,"* (Luke 15:29/NIV). So, he took one. He took the *Compassionate* Lamb and made him a scapegoat, and in religious rightness celebrated with his friends.

As the eternal Son hung on the cross, impaled by the older brother, He said, *"Father forgive them..."* What's interesting is, in all the key moments we hear the Father speaking, like at Jesus's baptism, the mount of transfiguration, the feast where the people hear the Father's voice as an angel or thunder; but at the Cross, there's only silence. Why? For the same reason the father didn't acknowledge the younger son's plea, *"Father, I've sinned against heaven and you. I'm not worthy to be called your son." Grace* and *Rest, Divine Pleasure,* and *Compassion,* have nothing to say to what isn't real. It's not that the crucifixion didn't happen, with all its suffering and torment. Rather, it's an issue of Divine reality. Like in Jesus's parable, the father approached both sons from the standpoint of *Compassion* and *Life,* not the world of moralism, right and wrong, good and evil, thus, a religious world He didn't desire (Psalms 50:7-15). That was a world we created. He never desired to eat flesh or drink blood. We used our Divine power, coupled it with the Knowledge of Good and Evil, and formed this world of egoistic illusion. In other words, in the upper worlds where the Limitless God abides, if He didn't create it, He's not bound to it, nor obligated by it. If He enters anything we egoistically created, He does so to liberate us from it.

Because we desired sacrifice in our religious reduction, He gave it to us (Leviticus 17:11), and tolerated it till He could bring it to an end (Hosea 6:5-6). He profoundly saw the crucifixion from the standpoint of Life, something He entered for our sake and endured its suffering because of the greater joy He saw. When the Father finally spoke, it was three days later through the reality of the resurrection, and in Christ said, *"Peace be with you."* But He didn't stop at telling us there's no conflict and peace between us. Jesus then said:

> *"'Peace to you! As the Father has sent Me, I also send you.' And when He had said this, He breathed on them, and said to them, 'Receive the Holy Spirit. If you forgive the sins of any, they are forgiven them; if you retain the sins of any, they are retained.'"*
>
> *(John 20:21-23/NKJV)*

Again, He reiterates, *"Peace to you,"* and adds a commission, for them to go in the same manner as He was sent. He breathes on them and says to receive the Holy Spirit. But then He says this strange statement, *"If you forgive the sins of any, they are forgiven them; if you retain the sins of any, they are retained."* How many of us thought He was giving the Apostles the ability to forgive sins? How many of us thought He also gave them the right to retain a person's sin upon them? Some turned this into forms of confession and penance. Others, into prayers of specific renunciation for the hope of deliverance. But what if it was consistent with the Life, message, death, and resurrection of Jesus? Jesus didn't come and say, "I forgive you, because I was offended that you broke My Laws." Nor did the Father bellow from Heaven, "This is my beloved Son, Whom you crucified! But I forgive you anyway." Nope, none of the above! Rather, "Peace and receive." What if that following statement was exactly what we see throughout Jesus's ministry, rather than the doctrines we created? Think of it, forgive someone's sins, or retain someone's sins? Since when would any of us want the power to literally retain a person's sins to them? By doing so, aren't we actually saying, "God damn them! I chose not to forgive them!" Or was Jesus really saying, "I offer peace, all you need to do is receive. I'm not in the sin forgiving or retaining business; I never have been. But, if you still live in a religion of good and evil, right and wrong, you may choose to forgive someone who offended you. Or, if they offended someone else, or even think they offended me, you may choose to grant them forgiveness. So, in your thinking they'll be forgiven by all the aforementioned. But, if in your heart you don't forgive them, then they'll still be a wicked sinner. By doing this you'll give yourself permission to have self-righteous anger as the offended one. Or tell someone who was offended how that person will get theirs in the end. Or God must be angry and will judge such a one to burn forever. But as for me, I don't live in that world, and neither should you. So, peace and receive!"

The axis of *Grace* and *Rest* is that simple. It may be simplistic to some, thinking there must be some form of moral accountability. There is, but not in a world of good and evil. *Grace, Divine Pleasure, Compassion,* and *Rest* are not things you contrast to law, judgment, and condemnation. Rather, they're realities that exist in a world of their own, the world of the Tree of Life. We can try to apply them to a world of good and evil, but when we do, Divine truth gets skewed and our egoism starts to rate how bad someone is based on what they did. Thus, our judgmentalism precedes what we perceive as grace and compassion, and redefine them by offering a diminished condemnation. "Well, you should have gotten that! But since I'm going to be gracious you'll only get this with a little bit of that." The fulcrum is the issue of comparison. Till now our egoistic self has compared good with evil, however we've decided what they were. We even redefined God's Covenant of *Grace* with Law and sacrifice, claiming it's God who defined what's good and evil. Nonetheless, the only true choice and comparison is between the two Trees, Life, and the Knowledge of Good and Evil, no different than in the Garden. In other words, Life and Death, or better said, between Life and the absence of it. God was and is eternal *Grace, Compassion, Pleasure,* and *Rest.* What this all means is that we find our identity in our home, our Father's House of *Grace, Compassion, Pleasure,* and *Rest.* Embracing the knowledge of good and evil rooted in the Ego, is leaving that home and going out in the field of a distant country, trying to find our identity. But, as we return home, awakening to the Mind of Christ, we, in His Likeness, find that we always see with the eyes of our Father, full of *Grace* and *Rest* in *Compassionate Pleasure.* With our gaze, we say to ourselves and others, all with thanksgiving to our Father, *"Peace... Receive..."*

CHAPTER 14
I AM ETERNAL PEACE

"We clap hands and welcome the Peace of Christmas.
We beckon this good season to wait a while with us.
We, Baptist and Buddhist,
Methodist and Muslim, say come. Peace.
Come and fill us and our world with your majesty.
We, the Jew and the Jainist,
the Catholic and the Confucian,
Implore you, to stay a while with us.
So we may learn by your shimmering light
How to look beyond complexion and see community.
...
"We, Angels and Mortals, Believers and Non-Believers,
Look heavenward and speak the word aloud. Peace.
We look at our world and speak the word aloud.
Peace. We look at each other, then into ourselves
And we say without shyness or apology or hesitation.
"Peace, My Brother.
Peace, My Sister.
Peace, My Soul."

Excerpt - *Amazing Peace*
Maya Angelou, Written 2005

Our union with Christ in God is best described with the theological concept of the Trinity. Most of Christianity recognizes this teaching. It's the concept that the Divine is three aspects or persons, Father, Son, and Spirit, and they together are God. Hence, God in one respect is a They, not a He. When it comes to gender, as we have stated before, the Holy Spirit is referred to as a she and is in the feminine gender throughout the Tanak. Most importantly, the union of the Trinity is in a state we've called **περιχώρησις** (perichoresis), meaning, *the spinning dance.* This isn't a new idea. Even in the Old Testament, in 2 Samuel 6:14 & 16, we see that the Hebrew word **מכרכר** (m'carkeer), meaning *twirling dance,* is used. David did this before the Ark of the Presence, and it's the only place this word is used. It's no accident that David, who had a glimpse into the Melchizedekian priesthood, would gesture in this way before the Divine Presence; you could say it was a prophetic act. **περιχώρησις** (perichoresis) is the spinning desire of one who prefers the other and the same in turn. It doesn't matter if it's two, three, four, or more, it's the consistent altruistic preferring of the other, which makes the other and the one doing the preferring one in the same. This is equality with equity and equanimity. To take this into the Divine logic mentioned previously, we have to restate what we said in the previous volume: *"It's no longer Three-in-One, now it's ALL-in-ONE… God never intended eternal reality with only Three aspects of His Limitlessness. The Light requires much more! God always included all of us within the Three. So now it's not only Three, it's all as One,"* (*Melchizedek: Our Gracious King-Priesthood in Christ*, Chapter

17: "Being A Melchizedek," Part 2: The Journey of a Melchizedek).

Why is this important? Because a key definition of the Messiah is, **שר שלום** (sar shalom) *"Prince of Peace"* (Isaiah 9:6) which describes His very essence. The Apostle Paul expounded on this to a greater aspect when He wrote:

> *"For He himself is our peace, the One who made the both one, having broken down the middle wall of the partition, the enmity, in His flesh having rendered inoperative the law of the commandments in ordinances, in order that the two He might create in himself, resulting in one new man, making peace..."*
> *(Ephesians 2:14-15/Wuest)*

This is not just a reference to making peace between God and Man, but between Jew and Gentile as well. The notion is mind-blowing. How could Jew and Gentile become one? If you're a Jew, you'd have some serious Laws stating that being in union with a Gentile is forbidden, especially in a religious context. If you were a Gentile, there were serious religious and race issues that existed long before the time of Rome. Why would you want to be in union with those "inferior" Jews? When we expand these historical racial, tribal, and religious issues, we create caste systems, political factions, and other schisms that fragment us further. Nonetheless, Christ *is our Peace* and has broken down the hostile wall of division. The ramifications of this are far more reaching than just being nice to our neighbors or being friendly with someone with a different point of view. To add to the point, this "Peace," this breaking down of animosity, doesn't just apply to our fellow Christians. In other words, this doesn't only apply to people that think or believe like we do, but also to those who appear to think differently. As we awaken to this Eternal reality, this Peace becomes an awareness of our union of Oneness, which brings to an end all our rationalizations for any sense of separation. We become conscious to a reality that we all emanate from the same Source, whether someone is awakened to that or not. Hence, there's no Jew, nor Gentile, nor bond, nor free, and so on (Galatians 3:28). Remember, God didn't create the separation, it's our egoistic illusion that did.

Earlier we referred to the phrase *"Prince of Peace,"* which in Hebrew is שר שלום (sar shalom). The word for *peace,* שלום (shalom), is from the word שלם (shalam), which means *complete wholeness.* In relationship to the Hebraic meaning, when the Apostle Paul writes to the Ephesians, he uses the word εἰρήνη (eirene), meaning *freedom from war* and *being set at one again.* In the Greek world, the word was a description of a *state of being,* not simply a cessation of conflict. To reiterate, this is more than just being nice to our neighbors, or to those who have a different point of view; this is a complete transformation of our consciousness. This is an awakening from egoistic sleep and seeing ourselves at one with the whole of Creation. Most importantly, it begins with us seeing ourselves at one with all Humanity within the Trinitarian dance. In other words, we're both personally and corporately an emanation of God revealed in the totality of Creation, past, present, and future. We are "ONE new Man."

Part 1: Leaving the Illusion of Dualism

In the dualistic world of the Tree of the Knowledge of Good and Evil, we sleep. Together in our collective unconsciousness, we dream of the illusion of what it's like to be safe in our own rightness, to be in a special relationship, to be wealthy, famous, or whatever our fantasies conjure. Yet, as we stir with the dawn of Divine Reality, the illusion is challenged. Our sense of safety was founded on all the egoistic delusions that created a false tranquility, or you could say, "peace." However, when any disturbance disrupts it, we seek to regain it with a vengeance. This fabricated tranquility is not established upon, nor sought by, peace, but war. Like a Mafia Don who is relaxing with his family at a beach, he still must have armed bodyguards nearby to create a sense of safety. This sense of safety or peace exists with the constant threat of danger. It exists with the constant undercurrent of alertness and preparedness to respond violently. This is not the inner *Rest* of Divine Peace, but the posture of hostility. It's the constant waging of war upon every aspect that challenges the illusions we hold. We'll pummel whoever or whatever threatens it, and we'll keep our emotional guns poised to fire just in case of threat. The Ego's need to be in "a world of right" will attack whatever suggests otherwise. The violent response is the axis of the Ego's identity. For that matter, its rightness is based on the avoidance of being wrong. To be wrong is to be flawed. To be flawed creates insecurity in our fabricated identity. Such insecurity is what causes us to feel unsafe and vulnerable. This happens on a regular basis within the dream-world of the Knowledge of Good and Evil as we interact with

471

others. Thus we have classism, racism, nationalism, cultism (religious or not), and tribalism. All are built on the underlying fear of losing our fabricated self and losing the validation of the tribe and caste which affirms it. Compound that fear by the added dread of losing possessions, status, and power, and we're poised for war. This is the motivation of every unconscious person and people group. The writer of the book of Hebrews surmises this by calling it, *"the fear of death"* (Hebrews 2:15).

In contrast, what we're speaking of now is the awakening to the real world. This literally means, the complete deconstruction, reconstruction, and transformation of reality as we comprehend it. Thus, the peace the Ego attempts to gain wages war against the very One who offers it. The Ego isn't a peace bringer, but a warmonger. True peace doesn't exist in any "egoistic illusion." Regardless of what we deem as truth, righteousness, peace, and love, they do not exist in a dualistic world of good and evil. There's only an apparition of them. These wraiths take form and gain strength from our base nature. They form what we claim as truth, what we decide as right, and the appetites they bring. They're our creation and they culminate in our fashioning of relationships, tribes, nations, politics, and religions. In the same way we created this world at the Fall, we also create and empower the forces that hold the illusion together.

As we stir to consciousness, our Egoistic self sees this as Armageddon. Both the New and parts of the Old Testaments seem to portray a violent, world-ending return of Christ, which is misrepresented when seen with egoistic eyes. Christ is not returning to wage a bloody war on the very ones He loves just because they have not yet discovered a desire for Him (1 John 4:9). Nor does He demonstrate His Love for "saved people" by destroying "sinful ones" in some end-time battle. If one looks carefully at most of the eschatological approaches in modern evangelicalism, including their charts, novels, and art, they have Jesus Christ *in name only.* No! Divine reality is that the Love of God was revealed and that, while we were yet egoistic sinners, Christ died, offering His Life to us in true peace and reconciliation (Romans 5:8).

The perceived condemning return of Christ is not about vengeance at all, but a description of us becoming conscious. As the Light of Christ dawns with the opening of our eyes, a type of Armageddon occurs to the egoistic world we once created. The serpentine Ego may scream, "You're killing me! You're destroying my world! You're decimating my peace and bringing war!" Then, if we add its religiosity to the equation, it will cry out, "The terror of the Lord has come! The judgment of God is upon us! He's come to destroy sin and sinner! The end times are here!" But, when heard with a conscious heart, we hear, "Whoever desires, awake! Drink of the waters of peace and life freely," (John 7:37). "There's no desire to destroy! Rather, to destroy that which is destructive, we do through meekness, compassion, and peacemaking," (Matthew 5:1-12). In that moment, the world we knew, like a twirling wisp of vapor, transfigures into the reality of what always was, is, and shall be, *but seen for the first time with new eyes!*

473

Part 2: Returning Home and Seeing It For the First Time

We made a brief mention in a previous chapter, "Refresher: In the Beginning Again," about a book which later became a movie in 1939, *The Wizard of Oz*. We spoke of the event where the little dog Toto exposed the man behind the curtain. However, that's just a tiny moment in a grander story. Our becoming conscious to Divine Reality, our identity in Christ, and the Tree of Life, is awakening to what always Was, Is, and Shall Be, yet seeing it for the first time with new eyes. This is beautifully portrayed by L. Frank Baum in that same children's story. In broader philosophical circles the concept of the story is known as "The Eternal Return." (This is not to be confused with Frederick Nietzsche's idea of "Eternal Reoccurrence," which is not the same.)

Several years ago, while preparing to write this volume, I shared a series at our church called, "The Return." In the second lesson, "Home Again," I featured the Christ-centered message of the *eternal return* as depicted in the Wizard of Oz. (Before we continue, if you have never seen the movie, *The Wizard of Oz*, put down this book, view it, then continue on to the next paragraph. Enjoy!)

Think of the story (this is a condensed version). From the beginning we find Dorothy dreaming of a place other than home from a very egoistical view. In her self-centeredness, she wants something beyond the love of her uncle, aunt, and close friends. She says this illusionary place is *somewhere over the rainbow,* "where skies are blue." As she sings of the colors of the rainbow, the entire first segment of the movie is in black and white. In her eyes, she cannot see the color and beauty of what is right in front of her. Thus, she wants to leave and find what she desires elsewhere. In her discontentment, she unconsciously creates problems with a neighbor, Miss Gulch. Dorothy allows her dog, Toto, to eat Miss Gulch's flowers without stopping him. Miss Gulch, upset with Dorothy, goes to her home with letter in hand from the sheriff to take the dog to the pound. (It's clear from the accusation that this happened more than once.) Confronting Dorothy's aunt and uncle, Miss Gulch shows them she's been granted the right to take the dog by "law." They reluctantly give the dog to Miss Gulch, putting the dog into a basket, and Miss Gulch rides off on a bicycle to the pound. Toto manages to open the basket, escape, and return home to Dorothy. In fear of Toto being taken again, Dorothy runs away.

On her journey, she meets a carnival magician who persuades her to return home. But as Dorothy starts the return journey, there are gale force winds conjured by a pending tornado. When she arrives home, the storm intensifies. Her house is empty because her family and friends took shelter in their storm cellar. As she runs throughout the house calling for her aunt, she's blown about by the winds. She runs into her bedroom with Toto in her arms, but now the tornado is very close. The house is caught up in the turbulent winds and Dorothy is struck on the head by a windowpane that's flown loose. Knocked unconscious, her reality changes into a dream (or is it?).

The house, with Dorothy and Toto in it, is caught up in the spinning tornado. Dorothy regains consciousness and looks out the window. As the wind continues to carry the house high up into the sky, she sees debris, livestock, and even an occasional person fly by. They change from their real-world appearance into something different. Miss Gulch is apparently caught up in the tornado as well and riding that same bicycle. She transforms right before Dorothy's eyes into a wicked witch, dressed in black, riding a broom.

The house finally drops out of the sky and lands in a very different, dreamlike world called Oz. It's an illusion with fragmented prisms of the real world left behind. It's here that one of the most famous lines in all of movie history is said, *"Toto, I've a feeling we're not in Kansas anymore. We must be over the rainbow!"* The very imaginary world she dreamt of before she left home, **is the dream world she has created and fallen into.**

There are many important events that take place in both the book and movie that speak to our topic, but here are a few key points that relate to what we're discussing. When her house fell into Oz, it landed on the Wicked Witch of the East and killed her. The Witch of the East had the coveted ruby slippers of power, which at her perceived demise, were instantly transferred to Dorothy's feet. The background story of the Wicked Witch of the East is that she had the power to control weather and create tornados. Why did the house land on her? Because Dorothy is actually the Witch of the East. Consider, her name is Dorothy "Gale." In the movie, the ruby slippers are not taken by Dorothy, they are instantly and mysteriously transferred to her. The shoes disappear from the witch's feet, reappear on Dorothy, and then the witch seems to melt away under the house. The segment when the house lands on the Witch of the East was a storytelling mechanism, transfiguring and merging the illusionary witch and literal Dorothy.

As the story continues, Dorothy discovers three friends: a scarecrow, who needs a brain to reason; a tin man, who needs a heart to feel love; and a cowardly lion, who needs to find courage within himself. They go with her on the journey to help her find the path to "return home." They encounter many obstacles conjured by the Wicked Witch of the West, who is the sister of the Wicked Witch of the East. She covets the power of the ruby slipper and the only way to gain them is to destroy Dorothy. In exploring the mysterious Wicked Witch of the West, we find she's Dorothy's alter ego. Hence, the dualistic aspects of Dorothy Gale, like the contrasts of East and West, The East is where the sun rises and the West is where the sun sets, but there's only one sun that migrates from one state to the other, from its setting and rising. The same is true with the Ego and its Knowledge of Good and Evil. It's the same Serpent and same Tree, but they're polar opposites which exist in the same space. Whether its Dorothy, or each one of us, we all seem to experience polarizing attitudes, ideas, and most importantly, contrasting desires. As the Apostle Paul said, *"For what I want to do I do not do, but what I hate I do."* (Romans 7:15). You could say, when we look at the sun from *the World Below* standpoint of dualism, there's an East and West, opposite passions that exist in each of us. However, when we look from *the World Above* singular, Tree of Life standpoint, it's as if we stand upon the sun itself and emanate light. There isn't an East and West, or opposite passions, only that which emanates Life with all its glimmering facets.

Dorothy's journey begins mirroring all our stories. She is dominated by the lower nature, the ego, and its desire for something other than her true self and the reality in which she lived. While the Wicked Witch of the West may be a projection of the evil Miss Gulch, the entire dynamic was Dorothy's creation. If Dorothy hadn't been so self-centered and self-focused, Miss Gulch would never have had a reason to come to the house and demand Toto. As with most of the perceived evil in our lives, many times they are the stories we've told ourselves about events and people, rather than realizing they are projections of our own creation in a world of contrasts. For that matter, the entire world of Oz is all within Dorothy, and a projection of her inner state.

Her three friends are aspects within herself: the scarecrow, the need to think beyond herself and include others; the tin man, the need to love beyond herself and have compassion for others; and the cowardly lion, the need to discover a courage to go beyond her egoistic self and reveal all these qualities. Without them, the ruby slippers (the ability to awaken to reality) stayed dormant on her feet, using such power only to run from all that the ego conjures. Hence, her alter ego, the Witch of the West, coveting the power of the slippers, is that strong, polarizing, self-centered desire doing all it can to survive and reign. The last thing the ego wants is for us to realize our true inner qualities, because when we do, it can no longer thrive.

Finally, there's little Toto, similar to, but not exactly like Jiminy Cricket, as an externalized type of Dorothy's inner consciousness. In the beginning, it's the egoistic self, unrestrained and doing whatever it pleases, like running through Miss Gulch's garden, eating her flowers. When Miss Gulch tries to stop Toto, the dog bites her on the leg. This is what finally moves Miss Gulch to go to the sheriff and take the dog to be euthanized. The bottom line is that, at this point, Toto is unbridled and dangerous. However, when Miss Gulch arrives with a legal demand, Dorothy cries foul. Even her guardians are upset, though they yield to the legal demands. While Miss Gulch may appear to be the evil enemy, she's actually the victim, and her demands are the product of Toto, who is Dorothy's unrestrained egoism. As Dorothy goes through her journey in Oz, we watch Toto transform at each stage. Eventually, Toto becomes a little hero, leading Dorothy's three friends to where she's being held captive by the Wicked Witch and eventually revealing the man behind the curtain.

With little Toto in arms, Dorothy and her consciousness, along with her developing three inner friends, braves the obstacles her alter ego presents her. The quest of the journey is to find the one whom she hoped would help, the Wizard in the Emerald City. It's also important to point out that in most of the key stories that originally framed the concept of the Eternal Return, long before L. Frank Baum, were the Grail legends. Before the Grail took on the form of the cup of Christ in the medieval stories, it was originally an *emerald platter.* You could say that the Wizard of Oz is another retelling of those ancient Grail legends. While we see the stories of Oz as being meant for children, they have much to say to all of us.

The purpose of Dorothy's journey from the time she landed in Oz was to *return home.* The return is ultimately about discovering her identity, values, and seeing her home world *with new eyes.* Once they all arrived at the Emerald City, they found that the Wizard was not able to help her get home. He, like all the rest, was Dorothy's dream creation, which gave the Wizard his false external power. The Wizard had to be revealed as the man behind the curtain, the one who was not who he claimed to be, so that in the end it would all rest on Dorothy's inner identity, power, and most importantly, *desire.* The Wizard (who looks like the carnival magician who encouraged her to return home in the other world) was about creating an earnest desire to do so. With every step on the yellow brick road, and every challenge afforded her, a "pure desire" to return was created. The Wizard served as a transformational motivation. Within that pure desire came compassion, thinking of others, and the courage to confront the evil projection of her once large Ego. When Dorothy, Toto, and her three friends finally have an audience with the Wizard ("the man behind the curtain" hadn't been revealed as of yet), he says:

THE WIZARD: I am Oz! The great and powerful! *(with flames and a booming voice)* Who are you? WHO ARE YOU?

DOROTHY: *(with a gulp),* I am Dorothy, the small and meek.

Finally, we see the budding fruits of her transformation. When posed with the same question that Satan posed to Jesus in the wilderness, "Who are you?" usually translated, *"If you are the Son of God..."* it amounts to the same idea. He doesn't first ask, "Why are you here?" Or "What do you want from the great and powerful Oz?" But "Who are you?" She responds "Dorothy, the small and meek," which can seem to be a good, even fearful, religious answer. Yet, when the Wizard confronts the cowardly lion with a similar question, the lion faints from fear. Dorothy stands up to the Wizard, saying that he should be ashamed of himself for frightening the lion after he came for help. This is not her egoistic pride nor angry demand taking a stand, but her newly found "compassion with courage." The Wizard, with menacing speech, then tells them that he will grant their wishes under the condition that they bring the broomstick of the Wicked Witch of the West. More adventures ensue and they are finally successful. Like all our egos, it is housed by a castle of terrors with strong armies of illusion and fables to protect it. In the final conflict with the Witch, the Witch sets the scarecrow on fire. Dorothy, moved with compassion and courage, quickly grab a water bucket and puts out the fire. However, the Witch is doused with the water as well and instantly starts melting away. Her final words are:

WICKED WITCH: What a world! What a world! Who would have thought a good little girl like you could destroy my beautiful wickedness! Look out! Look out!

Toto inspects the remains of the Witch, which is only her garment. The powerful ego, now being diminished, breaks the captive illusion over the Witch's guards and they rejoice over Dorothy's victory.

Dorothy and her friends return to the Wizard with broom in hand. It's in this moment, despite the bellowing declarations of, "I'm the Great and powerful Oz," that he too is exposed. Toto peels back the curtain where the Wizard is hiding. We find he isn't great and powerful, just a jolly old carnival performer hiding behind an aggrandized false persona. Now that Dorothy's Ego has been exposed and put in its proper place, we find the Wicked Witch has melted and the Wizard has been reduced to his actual size. In both external apparitions of the dual egoistic opposites, the Witch and the Wizard, both have been significantly minimized. This is also why the Wizard doesn't have the capacity to escort Dorothy and Toto home. The dualism of the Serpentine-Tree, whether it's the evil Witch who opposes *the return home,* or the all-powerful Wizard who claims the ability to grant our desired *return;* neither are capable. Rather, through humility, the Scarecrow is now conscious enough and can think in new ways, the Tin Man has compassion to empower the journey, and the once Cowardly Lion has the courage to keep the ego in its place. By the end, we once again find what was true from the beginning. Dorothy had the ability to return home all along, she just needed to discover it. Like us, who always were, and are, the Image of God, from which our true identity emerges, if we're unconscious of it, we cannot walk in its reality (like the ruby slippers). Though we may religiously be aware of the notion of a doctrine that claims our Likeness, it doesn't mean we've awakened to it. For that matter, nor can we be in a world of egoistic duality. Rather, our feet are just shod with pretty slippers. We may even be "proud" that they look so good on us. On the other hand, it doesn't mean we're deformed or corrupt, we're just asleep. With that aspect of our godlike quality, which is that right to choose, we empower the egoistic desires for something "other" somewhere over the rainbow. We use that power to conjure a world of illusion with the stories we tell ourselves. Thus, like Dorothy, sleeping in an unconscious dream world, we journey through it finding hints and glimpses of who we are, like peering into a fractured mirror.

Prior to the final scene in Oz, the now diminished Wizard, along with Dorothy and Toto, get into a hot air balloon. He still arrogantly parades himself as the great Oz, claiming that now, as he embarks on the journey to take Dorothy home, he will assemble with his great fellow wizards. As he continues his narcissistic speech, he presses the rule of Oz upon the Scarecrow, Tin Man, and Lion. Yet, if we watch the scene carefully, once again Toto takes center stage. We see Toto attracted to a cat that's held by a bystander, so he jumps out of Dorothy's arms to chase it. Dorothy leaps out of the hot air balloon to chase after Toto. Then, as if thoughtlessly behind the scenes, we can see the Tin Man (compassion and love), who's holding the rope that tethers the balloon to the ground post, quietly loosen it, letting the Wizard float away. Now both Witch and Wizard are gone! Both the dualistic desires that oppose and claim fulfillment are no longer of influence. One may think, "Well, maybe he did that on purpose so Dorothy wouldn't leave." But not so. It's at this point we arrive at the final scene in Oz. Glinda, the Good Witch of the North, arrives in the Emerald City and encourages Dorothy about returning home. In that dialogue there are some powerful New Testament truths:

GLINDA: You don't need to be helped any longer. You've always had the power to go back to Kansas.

DOROTHY: I have?

SCARECROW: Then why didn't you tell her before?

GLINDA: Because she wouldn't have believed me. She had to learn it for herself.

TIN MAN: What have you learned, Dorothy?

DOROTHY: Well, I -- I think that it -- that it wasn't enough just to want to see Uncle Henry and Auntie Em -- and it's that -- if I ever go looking for my heart's desire again, I won't look any further than my own backyard. Because if it isn't there, I never really lost it to begin with!

Dorothy is then told to click the heels of her ruby slippers three times and repeat, "There is no place like home," and she will return. She does. She awakes in her bed, repeating those words, and surrounded by Auntie Em, Uncle Henry, Hunk (the

Scarecrow), Zeke (the Cowardly Lion), Hickory (the Tin Man) and even Professor Marvel (the Wizard of Oz).

DOROTHY: Home! And this is my room -- and you're all here! And I'm not going to leave here ever, ever again, because I love you all! And -- Oh, Auntie Em -- there's no place like home!

The story of Dorothy Gale is the story of the Human condition, a beautiful retelling of the Grail stories and, most importantly, the parable of the Prodigal Son. Like us, The Adam, who desired more than their home in the eternal world of the Garden of Pleasure (Eden), they egoistically desired something else. Like Dorothy, they left their home in Eden by choosing another path, the knowledge of good and evil. The resulting death was far more than just a physical finality, but a dream world of their own creation. Yet no sooner did they leave that they embarked on a journey with obstacles, calamities, and fortunately, three spiritual friends. In Dorothy's world they were the Scarecrow, Tin Man, and Cowardly Lion. The Scarecrow who desired to think, the Tin Man who desired to love, and the Cowardly Lion who desired courage, were the internal aspects of Dorothy that needed to be realized so she could return home with *new eyes.* In the same manner, we too are to discover three friends, Father, Son and Spirit, not as external entities, *but internal realities.* The world of Oz was one of Dorothy's own imaginative creations, just like the world we created that we now live in, which is seemingly more real than the thought of a greater, spiritual world. Yet, like in the land of Oz, there is a deep inner yearning that keeps beckoning us. That yearning or internal realization is an arousing to a whole new value of ourselves and most importantly "home," Like Dorothy, as we become conscious, with the egoistic dream melting away, we see what was, is, and shall be, with a whole new awareness.

Part 3: Awaking To the Reality of Oneness

In the world of the Tree of the Knowledge of Good and Evil, we exist in a realm of conflict and contrast which sets the criteria on how we learn and make decisions. There must be a wrong to contrast with that which is right. If wrong doesn't exist, then right can't exist either. Consequently, the Ego, the lower nature, and its cosmos, can't survive in its current form without such a criterion. How does one describe a world of oneness, the Tree of Life, the reality of Christ, where there are no conflicting contrasts, only dynamic complements? For example, if we approach this from a *World Below* perspective, the concepts of being awake or asleep, conscious or unconscious, still fit into the binary world of good and evil. Referring back to the concepts of faith below, within, and above reason, just because we "believe the right thing" doesn't mean we're conscious. We've established that the Ego is quite content in its certainty that what it believes is right. In the same way, we could say that those who are awake, or conscious, are "in" and those who are asleep, or unconscious, are "out." On the other hand, if we see with a touch of the *World Above*, the ideas of being enlightened, awake, and conscious, are not an "either/or" notion, but a progressive awareness. What we're discussing is a process of uncovering reality. We're not losing one for the other, but are effectively transforming from one state to another, like climbing a ladder. We're not losing sight of where we were, but as we climb, an elevation of consciousness unfolds and a broadening of awareness occurs. Although Dorothy awoke in her room after her Oz experience, it was technically the same place she'd been just hours before while she was unconscious. Yet her awareness completely transformed and she was able to see with a new set of eyes. She was able to comprehend *both states* simultaneously. She was aware of the values of her newly conscious life, which brought rest and grace, as well as her relationship to the unconscious world she'd created. In the *World Above,* she was able to recognize how she related to the *World Below,* yet with a completely different point of reference.

Another way to describe this is with a light switch. From the *World Below,* we see a person who is awake or conscious as if their switch is turned on. In contrast, we perceive a person who's asleep or unconscious as if their switch is turned off, in effect, living in darkness. But what if the egoistic knowledge of good and evil, *in* or *out,* the *on* or *off* switch, wasn't our reference point? What if we saw from the *World Above,* from the Tree of Life? Our tools and reference points would be very different. Therefore, what if we had a "dimmer" rather than an "on/off" switch, as well as another necessary component we haven't discussed yet, a focus lens? This would give us a very different perception than simply on or off. Having only an on and off switch of the *World Below* is no better than trying to perceive the entire area with a flashlight. Though the light is on, because of its binary focus, the view is incomplete. So, while one person points the flashlight in one direction, another person may point it in a different direction. The result is differing, segmented views of reality because of limited focus. This egoistic limitation creates a sense of separation, and many times an inability to find a way to interact. Being that a base ingredient of egoism is fear, this results in the continued argument of right and wrong, good and bad. But if have a dimmer connected to a light hanging from the ceiling, it provides a very different experience. Now it's a process of light gradually brightening and us bringing what's illuminated into focus panoscopically (like a movie projector). The light brightening is wonderful, but it's only part of the process. In addition to the light, there is the process of *focal convergence.* The light helps create the atmosphere which gives us the potential for clarity. As the dimly lit room is illuminated, we still must focus on the images the light reveals. Obviously, the brighter light provides more potential for clarity, which suggests this is an ongoing adjustment of these relationships. Herein is yet another important element; if we've never seen something in the proper light and focus, how do we know if it's fully in focus when we see it? More so, how do we know what we're seeing without some kind of reference or instruction? The quick and simple answer is, we wouldn't. This is why the parable of the Prodigal Son, and the allegory of the Wizard of Oz, are so profound. We do have a reference! *We were there, we were in the Upper World before we ever fell asleep and created this one.* The reason we experience what is considered as "revelation" or the "ah-ha" moment, isn't because we haven't seen something before. It's because we have seen it before! But this time, we see it with renewed Life-giving eyes! It's a form of remembering, but from a completely different reference point. For example:

> *"They came to Bethsaida, and some people brought a blind man and begged Jesus to touch him. He took the blind man by the hand and led him outside the village. When he had spit on the man's eyes and put his hands on him, Jesus asked, 'Do you see anything?' He looked up and said, 'I see people; they look like trees walking around.' Once more Jesus put his hands on the man's eyes. Then his eyes were opened, his sight was restored, and he saw everything clearly. Jesus sent him home, saying, 'Don't go into the village.'"*   *(Mark 8:22-25/NIV)*

This entire chapter of Mark's gospel is about seeing. In the verses above, we see a man who was blind. When Jesus first touched him, he didn't see with clarity. You could say he saw the light brighten, but didn't have the ability to focus. Can you imagine if Jesus and the man simply stopped there? In that man's reality, people as trees would be an unconscious confusion. While in the sense of spiritual metaphor there's a truth to be taken, from which Tree do we as people emanate, that wasn't the point just yet. It wasn't enough for the eyes to perceive light, they had to be able to focus in order to see reality. I would suggest that many of us in Christendom have seen the Light, but haven't learned to focus. To refocus our perception to see with Divine Eyes, we must move our point of reference from egoism to one of *Grace, Rest,* and *Compassion.* Without any spirituality (or a minimal sense of it), the Ego sees with a flashlight focus. When we break the barrier and begin to awaken, while still groggy from the Egoism of good and evil, the room is lit, yet without focus, hence seeing men as trees. To focus the lens of our Divine Eyes, we must connect to the Divine Source within, which is *Grace, Rest,* and *Compassion.* These vectors create the necessary *focal convergence* to clearly see panoscopically.

In the broader picture of this chapter, Mark tells us that the mass of people who were following Jesus hadn't eaten for three days. Jesus asks the disciples for the loaves and small fish they had. He tells the people to sit, gives thanks to the Father, and then has the disciples distribute the food. As the disciples share what was blessed, what was a few are multiplied, and are more than enough to feed everyone. No sooner are they finished and the people disperse, than Jesus and the disciples meet the Pharisees who challenge Him to give them *a sign* to validate His identity. In other words, *"Let me see something that will convince me."* Interestingly, they just missed a major miracle, yet that's a key part of the point. There's a difference between the people, the Pharisees, the disciples, and Jesus. There were at least four aspects of seeing in that moment. Jesus was conscious to the point where He could see into all the existing worlds around Him. You could say, He saw into several dimensions at once. Jesus saw with panoscopic vision. In one, a mass of hungry people and only a few loaves and fish. At the same time in a broader dimension, multitudes were fed till they were full and even had loaves and fish left over. It was about how Jesus saw reality that defined it in the moment. He didn't deny the one for the sake of the other, rather He looked into the all-inclusive one and that became reality. Yet, for the Pharisees, that reality never occurred. Nonetheless, for this also to be possible, simultaneously both the people and the disciples had to be in an inner space that would be receptive to that same *Upper World.*

In the case of the people, they humbly followed and stayed with Christ to this point. Their "focus" was not on external needs, but internal fulfillment, another way of saying *Divine Peace.* Mark's gospel doesn't describe people complaining about hunger, being unsettled, or making demands. Rather, one could say they were trusting Christ with their *being.* The people didn't work up their faith for a food miracle using will power, nor build it up by scrutinized study. No, it came down to the element of focus. Not eating for three days just wasn't as important as being with Christ and the inner food He was imparting. This is why *Divine Peace* is at the center. It doesn't require an intellectual understanding, just the inner sense of union with Christ and reality (Philippians 4:7). Understanding follows, but not in the type of knowing that comes from the Ego. Rather, it's an unfolding with a brightening of awareness, and an intuitive refocusing of our consciousness. Thus, a spiritual synonym for "Peace" is "Oneness."

The people, now spiritually and physically full, were sent along on their way while Jesus and the disciples got into a boat and continued their journey. When Jesus and the disciples arrive at their destination, there is an interesting designation given. In the Gospel of Mark, it is called, **Δαλμανουθά**

491

Dalmanutha, and in the Gospel of Matthew it is called, **Μαγαδαν** *Magadan,* which in Hebrew is מגדון, *Megiddon.* Unfortunately, in the Textus Receptus, it's erroneously scribed as *Magdala.* Translations that use the Textus Receptus as a source inadvertently misdirect the point of the text. While Magdala is a place on the shore of Galilee, the fact that both Matthew and Mark use different names points not to a physical location, but to define a spiritual condition. This isn't unusual to the Biblical writers. An obvious example is found in Revelation 11:8, where *Jerusalem* is called *Sodom* and *Egypt.* All three cities are in very different locations, but the focus is that their spiritual qualities were all the same. So the issue isn't where they're located physically, but spiritually. We see this occur in the Tanak as well. In one reference in Zechariah 12:11, we see *Jerusalem* equated to *Magadan,* which is the condition we just stated in Matthew's gospel. It was there that King Josiah was murdered by Pharaoh Necho, which resulted in great mourning. By word definition, Josiah יאשיה means *Foundation of Yah,* and Necho נכה means *to smite.* Can you imagine? It's speaking of the *Foundation of Yah* being smitten? With that notion as the backdrop, in the Matthew discourse, he equates the Pharisees and Sadducees receiving no other sign than *that of the prophet Jonah,* a prophetic forecast of Jesus death and resurrection. We could effectively say that the crucifixion was a type of smiting the *Foundation of Yah* (1 Corinthians 3:11). Regarding *Dalmanutha,* there's simply no such place on a map to reference. However, its definition is telling. It means *The Shepherd's Way.* Herein is a major point of divergence of an egoistic knowing of good and evil, and an altruistic emanation

492

of Divine Life. As later pointed out in the Gospel of John, Jesus calls the Pharisees hirelings, thieves, and spiritual murderers, and refers to Himself as one willing to give His life for the sheep. (See the entire tenth chapter of John's gospel.) The spiritual setting *Magadan - Dalmanutha* reveals both kinds of shepherds. Hence, they may occupy the same location for a moment, but in spiritual reality, they're forever worlds apart.

When the Pharisees arrive—the alleged shepherds of those same people Jesus just fed—they demand to see a sign. Unfortunately, regardless of how demanding we are to see something spiritually, it's ultimately pointless. We can't demand ourselves to see anything from that inner posture. Nor can we demand God to open our eyes, simply because we want Him to prove Himself or an aspect of Himself to us. Such demands are commonly born of our egoism. If being in the Likeness of God, as Christ demonstrated, is through humility and meekness, then such demanding only enforces our unconsciousness. Then add Bible verses to that unawareness, and we have righteous arrogance walking around unconsciously. Welcome again to the Christian Zombie Apocalypse. In the same way, God doesn't just randomly open the eyes of the blind, though it may seem that way to the observer in *the World Below*. Nothing is random or accidental.

When light enters the natural eye, technically everything it sees is illuminated. But it's the mind and heart that determines what it wants to see. It's the mind that focuses the lens of the eye, deciding what to emphasize. Then that same heart and mind defines what is emphasized based on the stories in the memory it references. Thus, what we "think" we see and what's seen can be completely different, even worlds apart. The challenge is, it's irrelevant as to what's truly seen. The only thing that's seen is what's validated by the memories of our emotional egoism. Therefore, the gateway, or as Jesus said, *"...the gate is narrow and the way is hard that leads to life..."* (Matthew 7:14), is through *Grace, Rest,* and *Compassion.* These vectors of Divine Life are why the gate seems so narrow. In short, our Ego, regardless of how small we think it is, is still too big to enter. Consider all those who sit at the gateway, religiously proud of their resistance to immorality and their offerings to others, but never enter. Worse yet, they don't even realize they haven't.

How many of us have had a car accident, or missed our exit while driving, simply because we were focused on something else? For that moment, the exit didn't exist, even if a few miles or kilometers earlier we'd thought to look for it. Then there's that moment after the accident when we claim in shock, "I didn't see it! That car just came out of nowhere!" If that can happen in very practical ways, how much more can it happen in regard to our true self and spiritual reality? For the most part, when our inner egoistic Pharisee is demanding to see, it has already decided what it wants to see and what it should look like, all for the purpose of gratifying itself. This culminates in not seeing anything, only the illusion it wanted to see from the beginning. This is why the Pharisees weren't present when the miracle of feeding the multitude occurred. They couldn't be because they were not in the same inner space as the people and the disciples. This would be no different than pulling our car over on the side of the motorway and demanding our exit to appear, or declaring this is where it should be, though it's miles away. Nevertheless, such is the inner Pharisee. It struts around the car claiming that the exit must be here somewhere, and if more people would pull over and prayerfully agree then it would be revealed. Then sitting on the curb, full of itself, adds, "If those who keep driving by would just stop and listen to my knowledgeable proclamations and laws, they too would know about the exit!" Then, once the arrogance forms frustration because the exit still hasn't been found, our inner religiosity thinks, "If I only pray harder, speak in tongues longer, and study more intently, the miracle of the roadside exit will appear." Nope, it's not going to happen! Not that way. Why? Because the motorway exit is exactly where it needs to be for our journey. The only way we will get to it is if we walk (or drive) farther along the way. Then, we will perceive it in the distance getting closer and closer, like a light growing brighter and brighter. Finally, when we arrive at our exit, or better said, when we *realize it,* all the scenery will start coming into focus. This is why God doesn't randomly open eyes or do miracles to prove Himself to our egoism. It's not that the Almighty doesn't want us to see, nor is incapable of giving us the miracle of sight. But if He compromised reality in doing so, He would only seal our blindness. This is why God said in the Garden after we partook of the Knowledge of Good and Evil, *"...He must not be allowed to reach out his hand and take also from the tree of life and eat, and live forever,"* (Genesis 3:22/NIV). To allow the mingling of the Tree of Life with the Egoism of the Tree of the Knowledge of Good and Evil would've sealed Mankind in the Death Sleep forever. For the same reason that He allowed us to choose the illusion of the Tree of Death, He also allows us to awaken when we're humbly ready. You could say that the occurrence of our inner resurrection isn't up to God, but up to us. Nonetheless, as we take this journey in *the World Below,* He, all the while from *the World Above,* walks with us on it. He never leaves us nor forsakes us in our unconsciousness. He's the very spiritual air we breathe as we sleep. Note the words of Jesus:

> *"'I have come to judge the world's blindness - so that they who are blind may see and those who think that they see may become blind.' Some of the Pharisees overheard him and said, 'So, are we also blind?' Jesus said, 'If you were blind you would have no sin, but now you say you see and your sin continues!'"*　　　　　(John 9:39-41/MIRROR)

This verse has many sides to its block logic, and bears repeating in many forms. However, the notion of the blind having no sin while those who claim to see continue having their sin, doesn't make sense on the religious surface. For that matter, some translations use the phrase, *"...your sin remains."* You would think those who see, being enlightened, would have no sin by avoiding it, and those who are blind would be the hard-core sinners, relentlessly running into it. However, as Jesus points out, the reverse is true! Consider the creative power of the Image and Likeness of God, the Human Being. The Adam had the power, through its choice in the Garden, to create the phantasm in which we now live. Similarly, Dorothy created, and experienced, a world in which witches, Winkie guards, and flying monkeys repeatedly attacked her and her friends. These were external creations she fought because she wasn't yet capable of seeing their inner realities. Accordingly, we too have created similar enemies in our world. We create the necessary forces of demons and devils, who seem to attack out of nowhere. Then we, in due course, fall prey to wicked sins and become victims of their evil calamities (Galatians 5:19-21; Rev. 12:9). Of course, the ego then adds that this must be happening because we're doing something right and the enemy doesn't want us to succeed; he is afraid of what that would mean. This is not to say that devils and demons aren't real, they are. They are as real as the flying monkeys were to Dorothy, and the flaming broom that painfully burned the Scarecrow. Yet, when the religious Pharisees met with Jesus, the multitude already had full bellies and were content on all levels. While the people ate in spiritual rest, the Pharisees were agitated, ready to enter spiritual war as they set forth to make their demands. Hence, the Pharisees remained blind, ignorant, and in effect, unknowingly malnourished.

Finally, we come to the disciples, who are the most interesting in light of the three aspects of sight we mentioned so far. They didn't just observe a miracle with the people, they participated in the process. Yet, it wasn't their "obedience" to Jesus that helped the miracle. Their involvement wasn't so much about doing as it was about seeing. Sheer obedience doesn't bring forth spiritual insight. If it did, the Law-abiding and Scripture-doing Pharisees would've been spiritual giants by now, seeing all things in Christ. It wasn't about searching scripture and obediently doing, rather it was about seeing. Jesus asked the disciples, *"How many loaves do you have?"* (Mark 8:5). Why ask such a question? After all, shouldn't the miracle worker know the answer? If they had five, ten, or even a hundred loaves and fishes, would it have made a difference? Can you imagine Jesus saying, *"Oy vey! Only five? If you had at least ten I would've been able to pull this miracle off! Ugh! Oh well, let's take an offering from the people and then a couple of you guys run to the grocery store."* In this instance, the disciples were a bit further down the proverbial motorway, heading toward their proper exit. Why? Because Jesus had already fed a multitude in an earlier situation. He'd said to the disciples:

> *"You give them something to eat."*
> > *(Mark 6:37/NKJV)*

Jesus was kindling a change in their point of view, from God being external to God being internal. This was a major refocus for the people of His day, and in some cases, even heretical. It was like He was pointing to an exit on the motorway they wouldn't have recognized, or at the very least considered using. Hear the words of Jesus that immediately followed:

> *"How many loaves do you have? GO AND SEE!"*
> > *(Mark 6:38/NKJV)*

At that point, Jesus was stirring the disciples to perceive from one level of reality to another. After that first experience, although the disciples still seemed to display some uncertainty about how to feed the multitude, Jesus didn't have to tell them *to go and see.* Now they were aware and they responded. While they could see there wasn't enough food in one world, they were ready to see another reality taking on a Christ point of view. There are accounts of Jesus feeding multitudes with loaves and fish in all four Gospels. In Matthew's and Mark's accounts, they tell us how the disciples saw and gave what they had to Jesus, who blessed it. Then when Christ returned it to them, they went and fed the multitude. The first aspect to consider is that Jesus never fed the multitude directly, the disciples always did. You could say they became an emanation and expression of Christ to the people. But how? How did this awakening occur? In the Gospel of John, there's added insight:

> *"Then one of his disciples, Andrew, the brother of Simon Peter pointed to a little boy who had five small loaves of inexpensive barley bread and two small fishes and remarked how insignificant they appeared amongst such a multitude of hungry people! Jesus asked his disciples to get everybody seated ... Jesus took the bread and fish and thanked God for it, then distributed it amongst the people; everyone was free to take as much as they wanted!"*
> *(John 6:8-11/MIRROR)*

The text specifies that *"Andrew, the brother of Simon Peter pointed to a little boy."* By word definition, and not only translation, this part of the sentence can read Ἀνδρέας ὁ ἀδελφὸς Σίμωνος Πέτρου Ἔστιν παιδάριον ὧδε, *"a man, a brother (or kindred) of 'the hearing piece of the rock,' there exists a little boy in this manner.* Consider, a person, a mere man, who recognized *the rock of revelation [Christ],* realized *the key was with a little child.* We know throughout the Gospels that *humbling oneself as a little child* is how we gain entrance to receive from, and manifest the Kingdom of God (Matthew 19:4; Mark 10:15; Luke 18:17). Once again, we have the message of letting go of the Ego and humbling oneself, thus unfolding Christ and His Kingdom from within us. The focus is the humility in childlikeness that manifests and reveals Christlikeness. In John's account, he presses us to see the inner workings of what appears to be an outward miracle. It's not God breaking through and usurping this world's natural laws to reveal His purpose. Nor is it to show how great and powerful Christ is so people will believe and follow. Apparently, they already believed, followed, and hadn't even addressed their physical hunger before the miracle occurred. In Divine reality, there's no breakthrough or defiance of any natural law. Consider the stature of childlike humility which, by extension, *is Christlikeness;* what happens thereafter is nothing more than the "natural course" of things. In other words, it wasn't breaking through this world's natural laws and bending them by a higher power's demand. There's that word again: *demand.* For the record, childlike humility doesn't demand anything, it just sees panoscopically from an inner space where this world's natural principles are coupled with the fullness of the Divine universe in which it abides. Another way of saying this could be that the natural laws of this world were reattached to Divine reality and simply functioned according to design. Feeding the multitude

was no different than feeding one person. In the accounts in Matthew and Mark, there's no mention of a little boy. However, if one can receive it, the humble little boy giving his fish and bread is mentioned, just in another spiritual form:

> "...Jesus called His disciples to Him and said to them,
> 'I have compassion on the multitude...'"
> *(Mark 8:1-2/NKJV)*

Compassion is the humble little child that empowers Jesus to feed the multitude. One may think it's absurd that God would need to be empowered. But therein is the Divine lesson and the long-awaited, seemingly invisible, exit off the motorway. We know God is love, in other words, we know God is *Compassion,* therefore God in Christ *is* the humble little child. God, *Compassion,* the humble child, are all the same, just different expressions of the same block. Remember, the infinite God's entrance into this world was as a babe in a manger, wrapped in swaddling clothes. He's the Child whose name is Wonderful, Counselor, Mighty God, Everlasting Father, and Prince of Peace (Isaiah 9:6). When we're unconscious, asleep in *the World Below,* we're not childlike, but more so childish, irrespective of age. Childlikeness is humility, *Compassion,* and *Divinity.* Childishness is self-centered, *egoistic,* and the Serpentine Tree. However, when we stir toward awakening, we fit the description as the Apostle Paul shared in his Epistle to the Corinthians:

"When I was a child, I talked like a child, I thought like a child, I reasoned like a child. When I became a man, I put childish ways behind me."

(1 Corinthians 13:11/NIV)

In the context above, becoming a man, or a full-grown adult, is not ceasing to be a child, it's simply the removal of childishness. It's embracing our childlikeness through humility, in which we find the *Compassionate* Christ. This is a true adult and *pure child,* thus a spiritually mature person who is an emanation of the Everlasting Father. Again, Jesus says:

"Whoever receives one of these little children in My name receives Me; and whoever receives Me, receives not Me but Him who sent Me."

(Mark 9:37/NKJV)

Was He just speaking of children in the neighborhood and the world? Not only the children in our neighborhoods and the world, but each one of us regardless of our age! How many of us have aged chronologically, consider ourselves adults, and yet are still asleep in spiritual childishness? Many times, our so-called adulthood is so congealed over the years, that our fabricated sense of egoistic certainty isn't addressed until some calamity happens. This isn't to say if we're humble, calamity won't happen; that would be a false Gospel. The issue is, while calamity does happen in this world, the key is how we respond to it. An adult who's still in spiritual childishness may manifest by being one who cries out and rages against the system, and/or God, shaking their fist in defiance. Such things only aggravate matters and empower more of the same. On the other hand, childlikeness is found in humility and *Compassion,* which is not simply "the point," but "the key" that opens the narrow gate to the Kingdom, and results in a transformative response, even a miracle.

All these are connected, all these are *One.* In the accounts where Christ feeds the multitude, we find the disciples giving to Jesus, and then Jesus blessing the gifts and returning them. Then the disciples give what they have to the multitude. What happens internally, or in *the World Above,* is the disciples became the agent of the humble child, *Compassion.* They became the conduit of the Source, and the miracle occurred. Once again, this may be a bit challenging to receive, but Jesus didn't even need to be there physically for the miracle to manifest. Let me explain, taking a moment to follow this thought through to its conclusion. For the moment, let's remove the label *disciples* , which can suggest different things based on the reader's background, so we can address the inner state of what that means. What about a person who's come to a point in their life where they're desiring more than just what the Ego offers, and is awakening to something greater? What about that same person, religious or not, moved with *Compassion,* takes what they have and gives? Whether they're wearing a Jesus t-shirt or not, know of the Bible and its contents or not, we're seeing the stirring of Christlikeness. In the realm of God's Kingdom, it's far more reaching to "BE" than to have the "correct label" in our doing.

Consider again Jesus's words:

> *"Therefore whoever humbles himself as this little child is the greatest in the kingdom of heaven."*
> *(Matthew 18:4/NKJV)*

> *"...then I shall know fully, even as I am fully known."*
> *(1 Corinthians 13:12/NIV)*

Living in the Peace of God isn't just experiencing a calm during a storm. It's seeing the storm with new, or more inclusive eyes from *the World Above*, our home. Peace is an emanation of the inner space from which we live, emanating our union with the Source. In some respects, one may not see a storm at all anymore. This comes from us knowing as we are fully known. How does the Eternal Source of All Creation know us? How are we seen? We're seen as He sees Himself. This is called the Image of God. Seeing ourselves as just a replica, but separate, is like having a carved statue and calling it the Image of God, which is rejected in both Old and New Testaments as idolatry. We're not itemized replicas, but the express Image itself. This isn't believing it because we have the correct Biblical information. It's beholding the reality of our inner self.

If we know fully as we're fully known, in other words, see fully as we're fully seen, then we're seen as He sees Himself. This is true *Divine Peace*. This is שלם (shalam) *complete wholeness* and εἰρήνη (eirene) *being one*. We see ourselves as He truly Is, which means we see Ourself as We truly are.

CHAPTER 15
I AM THE SAME YESTERDAY, TODAY AND FOREVER

"This is the crime that I must expiate
Hung here in chains, nailed 'neath the open sky.
Ha! Ha!
What echo, what odour floats by with no sound?
God-wafted or mortal or mingled its strain?
Comes there one to this world's end, this mountain-
girt ground,
To have sight of my torment? Or of what is he fain?
A God ye behold in bondage and pain,
The foe of Zeus and one at feud with all
The deities that find
Submissive entry to the tyrant's hall;
His fault, too great a love of humankind."

Prometheus
Prometheus Bound
Aeschylus, 430 BC

Since the dawn of time when humans first filled the earth, long before Moses ever penned the words of the Torah, long before Abram agreed to follow a voice, inner or outer, proclaiming that he would become a father of many nations, the notion of a godlike being in human form, dying and rising from the dead, was nothing new. Not only does the story occur repeatedly, but the circumstances around the death and resurrection are a focus point. As we've discussed in the previous volume, we find Judas (whose name means *praise* in Hebrew), betraying Christ to the legalists and literalists (the Pharisees and Sadducees) whose use of geopolitics intended for His life to end in crucifixion. The truths put forth were that such *praise-worship* in any legalistic or literalistic form will betray, even crucify, the revelation of the Living Christ in our true identity and origins. However, if we refocus our *praise-worship* to the yielded, crucified, and resurrected Christ, it will actually put to death our legalistic, literalistic, base nature of this cosmos, and unveil our true self. As the Apostle Paul says:

> *"May my only boast be found in the cross of our Lord Jesus Christ. In him I have been crucified to this natural realm; and the natural realm is dead to me and no longer dominates my life. Whether a man is circumcised or uncircumcised is meaningless to me. What really matters is the transforming power of this new creation life."*
>
> *(Galatians 6:14-15/PASSION)*

Once again, this is one of those times when if you try to get the square peg in the round hole, it just won't work. Thereby, we find the Sanhedrin, along with others, conspiring to kill Jesus because they just couldn't get the revelation of the Father-peg, which the Messiah Jesus brought, in their political-religious-hole. As we continue this section, we may find ourselves in a similar dilemma at times. May I suggest the possibility of emptying ourselves to whatever capacity we can of any preconceived Sunday school type thoughts, and open our hearts to potentially broader, Christ-centered ones which we may not have considered before.

At times, our passion plays and cinematic dramatizations seem more like a Middle Eastern Godfather movie than the message the Gospel brings. It's as if we see Emilio "Levi" Barzini plotting a hit on a neighboring family member, favored son of the Godfather, Sonny "Melchizedek" Corleone, by having him ambushed at a Gethsemane tollbooth. Was that the kind of plot emphasis the writers of the New Testament wanted us to grasp? Was it meant to be a Mafia-like murder drama, but with a happy ending? Such has made wonderful theatrical plays, great movies, moving television mini-series, and of course, incredibly beautiful art. All the same, were the actual writings laid forth meant to communicate something far more profound? The copies of the Apostolic letters we have make the message relatively clear. Despite the fact that no original scrolls exist which were written by the hand of the Apostles, and all the historical aspects of the events from 2000 years ago are based on the copies of the copies that we have, the central theme still comes through. There really is something greater than just a powerful, dramatic passion play. If we can imagine something beyond a man being heinously betrayed by a friend, then painfully nailed to a cross and buried in another friend's grave, we may be on to something. Aside from that horrible murder, if we can also imagine something beyond an amazing occurrence where that same man rises from the dead, we're ready to awake. The "something beyond" we're referring to is what the New Testament proclaims as the Kingdom within us (Luke 17:21; Romans 2:29), the Christ within us (Romans 8:10; Colossians 1:27, 2:10; Philemon 6; 1 John 5:20), and us abiding in Him (2 Corinthians 5:21; Ephesians 1:4; 1 John 4:13; 5:20, to mention a few verses). This awareness of the Kingdom, Christ, and us within each other, is what can move us beyond a dramatic story of what took place a couple of thousand years ago, and usher us into the eternal realities of these occurrences.

More heinous is when our legalism and literalism arrogantly betray and crucify the Christ *within us.* Yes! When we crucify Christ within us, it's more heinous than if we nailed a person, like Jesus, to a cross! Why? Because to perform the external violence, we must first do it within ourselves. In other words, when we approach any aspect of our spirituality legalistically, in whatever area we do, the Eternal Christ is crucified to us. When Christ within is crucified, either in full or part, that aspect of our true self is as well. When our Ego veils the Christ within, it's an act of violence. That may sound harsh, but that's precisely the point. Most anything the Ego does has some form of self-centered violence within it, whether to another person or toward ourselves. The very notion of pointing the finger at someone and saying, "You're wrong!" comes from a violent root. The Apostle John equates us not loving our brother to actual murder (1 John 3:10-15). He's emphatic in verse 14 when he says, *"Anyone who doesn't love, remains in a state of death."* If not loving our brother is a type of murder, how much more is it a murderous suicide of our true self when we don't lovingly embrace, in full or in part, the reality of Christ within us? However, the Life-giving aspect is that, regardless of how violent our Egos are at first, there's nothing that will keep Christ within us in His fabricated grave. Eventually, the stony seal of our inner tomb will roll away and our true self in Christ will emerge. As Peter said regarding *the World Above, "...one day is as a thousand years and a thousand years as one day,"* (1 Peter 3:8). In other words, this emergence occurs in the inner world of timelessness, so the Divine intention will be realized whether it takes days, years, or beyond.

What Paul and John were sharing was nothing new to their audience. For that matter, they borrowed from other religions, philosophies, and mythologies when necessary to help make their point. Why? Because truth, regardless of where we find it, is still truth. In many cases, the Apostles used the known religions and philosophies of the people they spoke to in order to uncover the reality of Christ. Encrypted in these stories and myths, the idea of a dying and rising god wasn't just meant to display the power that god had over death, but to shed light on why both humans and other gods wanted them dead. It posed the question, "Why the violence?" What was it about the dying and rising god that warranted such a reaction? What was the "quality" of character the dying and rising god had that was so unique, it couldn't be quenched, and resurrection or rebirth was imminent? The next question is, why do stories simulating Christ's death and resurrection appear in other religions and mythologies long before Jesus walked the earth? The simple answer is, from the beginning there's only "one story" and "one reality." Yet, in its omnipotence, there's much more to comprehend. It's an impression of Divine reality that has been seared in us since we fell asleep in Eden. Each one of us has it branded deep in our consciousness, and it rises in dreamlike ways amidst all the outer noise our minds conjure. Thus, it finds its way into our thinking and feelings, both real and mythical, calling us to our higher self. It comes in many forms and apparitions in our world of illusion, but the Source is the same. While we may not have always understood it, nor always defined it with clarity, it was there throughout the ages like a nightmare that's also the most wonderful dream.

Part 1: A Limitless Life Through the Mystery of the Ages

The myths of the dying and rising gods and their effects on civilization have been around from the beginning of recorded history. In a similar manner that paganism gave us the horrific penal substitution rituals, it also gave us, obscured in them, a message of redemption, rebirth, and resurrection. Even the early church fathers, like Justin Martyr and Clement of Alexandria, referred to these historical pagan correlations. Clement of Rome, the fourth Bishop of that region, who some would consider seriously legalistic, also referenced such myths like the Egyptian Phoenix arising from the ashes:

"Let us consider that wonderful sign [of the resurrection] which takes place in Eastern lands, that is, in Arabia and the countries round about. **There is a certain bird which is called a Phoenix.** This is the only one of its kind, and lives five hundred years. And when the time of its dissolution draws near that it must die, it builds itself a nest of **frankincense, and myrrh,** and other spices, into which, when the time is fulfilled, it enters and dies. But as the flesh decays a certain kind of worm is produced, which, being nourished by the juices of the dead bird, brings forth feathers. Then, when it has acquired strength, it takes up that nest in which are the bones of its parent, and bearing these it passes from the land of Arabia into Egypt, to the city called Heliopolis. And, in open day, flying in the sight of all men, it places them on the altar of the sun, and having done this, hastens back to its former abode. The priests then inspect the registers of the dates, and find that it has returned exactly as the five hundredth year was completed." (1 Clement 25)

Why would Clement refer to the Phoenix? Because the early Christians were aware of the consistent correlation of the myths of the dying and rising gods with their respective messages of redemption, rebirth, and new life. Most all the writers of the New Testament laced their messages with these associations in some way. They were more concerned about *speaking the truth in love* (Ephesians 4:15) than getting caught in the thorny branches of the Tree of the Knowledge of Good and Evil. Consider, while Paul tells the church at Ephesus not to be tossed with every wind of doctrine, he just told them that *the Mystery of the Ages,* which was hidden in God from the beginning, was to be revealed through the Church. So far so good, right? Well, the notion of the *Mystery of the Ages,* a phraseology not unfamiliar to the Greco-Roman world, is now being used by Paul in an augmented way. When Paul wrote and spoke to his audience, he used terms they understood. Since the notion of the Gospel was already a radical message, he didn't invent new phrases and ideas. In the old world, dating back to before 500 BC, they had what was called *the mystery schools.* These were religious-philosophical groups that taught the initiated " mysteries of the spiritual world." One of the more famous of those schools was the Orphic Mystery School. They taught, of course, Orphism (see *Melchizedek: Our Gracious King-Priesthood in Christ,* Volume I, Page 422), which the writer of the epistle of Hebrews directly references in chapter 12. One aspect of Orphism teaches that *sin continually weighs human beings down,* preventing us to stay in the heavenly world. Thus, when humans physically died, the sin of their soul weighed them down, causing them to perpetually reincarnate until all their wrongs, past and present, were corrected,. The writer, rather than accuse the myth as being demonic, cultic, or false, simply referenced the myth focusing the reader to the truth of the Gospel, saying that through faith in Christ's *Grace,* every weight of sin is removed. Hence, the *Mystery of the Ages* fulfilled.

The epistles of the Apostles are full of these references. In the same manner again in Ephesians, Paul references another myth that was around for a very long time. Developed by the early Greeks and later adapted by the first century Gnostics, it was known as "The Descent of the Goddess," and "The Fallen Goddess (Sophia)." We can trace the origins of these myths as far back as 4000 BC, starting with Inanna of the Sumerians, followed by Ishtar of the Assyrian/Babylonian's at approximately 3500 BC to 2500 BC, then retold and further embellished in the Isis myths of Egypt from the Old Kingdom in 2600 BC, and then again in the New Kingdom, approximately 1500 BC. Finally, the Greeks took the myth even further, as told in Platonic form several hundred years before Jesus.

Paul is clear that the *Mystery of the Ages* is the revelation of Christ through the Church. He's relating, as in the epistle of the Hebrews, that Christ is the fulfillment of the *Mysteries* rather than refuting them, as if that should be necessary. All of us today have grown up in a world highly influenced by a version of Christendom born in the West, and since the early Middle Ages it's been diligent in developing a religious-political-social order where all other systems are anathema. This reshaped what was once known as *the Gospel of Grace* (Acts 20:20; Galatians 1:6; 2 Timothy 2:1), to merge both Church and State, something Jesus never ascribed to. Originally, being a part of the Kingdom of God meant not being part of the Kingdoms of this World the way a non-believer was (Galatians 6:14). Rather, we were to be ambassadors of Christ, having an occupancy in the nations of the world and carrying out His business in them (2 Corinthians 5:20; Luke 19:13). Nonetheless, that reshaping changed many things. At that point, being contrary in thought or deed to the beliefs of the Church was also to be an enemy of the State, and being contrary to the State was being an enemy of the Church and God. Technically, we're right back to where we were in Chapter 5 with the pagan kings and priests, there's just a change in religion. Thus, much of how we see the New Testament is influenced by the beliefs of that era and reflected in the Latin, followed by the early German and later English translations. Before you know it, we're submitting to the government, claiming it's ordained by God and that submitting to it is like submitting to Him. Therefore, Christendom claims it's important to have Christians in governmental positions so the ungodly won't misuse God's authority. Yet, as far as Christendom is concerned, history has been clear for more than a millennium and a half, including the present day, that many of those who have attempted to carry Cross and Flag do as much damage as those who don't, just in a different form. As we've said previously, when asked the question of whether Christians should occupy seats in government, the answer is, "Yes!" However, the primary purpose of a Christian in government isn't to enact laws to make a country more Christian, which the New Testament has proven futile and inspires the reverse (Romans 7:5). Rather, like any other vocation, it's to first work with integrity while emanating the Love of Christ with those you work with and with whom you work for.

Even though we now have many translations after a broader use of Greek manuscripts, much of our theology continues to uphold the "valued traditions" from that period, making them part of the present day so-called righteous theology. Most importantly, regardless of translation, the front-loaded doctrines which define such scriptures shaped much of how we see Christian religious life in the secular world. For well over 1500 years that merge between Church and State lived on in different forms. This is the tension between what the Kingdom of Christ brought to humanity 2000 years ago, and the Kingdoms of the World, or Ego, have had since the beginning as it securely holds onto its rule. Yet, as God continued to move forward in the shadow of such tension, when the Pentecostal outpouring occurred in the beginning of the 1900s, even with the beauty and power of what that meant, aspects of it still stood on the displaced foundations of those doctrines and took them into the prophetic realm. Though the Apostle Paul is clear that *"the spirits of the prophets are **subject** to the prophets,"* (1 Corinthians 14:31-32), which includes several themes of discussion, one of which is that the prophetic impression one perceives will be influenced by the doctrines they've been instructed in, and thus believe in. This will directly affect how prophetic people see that impression, and how they see both God and the world around them. What makes a prophetic view or utterance false, or errant, isn't necessarily the Christian who sees or hears something, but the lens and filters through which they see and hear. The result can be quite harmful. To complicate the issue, if that person, or minister, is a part of a group in which everyone believes with the same lens, then regardless of how divergent from the Gospel of Grace the prophecy is, to them it is true, affirming, and correct. This can empower the Serpentine-Ego with ideas like, "We're the special, informed ones who are in the know of what God is saying and doing. Those other people are deceived." When you think of it, it sounds like we're back to just another *mystery school.* Only a short time after the outpouring on Azusa Street, it became evident that when any prophetic ministry with some accuracy claimed, "God said…" regarding the religious-political-social order in North America, or anywhere else for that matter, it was the "word of the Lord" and needed to be heeded and obeyed. From that point on, prophetic people began prophesying which candidate running for office a believer should vote for, and who was supposedly "God's man or woman" for a political purpose. In addition they proclaimed which laws should be enacted in order to make a nation reflect Christian values so they'd maintain the blessing of God, as well as which infamous people or laws the "enemy" was using against those values. This isn't within the parameters of the true prophetic ministry of the Holy Spirit, and something you'll never see in the texts of the New Testament. In our teetering post-modern Christendom, there's another kind of a double-edged sword besides the one called the Word of God (Ephesians 6:17; Hebrews 4:12). Rather, it's very similar to the one Peter used against the High Priest's servant, cutting off his ear (John 18:10). Today, on one edge of this sword, we *believe the prophets* (2 Chronicles 20:20) in an Old Testament veiled form, rather than through the revelation of Christ. In other words, this sword has its roots in the Serpentine lower realm of good and evil, rather than being evaluated by the upper world of the Nature of Christ and His Kingdom. Regarding prophetic insight and to encourage the younger ministers I was developing in our church, the Holy Spirit once impressed upon me, *"Prophetic accuracy doesn't mean Divine truth."* The other edge to this sword is that a good portion of the Biblical text translations are interpreted through those same lenses and reinforced accordingly. So now we claim we have both "Word and Spirit" in agreement about our view of God and Country. The result isn't just a misuse of the written Word, or just a disfigured lens of how we interpret the prophetic, but now we've cut off the ears of those who need to hear the Gospel of Grace. Keep in mind, this marriage bed of religion and politics is contrary to Christ and His Kingdom. It's important to point out that the name of the High-Priest's "servant" whose ear was cut off was Malchus, which is Hebrew

for מֶלֶךְ (melek), *king.* In these Serpentine relationships, while kings and religious leaders are in bed together to help keep social order and their beliefs secure, one always becomes the servant of the other. In the end of the situation with the kind of sword Peter wielded, though in his mind it was on behalf of Jesus, it only prevented those who needed an ear to hear to even have an ear at all. It's amazing that Jesus had to then stop and take the extra time to heal the ear of someone who *seemingly opposed Him,* because of the actions of someone who *supposedly was supporting Him.* Selah. (Interesting point, while writing this very paragraph, I received a text from a minister friend who asked for prayer because of a person in their congregation who seriously offended another person with the infamous, "God told me to tell you..." Ugh! How many times have we attached God's name to our egoistic critical impulses and called it a "word from God"? Another listening ear just got cut off! Now we must spend time healing that person's ear, while trying to pry the bloody prophetic sword out of the other's hand and explain why, in their so-called prophetic certainty, they seriously wounded a person with doubt and fear.)

What we're faced with today isn't only a reshaped view of Christ and the Church's involvement in secular government, we've also displaced the use of the Apostolic message as they were being good missionaries to the world around them. They weren't concerned if *the mystery schools* were of the Devil or not; they weren't that shallow in their thinking. Rather, they were able to discern truth where it was, even in a *mystery school,* and utilized it to preach Christ. In the same way, when a person with a distorted lens sees something prophetically, rather than throw the baby out with the bath water, we need to refocus, or polish, their lens. The Apostles simply took the truths encrypted within the mystery schools and refocused them to reveal Christ. In the Apostles' day, pagan religions and governments were interwoven, and when advantageous, the Apostles extracted truths from *the mystery schools* of those systems to reveal Christ and His Kingdom. In other words, Christ is both a revelation of what is encrypted in the Torah as well as those shrouded in *the mysteries,* and His Kingdom is a revelation of a completely different form of government outside of them all.

Despite our present-day, reshaped thinking of the New Testament, when the texts are seen in their raw form, the evidence strongly points us in a different direction. For example, when Paul wrote Ephesians, there's virtually no mention of Jewish or Old Testament references. Rather, the entire epistle references *the mysteries* and the shades of truth in them. Thus, by virtue of Christ revealing this *manifold Wisdom,* **πολυποίκιλος σοφία** (polupoikilos **sophia**), to the principalities [**ἀρχαῖς** (archais) plural for **ἄρχων** (archon)] (Ephesians 3:10) through the Church, His Bride (Ephesians 5:23-24), who IS the **πλήρωμα** (pleroma), *fullness* of God (Ephesians 1:23), we find another *mystery* brought to fullness and conclusion. This is right out of the writings of the Greek mythos regarding the Goddess Sophia mentioned earlier, and Paul used it to speak to the thinking of the Ephesians. It's no different than what Paul did at the Areopagus (Acts 17:22). On the other hand, if he were part of Christendom today, he would be pressed to conform to its predetermined view and refute such myths rather than borrowing from them, being told, "That's Gnosticism! That's error!" Can you imagine the finger pointing, even at Paul? How many of us have heard that throughout the centuries some church leaders refuted such "Gnostic teaching" in that way? Why did the question of Gnosticism even come up in the Church? It really wasn't because demons were trying to creep in and pervert the Gospel, it was because the Apostles started it by referencing similar ideas at points. This isn't saying that everything in Gnosticism was truth, but there were and are truths present, and the people of that day were familiar with such teaching. It's no different than New Testament references to pagan penal substitution, or Jewish ritual practices. What's happened over time in Christendom, is that we distanced ourselves from aspects of New Testament texts for "fear" of false teaching, redefined them and thereby skewed what they were saying. We could say, we made sure the very thing we feared came upon us (Job 3:25). The New Testament writers didn't have "the fear of being wrong" or "the need to be right" as their security; their righteousness was based in the Love of God by faith in His *Grace,* and they were sharing that with humanity. Notwithstanding, Paul, as did John, utilized the myths and expounded on them. Paul shared the truth of Christ based on the mythos his hearers understood. Of course, this was dependent upon to whom he was speaking, the Ephesians, the Corinthians, the Hebrews, and so on; he tailored the message to reveal Christ. He wasn't trying to move them away from what was wrong and toward what was right. He was trying to empower them to awaken to Divine Life. When we're awakened to such Life, anything else is earnestly less relevant.

In the case of the Sophia myths, the goddess of Wisdom referred to in Ephesians by Paul, here's a condensed summary of her story. Sophia, Wisdom, fell from the Pleroma (the fulness of the heavens), because in pride she tried to emulate the Creator by creating independently on her own. Thus, she conceived a creature, a serpent with the head of a lion. In her horror, Sophia cast the creature from the Pleroma (the fullness of the Heavens) into a dark cloud below. In that moment, the creature seized her power and trapped her in the darkness in its stead. This harsh beast became the first of an order of beings called *the archons* (the principalities) who would rule and enslave the physical world. It then created twelve additional archons to solidify its rule of the cosmos. [Note the consistent use of the number twelve throughout most all religious systems, such as the number of the Greek Titan gods, followed by their Olympian gods, the number of names of the Hindu god Surya, the number of the tribes of Israel, the number of sons of the Norse god Odin (Wotan), the number of the Apostles, more recently, the number of the days of Christmas, and most importantly, the New Jerusalem (Revelation 21:9-21). This numerical value in all these cultures, and even in the Bible, was the universal symbol of the ruling cosmic order.] At the same time, Humanity, the image of God, also existed. (Humanity being in the image of God wasn't exclusive to the Bible, the Greeks also believed this). They were full of Light and dwelled freely throughout the heavenly worlds. Because of their liberty and likeness of the highest god, they became a source of jealousy for the archons, so the archons plotted against the Humans. Through deception they encased their souls in flesh, weighing them down and imprisoning them in the lower cosmos (world). The Humans and all their offspring where trapped on the Earth from that time forward, living under the rule of the archons. If at the end of a human's life they hadn't gained the necessary knowledge (the gnosis) to ascend past the archons to enter their original heavenly abode, they would fall again to the lower world and reincarnate under the archon's rule. (Note the similarity of the Orphic Myth mentioned earlier.)

Throughout Ephesians, Paul is telling his readers that Christ *is the fulfilment of the mysteries of the dying and rising god,* who has broken the power of the *archons,* and liberated *Sophia,*

521

wisdom, which in their understanding was the key to attaining salvation in their original higher world. The Church, like Sophia, is that feminine quality who embodies *the polupoikilos sophia (the manifold wisdom)* and is the *pleroma (fullness)* of God. It's through Christ's Bride that He has made known to the archons this victory, passing *knowledge* (gnosis) and being rooted and grounded in love (Ephesians 3:17-19). Paul's message takes the Gnostic myth to another level. Until Paul's Gospel, Mankind had to attain a special *gnosis* to break through the power of the archons and return to their heavenly dwelling. However, whenever they would try, the archons would interrupt the process with confusion and chaos, and Mankind would remain trapped. Paul's conclusion for them was that *gnosis* is not gained by direct pursuit, which will always result in failure. It is attained by a higher power, *Love.* By being grounded in the *Love of God,* it surpasses the power of the archons, and *Love* itself is the special gnosis. In conclusion, the way for Mankind to return to their heavenly dwelling was by being rooted in Christ's Gracious Love. This not only gained the gnosis necessary, but also unveiled their true form as the *Divine Image and Likeness.*

In similar fashion, Clement of Rome had a scriptural basis when referring to the Phoenix: the book of Job, which used Egyptian mythology:

> *"I said, 'I will die with my nest, and I will live as long as a phoenix.'"*   (Job 29:18/CJB)

Some translations use the phrase, *"like sand,"* or in more rare cases, *"like a palm tree,"* however the Hebrew phrase is וכחול (v'ka'ol). The notion of *sand* can make a bit of sense, being that sand is numerous and to count it on the seashore would seem to go on forever. On the surface, the notion of a palm tree doesn't make sense within the context unless we see it as a type of the Tree of Life. Nevertheless, the most accurate translation is *Phoenix.* Even the Complete Jewish Bible, quoted above, and The Jewish Publication Society edition of the Tanak uses *Phoenix.* Why? Keep in mind that by the time the beginning verses of the Torah and earlier Job were written, Egyptian mythology had already been in existence for thousands of years. The point is, Clement understood the correlation to the myths of the dying and rising gods, along with their concurrent teachings of reincarnation, resurrection, and rebirth. While the message of Job clearly has its place in the Tanak as a whole, the writer didn't have the legalistic trappings of the tabernacle, priesthood, nor the Law with all its injunctions. The notion of sacrificing to appease a god, fear of judgment, and giving offerings for a blessing, came solely from the paganism of the day. This isn't to say that the teachings of God Most High יהוה weren't around, but they were communicated by the oral tradition. To many at the time, He was just another of the many gods spoken of. One of the purposes of the book of Job, like the story of Noah, is to reveal that יהוה was different from the pagan gods of judgment, sacrifice, and condemnation. The writer of Job understood the concept of sacrifice and burnt offerings, though such are only mentioned twice throughout all 42 chapters. When burnt offerings were mentioned, they had the same implication of pagan penal substitution. However, as we see when we reach the end of the book, this meant little to the God of Elihu. While the three friends of Job are each told to give a burnt offering, being this is what their beliefs accepted (something consistent throughout the Old Testament), it was the intercession of Job that would make the difference. *"I will accept him..."* and *"...the Lord had accepted Job,"* (Job 42:8-9). It never says that God accepted the burnt offerings, it was the prayers of Job, and Job himself. The fact that the book of Job may have been written at the time of, or just prior to, Moses writing the Torah, it seems to present more of a Melchizedekian view in its scope, contrasting the legalistic religious ritual sacrifices and the message of Job's three friends. For that matter, we could say that Job's three friends were a type and shadow, and maybe even a precursor in thought, to the coming Aaronic-Levitical priesthood. They spoke of good and evil, judgment and wrongdoing, as possible reasons for Job's dilemma. While Elihu, who appeared much later in the story, like Melchizedek, speaks of a wondrous Creator God of *Grace* and *Compassion*. Thus, Job's religious worship, which starts no differently than his three friends, ends with finding himself a priest of God Most High. Job, though not a moral sinner (Job 1:1), still finds himself repenting of a possibly worse sin, his ignorant religiosity!

> *"...Surely I spoke of things I did not understand, things too wonderful for me to know. ... Therefore I despise myself and repent in dust and ashes."*
>
> *(Job 42:3-6/NIV)*

Job, with his new understanding of the nature of God, intercedes for his friends in similar fashion as Christ (1 John 2:1). He presents a Divine Grace, transformation, and restoration with equity (Job 42:12-15), and like Christ, a type of *Phoenix* rising from the worm filled ashes (Job 2:8; 7:5; 42:6). The Satan roaming the earth at the beginning of Job reappears later as the mythological creature, Leviathan לויתן, the Serpentine egoistic legalist swimming through the seas of people, looking for those who violate their religious rules to bring judgment and calamity. The Satan who roams both land and sea with devouring judgment demands blood, either human or animal, to be appeased. Toward the end of the book of Job, Leviathan לויתן is contrasted with Behemoth בהמות. Behemoth בהמות is called, "...*the first of the ways of God*..." (Job 40:19/NASU), who is made along with Mankind. He's the strength, peace, and the unity of Creation. However, Leviathan לויתן is called, "...*king over all the sons of pride*," (Job 41:34/NASU). [It's interesting to note that the word *Leviathan* לויתן, contains the priesthood, Levi לוי , see The Genesis Factor, Class 4, for details.]

The ultimate point is that these mythological stories were well known by both the Apostles and the Apostolic Fathers who succeeded them. As time went on, the Church digressed into a ritualistic political-religious structure, whose height was the Holy Roman Empire. Proper belief in its doctrine, adherence to its rituals, and allegiance to the Roman government was its newfound purpose. Of course, it took about 200 years to bring the Church to this point, like slow cooking a frog. One of its ways of establishing its ascendancy was the removal of all things "not Christian" despite the writings of the Apostles and their successors. The Apostle Paul grievously warned the Church of this (Acts 20:28-32) commending to them, *"...the word of His grace..."*, rather than a new religion with Jesus only as its figurehead. Thus, of all we have said, including the Zoroastrian Magi mentioned in the Gospels, there are those who attempt to discredit these correlations. The basis of the argument is built on the same doctrinal issues that formed the Roman Church's ascendancy. However, to attempt to discredit these relationships, one would have to discredit all of them, which is historically impossible. We would have to rewrite both history and the New Testament, though there could be the solid argument that the old Holy Roman Church and aspects of modern Protestantism have attempted to do so.

Let me state my point before I proceed. The message of Christ isn't simply a message of a Hebrew Messiah who declares to be everyone's Savior. Nor is the message of Christ what Western Evangelicalism has morphed it into over the last 500 years, making Him the Savior of those who are part of Christendom as they define it, and making themselves the perfected vehicle to be its herald. Rather, as the writer of the Book of Revelation makes clear, Christ is the Savior and Redeemer of the world, including both Jew and Gentile equally, referencing multiple mythologies and Hebraic symbolism at the center. To put it another way, the Christ, the Eternal Creator, isn't limited to a religion, be it Jewish, Babylonian, Egyptian, Zoroastrian, Mormon, Catholic, Protestant, Buddhist, Muslim, or whatever you like. The

Eternal One just IS! If we consider what we've said in the previous chapters, we also are eternal. It's our lower base nature, the Ego that we misuse, who says to us otherwise. Like Peter at the Mount of Transfiguration (Mark 9:4-6), who in the moment of revelation wanted to build a tabernacle to enshrine the experience. Hence, we too have done the same. Whether it was Babylonian, Egyptian, Greco-Roman, or some other mythology, even present-day Christendom, we've tabernacled into confinement who God is and, therefore, who we are. As we said in the previous chapters, it's as if we stirred from sleep for a moment, slightly opened our eyes, then turned over, went back to sleep, and a religion emerged in our dreams.

This is why when we look into the religious systems of the past, before Christianity, we see the repetitive similarities, including the death and resurrection of Dionysus, Tammuz, Horus, Osiris, Hermès, and on we can go. The point is, truth is truth, reality is reality, God is God, and who we are is who we are. This message has been heralded in different forms throughout the ages and the most evolved, or clear, is the Gospel of Jesus Christ (assuming it's left untouched by the very religious trappings the Apostle Paul and John, the writer of Revelation, warned us about.) For us to simply believe that thousands of years passed from the Fall to the birth of Jesus, during which time all of humanity worshipped demons until their end and then burned in eternal torment, shows something very wrong with Christendom's picture of Christ. Yet many today still think that when Jesus arrived on the scene, then and only then did humanity have an opportunity to be saved. Prior to that, you were toast. Literally. Even then, if people were in a part of the world where the message hadn't yet been heard, they too were subject to fiery torment. Considering the red letters in the Gospels, there's something seriously wrong in how we apply them if that's our conclusion. After all, long before Christ, God spoke to the polytheistic King of Gerar, Abimelech, because of the "integrity" of his heart, though Abraham lied to him regarding Sarah (Genesis 20:6). It's interesting that God Most High doesn't condemn His lying covenant partner, yet He speaks to a polytheistic, non-covenantal King who keeps his integrity. The Creator of the universe has had no problem speaking to anyone of any persuasion, whether monotheistic or polytheistic, regarding the truths of spiritual reality.

Part 2: A Limitless Life Through Death and Rebirth

In the story of Dionysus (whose Roman name was Bacchus) there were multiple cases of death and resurrection. We can summarize his myth as follows:

Dionysus is the son of Zeus, the King of the Olympian Gods, and Semele, a mortal woman, daughter of Cadmus of Thebes. In the Orpheus version of his myth, he is first the son of Zeus and Persephone, Queen of the Underworld (after her abduction by Hades). In both versions we have Christlike origins. Dionysus was born of both god and a mortal woman, and was resurrected by his father from the underworld and elevated to godhood.(He is the god of agriculture, in particular grapes, and the creator of wine.) As the story goes, when Hera

(Zeus's goddess wife) found out about Semele, Zeus's mortal mistress, she approached her, disguised as a human woman, and befriended her. She persuaded the pregnant Semele into asking Zeus to reveal his true form as a god. Until then, Zeus would only come to her in human form because, "No one could see his glory and live." Sound familiar? Zeus, in love with Semele, yielded and revealed his glory. Instantly, she burst into flames and turned to ash, yet out of the ashes was the unborn Dionysus who Zeus quickly took and hid in his thigh. (Note the notion of life coming forth from the ashes as the Phoenix.) In the Book of Revelation, when Christ returns, He treads the wine press (grapes) of God and has His name written on his thigh. Why? With yet more similarities to Dionysus, which we will mention, John of Revelation is equating the Christ message to ALL. He didn't, as many of us modern Evangelicals do, negate all other religions as false and claim that we "and we alone" have the truth. Actually, that was one of the key warnings of Revelation.

The Orphic myth of Dionysus (known in the prior myths as Zagreus) takes the story to a time prior to Semele, but ends with her. This was a point of transition where the Titan gods were being rivaled by the Olympian gods. Once Persephone gave birth to Dionysus, Hera incited the Titans to kill the child. Not only was it inflammatory to her that Zeus have a mistress, but to have a child brought forth from Persephone of the underworld and who would ascend as the ruling god over both Olympians and Titans was unthinkable! Zeus's intent was to give the supreme throne of all the gods to "the half-breed" Dionysus. To the Titans, Dionysus was a half-breed because he was born of both god and man. (Sound familiar?) It's important to point out at this juncture that, as the story progresses in Greek mythology, the Titans, despite their rule from Mount Othrys, were compared to the base, fleshly desires that warred against the higher Dionysian spiritual nature. When the twelve Titans finally caught Dionysus, they literally tore his body into pieces, and each ate their portion of his flesh. Because of this, the Greeks were taught that within our human nature, the lower fleshly Titanic nature would always war with the higher, Dionysian. Therefore, the Apostle Paul used the same imagery and language in Galatians. He states how our base nature devours and consumes one another, and how flesh and spirit, "*...are opposed to one another...*" (Galatians 5:15-17). This was a common understanding for his audience. In the same manner, Peter says, "*...the passions of the flesh, which war against the soul...*" (1 Peter 2:11). Here again in the New Testament writings, we see neither Peter or Paul telling their listeners that such mythology was evil, or demonic, or a lie. Rather, both referenced the mythology. Why? Because there was honest spiritual truth contained within the stories.

Taking the myth further, Athena, rather than eating her portion, took the heart of Dionysus from his broken body and gave it to Zeus, who consumed it to preserve it within himself. Then at the opportune time, Dionysus came forth from Zeus's bosom (like John 1:18) and during a time of intimacy with Semele, he impregnated her with Dionysus's heart. She in turn gave birth to a son. Unbeknownst to her it wasn't just a regular birth, but a rebirth. Dionysus was now resurrected and restored to life. Looking back toward the Titan's eating Dionysus's flesh, again we see a similarity with a twist at the Lord's Supper. The *twelve* apostles, along with the god/man Jesus, where seated and *"...Jesus took bread, and when he had given thanks, he broke it and gave it to his disciples, saying, 'Take and eat; this is my body,'"* (Matthew 26:26/NIV). While the Jewish aspects of the Passover were being fulfilled (which many Christians grasp today), in the same way, so was the fulfillment of the other surrounding mysteries. Everything was culminating from all paths of life in that moment. The challenge we continually face in modern Christendom is that we still view God from our base "Titan" fleshly nature, who wants to approach these things from a good and evil perspective, rather than a Tree of Life vista. From the virgin birth, the Father inseminating a mortal woman, to the disciples figuratively eating the body of "the Son" of both a mortal and God, we have the prophetic fulfillment of Gentile and Jewish religions through the *Mystery of the Ages,* Christ. The difference with the Gospel of Christ is, while the myths continue with repetitive death and rebirth because of the warring of flesh and spirit, Christ reconciles the one with the other, making peace (Ephesians 2:15). In similar fashion, the Jewish myth has the constant demand of death as payment for sin, insistent for fresh bloodletting, which would still be going on today if the Temple wasn't destroyed. However, Christ not only puts an end to such sacrifices, removing the notion for penal substitutionary sacrifice, He also nails that very same Law, which demands such death to His Cross, triumphing over all *the principalities (the archons)* that used it to enslave us (Colossians 2:14-15). Now in Christ there's neither Jew, nor

Greek, nor Egyptian, nor Gentile, nor bond, nor free, rather we are all ONE, and with awakening, an expression of the *Mystery of the Ages* (Colossians 3:9-11).

It's also interesting to point out that at the last supper, only eleven of the twelve ate; Judas left to betray Jesus. The same was similar with Dionysus. Only eleven of the twelve ate the broken body, Athena giving his heart to Zeus. Yet, despite Judas's betrayal, which ended in Christ being crucified, Jesus said, *"Father into your hands I commit my spirit,"* (Luke 23:46). Once again, a similarity of "the Father receiving the heart of His Son." The cycle then continues with Christ going into the underworld (Persephone) and being reborn, resurrected from the dead.

While there's much more to the Dionysus myth, another key point was in Roman art. Modeling earlier myth depictions, the way Dionysus died was by being hung on a cross. Hence the "Cruciform" representation. There's a famous piece of art engraved in hematite (a blood red stone) that is from Rome in the third century, prior to the establishment of the Roman Catholic Church. It depicts Dionysus being crucified under a crescent moon with the Pleiades overhead. This repeating cruciform of gods and goddesses goes back long before Jesus.

Our prologue story of Prometheus being chained comes from ancient art and literature dating back as far as 800 BC Greece. He's depicted as chained to the rocks of Scythia in *cruciform*. Why did Zeus banish him from Olympus? At this point in the mythos, the gods had dethroned the Titans and banished them to the dark underworld of *Tartarus* (translated *Hell* in 2 Peter 2:4). Zeus, the newly acclaimed ruler, took the throne and for a short season there was peace. Prometheus was given the task of creating Mankind and did so, making them in the image of the gods. Enraged by humanity being in their image, Zeus was going to wreak severe wrath upon them. Prometheus, on the other hand, loved humanity and reasoned that the way to save humanity was to give them fire, which would withstand *the wrath of the gods.* To add more insult to Zeus, Prometheus claimed he had a vision of a son of Zeus that would dethrone him. Now even more enraged by Prometheus's *compassion* and vision, he condemned Prometheus. Prometheus was chained in *cruciform* with his arms stretched out, and eagles were given the daily task of consuming his liver. Once again, we have an eating of the body of the one who is crucified. During the night his liver would regenerate, and the torture would start all over again in the morning. The reason Prometheus's liver was the focus was because the Greeks believed the liver was the seat of life and soul, which couldn't be destroyed. Rather, the life force was so great that it would regenerate. While this was very primitive in the Greek side of the mythos, it was still a type of death and resurrection each day. While Prometheus was sentenced to death, his life source would regenerate, and he would live again and again. Finally, with the sacrifice of a centaur, a creature that was half-man and half-animal, usually a horse, made by Hercules (another son of Zeus, who was both god and man), Prometheus was freed. In this case the imagery of a centaur was a depiction of the animalistic, egoistic, base nature that was quelled. Thus, within the dying and rising gods' mythos was a love and compassion for humanity, as well as the elimination of the base nature, with a willingness to withstand the wrath of the demigods, the principalities (the archons). Regardless of how many deaths and resurrections would be necessary, throughout the mythologies told and retold, it was the dying and rising god destined for the throne. (On a side note, three millennia have passed since these myths were established and evidently the Greeks knew something. In the experimental work of Higgins and Anderson in 1931, they found that the liver, after partial hepatectomy would regenerate partial mass within a few hours. In their experiments with lab rats, the liver was completely regenerated within 72 hours.)

Of course, there are aspects of these pagan myths that have no correlation at all, like the wrath of the gods, judgment, blood covenant and ritual sacrifice (as we pointed out in Chapter 5). Yet, neither does that fit the revelation of Christ in the New Testament, which is the point. Like in the appearance of Melchizedek, which is in a completely different realm than the sacrificial temple and the Aaronic Priesthood, so are the myths of the dying and rising gods. For that matter, the Levitical temple system is an amalgamation of the aforementioned pagan systems. The interesting aspect of the Torah, compared to the pagan religions, is that it addresses more aspects of those areas. It seems as if God, through the Tanak writers, filled in the blanks, showing the futility of such priesthoods, both pagan and their own, with rituals and their respective bloodletting. In the same way that the dying and rising gods, who in those same myths stand apart from the legalism and literalism, the Apostle Paul says:

> *"But when the fullness of time had come, God sent forth his Son, born of a woman, born under the law, to redeem those who were under the law, so that we might receive adoption as sons. And because you are sons, God has sent the Spirit of his Son into our hearts, crying, 'Abba! Father!' So you are no longer a slave, but a son, and if a son, then an heir through God."*   *(Galatians 4:4-7/ESV)*

In the same way that Dionysus came with celebration, wine, and joy, so did Melchizedek and, of course, Jesus. Homer said that Dionysus, with wine and food in hand, was the "joy of man!" Of course, we know that we are to *"eat the fat and drink the sweet"* because *"the joy of the Lord is our strength,"* (Nehemiah 8:10/ESV). Then there was the time when Dionysus was taken captive by a group of men. Dionysus turned into a lion and scared them away, causing them to jump into the sea. It's interesting to note that Jesus is also called the *"Lion of the Tribe of Judah"* (Revelation 5:5) and when dealing with the possessed man with the "Legion" (approximately 6000 soldiers of ten cohorts of six centuria) at the Gadarenes (Gerasenes), caused the Legion to enter local pigs which then jumped into the sea (Mark 5:13). Also in the myth, Heramade Dionysus go mad for a time. Thus, during their worship celebrations, his followers were many times accused of drinking wine to the point of mindless intoxication, appearing to be mad as well. Those accused would proclaim that drinking the wine opened their hearts to the spirit of Dionysus which entered them during the celebration. Like Hera, the Jewish leadership accused Jesus of being demon possessed and *"raving mad"* (John 10:20). From the raving-mad Jesus to the day of Pentecost, we have, *"All of them...filled with the Holy Spirit and began to speak in other tongues...Then Peter stood up with the Eleven, raised his voice and addressed the crowd...'These people are not drunk, as you suppose. It's only nine in the morning!'"* (Acts 2:4,14-15). Why was Peter having to explain it was only nine in the morning? Because the followers of Jesus were accused of being drunk with wine. (Acts 2:13).

Why say all this? For some, this section may have brought on responses like, "What does this have to do with God and Melchizedek?" or, "That can't be true, you're trying to make things fit!" and let's not forget the ever popular, "Jesus is the truth, all the others are lies!" If those were our thoughts, even a little, it may be time for us to seek the Kingdom of God within us and sense what "Eternal Life" in Christ means. These discussions, including all the other dying and rising gods we haven't mentioned, have been part of scholarly discourse in religious, philosophical, archeological, and paleographical studies for centuries. What's the point? King Solomon said, after he built the famous temple in Jerusalem, *"But will God really dwell on earth? The heavens, even the highest heaven, cannot contain you. How much less this temple I have built!"* (1 Kings 8:27/NIV). Consider what Solomon was saying. If the Temple in Jerusalem could not be, and ultimately wasn't, the dwelling place of God, then what was the point? Then hundreds of years later, Jesus comes along saying virtually the same thing (Mark 14:58). Then add, at the very moment of His death on the cross, the veil of that very same Temple was torn from top to bottom. The ripped curtain revealed nothing more than an empty chamber, with no Ark of the Presence. Maybe we should finally take those words to heart and apply them to our lives today. We're quick to apply scriptures regarding some perceived prophetic event, eschatology, healing, and of course, morality; maybe it's time we do the same to these statements of Solomon and Jesus. In other words, the Eternal Creator, the Father of us all, the Living Christ, cannot be contained in the shrines of our religiosity, whether in Christendom, Judaism, Greek Mythology, or any other Western or Eastern belief system, regardless of what truth we think we know and how awake in the moment we think we are. The second we think we have the final word on Divine Reality, we've potentially imprisoned the infinite Creator back into the empty chambers of our temples, whether physically made with our hands or in the restrictive shackles of our egoistic minds.

It's undeniable that the Gospel was preached to Abraham (Galatians 3:8), long before the Torah was written and Solomon's Temple was built. Remember, Abraham and Sarah, as well as Noah and his family, were all technically pagans at the time. They were not a nice practicing Jewish or Christian family. They knew nothing of the Holy of Holies, doing mitzvahs, keeping the sabbath and honoring dietary laws, much less speaking in tongues, conducting spiritual warfare, and arguing the inerrancy of scripture. In the same manner as

Noah and Abraham, throughout the ages and cultures, anyone, pagan or not, who was of humble heart with a desire to respond to the inner pining of Divine identity, would find themselves stirring to consciousness. They would perceive the revelation afforded them in the capacity they could. Nonetheless, in humble desire, the mind of Christ within anyone would arise and speak the Divine mysteries of wisdom and salvation. Remember, when we are speaking of antiquity, a Greek word like **Χριστός** (Christos), *the anointed one,* comes from what's known as the *apoxyomenos,* the anointing of an athlete, as well as the scraping of oils and dirt from his body. It was adapted by the translators of the Septuagint for the Old Testament Hebrew/Aramaic word מַשַׁח (Meshach). Before either Greek or Hebrew, in the Sumerian Kingdom of 4000 BC, such a word didn't exist, but the concept, though a primitive one to what we know today, did. Despite the terminology, those truths were still made known by the Holy Spirit to the humble of heart, whether Sumerian, Hebrew, Greek, or whomever, along with the realities of redemption, death, rebirth, and resurrection. Think of it, when the Gospel was preached in Abraham and Sarah's time, it was done as a journey, an unfolding path of truth. It began for them as pagans in the land of Ur, then in childlessness, to a promise, to miracle fulfillment, to a withheld sacrifice, and a transformational provision. Irrespective of religion or myth, the symbology of the eternal nature of God as the god-man, as well as his death and rebirth, were revealed, and ultimately undeterred by any opposing god or goddess. One of the greatest ways this has been expressed is through the virgin birth, death, resurrection, and rebirth in the heart of Man as revealed in the Gospel of Jesus Christ. It's the never-ending revelation of true Divine Love, Light, and Life, which in no way can be silenced, obscured, or killed. Throughout the ages there was the constant telling and retelling of how what is totally Divine can live in mortal form, conquer mortal death, and be reborn to life once again. Like Melchizedek, who was a revelation of an endless life, who existed long before Abraham and long after, these manifestations of limitless, unchangeable, eternal life and truth, were a part of human consciousness.

In many respects, this made the Apostolic message a lot easier. They would reference these myths to stir the listener, like the concept of the *principalities* and *powers* of Paul's letter to the Ephesians, which came directly from Greek mythology. Paul was not saying, "Let's pretend your fake story is true for a moment so I can tell you my story which is the real truth and show you wrong." No. Paul not only knew his audience and used language they would understand, but he used the myths that matched the message. If the myth didn't match, then how would the language or message-reference be valid? It wouldn't! The fact that Paul referenced ancient myths wasn't only something the audience understood, but also held a spiritual truth and dynamic that assisted in unveiling what he was communicating. For some in Western Christendom, in order to make our beliefs the "only truth" we have objected to these consistent correlations, even overlooking that the Apostles themselves used them. Regardless of the legalistic or literalistic objections, some of which have a presentation of academic study, the intention is to validate our unerring religious beliefs rather than uncover timeless spiritual realities given by the Spirit to humanity. Such a mindset only places us back in the jaws of the Serpentine-Ego, which keeps us asleep in the Light (2 Corinthians 4:4). The common fear is that somehow opening our hearts to such things would be "contrary to scripture." However, if we resist humbling ourselves, our arrogance of assumed "knowledge" will only veil our true "knowing" available from the Grace of Christ within.

For many who sleep, the message of Jesus dying on a cross is to appease an angry Father who, justified by His own laws, was going to toss humanity into everlasting torment or complete annihilation because of their sin. But the Gospel of Jesus Christ is just the opposite. It's the restoration of our Divine Identity being the Image and Likeness of God. It's the message that though we may perceive ourselves as fully mortal, it also means we are fully Divine, created in His Likeness.

One of the key attributes of awakening and becoming conscious is being able to see His and Our Divine Identity, in ALL and through ALL (Ephesians 4:6; Colossians 3:11).

> *"And the LORD shall be King over all the earth. In that day it shall be-- 'The LORD is ONE,' And His name ONE."*   *(Zechariah 14:9/NKJV)*

Jesus said:

*"He who overcomes, I will make him a pillar in the temple of My God, and he shall go out no more. I will write on him the **name of My God** and **the name of the city of My God,** the New Jerusalem, which comes down out of heaven from My God. And [I will write on him] **My new name."**   (Revelation 3:12/NKJV)*

In true consciousness, it's no longer essential for Jesus to be one's *Savior*; He's accomplished that for us. In true consciousness, it's no longer essential for Christ to give one *Wisdom*; He's forever an emanation of that within us. In true consciousness, it's no longer essential to feel God's *Love*; He's that alive in us. Nonetheless, in true consciousness, Oneness is always essential. There's always the awareness that We are One. Father, Spirit, and Son are One. They are Him, He is in Us, We're in Him. He is One, We are One, He and We are One, with gentle distinction, yet no sense of separation. This is the real *Knowing*, "Gnosis," the real *Wisdom,* "Sophia," rooted and grounded in THE ONENESS OF DIVINE LOVE, never changing, yet always becoming. The same endless Light, yesterday, today, and forever, in the cycle of eternal Life, together in Love as One.

CHAPTER 16
I AM REALITY

"The Baal Shem Tov said that he who says that there is another force in the world, namely Klipot (shells), that person is in a state of 'serving other gods.' It is not necessarily the thought of heresy that is the transgression, but if he thinks that there is another authority and force apart from the Creator, by that he is committing a sin."

Shamati
Rabbi Yehuda Ashlag
February 6, 1944

Awakening to Reality and, like Jesus, living from *the World Above* though existing in the physical *World Below,* can only be done from a completely different consciousness. The more we move away from the binary world of good and evil to a more liberated world of Life, the more we unveil our Divine identity and live from that Likeness. However, it's a tough pill to swallow that *the World Below,* in which we seemingly live, is nothing more than the good and evil stories we tell ourselves about our experiences, and the illusions we fabricate from their memory about what's facing us. The Apostle Paul was clear that the incarnation of Christ wasn't about validating this egoistic world of flesh and blood: *"Now I say this, brethren, that flesh and blood cannot inherit the kingdom of God..."* (1 Corinthians 15:50/NASU). Nonetheless, on the heels of connecting flesh and blood, as some translate *the natural body*, with the egoistic base nature, **σῶμα πνευματικόν** (soma psuchikon, 1 Corinthians 15:44), Paul equates this mortality to corruption, and such corruption as *Death*. He then declares, referencing a promise in Isaiah 25:8, that this *"Death, is swallowed up in victory."* But He doesn't stop with a mere promise of heavenly afterlife, or us receiving another, incorruptible body at some future time. Rather, he gives further definition by establishing the source of this corruption, and how this thing called *Death* can pierce us terminally: *"The sting of death is sin, and the power of sin is the law,"* (1 Corinthians 15:56/NIV). By naming "the Law" as the infectious agent that empowers sin, making it a venomous toxin, he points us right to the definition of Death that God gave regarding the Tree of the Knowledge of Good and Evil (Genesis 2:17). He adds that Christ has given us a consuming victory over Death, neutralizing its poison by annulling the religious formulas and rites we once embraced. With that in mind, if the legalism of decreeing what's good and evil is nailed to Christ's cross (Colossians 2:14), what then does the incarnation reveal? It's the conclusive apocalypse of all religious injunctions, along with its bedfellows of political ascendancy and dominance. It declares we're no longer subject to their jurisdictions, and reveals them for what they are, "...*the weak and worthless elementary principles of the world...*" (Galatians 4:9/ESV).

Think of the message, miracles, and life of Jesus; He didn't have authority simply because He was special, or a really good person, or more holy, or more powerful than the opposition was evil or demonic. It wasn't even because He held the title of Messiah, or had a unique endowment from the Spirit, though both are true. No! It's because He wasn't part of a kingdom that was antagonistic to itself. Consider, the Tree of the Knowledge of Good and Evil is a system that opposes itself. Its accuser accuses itself. In other words, evil accuses good of being evil, and good accuses evil of being evil. Both stand with their fingers pointed at each other in opposition and yet, it's supposedly one kingdom. Its end is ruin and destruction, it cannot stand, and the incarnation was and is its eschaton. Jesus didn't gain victory over Death at the resurrection, He had the victory over it long before He was ever conceived in Mary's womb. The resurrection three days after the crucifixion was the proof of what always was. As Jesus said:

> "*How can Satan cast out Satan? If a kingdom is divided against itself, that kingdom cannot stand. And if a house is divided against itself, that house cannot stand. And if Satan has risen up against himself, and is divided, he cannot stand, but has an end. No one can enter a strong man's house and plunder his goods, unless he first binds the strong man. And then he will plunder his house.*"
>
> *(Mark 3:23-27/NKJV)*

The Serpent and its Tree, springing forth with all its illusions of literalism and legalism, is a kingdom that's divided against itself; it cannot stand against what's Real. While Jesus was responding to the scribes and Pharisees who called Him Beelzebub, the ruler of demons, because He healed a blind man, He makes the point that their rationalization doesn't work. At the same time, He wasn't saying that Beelzebub's kingdom was undivided and strong. Nor was He saying that He can do what He did because He's God and much stronger. Rather, the strongman in the parable isn't strong at all. There isn't even a strongman guarding the house! Rather, there's a divided ruler opposing himself, and is easily vanquished because of it. Why? By virtue of being divided he creates his own end. Thus, Jesus tells His accusers that they are divided against themselves, calling the Holy Spirit unclean, and by virtue of their own Law (Leviticus 24:16) condemn themselves. Luke's account (Luke 11:14-23) adds that the strongman was fully armed, but with what? Based on how Jesus ends the discussion, the armament was nothing more than the attractive legalistic trimmings of an empty religion. The so-called guardians of the house are, at most, accusers of a blind man, charging why he should remain blind, and accusers of Jesus, concocting why He didn't have the right to do what He did. In their empowered egoism, they've bound themselves by violating the very religious Law they attempted to defend and blasphemed the Holy Spirit in an attempt to safeguard its purity. What made Jesus the stronger one who could enter their house and plunder their goods, was that the so-called guardians were already bound without Jesus having to lift a finger. Christ was of a different House, a different

Kingdom, where there's no conflict of right and wrong, good and evil, accuser and accused. In His Kingdom, there's only the steadfast immovability of Resting in the Loving Compassion of Grace and Life. So when Jesus waltzes into the house, the guardians are already bound by their own doing, and He takes their goods. In other words, He heals the blind—both physically and, most importantly, spiritually—who are captivated by a paper tiger religious system. Another way to say this is, Jesus is Reality who, like an apocalypse of morning Light, awoke people from the illusion of what kept them asleep. Like our example in Chapter 14, where Dorothy is far from home, trapped in the land of Oz with its witches, flying monkeys, and winkie guards, but in the end, all were easily vanquished. How? It wasn't because Dorothy utilized the powerful ruby slippers to defeat them. Nor did she make her way home because she found the path to a great and powerful wizard who had the magic to take her there. No! **Her foes were vanquished and she found her way home *because she woke up!*** The moment she became aware of reality, there were no witches, flying monkeys, or wizards to be found! The same is true with demons, sin, and the like. It wasn't that Jesus had more power, or was even more holy, but that in Jesus's world, *the World Above,* such didn't exist! In Jesus's World of the Tree of Life, consider the following:

> *"And when Jesus saw their faith, he said to the paralytic, 'Child, your sins are forgiven.' Now some of the scribes were sitting there and reasoning in their hearts, 'Why does this man speak like this? He is blaspheming! Who is able to forgive sins except*

God alone?' And immediately Jesus, perceiving in his spirit that they were reasoning like this within themselves, said to them, 'Why are you considering these things in your hearts? Which is easier to say to the paralytic, 'Your sins are forgiven,' or to say 'Get up and pick up your stretcher and walk'? But so that you may know that the Son of Man has authority on earth to forgive sins,'—he said to the paralytic— 'I say to you, get up, pick up your stretcher, and go to your home.' And he got up and immediately picked up his stretcher and went out in front of them all..."

(Mark 2:5-12/LEB)

What did Jesus see? For that matter, what didn't Jesus see? First, Jesus saw a small group of people who didn't see a paralytic or the religion that said the man had to be that way. Second, Jesus went to the core of the paralytic's problem, sin. The paralytic believed he was ill because the Law said that if we didn't carefully observe the rules, serious sickness would come upon us (Deuteronomy 28:58-61). Remember? The power of sin is the Law. So, what does Jesus do? Nothing! He doesn't even touch the man. He simply tells the paralytic what he needed to hear, *"Your sins are forgiven."* Wait...what? What about an appropriate blood sacrifice, maybe a goat or something else? What about some form of penance? Nope, nothing. Just, *"You're not a sinner anymore."* Immediately, the literalistic legalists are conflicted as anyone would be who's bound by the Tree of the Knowledge of Good and Evil. Hence, their house is divided. To them, Jesus was blaspheming by saying the man's sin was forgiven, as if He were God. In their world, the only way God forgives is if He's paid to forgive, which as we've seen in previous chapters isn't forgiveness at all. However, Jesus didn't see their view of the תורה Torah as binding or dictating what He could or couldn't say or do. To Jesus, neither their Law of sin and death, or the paralysis it caused, meant anything, it was now superseded by His Law of Life (Romans 8:2). Then, as only Jesus can do, He calls their religious bluff, saying, "I see your bet, and I'll raise you a stretcher." However, rather than responding within the confines of their belief system which said, "Only God can forgive sins," Jesus says, "*...so that you may know the* <u>*Son of Man*</u> *has authority on earth to forgive sins...*" another apocalypse happens! He says to the paralytic, "*...get up, pick up your stretcher, and go home!*" In other words, "Reality is here, the illusions that declare you're a sinner and keeping you paralyzed are irrelevant!" The difference between, "Only God can forgive sins," and "*...that you may know the* <u>*Son of Man*</u> *has power (authority) to forgive sins,*" is that their version of God wouldn't forgive without an acceptable sacrificial payoff, and Jesus was approaching the situation from a Reality where He and His Father (God) weren't offended to begin with. The notion of saying He's the "*Son of Man*" makes the point all the more emphatic. He's saying, "In my World, Mankind thinks Tree of Life thoughts, and all who think those thoughts can just get up and come home!" You could say that by telling the paralytic to get up and go home, it's no different than the prodigal son in the distant country bound by the illusion of famine and want, getting up and heading home to his father. It's as if Jesus is saying, "Hi there! I AM a brother of another Mother, the Jerusalem from Above (Galatians 4:26). You've

549

been joined to these religious citizens who have offered you nothing but paralysis. Come on, it's time to get up and go home. Our Compassionate Father is waiting for you with a celebration!" As far as the *Son of Man* being a messianic reference as some assert, the Christ, the Anointed One, was a person who knew their Divine Identity and functioned according to its design! In other words, an anointed one, Christlikeness, is truly being Human (2 Corinthians 1:21).

In the *Mind of Christ,* the only reality is Divine Reality. The dream world we created when we partook of the Tree of the Knowledge of Good and Evil may seem real to us, but not to God. In "Real Life" the only reality is what's eternal, what God created. If God didn't create it, meaning if God didn't provide the "Life force," it's not lasting and therefore not real. Like the goddess Sophia, who attempted to create apart from God, we created something by our own egoistic choices and desires, which means it has a quick expiration date. We were designed to be co-creators with God, not to misuse our ability to define reality egoistically. As always, Hebrew is multifaceted, and its logic cannot be viewed from a surface reading alone. Hence, for the Hebrew text of Genesis 2:19, we usually see translations with the following:

> "Now the Lord God had formed out of the ground all the beasts of the field and all the birds of the air. He brought them to the man to see what he would name them; and whatever the man called each living creature, that was its name."
>
> *(Genesis 2:19/NIV)*

What can be limiting begins in the phrase, *"formed out of the ground all the beasts of the field."* The Hebrew phrase is:

מִן הָאדמה כל חית השדה

(min ha'adamah kal hayyat ha'sodeh)
from the soil [the I will be like] all life spread out.

While we commonly translate **חית** (hayyat) as *beast*, it's more precisely *life*, and specifically, *her life*. When we add the word **השדה** (ha'sodeh) which we translate *field*, like all other Hebrew words it has a multidimensional meaning. Its root is **שד** (shad) which is *the breasts of a woman*. When God appears to Abram, the phrase used is, *"I am God Almighty."* The Hebrew is **אני אל שדי** (ani el shaddiy), *I AM [God] strong my breasts*. Keep in mind that at this moment, Abram was seeking an heir for his legacy, and Sarah had been barren. The same is true throughout the Book of Genesis when it comes to the notion of procreation, as in Genesis 28:3 when God speaks to Jacob about multiplying his lineage. Thus, God comes to Abram and Jacob, revealing the feminine aspect of God, the Strong One who has the Life Force, as a woman who has the life-giving nourishment of her breasts. Like in the opening verses of Genesis, God is revealed as both masculine and feminine. This is not about making beasts, but God's breasts (yes, I was being punny). It's not about animals, though that can be a part of the equation, but about the very essence of what Father, Spirit, and Son is: Life and that which emanates from them.

551

The next phrase that needs to be considered is *"and all the birds of the air":*

ואת כל עוף השמים

(v'et kal oph ha'shamayim)
and all covering the heavens

While we translate עוף (oph) as *birds,* we do so because of their wings that *cover over.* Thus, translated in Judges 4:1 *"...while he lay fast asleep, exhausted..."* and in 1 Samuel 14:28 *"That is why men are faint,"* we have the same word in verb form. עוף (oph) is about a state of being. The idea is that our eyelids *cover over* our eyes when we sleep. The word is also used to describe something that *shines* in the darkness, as in Job 11:17 *"...and darkness will become like morning."* Here it's the idea that when our eyes are closed, they're covered over in a type of darkness, just like the wings of the cherubim cover the veil of the Holy of Holies. However, when we uncover them, opening the wings of our eyelids, we can see the morning light as it shines. Lastly, describing what the Adam is about to do by bringing definition to the Life God emanates, the letter definition of this Hebrew word is quite telling. ע (ayin) the eyes (seeing), ו (vav) joining, the light that comes down, ף (final - pei) the mouth (speak). By letter definition it's also describing the eyes see the light that comes down from above, and the mouth speaks. Thus, what the Adam saw, he spoke and gave it definition.

The text, not only in concept, but also the words and their letter definitions, point to God providing the Life force of Creation, and the Adam giving it definition using the enlightenment from *the World Above*. If we return to Chapter 4 - The Other Creation Before Genesis, we discussed the word רע (ra), usually translated *evil,* taken from the Egyptian sun god; the letter definition is, *the eyes in the head.* In other words, it's only seeing based on what one thinks in their mind through *the natural eye.* thus, seeing egoistically. This is in contrast to being enlightened in the mind from *the World Above* and seeing with that insight. When we egoistically perceive and give definition to our world without awareness from *the World Above,* the Real World, it's just a momentary vapor, an illusion. When Jesus says, *"You are from below, I am from above..."* (John 8:23/NIV), He's not just saying I'm from Heaven and you're from the Earth, but, "You live from an illusion fabricated by your Ego, I AM from the Real World."

The Apostle Paul says:

> *"...we look not at the things which are seen, but at the things which are not seen; for the things which are seen are temporal, but the things which are not seen are eternal."*   *(2 Corinthians 4:18/NASU)*

The word we translate as *temporal* is **πρόσκαιρα** (proskaira), and it's only used about four times in the New Testament. When seen through the illusion of the Ego, time is chronological, appearing as something that exists, sure and steadfast. If the Apostle Paul used a word or phrase like

χρόνον τινὰ (chronon tina), meaning *some portion of time*, as Luke does in Acts 18:23, he would be speaking of a measured portion. He also could have used **ὀλίγον** (oligon), as James and Peter do in their epistles, meaning *a while* or *a little bit.* But he doesn't. Rather, he chooses **πρόσκαιρα** (proskaira), meaning *transitory, ephemeral, evanescent, vaporous,* and *flitting.* The root to this word is **καιρός** (kairos), *a moment in time* where duration is irrelevant. In other words, we can have a **καιρός** (kairos) experience that lasts for seconds or for centuries. In one sense, when the physical is seen with the egoistic eye, it's solid, material, and long-lasting. Again, this is only an illusion, but understandable. If we lived together in a valley, we could say that its surrounding mountains are solid, material, and enduring. We could add that the mountains will last forever and will outlast not only our physical life, but most likely many generations. But in the same way that a butterfly, who lives only eight to ten weeks, lands on a black willow tree, which lives for a minimum of 40 years, many generations of butterflies have and will live on this "everlasting tree." Yet, if that same butterfly could see outside of time and space, it would know that the willow tree is just as **πρόσκαιρα** (proskaira) ephemeral by Eternal standards. Thus, when seen with Divine Eyes, the physical world with all its components is evanescent, a vapor. The only true reality is Divine Reality, which can't be seen by the egoistic lens. For that matter, **καιρός** (kairos) has a double meaning. In similar fashion, when someone has a "spiritual experience" in the physical world, and perceives it with the egoistic lens, it becomes a

καιρός (kairos) moment in chronological time. It's as if, like a vapor, the spiritual world broke through into physical reality, touched us for a moment, and then disappeared. The irony of the latter perception is that the reverse actually happened. We induced our Ego to acquiesce for a moment and touched Reality.

Part 1: A Father Who Throws His Children In Hell

If there's a skewed doctrinal concept that has developed in Christendom over the last two millennia, it's regarding the horrific place called *Hell*. While we spent some time discussing it in the last volume, it seemed proper to bring it up again at the conclusion of this one considering all we've discussed. What's most interesting is that, for most of Christendom in the West who highly support Israel and their so-called "Jewish roots," there's a complete departure from them on this topic. From the time of Adam through the time of Solomon's Temple, the notion of an eternal fiery afterlife didn't exist. However, since the building of the second temple, commonly known as Herod's Temple, there was a shift in Jewish mythology, which we will discuss. Thus, for the average present day rabbi and Jewish mystic, a fiery afterlife is only a momentary, twelve-month maximum experience to purify a soul in preparation for another incarnation in this world, or if they were pure enough, to return to the Garden of Eden and live on. With that in mind, if there was anyone who spoke more about *Hell* in the New Testament, it was Jesus. To be specific (depending upon translation), He spoke of it 15 times. However, He didn't discuss it because He believed in, or acknowledged, a fiery eternal torment for sinners, nor the burning annihilation of a soul. Rather, it was because the Jewish leaders, in particular the priests, scribes, and Pharisees, began adapting some of the paganistic mythologies around them and incorporated aspects of it into theirs. Jesus was responding to what they preached, and flipped their own myth on them. On the other hand, the Sadducees at that time, didn't acknowledge any of it, including any type of reincarnation or resurrection.

It's important to understand that when Jesus arrived on the scene, all these myths collided with each other. Consider all the different religions present in the region at the time: the Greco-Roman Western myths, the Egyptian, Hindu, and Persian myths, along with the Essenes mystical view. All of these influenced the culture. However, if we investigate the Tanak and see what it said about people going into a fiery grave, we see a point of view that is very different than where we land in Christendom today. Consider these key verses:

> *"You must not worship the Lord your God in their way, because in worshiping their gods, they do all kinds of detestable things the Lord hates. They even burn their sons and daughters in the fire as sacrifices to their gods."*
>
> *(Deuteronomy 12:31/NIV)*

> *"Let no one be found among you who sacrifices his son or daughter in the fire..."*
>
> *(Deuteronomy 18:10/NIV)*

"He walked in the ways of the kings of Israel and even sacrificed his son in the fire, following the detestable ways of the nations the Lord had driven out before the Israelites." (2 Kings 16:3/NIV)

"He burned sacrifices in the Valley of Ben Hinnom and sacrificed his sons in the fire, following the detestable ways of the nations the Lord had driven out before the Israelites." (2 Chronicles 28:3/NIV)

"They have built the high places of Topheth in the Valley of Ben Hinnom to burn their sons and daughters in the fire — something I did not command, nor did it enter my mind."

(Jeremiah 7:31/NIV)

"They built high places for Baal in the Valley of Ben Hinnom to sacrifice their sons and daughters to Molech, though I never commanded, nor did it enter my mind, that they should do such a detestable thing and so make Judah sin." (Jeremiah 32:35/NIV)

Think of those last two verses where God says, *"...something I did not command, nor did it enter my mind..."* Literally:

ולא עלתה על לבי

(v'lo alta al libiy)
and nothing ascended over my heart

In every verse, the idea of Israel throwing their sons and daughters into the fire was something abominable and detestable to God. He emphatically says it's something He never commanded, nor did it enter His mind, nor the notion ever ascend to His heart. Yet in Christendom, we've refashioned the very thing that God claimed to detest, and we have the Father throwing His sons and daughters of humanity into the fire. In addition, He didn't just throw them into the fire as a sacrifice to appease His wrath, but for eternal conscious torment, and/or slow annihilation. It's claimed that He did this as a type of satisfaction for His Divine Justice. How did we get here? How did the God that Christendom claimed as Creator move from being one who sees such an act as an abomination, to being the perpetrator of it? How did Jesus's Father become Molech? Excuse the expression, but... "What the *Hell?*"

To address this, let's lay out the modern view of Western evangelical theology that leads up to a fiery Hell. Even though we've romanticized it with a poetic approach, let's strip it down to its raw form and reconsider it. It begins with God having a couple of children named Adam and Eve. He raises them to be caretakers in His Garden. He tells them they can eat the fruit of any tree, except the one in the middle of the garden, the one with the Serpent, and gives them a stern warning. If we assume they're ignorant and innocent, then what happens next seems like a natural progression. Tell a couple of ignorant young adults not to do something, and what do they do? The second you're not looking, they do it! They ate and were caught with fruit juice all over their mouths. Now

God, the "perfect parent," becomes infuriated. Rather than giving them a spiritual time-out, telling them to sit under the tree and think about what they did, He just kicks them out of home and garden! One misdeed and they're out, with the sound of a slamming gate behind them. As if locking the gate wasn't enough, He also posts an enchanted, flaming-sword-wielding cherub, like an angry watchdog, to keep them from approaching it. On the way out, before He shuts the gate, He says, "Anything you plant in the ground, you're on your own. You'll toil to get something to grow, and the ground will yield thorns and thistles." He then hands them each a set of clothing—apparently having killed a couple of animals to make them—and finally slams the gate shut.

Great! So, there they are, two totally ignorant young people out in the cold, with no food, one set of clothing, and a growling, fiery watchdog guarding the gate back home. What do they do? What any pair of rejected, disowned young adults would do before they even find a place to live, and have something to eat: have sex, what else! Obviously, Eve gets pregnant. But, if that wasn't enough, with still no real home or food (at least from what we know of if we are taking the Bible literally), they're at it again, and baby number two is on the way. The first child now has a brother, and evidently, he's asked to babysit his younger brother a lot. Sibling rivalry is inevitable! (If this was in our day, you could see Eve bringing Cain to a Christian therapist saying, "I don't know what's the problem, he just hates his younger brother. He's always shouting, 'I'm not my brother's keeper!'" Can you imagine the therapist offering, "Well, I don't think it's just his problem, it seems to be a parental issue." Eve with a stunned look on her face responds, "No way! We're a good, God-fearing home. We're raising both boys in the fear of the Lord." The therapist continues, "From what you said, it appears to be related to the rejection you experienced from their Grandfather, and how that affects your relationship with your husband. Why are you frequently leaving Cain in charge of his younger brother to the point He resents him and you?") Nonetheless, at the yearly sacrifice, feeling like the overburdened first born, Cain seems to feel like Granddad likes his younger brother better and favors him. Being there were no therapists, pastors, or priests to talk to, Cain takes the easy solution: he kills his younger brother. This gets Granddad, God, upset enough to leave Eden for a moment and wreak more judgment and condemnation on the Adam's family. So, bypassing mom and dad, Granddad goes straight to the older brother and punishes him, cursing him to wander the earth. Okay, so Granddad dealt with the situation, right? Maybe He was thinking, "Where were mom and dad when all this sibling fighting was going on? Surely, if these boys' parents were more involved, this wouldn't have happened." Something to think about, later on, according to the book of Leviticus in chapters 18 through 20, incest is wrong. But since there wasn't anyone else to have sex with at the time, assuming one believes that Adam and Eve were the only two people on the planet, Granddad was seemingly okay with it, at least for a while. Maybe that's why humanity is in such trouble, we're all inbred! No sooner does this happen than the couple is at it again, and replacement baby number three is on the way.

As time goes on, Granddad God decides for some unannounced reason, that He wants his inbred grandchildren to come back home. However, in order to be allowed back in Eden they'd have to perfectly keep a bunch of religious laws.

Let's stop and think this through for a moment. If they were kicked out of the Garden the first time because they couldn't cope with one directive, "Don't eat from that tree," you'd think the "all-knowing-Granddad" would be aware that there's a problem with rule keeping. If they couldn't follow one command to keep their hands away from a fruit tree, how in Heaven's name could His grandchildren keep 612? Not to mention the big 10!

However, Granddad, has a solution. If anyone breaks any of the rules, they're to make a special altar, put the rules He originally wrote inside of it, and call it the "mercy seat." Then, have them kill an animal, and sprinkle some of its warm, freshly shed blood on the mercy seat. Why? Because as with eating the fruit, Granddad gets extremely upset with anyone breaking His rules. Killing a living creature and shedding its blood seems to calm Him down, at least until the next rule is broken. This can sound like some kind of blood thirst or a bloodletting, or more accurately, zoosadism. So, let's not call it that; let's call it a "holy sacrifice" to appease the righteous wrath of God. Wait...Let's think this through again. The grandchildren of the two people who couldn't obey one command and keep themselves from a piece of fruit are told that when they break any of the 612 new rules, they should start killing things.

According to scholars, by the time the second temple was built, there was a dual drainage system in the altar so the constant flow of blood could evacuate the temple into the Kidron Valley. Think of all the animals that had to be killed to create such a blood flow. But, as many say, "There's nothing wrong with that because at least it's not like those other religions that perform human sacrifice." Really? On the other hand, what's up with Granddad, who needs all this rule keeping and bloodshed? If it was just to prove the point that we can't keep rules because of our unholiness, then after the Adam's family sinned, or at the very least after Cain killed his younger brother, then he should have stopped there and completely dealt with the issue. But that's not what happened from Christendom's point of view. Let's not be so quick to give up on the idea of human sacrifice just yet either.

Granddad has a better solution to all this law breaking and bloodletting, which has obviously gotten out of hand when you must put a drainage system in your altar. His solution? He wants His favorite Son to be murdered as a final blood payment! This is where it all becomes very interesting. He sends this Son, born of a virgin, so everybody will know His special son is completely sinless and a worthy sacrifice. After all, Granddad is so pure that He demands the murder of a perfect person, like His Son to resolve all this. Thus, He has His boy raised in the middle of the very nation with all the law breaking and bloody sacrifices, which are now performed by priests of this same God. Expanding the notion a bit further, because of all the human immorality and imperfection, this Son is being sent because his "loving Father" needs to satisfy

His unsatiated wrath and the best way to do it is by draining the blood of His own Son. Why does He need to be gratified by watching His "special Son" be spit upon, punched, whipped, beaten, nailed to a cross, and then speared in the side? Why does such a ritual satisfy whatever anger He has? Or does it? Pardon the pun but, "Hell no, it doesn't!"

Let's be honest, it didn't stop there, did it? Nope! Not even close! To get back home and live in the Garden again, all His grandchildren will have to "properly select" His tortured Son as their penal sacrificial representative. If by chance they don't properly choose, Granddad adds one more item as the result of "not obeying His new command of accepting by faith" His Son's substitutionary sacrifice, *the eternal torture chamber!* Yes, now we've gone from killing to eternally tormenting. It's a fiery oven that never stops burning! Yep, choose wrong, and we're going to burn forever in screaming torture. If you're lucky (and we Christians don't believe in luck, that would be of the devil), and opted to believe a doctrine that says those who choose wrongly will be sent to the inferno only to be tortured for a while until complete annihilation is accomplished. At least the torture is short. Wait, let's think this through yet again. If there's no time or distance in the spirit world, how does only roasting in an oven for a "short time" work out? If we continue with this line of thinking, if King David is right when he says that if we make our bed in *Hell* (as translated in some Bibles), God is there (Psalms 139:8/KJV). What's wrong with this picture? Granddad is still keenly aware of the screaming torture of billions of people, and He's okay with it? He even feels gratified with that kind of punishment because we deserve it.

Have you noticed a serious pattern? This God seems as pagan as any other, if not worse! What's wrong with this line of thinking? He's been made out to be the Creator of all life, but for some reason He finds satisfaction by killing it when He's angry. Moreover, it's not just a quick kill, it's a ritual! When it came to His special Son as a substitutionary sacrifice, it took a week of torture to finally kill Jesus on the cross, and once He was crucified it took another six hours before He died. Move over Hannibal Lector, Jeffery Dahmer, Ted Bundy, Igor Mirenkov, this Guy makes you look like Sunday school teachers! But wait, isn't that the point? This bloody God *is* being taught in Sunday schools! Nonetheless, Christendom in the West justifies their worship of this judgmental, wrathful, condemning, blood thirsty, eternal fire burning, torturous god with, "He wants us to vote against the evils of abortion and gay marriage because people who do such things are of the devil!" Think of it... It's okay to slowly kill his own Son at the age of 33 for a blood payment He requires, by the system of religion He's set up, but if you do it while your son is in the womb, He'll have none of that! Think of it, if it was the death of His Son that was enough to satisfy the debit, why not Mary have an abortion? Done deal. We know historically abortions were occurring at that time. But no, the gruesome agony was a requirement. To make matters worse, while He's torturing His Son and having His blood slowly drained for six hours, this Father points to humanity and says, "Understand, you made Me do it! It's all your fault! I need to satisfy My justice with the blood of My own Son so I can forgive you, and you can come back home and live with Me." Why would anyone want to live with that kind of God in a supposed Garden anyway? What if once you're back home you eat the wrong fruit again, or you step on the wrong flower? Or worse, at the daily worship service you forget to tell this Father how wonderful He is for killing His Son to pay for your forgiveness so you could come back home? Maybe this isn't the Garden of Eden, but the Garden of Arkham!

Part 2: How the Hell Did We Get There?

There's a lot of great scholarly theological books available that address the false mythology of *Hell* as we've come to know it. Nonetheless, before we conclude this volume, it stands to reason that we should address this before we investigate the final section. First, the word *Hell* is a non-Biblical word; it's an adaptation of the Old High Germanic language for the Norse legends. *Hell* (also Hel, Hella, Helia, and Helja in Porto-Indo-European, and there are more regional versions of the word), was the Norse goddess of the ice-cold underworld of the same name. There she would receive the dead, but it wasn't a place of torment like in Christendom. It was simply the alternative to living in their version of a festive heaven with Odin (Wotan) in Asgard (Walhalla). In *Hell* people lived on, eating, drinking, and fighting, in the icy regions apart from the festivities of the gods. The English adaptation of the word started in approximately 725 AD, 400 years after the establishment of the Holy Roman Empire. Those 400 years prior, the Latin translation called *the Vulgate,* came into being. It was commissioned by Pope Damasus in 382 AD and by the turn of the century, Jerome of Stridon completed it. This was the first official translation of the Greek and Hebrew Bible for the western world. However, now enters both the changing of the meanings and the merging of words.

In the known Greek texts of the time, there were three words that would morph into the *Hell* we know today with the help of the official Latin translation, and the subsequent ransom doctrines. The words are ἄδου (hades), γέενναν (gehenna), and ταρταρώσας (tartaroosas). The last word, ταρταρώσας (tartaroosas), is only used once in the New Testament, which is in 2 Peter 2:4, referencing the Greek mythological place where the Titan gods were held: Cronus, Oceanus, Theia, and Phoebe, to mention a few. As we will find regarding *Hell,* Tartarus was both a deity as well as a place, far deeper than what we know as *Hell* itself. It comes from the Orphic religion, also mentioned previously, and later written about in detail by Virgil in *the Aeneid.* For this volume we're not going to discuss this in depth, other than what was just referenced, being that its incidental usage is only in 2 Peter, and doesn't divert from, or add to, the two major words that formed the *Hell* myth we've come to know.

First, let's review some background. In the Tanak, the Old Testament, the word that became *Hell* through translation is שׁאול (sheol). This word never had the connotation of a fiery afterlife in the Hebrew mind. The word actually means *unknown.* It comes from the word, שׁאל meaning *to ask,* from the root, שׁל meaning *quiet*. It's not to be confused with the word, קבורה (keboorah) or its root, קבר (kabar) meaning *sepulcher* or *tomb*. שׁאול (sheol) received the primary translation as *the grave*, not because of the tomb itself, but because it's descriptive of what it means to lie in the grave. As in the Hebraic mind with word relationships and its respective block logic, this word makes sense as a description. When someone dies, they are buried and placed in a tomb. Accordingly, what lies beyond *the grave* was *unknown*, meaning it was an *unanswered question* as the person's body lies *quietly.* (Regardless of how modern Christendom wants to claim it goes back to its Jewish roots, not so on this topic! Rather, we partner with the Pharisaical doctrine, which you could call a Jewish root, which Jesus was addressing to the contrary at the time of His ministry throughout the Gospels. It was the Pharisees that will add the concept of a fiery place. We'll come back to this point.)

The word שׁאול (sheol) appears in the Tanak approximately 66 times in 64 verses. By the time we get to our English translations, of the 66 times, 55 will choose the word *Hell* rather than *grave* or *unknown*. As we move from the Hebrew into the Greek Septuagint (the Greek translation of the Hebrew) the word ᾅδου (hades) is used because of its meaning, *unseen.* Thus, what's *unseen* is *unknown,* so far so good in translation consistency. This is also one of the two major words used in the New Testament. It's used ten times, only four times in the Gospels of Matthew and Luke, twice in the entire book of Acts and only in the second chapter, four times in the Book of Revelation, and *never* in any of the epistles by any apostle.

Then enters the other major word, **γέεvvαv** (gehenna), which is referenced in the verses in the previous section (Deuteronomy 12:31, 18:10; 2 Kings 16:3; 2 Chronicles 28:3; Jeremiah 7:31, 32:35). **γέεvvαv** (gehenna) is the Greek rendering of the Hebrew phrase **גֵּיא בֶן הִנֹּם** (gay ben Hinnom), *valley of the son of Hinnom.* This valley, a narrow ravine, was located between Mount Zion and the Mount of Evil Counsel, southwest of what will become the Temple site. Jesus uses this place as an illustration when He speaks of Abraham's bosom and the great gulf between it and the hot, dry place of the rich man (Luke 16:19-31). This word is used twelve times in the New Testament: eleven in the Gospels and only once in the Epistle of James (James 3:6), not in relation to a place that a person is sent where they burn forever, but as a metaphor for the power of misspoken words. Once again, it's *never* used in any other apostolic epistle.

In total, **ᾅδου** (hades) and **γέεvvαv** (gehenna) are used by Jesus fifteen times in the Gospels. Each time **γέεvvαv** (gehenna) is used it's in some way connected to the doctrine of the Pharisees, for example:

> *"Woe to you, scribes and Pharisees, hypocrites! For you travel land and sea to win one proselyte, and when he is won, you make him twice as much a son of hell as yourselves."*   *(Matthew 23:15/NKJV)*

From the time of the destruction of Solomon's Temple through the Jewish exile to Babylon and the building of the second temple (later known as Herod's temple, but completed in 516 BC by Zerubbabel), the Jewish leaders began proselytizing both Jew and Gentile, saying that if they didn't follow them, they would wind up in Gehenna. Consider that just over 100 years prior they were being called an abomination by Jeremiah for offering their children in fiery sacrifice to Molech at that location. It would then be Josiah (2 Kings 23:10) that would destroy Tophet in the Hinnom valley and attempted to restore proper worship to God. What was once a place of fiery child sacrifice to Molech was turned into a flaming garbage dump. From this idea came the notion that if you weren't a follower, you would be thrown into the fire. It didn't just mean you were worthy to be thrown into a garbage dump, but that you were given to Molech of Tophet, מֶלֶךְ הַתֹּפֶת, the King of the Drumfire. You can see how, 1000 years later, we create the picture of a devil with a pitchfork, standing in fire, and welcoming sinners.

When Jesus arrives on the scene, we see Him upending the doctrines of the Pharisees and using their teachings against them; we see this in other matters as well (continue the example: Matthew 23:16-22). Hence, literally from the Greek, Matthew 23:15 says, "*...he is born a son of the Valley of Hinnom two-fold more [than] yourselves!*" It wasn't that Jesus was affirming a fiery *Hell* of eternal conscious torment, but confronting the Pharisees with their own teaching. He was pointing out that, while they were saying people who weren't their proselytes were going to Molech's Gehenna, he was telling them that their followers were born of it, just as they were, only worse! At the time, the Pharisees were not only bringing this teaching to the Jews, but they were proselytizing the Gentiles as well. This was also a major point of contention among the Jewish people. Consider, not only were they under Roman rule, no longer owned their land, had a temple repaired by a pagan, and no Ark in the Holy of Holies, now they were adding Gentiles to their community. In their thinking, the gentile proselyte was the last straw, causing the purity of the Jewish people to vanish. The known zealots of the time called these proselytes "the scabs of Israel." When Jesus spoke to both the Jewish leaders and the people, these were all references within their theological thinking. What's interesting is, in Jesus's teaching, we never see the mention of His Father and ἅδου (hades) or γέενναν (gehenna) in the same sentence. Moreso, in Jesus's discussion of fiery places after addressing the Pharisaical doctrines, He refers to a teaching of purification; we will discuss this in the next section of this chapter.

When Constantine came to power in Rome in 306 AD, he claimed the Christian God was the source of his victory. This gave the West a new addition to whatever Gospel they understood. Not only was Jesus the Prince of Peace, He was now Prince of the Roman Empire, under the emperor of course, and condoning the violence of war to assert its purpose. Then, in the name of a unified empire, Constantine commanded the bishops to assemble what they agreed upon as valid scripture and canonize it. In many ways, aspects of this were already done, but not as an official distribution in

Rome. Hence, the New Testament as we know it was born. Prior to then, more scrolls circulated among Christians besides those included in the New Testament we now know. This at times created factions among Roman Christians, and Constantine didn't want that. He envisioned a unified Rome. So far so good, Constantine helped ratify the New Testament. However, a serious problem arose years later as a result. The Greek scrolls had some variants in them, changing the text in some cases. Also, not all of the Church of the Holy Roman Empire read Greek or Hebrew, not to mention there was an acute antisemitic attitude throughout the Empire. In keeping with the Empire's expansion through violence, it was no accident that Pope Damasus came to the papacy through the same, massacring his opposition at the Basilica. Once in power, he commissioned the Latin translation. When Jerome translated the texts, he imposed the known doctrines of the time into them. Thus, the words ᾅδου (hades) and γέενναν (gehenna) were merged and replaced with the Latin words, *inferi, infernum,* and *inferno.* So now, when the Book of Acts says, *"because you will not abandon me to **the grave**..."* (Acts 2:27/NIV), it becomes *"quoniam non derelinques animam meam in **inferno**..."* (VUL). Now we have the notion of a *fiery blazing inferno.* Then, when it came to the word γέενναν (gehenna), it was replaced at times, like in Mark 9:43-47, with *extinguitur* (which is where we derive the word " *extinguish"*), it means to *annihilate.* So between those two Latin words, Christendom in the Middle Ages developed the afterlife doctrines of a tormentous, fiery inferno where lost souls go for eternity and, in some extreme cases, a fiery annihilation. This mythos was further established by

Augustine of Hippo around the same time of the Vulgate translation. In his writings, *Enchiridion Fidei, Spei et Caritatis* (*The Handbook of Faith, Hope and Love*) along with his famous book, *De Civitate Dei* (*The City of God*) he states that the inferno was a permanent place for sinners without Christ, but those who received Christ and subsequently sinned would go to the inferno for a short time to be purified. By the time Dante Alighieri was writing *The Divine Comedy* (1320 AD), it was well established with the different levels of a tormentous, blazing inferno.

Part 3: When Hell Freezes Over

As we stated earlier, around 725 AD the word *Hell,* the name of the Norse Goddess and the dark, icy underworld she ruled, began circulating in the English world. Hence, the first English translation of the Bible would be done by John Wycliffe in 1382 AD, but not from the original languages, only from the Latin Vulgate. Wycliffe will employ the name and realm of the Norse Ice Goddess for *inferno.* Since then, scriptures like Acts 2:27 read, *"For thou shalt not leave my soul in Hell..."* Yes, Hell has frozen over! But only in name. While the word is now translated *Hell,* the frozen place and ice Goddess, the theological definition still remained as *the fiery inferno.* In the more polished English translation by William Tyndale in 1535 AD, while using the Greek and Hebrew texts as a source, he still left *Hell* in all the places for the *inferno.* With the establishment of Protestantism during that time, the notion of a fiery, eternally conscious torment remained engrafted in both Middle Age and Modern theology, though it was never taught in that manner by the early Church.

As the *Hell-inferno* doctrine grew from the 300s to what it is today, the message of the redemptive work of Christ had to alter to match it. From 33 AD to approximately 200 AD, as we mentioned in previous chapters, early Christianity taught what was known as *Christus Victor*, the total *Victory of Christ.* They saw the passion, crucifixion, and resurrection of Christ as the recognizable restoration of our identity as the *Image and Likeness of God.* In so doing, this also aroused the inner awareness of the Kingdom of God. Not long after that the Church father, Origen of Alexandria, would develop the *ransom doctrine,* which would prevail, with modifications, from approximately 150 AD till 1500 AD. We can call it the *Ransom Doctrine 1.0,* which proclaims that Christ's sacrifice paid Satan for humanity's freedom, which was further developed by Gregory of Nyssa and Rufinus of Concordia 100 years later. However, the context of that statement was within the framework of *universalism,* still standing on the concept of Christ's total victory. As this theology developed, universalism was removed from the picture, and Origen's meaning was distorted without that component. This is not to say that the *Ransom Doctrine 1.0* was totally correct, it was still a departure from what was taught for the first 200 years. However, keep in mind that when a pilot flies an airplane, if there is a minor deviation in his course trajectory, he and his passengers will end up hundreds of miles off course. The problem with Origen's doctrine is that it put God and Satan on equal footing, leaving the realm of the Tree of Life, and brought us back to the Tree of the Knowledge of Good and Evil with right and wrong, holy and wicked as comparable powers. While many would suggest that God is still more powerful, it becomes evident that it's not so in practice! Now we're constantly in conflict with the enemies of God: Satan, fallen angels, and demons. Consider this, you're not a defeated foe when you've just been paid off. When you think about it, if someone is paid off in a deal, at one point they had the upper hand, and maintain their authority if a future debt is owed. Now salvation is a transaction with Satan or the devil. In each generation there are many who need to discover Christ. Within those theological parameters, Satan has a very profitable business. As each soul realizes Jesus as their payment for liberation, Satan cashes in. If we follow this logic to its ultimate end, if Jesus's life was paying for a soul's liberty, when all is said and done, who owns the life of Jesus? Evidently, Jesus is bound in the devil's chains. Some will shout, "That was the Divine deception! Jesus was innocent, so Satan couldn't hold Him! The Bible says so!" This thinking is only possible when scripture is mismatched and used out of context. If we follow Jewish Law, under which Jesus was crucified, this doesn't pan out. The fact that Jesus was sinless is what gave Him the value for Satanic payment in *Ransom 1.0.* For that matter, in any ransom doctrine or theory, the one who's paid keeps the payment! If a collector of a debt is somehow deceived, or a slight of hand is taking place, that's a covenantal breech, or to say it another way, *"False scales are an abomination to the Lord..." (Proverbs 11:1).* Now we're saying God has no integrity with a debt or promise. Really? God becomes a deceiver, to deceive a deceiver, and somehow that's righteous? On the other hand, being that *Ransom 1.0* is saying Satan needs to be paid because he owns the sinner, fast forward to present day, and this doctrine becomes the basis for most of our fabricated spiritual warfare teachings. Now we must fight the devil and so on, it's really a return to a Greco-Roman mythological root (like we see in the movie, *The Immortals*), but with a Jesus stamp. Remember, we are the *Image and Likeness of God,* which means we do give Creation definition. So, if we take our creative power and use it in a certain way, then good and evil "forces" can exist as a result and will impact how we live and see the world.

Moving on from Origen's day, it would be around 940 years later when Anselum du Bec, better known as Anselum Archbishop of Canterbury, would construct an additional dynamic to *Ransom 1.0,* calling it the *Satisfaction Doctrine.* In keeping with our programing lingo, we could call it *Ransom 1.5;* it's not a complete version change, but there is a modification. When we think of those days over 1000 years ago, there wasn't a massive, lightning-fast social media network where such teachings could be communicated quickly. It took years, sometimes centuries, for major changes to occur. We did mention this doctrine before, but it's a necessary addition here because it helps define what happens next. What Anselum added in 1095 AD was that Mankind's sin defrauded God of the glory due Him. So, at this point, Christ is sent to be crucified and pay the price for our shaming God. His obedience isn't just about paying off Satan, but it's what restores God's dignity. Think of it, not only is it necessary to pay off Satan, but to restore God's damaged self-importance.

Our debt, or sin, is now an issue of disgracing God. This suggests that the Father was pacing around Heaven saying, "Jesus, you better do something. Their sin has disgraced Me, and I can't rule the universe with such shame! What will the angels, Satan, and the demons think? How can I be worthy of any human bowing and worshipping Me if I've been so stigmatized?"

Then, after the Lutheran reformation with its focus on grace and faith, John Calvin comes in 1500 AD with a reboot of Origen's and Anselm's teaching, which we can now call the *Ransom Doctrine 2.0.* This new version introduces Penal Substitution (aka Vicarious Atonement). The God who'd been dealing with shame for the last 500 years is no longer just focused on His imposed disgrace, He's outraged by it! Now, God the Father's wrath must be appeased. He demands a blood settlement to balance the scales of Heavenly justice. In this scenario, Jesus is sent as a sacrifice that will appease both His wrath and His need for payment. No longer is Satan the one who needs to be paid off, it's God Himself! Without a leveraging transaction, forgiveness and grace aren't possible. In *Ransom 2.0,* Satan is no longer the direct enemy of God, it's Mankind. Satan doesn't hold Mankind captive as in the *Ransom Doctrine 1.0,* rather he's fulfilling directly, or indirectly, God's purposes.

> "It is evident, therefore, that Satan is under the power of God, and is so ruled by his authority, that he must yield obedience to it. Moreover, though we say that Satan resists God, and does works at

variance with His works, we at the same time maintain that this contrariety and opposition depend on the permission of God."

(*Institutes of the Christian Religion*, Volume 1, by John Calvin)

But let's not stop there. He also introduces the condemnation of infants to *Hell*, the burning inferno, because of predestination and original sin. In Calvin's commentary of Deuteronomy 13:15 he writes, "If any should object that the little children at least were innocent, I reply that, since all are condemned by the judgment of God from the least to the greatest, we contend against Him in vain, even though He should destroy the very infants yet in their mothers' womb....We may rest assured that God would never have suffered any infants to be slain except those who were already damned and predestined for eternal death." Because of Calvin's addition of both the predestination and sovereignty of God doctrines, the notion of making any choices is already predetermined and controlled by God. So free will or choice is no longer an option. God had to be paid off, but only for a predetermined number of souls. Satan is inadvertently working on God's behalf and, to the horror of modern day North American Christendom, in Calvin's *Ransom Doctrine 2.0*, abortion isn't just permissible, it's the predetermined will of God.

Think of where we are and how far off course we find ourselves. It's as if we started in New York heading toward Hawaii, only to find ourselves landing in Antarctica. "Hey, where are the coconut palm trees?" Here, the God who's in control of everything has a serious self-esteem problem. He's angry as *Hell,* and without even a conversation, because of His self-proclaimed sovereignty, He's predestined people, including infants, to eternal conscious torment. Wait...are we sure His name isn't Molech? You could say there are some major problems with version 2.0's operating system. Well, John Calvin is barely cold in his grave (or was barely burning, if his assumptions about himself based on his own predestination teaching were wrong), when other reformers seriously questioned the validity of his theology: Jocobus Arminius of the late 1500s from the Church of England; Thomas Helwys and John Griffith of the early Baptists in the 1600s; John and Charles Westley of the 1700s; and Charles Parham, who introduced the foundations of modern Pentecostal theology in the late 1800s, 25 years prior to the Azusa Street outpouring. We now have another reboot and new operating system, the *Ransom Doctrine 3.0.* This version is basically the current situation for most of Western Christendom. It's a combination of Calvin's penal substitution and Origen's satanic payoff, without universalism. In this version, because of our sin, the wrath of God still needs to be appeased and our sinfulness gives Satan the legal right to hold us captive. However, because of the substitutionary blood sacrifice of Christ, God's anger is appeased most of the time and Satan loses his legal right to hold us captive, but only if (and that's a big IF) we properly appropriate it by faith. If we sin, even though we accepted Christ, we can still open the door for the devil and his minions to attack us, until we properly place our faith in the correct scripture, quote it in prayer, and use the name of Jesus as legal validation. However, if someone hasn't received Christ, the wrath of God has not been appeased for them, Satan still holds them captive, and they're still destined for *Hell*, the inferno of eternal conscious torment. There is a touch of something positive in this rebooted version 3.0, though. We trash the idea of predestination, choice is regained to a point, and infants get to go to Heaven if they die. However, because we keep parts of the previous versions, our choice is still influenced by the existence of a fiery *Hell*.

This "choice" model has several flaws. The listener of this "Almost-Good-News Gospel" must believe that after their death, they will find themselves burning in *Hell*, which is a real place. What this means is, if you are afraid to die and burn, there really isn't much of a choice. However, this Almost-Good-News Gospel requires a belief in a fiery end. Just in case a person doesn't know anything about *Hell*, they must hear strong preaching regarding their sin, the judgment of God, eventual condemnation, and the destination of eternal damnation to understand that it's all real and pending. Yet, sprinkled in at some points (like on the mercy seat) we add the idea that God loves them. It's just that in their sinful state, He really doesn't like them. So after we scare the *Hell* into them, we give them a distorted caricature of Jesus and His Father, having Jesus be the sacrificial blood payoff to the Father who's appeasing His wrath and need for justice. Let's not forget, while both are allowing us to go to *Hell*, if we so-called choose to go, we're already on the path to go anyway. Thus, in *Ransom 3.0* there's another quandary. We are to choose Heaven and shun *Hell,* but what about those who never hear the message to make the choice? Some denominations have long explanations to say, either they are supposed to go to *Hell* anyway, rekindling a neo-Calvinistic predestination idea, or that's the reason we have to preach the Gospel to everyone we meet; we don't want their blood on our hands. Yet, somehow, someone somewhere slips through our hands.

To add to the point, the *Ransom Doctrine 3.0* is what's known as a "Hobson's Choice." It's a choice which really doesn't offer much of a choice. For example, in *The Godfather*, Don Corleone says, "I'll make you an offer you can't refuse." In Mafia language, it's not that the choice is so good that we can't refuse it, but because the consequence of not choosing is so threatening we wouldn't dare refuse. Another type of Hobson's Choice was offered by Henry Ford when it came to purchasing his new car, the Model T. "You can have any color you want, as long as it's black." The choice is simple, buy a Model T with the colorful choices of black, black, or black. After all, there are so many blacks to pick from! In version 3.0 our choice is to choose Jesus and go to Heaven, or don't and go to *Hell* and burn in eternal conscious torment forever, (a place you were going to anyway). On a more positive note, in this reboot of the *Ransome Doctrine,* all babies are now allowed back into Heaven because they're innocent until "the age of accountability." This keeps Calvin's version of original sin but vindicates babies. However, now that babies get to go to Heaven, at what point do they automatically become *Hell* bound like the rest of unsaved Mankind? In Catholicism and other similar denominations, they use the vehicle of infant baptism to mitigate original sin, which basically gets them to their first communion. If the infant isn't baptized by their parents and a priest, *Hell* is still ahead of them, just a nicer version located at the border, called Limbo. However, if they're baptized as an infant, raised in the Church, had their first communion and confirmation, it's all good. Modern Protestantism takes a different course, called "the age of accountability." Borrowing from Judaism's Bar Mitzvah and Bat Mitzvah, it falls somewhere around the age of 13, depending upon the denomination. Yet, what a contrast! In Judaism it means a young adult gets to partake in worship, become responsible to practice Torah for themselves, and officially be engrafted into the Jewish community as an adult. In Christendom, you get to go straight to *Hell* if you die. So, rather than a celebration of a rite of passage, it's accept Jesus or else; it all comes down to one second in a child's life. Prior to the age of accountability, you're Heaven bound, all is well. The second (literally) you reach the age of accountability, your destiny instantly changes and now you're on a bullet train bound for *Hell.* If something happens to the child, it all depends upon the day and hour: 11:59:59 PM, they go to Heaven; Midnight, 12:00:01 AM, nope! You should've known better and gone to Sunday school. Say hello to the fiery oven, gingerbread boy!

Part 4: Thawing the Fiery Ice Queen into Reality

So here we are. *Hell* is an ice goddess refashioned to fit a burning *inferno,* to substitute both the raging Ego and what's *unknown* and *unseen* to the *World Below.* You may ask, "What's all this talk about eternal *Hell* fire that people are thrown into?" To be blunt, it doesn't exist in the manner we've been taught to think for the last approximately 1700 years. Rather, it's important to reference proper hermeneutics at this point. Jesus says something that has frustrated commentators for some time:

> *"For everyone will be salted with fire. Salt is good; but if the salt becomes unsalty, with what will you make it salty again? Have salt in yourselves, and be at peace with one another." (Mark 9:49-50/NASU)*

Regardless of all that preceded this statement, Jesus was specifically talking about being thrown in Gehenna. He concludes with, *"...everyone will be salted with fire."* Hold on, the fire is actually a good thing? In the Jamieson, Fausset, and Brown Commentary, they call it, "A difficult verse, on which much has been written—some of it to little purpose." In the famed Matthew Henry Commentary, before he gives a lengthy, ambiguous explanation that starts with, "The two last verses are somewhat difficult, and interpreters agree not in the sense of them." In Adam Clark's Commentary, he states, "...there is great difficulty in this verse. The Codex Bezae, and some other MSS., have omitted the first clause; and several MSS. Keep the first, and omit the last..." In Barnes' Commentary Notes, he writes, "Perhaps no passage in the New Testament has given more perplexity to commentators than this..."

Why is it difficult to make sense of this verse? Because, if our theology is rooted in Augustine, Anslem, Calvin and the like, the *Gehenna* is for the lost to be tossed in and burned forever, or slowly annihilated. But, if we leave the New Testament in the context of its time, the verse really does makes sense. However, for it to make sense we must then put all the other fiery-ice verses back into their original Hebraic context. When we look at the Old Testament and Jewish thought at the time of Jesus, we find that fire wasn't a bad thing, or a place of eternal torment. Actually, it was a type of purification and representation for the presence of God. Here are a few examples:

> *"There the angel of the Lord appeared to him in flames of fire from within a bush.* (Exodus 3:2/NIV)

> *"As the flame blazed up from the altar toward heaven, the angel of the Lord ascended in the flame.* (Judges 13:20/NIV)

> *"I looked, and I saw a figure like that of a man. From what appeared to be his waist down he was like fire, and from there up his appearance was as bright as glowing metal."* (Ezekiel 8:2/NIV)

We established earlier that God never considered such a thing, nor did it arise in His heart to burn anyone. Rather, in Jesus's words, fire is a purifier and a symbol of Divine presence when it describes God. The only other representation is the burning desires of the Ego, along with anger and malice. We spent ample time discussing this in the previous volume (see Chapter 10: Adam and Religion, and endnote 46).

It's also interesting to point out that the most common Greek word for *fire* in the New Testament is πῦρ (pur), and as we shall see, within it is its meaning. It's from there in the Indo-European that we arrive at *fūr* and *pūr.* In English we simply add the "e" and we have *pure.* According to *The Theological Dictionary of the New Testament* by Kittle and Friedrich, "In cosmological dualism fire and the snake represent truth and falsehood. In the human struggle for good conduct, fire is on the good side. Worship is thus paid to it as an embodiment of spiritual divine power. It belongs to the kingdom of Ahura Mazda, whose body is always a fiery one in Persian orthodoxy, a flame blazing forth in uncreated light. Fire is very often addressed as the son of the wise Lord, Yasna." We can see the parallels with the Book of Revelation (based in Persian performance theater) as the Son of God is depicted as a flaming persona. We also see how in Ezekiel, mentioned earlier, God's persona is depicted as a flame. The explanation continues, "Nothing connected with deformity or death must come into contact with it; thus corpses are exposed to beasts of prey, which embody the world of the evil spirit." Here again, we see the parallel when Jesus describes to the disciples, *"And answering they said to Him, 'Where, Lord?' And He said to them, 'Where the body is, there also the vultures will be gathered,'"* *(Luke 17:37/NASU).* In the same article, Kittle and Friedrich point out, "...fire is an antidote to evil influences." At the time of Jesus, the Persians, some Greek philosophers, and most certainly the Jews, saw fire as something every human must pass through for purification. As we mentioned in the first section, rabbis believed that passing through the fire was part of our purification to either enter Eden or, if there was still "soul work" that needed to be done, to prepare us for another incarnation on earth. Truly, this is our Jewish roots. Consider the Apostles Paul and Peter's words:

> "...each man's work will become evident; for the day will show it because it is to be revealed with fire, and the fire itself will test the quality of each man's work." (1 Corinthians 3:13/NASU)

> "...so that the proof of your faith, being more precious than gold which is perishable, even though tested by fire..." (1 Peter 1:7/NASU)

If we consider the Nordic usage of *Hell* being a cold, icy place where people eat, drink, marry, and fight, it's not much different than being alive on earth; all we need to do is turn up the inferno a bit to a temperature of 85° Fahrenheit (29.4° Celsius) and there we are, welcome to Southern California in the spring. For that matter, adjust the temperature and weather to wherever you are, and...welcome to *Hell!*

As the Apostle Peter continues:

> "Beloved, do not be surprised at the fiery ordeal among you, which comes upon you for your testing, as though some strange thing were happening to you..." (1 Peter 4:12/NASU)

In regards to testing by fire, the Mirror translation has a series of interesting notes, such as, "The word **βάσανος**, from the

585

verb *basanizō,* to test metals; from *basis* - to get to the bottom of a thing; often associated with the idea of torment. ...they shall be tested as one tests gold or silver with a touchstone; with fire and brimstone in the immediate presence of the Lamb and of those who have discovered their wholeness mirrored in Him - the dross of their deception will be exposed and cleansed," (MIRROR Notes). Add to this the notion of a New Heaven and New Earth (Revelation 21) and the fact that it's not over yet, stating nothing impure outside of the New Jerusalem, "...*anyone who does what is shameful, or deceitful...*" (Revelation 21:27/NIV), shall enter into it. Wait...didn't we all think it was over and everyone lived happily ever after? Rather, "...*the unbelieving and untrustworthy and abominable and murderers...*" (Revelation 21:8/NIV) have their place in "...*fire and in the presence of the Lamb,*" (Revelation 14:10). As we stated earlier, if God is going to enjoy the torment of souls in His presence forever, it's a contradiction to everything we know about the Trinity. However, we've read these verses with all the Ransom Doctrines that preceded today's theology and many times still see both Old and New Testaments through their lens. Because of it, we have confusion and contradiction, with Molech dressed in a Jesus t-shirt, claiming to be His father while rockin' out at a death metal concert. Instead, it's time to read the New Testament with the hermeneutic of its time. In Eastern theatrical terms, the presence of the Lord is the Eternal Fire from which all things are created (Genesis 1:3). What makes the fire eternal is that it's God Himself. It's an issue of awakening. Those who have awakened to God through Christ see themselves as Himself, the Eternal Flame illuminating the New Jerusalem. Those who haven't awakened experience the brief pain of purification for another incarnation on a new earth. This was the common teaching of the time. Listen to Jesus's disciples as they ask Him a very pertinent question:

> *"Now as Jesus passed by, He saw a man who was blind from birth. And His disciples asked Him, saying, 'Rabbi, who sinned, **this man** or his parents, that he was **born blind**?'"*　　　(John 9:1-2/NKJV)

It's one thing to ask if a man is born blind because of his parents' sin; it's another thing to ask if the man was born blind because of something he did. If so, when did he do it? A previous life? Of course! This is what was believed, and still is believed, by our Jewish brothers and sisters. For that matter, both Old and New Testaments refer to reincarnation on several occasions, though we've redefined those verses. What's most important is Jesus's response:

> *"Neither this man nor his parents sinned, but that the works of God should be revealed in him. I must work the works of Him who sent Me while it is day; the night is coming when no one can work. As long as I am in the world, I am the light of the world."*
> 　　　　　　　　　　　　　　　(John 9:3-5/NKJV)

Whether the man sinned in a previous life and was reincarnated to address his sins through blindness, or it's a generational hand-me-down because of the sins of his parents, both are irrelevant! In a consciousness that's awakened to the *World Above,* none of those things matter. Christ is both the Savior and the Purifier of all things. Keep in mind that the Christ is not just the person of Jesus who lived two millennia ago, but the Eternal One from and through which all creation emanates, who manifested in the person of Jesus two millennia ago. The notion of burning in eternal *Hell* would be completely off during that time. Sure, there were a marginal few that believed such things, but that isn't our Jewish roots, nor the Gospel. Spiritual awareness isn't just knowing Bible verses, fundamentalist theology, speaking in tongues, or knowing how to pray, it is something we come to as we awaken to the indwelling of Christ as a reality; it really is that simple. The Apostle Paul said:

> *"And I fear, lest, as the serpent did beguile Eve in his subtilty, so your minds may be corrupted from the simplicity that is in the Christ;"*
> *(2 Corinthians 11:3/YLT)*

τῆς ἁπλότητος τῆς εἰς τὸν χριστόν.
(tes haplotetos tes eis ton Christon)
the simplicity, [singleness, generosity] that's in
the Christ

The Gospel of Christ is simple. Sometimes the word **ἁπλότητος** (haplotetos) is translated as *singleness,* which means, *with no ulterior motive.* It also means *generous.* Christ has no ulterior motive, only to be the simple, generous Tree of Life to all. He isn't saving on one hand and finding satisfaction by letting people burn in eternal torment on the other. If there's a fire that burns us, it's our own self-centered Egoistic passions in this *World Below*. Many times, the consequences can be considered torturous, painful, and worse, self-deceiving. Nonetheless, the Christ, the Ultimate Reality, is consistent. None of our sins mean anything to Him, especially as far as our identity and destiny is concerned. If Jesus was asked today about our lives, "What about this situation or that one? Which sin opened the door to the attacks of the devil?" Jesus would respond, "Neither this situation nor that one opened any door. But that I may work the works of God in their life." The Eternal One is always emanating His works of Love, Light, and Life to us and within us, even if, as some believe, it may take fiery trials and several lifetimes for us to awaken to it. May we no longer allow our minds to be corrupted in any form, from the never-ending simple generosity of Christ. This is the only Divine Reality, the never ending, forever giving, continual Life emanating essence of God in Christ in Us.

CHAPTER 17
I AM THE CONCLUSION

*As my prayer became more attentive and inward, I
had less and less to say.
I finally became completely silent...
This is how it is.
To pray does not mean to listen
to oneself speaking.
Prayer involves becoming silent,
and being silent,
and waiting until God is heard.*
Søren Kierkegaard
1813 - 1855

Awareness of true Reality, God, is not something we can force, pretend, or assume. The Mind of Christ doesn't occur because we've read and memorized Bible verses, nor because we pray prayers to a deity in the heavens. Reading such is helpful when we realize it isn't the verse itself that's the real focus, but the consciousness behind its inspiration. When we seek beyond the verse and touch the mind and heart that inspired it, then we will begin to uncover the same within ourselves. To reiterate what we've already said in many ways, if it was the knowledge of the scripture itself that brought a consciousness of Reality, the Pharisees, Sadducees, priests, and scribes, would've been as revelatory as Christ Himself. Rather, it begins with a shift in the deep, quiet space of our heart, a place many of us fear to tread. As we attempt to bring this volume of the Melchizedekian priesthood to a momentary conclusion (how can we conclude something as vast as God in Christ in Melchizedek, and in Us?), let's recall the major mutations from a Christ-centered revelation, the Kingdom of God within us, to a return to a paganized moralism, blood sacrifice, a retributive external god, and how Christianized concepts were used to do it. While we may add that we believe this same god is also within us, because Bible verses tell us so, for most in Christendom it's exclusive. We add that this only applies to "the saved." The rest are either children of the flesh or of the devil. However, Luke writes in Acts, quoting the Apostle Peter, who was quoting Micah and Joel:

> *"And in the last days it shall be, God declares, that I will pour out my Spirit on all flesh, and your sons and your daughters shall prophesy, and your young men shall see visions, and your old men shall dream dreams..."*   *(Acts 2:17/ESV)*

Notice he said, *"all flesh."* This wasn't limited to people who realized the Gospel, or some mutated form of it. As we continue to search the Tanak, we find that this was the case all along, it was only realized in the last days. The founder of the Hasidic Jewish movement, Rabbi Israel ben Eliezer (1698 - 1760), also known as the Baal Shem Tov, said, "People should allow themselves the opportunity to really know what the unity of God means. To grasp a part of the non-divisible union is to grasp the whole." A successor, Rabbi Yehuda Ashlag, quoted at the beginning of the previous chapter, also said that if a person "...thinks that there is another authority and force apart from the Creator, by that he is committing a sin." These statements are not a refashioned Calvinistic Sovereignty of God type doctrine. Rather they speak of something that cannot be known with the mind, but that is sensed from a deep awareness within the heart. When Jesus was asked by a scribe what is the greatest commandment, He replied with the Oneness of God:

> *"The first of all the commandments is: 'Hear, O Israel, the Lord our God, the Lord is one.'"*
> *(Mark 12:29/NKJV)*

The scribe's response was profound in that moment:

> *"Well said, Teacher. You have spoken the truth, for there is one God, and there is no other but He. And to love Him with all the heart, with all the understanding, with all the soul, and with all the strength, and to love one's neighbor as oneself, is more than all the whole burnt offerings and sacrifices."*   *(Mark 12:32-33/NKJV)*

This man wasn't a Pharisee, a Sadducee, or a priest, but a professional copyist of the Torah. Thus, he had a solid textual knowledge of it. But clearly, his inner life was in a different place than where most of the other leaders were. Jesus's response to him was also profound:

> *"Now when Jesus saw that he answered wisely, He said to him, 'You are not far from the kingdom of God.'"*   *(Mark 12:34/NKJV)*

Listen to those words: *"You are not far from the Kingdom of God."* If Jesus's key message was that the Kingdom of God was both at hand and within us, what was He saying to this scribe? He was telling Him, "You're getting it!" Please note, there wasn't a message of Jesus saying you must receive me in your heart by confessing your sinfulness and asking for forgiveness. Why? Because this scribe was awakening to something far greater than simply the mechanics of "getting saved." This scribe was awakening to Reality. He was realizing that all the offerings and sacrifices prescribed by the Tanak paled in comparison to what He was awakening to. There was also no knowledge of Jesus's pending sacrifice and resurrection.

Jesus also said that he answered *wisely*. This word, **νουνεχῶς** (nounechos), which we translate *wisely, discreetly,* or *prudently,* finds its only appearance in the New Testament here. It's a combination of two words which come directly from Greek philosophy, Aristotle in particular. Why the writer of this Gospel would use this word is significant. **νουνεχῶς** (nounechos), means *to have control of one's mind.* When looking at all we've said thus far, the control of our thoughts comes by living from the I AM within, living from the emanation of an awareness of being one with God and Creation. In the account of the same discussion in Luke's Gospel (Luke 10:28), Jesus replies (from the Greek), *"You have* *concluded well, be a poet of this and eternally you shall live."* Remember, being a *poet,* which is many times translated, *be a doer,* or *do this,* is not to be confused with the Greek word, **πράσσω** (prasso), which means, *to do something,* or *practice something,* or *carry out something,* like obedience to the Law. Rather, it's the word **ποιέω** (poieo), meaning *to embody, to become,* and *create,* as one who *embodies a persona, and performs on stage, a poet.* Jesus is responding with this because the scribe was characterizing an awareness of embodying oneness with God, which means embodying Divine Love and becoming that Love to his neighbor, which is the synthesis of emanating the Kingdom within. In so many words, the scribe added that this was worth more than all the Law demands. Thus, he was awakening to a consciousness that no longer required the Egoism of the Tree of the Knowledge of Good and Evil. He was letting go of that *World Below,* and awakening to the *World Above,* **the Tree of Life.**

When we rewind 2000 years and look at the time Jesus and the Apostles were living in, we see a world that was soaked with human and animal sacrifice. Therefore, as we read the New Testament, we must remember the mindset of the recipients of the Gospels and Epistles. Everything was built around religious systems, Jewish and Gentile, that involved laws, ritual sacrifice, and blood covenant. Even though part of the message that the Apostles were trying to communicate was that Jesus was the end of all those sacrificial systems, it was a very small group of people who, like the scribe, were starting to *"get it."* According to Josephus and Philo, before the second temple was destroyed, the merged relationship of

Rome and Israel resulted in the priests offering sacrifices to God in behalf of the Roman Emperors and leaders. Then, after the second temple was destroyed, we find Roman conquerors offering sacrifices to Jupiter on its site, desecrating what was once considered holy. This was a prophetic fulfillment of the *Abomination of Desolation,* mentioned by Daniel and the authors of the three synoptic Gospels. However, what Jesus was awakening in "those who had ears to hear," was that none of those sacrifices mattered to the Creator of the Universe; actually, bloodletting of any kind was appalling. Rather, the Kingdom of God and the Mind of Christ was always within us. Yet, such a message was so upsetting to the Egoistic Mind, or we could say, the Mind of the Serpent, that we violently crucified Jesus and later killed those who followed His Gospel. The reality was harsh but simple. What comes with the Ego is justifiable violence in all forms, beginning with Cain and continuing to the present day.

Jesus made another profound statement in the Gospel of John:

> "...*If you abide in My word, you are My disciples indeed. And you shall know the truth, and the truth shall make you free.*" (*John 8:31-32/NKJV*)

How many of us thought this again referred to knowing Bible verses as the truth? It was something quite different. The context of this segment is very important. These words, uttered by Jesus, were prefaced with the woman caught in adultery, whom the scribes and Pharisees wanted Jesus's approval to stone (John 8:5). Here again, the deathly violence of their Egoistic religion surfaces in the name of godly moralism. Think of it, the premeditated murder of anyone is punishable by death (Exodus 21:12-14), but the "premeditated act of religious murder" against one who's deemed a sinner is justifiable. You can almost hear the voices of the Pharisees echoing as they stand with their stones in their hands: "The Word of God says she should be punished by death! We're doers of the Word, and God's Word is righteous!" However, Jesus, the Living Word, says to the woman, *"I don't condemn you, go..."* Think of what the Christ, the Living Word, says. *"If you abide in My word, you are My disciples, and in knowing the Living Word, you'll know the truth, and that truth will honestly make you free."* This was in direct response to that incident. The thought behind Jesus's words can be understood in the reverse. By obeying the religious moral law which results in killing the sinner, is the worst kind of bondage because it fuels the Ego in feeling righteous and enlightened, when it's in the darkest of places. Think of the religious people, including those in Christendom, who felt good about killing the unrighteous sinner. For that matter, after Jesus releases the woman without condemnation or threat, He adds:

> *"Then Jesus spoke to them again, saying, 'I am the light of the world. He who follows Me shall not walk in darkness, but have the light of life.'"*
>
> *(John 8:12/NKJV)*

The notion of stoning the woman came from *the ministry of death* (2 Corinthians 3:7). Jesus is clear that such thinking is walking in darkness, but He who follows Christ shall have *the Light of Life*. It's also important to note that the overly quoted verse, *"And Jesus said to her, 'Neither do I condemn you; go and sin no more,'"* (John 8:11/NKJV), has a concerning addition to it. The phrase *"go and sin no more"* was added by Bishop Papias of Hierapolis at the turn of the second century. Many commentators point this out, as in the Barnes' Notes, and the Jamieson, Fausset, and Brown Commentary:

"It should be added that this passage, together with the last verse of the preceding chapter, has been by many critics thought to be spurious [false]. It is wanting in many of the ancient manuscripts and versions, and has been rejected by Erasmus, Calvin, Beza, Grotius, Wetstein, Tittman, Knapp, and many others." (Barnes)

"The genuineness of this whole section, including the last verse of John 7—twelve verses—is by far the most perplexing question of textual criticism pertaining to the Gospels. The external evidence against it is immensely strong. It is wanting in the four oldest manuscripts—the newly-discovered Codex Sinaiticus, the Alexandrian Codex, the Codex Vaticanus, and the Codex Ephraemi Rescriptus—and in four other valuable Uncial manuscripts, although two of these have a blank space, as if something had been left out; it is wanting also in upwards of 50 Cursive manuscripts of ancient versions..." (JFB)

Why mention this? Because taking textual criticism into account shapes the point. The Bible is a wonderful tool for us to use to seek the Spirit beyond the verses and uncover within us the Mind and Heart of Christ. But the text has its flaws, mostly minor, but there are some major issues as well. Which means, rather than putting all our trust in translations and various, variant Greek manuscripts, our trust must be the Reality of whom it all speaks, "*Christ in us, the hope of glory.*"

Jesus's discussion with the scribe and the woman, who the Pharisees wanted stoned, is the necessary contrast of *the World Above* and *the World Below.* The challenge for many of us, even those who have begun to stir and awaken to the upper world of the Kingdom within, is that we still make these contrasts from the standpoint of good and evil, rather than Light and Dark, or Life and Death. When we see through the Egoistic lens of good and evil, they are simply opposing forces, depending upon where one stands. But Darkness and Death are not opposing forces, they are simply the absence, or better said, the *obscurity* of the Source. (New Testament Greek, **σκότος** [skotos], *shadiness, obscurity.)* When Life and Light aren't visible, Darkness and Death prevail. The same is true with Love, as we've stated previously. It's not that the Light isn't present, but it's been put under a bowl, or a shade (Matthew 5:15). Thus, like Jesus says to the woman (if we are going to leave the text as it was prior to Papias):

> "*Straightening up, Jesus said to her, 'Woman, where are they? Did no one condemn you?' She said, 'No*

599

> *one, Lord.' And Jesus said, 'I do not condemn you,*
> *either. Go.'"*   *(John 8:10-11/NASU)*

Immediately after this, the Pharisees engaged Him in conversation with accusations of false testimony, being a Samaritan, and having a demon. Then it all came down to this:

> *"'Your father Abraham rejoiced at the thought of seeing my day; he saw it and was glad.' 'You are not yet fifty years old,' the Jews said to him, 'and you have seen Abraham!' 'I tell you the truth,' Jesus answered, 'before Abraham was born, I AM!' At this, they picked up stones to stone him, but Jesus hid himself, slipping away from the temple grounds."*
>   *(John 8:56-59/NIV)*

The implications here aren't only about Jesus identifying Himself as God, as our modern theologies hold, but that Abraham also had a glimpse of the day when Mankind's true identity as the Likeness of God would be unveiled. The Apostle Paul said:

> *"You are all sons of God through faith in Christ Jesus, for all of you who were baptized into Christ have clothed yourselves with Christ. There is neither Jew nor Greek, slave nor free, male nor female, for you are all one in Christ Jesus. If you belong to Christ, then you are Abraham's seed, and heirs according to the promise."*   *(Galatians 3:26-29/NIV)*

"But when the time had fully come, God sent his Son, born of a woman, born under law, to redeem those under law, that we might receive the full rights of sons. Because you are sons, God sent the Spirit of his Son into our hearts, the Spirit who calls out, 'Abba, Father.' So you are no longer a slave, but a son; and since you are a son, God has made you also an heir."

(Galatians 4:4-7/NIV)

With this in mind, we can say as Jesus said, before Abraham was I AM. This isn't to demean Christ or to over-deify us, but to realize *the Gospel.* We are all *"sons of God"* and there's no distinction as it pertains to *the World Above* in *the World Below.* In the same way the Tree of the Serpent has Laws of Good and Evil, it also has Jews and Gentiles, slaves and free, male and female, and so on, with all the violence, separation, and alienation that such creates. Nonetheless, when we awaken and become conscious that the Living Christ, the Eternal Creator, the I AM, has always been our true identity, it doesn't just hold ourselves in that realization, but in synthesis with that consciousness throughout all Creation. This is true metamorphosis, or transformation. We're not leaving, as in distancing ourselves, from the Tree of Death, we are simply awakening to the Tree of Life, in which our true self has always been rooted. If Death is the obscurity of Life, then once Life is unveiled, Death no longer exists. Herein then is the question: why was the Tree of the Knowledge of Good and Evil created to begin with and why was the choice made available?

601

Part 1: The Path of the Two Trees

(In the following sections, please take time to ponder, read slowly and deliberately. This is a summary of Creation, the Adam, Mankind from the upper and inner world, from the two volumes, *Melchizedek: Our Gracious King-Priesthood in Christ*, and *Tree of Life Realities: Emanating Life from Our True Self*.)

Everything that follows is to be considered in the way the authors of both Old and New Testaments intended their writings to be perceived. We offered in both this and the previous volume the keys of block logic, roots and branches, hermeneutics, and allegory as important points regarding the thinking of the writers. Again, let it be said that this doesn't mean there weren't people who walked the earth like Noah, Abraham, Hannah, and David, to mention a few, but more so, they represent "inner spiritual realities" of the vast eternal world that abides within us. Jesus said that the Kingdom of God is within us. The Apostle Paul said that the eternal Christ is within us, and pointed out that we are not to know Him after the flesh, the lower world. When we think of the eternal Christ, the limitless Messiah who was in the Father from the beginning, it's hardly perceivable with the mind that such abides within us. Yet somehow, deep within the well of our awareness, we have a knowing that we are emanations of that limitlessness.

To summarize from the first volume, along with the refreshers at the beginning of this one, as well as being honest with ourselves, God, and the scripture, we find that the Tree of the

Knowledge of Good and Evil was *our* creation and part of *our* development. God gave us complete liberty to create our own path to discover the value of our true self and become conscious we're an emanation of His Divine Life. An element of this consciousness is farther reaching than just saying we can have a relationship with Him as with our next door neighbor, but it's that we're also an aspect of Him. In our Trinitarian theology, the relationship of the Three in One is the manifestation of God, and we're welcomed into that union. In Hebraic theology the Tetragrammaton...

י ה ו ה

...is a description of God, with the fullness of Divinity in the fourth letter. It's virtually the same concept as the Trinity, but not sounding as exclusive, as described by some. It's the fourth ה (hey) that fills out the final expression of the Creator revealed as Creation. Thus, it was to create a Creature that would be the fullness of His Image and Likeness, which means the Creature had to become *self-aware,* yet without *selfishness.* So, how does the Creature dwell in union with and as an emanation of the Creator? How does the Creature become *self-aware,* yet *selfless,* dwelling in the joy of receiving and giving with the Three?

We can call this the phases of Creation.

Creation Phase 1. The Creator, who is Love in the purist sense, created a Creature (נֶפֶשׁ [nephesh] the same word as

Soul), also defined as *the Desire to Receive*, giving it complete liberty to "choose" to Receive the Creator's essence, Light, Life, and Love, and freely Give in return (Reflect) whatever it desired, even to the point of not Giving at all. This "state of being" is called, **הילל** (heilel) Lucifer (from the Latin), the Vessel that *Receives and Reflects*. However, the Creature hadn't yet experienced both the value and what it meant to choose between *Receiving and Reflecting*, or to *Receive for Itself Only*. In its innocence, it was also ignorant. It hadn't experienced freedom's consequence to choose for itself alone. When it was created, it was in the state of *Receiving and Reflecting*. Thus, by being ignorant of what it meant to choose, it was also ignorant of *itself as a Creature* in the Image and Likeness of the Creator. (Be mindful, to truly be the Image and Likeness of the Creator it had to have the complete liberty to choose, because Love isn't true Love without unbound choice.) As the Creature became aware of itself it chose to explore what it was to *Receive for Itself Alone*. Thus, what we've called *the Ego* came into being. From this point, **הילל** (heilel) Lucifer, the Vessel that was to *Receive and Reflect*, became **נחש** (nachash) the Serpent, the Shining Enchantment, *the Desire to Receive for Itself Alone*.

Common in most theological circles in Christendom, we know this as the "Fall of Lucifer" and the transformation into Satan. We find these accounts in several places, the most common being from Ezekiel 28, Isaiah 14, and Isaiah 30. Another aspect is that, in those same scriptures, this Fall finds the Creature called *the dust of the ground* and *the Vessel shattered*.

Furthermore, there's an account of the same story in Ezekiel 31, using the imagery of a Tree in the midst of the Garden of Eden. Hence, *the Desire to Receive for Itself Alone,* the Ego, *the Dust of the Ground,* the Serpent, The Tree of the Knowledge of Good and Evil, Satan, are all attributes of the same quality, just described in the different facets of block logic. This occurred from the thickening of its *Desire to Receive for Itself,* the Ego. (We will discuss what Egoistic thickening or density means in "Part 3: The Path of the Tree of Life.") From the realms of the mountain of God (Ezekiel 28), it now became the dust of the ground (Isaiah 14, Ezekiel 28 and 31). Because of this decision, the Creature (the Soul)became aware of what it meant to choose, and more so, became *self-aware* through it.

Creation Phase 2. Like a loving Father whose child has just stumbled and fallen, the Creator then reached into *this dust of the ground,* breathed into it the Breath of Life, and once again the Creature was vibrant with Light; a Vessel resembling and reflecting the Divine Image and Likeness. Within it were all the same attributes as before, but now with the awareness of what it means to choose. The Creator told the Creature that in its midst were now two dynamic attributes: the Tree of Life, rooted in Divine Love and Light, and also the Tree of the Knowledge of Good and Evil, rooted in Egoistic selfishness, known as Death. The Creator gave the Creature full reign to eat from all the Trees of the Garden of Pleasure. In other words, the Creature can enjoy the fulfillment of all its Desires to Receive. Yet the Creature was warned that if it chose to partake of the Tree of the Knowledge of Good and Evil, *the Desire to Receive for Itself Alone,* it would obscure the Divine

Life, Light, and Love within it. While eating and enjoying all the pleasureful Trees of the Garden, the Creature was to cultivate the ground to produce more Life and Pleasure. This wasn't just an external Garden like in someone's yard, but an inner Garden of inner spiritual realities that were farther reaching than any future physical universe.

As the Creature cultivated the ground and enjoyed Divine Life, it was also aware that it still had the privilege to choose another path, another way of existence. Thus, while it lived in Likeness and Light, it had within it the voice of selfishness, the Ego, from its newly found self-awareness from the first phase. The Creature (the Soul) as it cultivated its vast inner Garden, was to guard it and keep it from its newly seeded self-centeredness. Rather, it was to nurture its self-awareness into freely *Receiving and Giving,* this is called Love. Finally, the moment came within its awareness when the volume of its selfishness increased and spoke; we call this, the Serpent. It knew previously what it was to choose, gaining its self-awareness, but it hadn't experienced a path of existence where it would only *Receive for Itself.* In other words, the Soul decided to cultivate its self-awareness into self-centeredness to the point of Desiring to leave the Creator and attempt to exist on its own. Of course, this is impossible. That would be like trying to live in this physical world without breathing. However, what if we were to become "unconscious" of the Creator, and shroud the Source of Life, so we can ourselves be the center of our universe. Then again, most of us go through our days without "being conscious" we're breathing, which makes the point. God is like the air we breathe, Who is forever lovingly present giving us Life, whether we choose to be conscious of or not. Nonetheless, the Creator did give the Soul the liberty to choose to believe it could exist in such a state of unconsciousness. This is what we perceive as separation. The self-centered Ego's density thickened to the extent that it could completely veil the reality of the Creator from its consciousness. To veil the Source of Life from the awareness of the Soul, is another way of saying that we choose to exist "unconscious" of *our* Identity.

The Creator knew it needed to allow the Soul this privilege so when it was ready, it could rediscover its connection, relationship, and identity in the Creator. This is the ultimate point, to create a Creature completely like the Creator, with the ability to discover its Likeness through its own self-awareness. Yet, to be completely like the Creator is to be completely Loving, which means it's self-aware, yet without selfishness, willing to *Give* itself away in Loving connection, relationship, and union. In other words, to be fully conscious of itself, yet part of the selfless imagery of Trinitarian union.

At this point, it chose to heed the inner voice of the Serpent and decided to take the journey of the path of the Tree of the Knowledge of Good and Evil. Like a flash of lightening, the Tree of Life was obscured, as if one closed their eyes to keep from seeing what was before them. To the realm of Life, if one now observed the Creature whose eyes were closed, it appeared to be in a deep sleep, a Death Sleep. In that moment, the Creature returned to the status of *the dust of the ground,* unconscious of the *World Above,* and completely selfishly aware. To say this another way, the Vessel once again shattered, and each fragment created its own separate reality, veiling the Creator. It took its creative power, given by the Creator, and obscured all the realities of the Divine Pleasure in the Garden. The Soul, who was once a union like the Creator, now created the illusion of separation, with each fragment believing it was separate from both the Creator and the other fragments. The Creator and the Garden were concealed as a distant memory within each of the self-centered pieces. Because of this, no individual fragment could fully comprehend its true self, nor the Creator, nor the vast Garden of Divine Pleasure. Perception of the Creator and the Soul's true nature required a greater consciousness beyond its *Egoistic self-awareness.* At best, it could only see small, veiled glimpses of the Creator and its true self, though distorted as if looking into a seriously shattered mirror. The Creature, designed to receive pleasure, closed its eyes to the Source of all pleasure. On its newfound path, its root form didn't change. It still *Desired to Receive Pleasure,* but was never fulfilled with the Source obscured. It took and consumed whatever it could from Creation to try and satiate its vast desire. The irony of this state of being is that, to obscure the Light meant more than merely closing the eyes, it was to consume It without reflection. There's only one Source of pleasure, Light, and to consume It without reflecting It is to obscure It. Thus, the Creator, and our true self, are obscured within us.

Whenever it sensed another fragment of the Vessel, if it didn't resemble what it believed would bring pleasure, or simulate its self-centered understanding of its desire, it would be repulsed by it. It would pleasure itself by pointing to its perceived differences, widening the gap of the sensation of separation, feeling superior by its rightness and the other's wrongness. In many cases, when the other fragments were appalling enough, the sense of the need for further separation would result in violence. Hence, rather than the fragments living in union, they fought against each other, each devising their own way of existence. Groups of fragments would create and agree on sets of rules and traditions, which created a false sense of belonging. This would calm their Egoistic fears, but there was still a sense of unfulfillment. In light of the distant memory of a Creator and a Garden, they created their own stories of what such would be like, making the Creator in their image, thus religion as we know it came into being. However, if someone from the group broke the tribal rules, or somehow did something they feared would enrage the gods they created, they would be punished with forms of penance, and at times with death.

Creation Phase 3. Amid all the fragmented self-centered violence and religious bloodletting, on occasion there would be a brief, momentary, genuine remembrance of the Creator and the Garden. This would occur when the Ego would tire of its self-inflicted suffering as it strived for peace and dominance through its tribal religions and wars. When this would happen, the thickness of its veil would thin, and a brief glimpse of the Creator with our true self would emerge. Even through it was just a peek, immediately there was a sense of loving grace and inner rest (Noah). Though seemingly foreign, it was undeniably there and real. The Soul saw a Creator with eyes of Love extending *Grace* to it. This remembrance caused a momentary "flooding of the Soul," causing it to rise above its Serpentine Egoism and *Rest* upon the waters of peace. Still, most of the fragments weren't ready to perceive the Creator as gracious, only in like manner as themselves: self-righteous, judgmental, violent, and punitive. Despite that, as the transformational waters of peace dissipated, the new perception of *Grace* and *Rest* within the Soul remained; it was like a new world surfaced. While the Egoism, with all its attributes, was still present, now within it was an impression of something greater. As self-centeredness—or as some call it, *sin*—abounded, so did this imprint of *Grace* and *Rest.* There was much struggle between the two Soul dynamics. One was of the Egoistic Tree full of law, judgment, punitive condemnation, and blood sacrifice, the other from the glimmering inkling of the Tree of Life, with its impression of *Grace* and *Rest.* Most of the time these inklings were overshadowed by the Egoism of Knowing Good and Evil, so the image of the Creator and the Creature, the Soul, were still quite distorted when glimpsed. However, this inkling, this remembering, was the beginning of an awakening to the Divine Nature within. Thus, while selfishly aware, down deep we began to stir to another aspect of ourselves, a greater one within us than the world we created around us. This wasn't just limited to our tribe and our way of ritual, but encompassed a rainbow of humanity.

Creation Phase 4. The Soul now developed to the point where it was stirring to the Nature of the Creator, full of *Grace* and

Rest, and found the inner whisper to *Trust* (Abraham). While there was still religious sacrifice and blood covenant from the Serpent's Tree all around, a notion of a new Life started to form, one based on the Love revealed by grace, without rules, ritual, and judgment. This stirring began to *Trust* the inkling within it saw. This inner trust was an *Awakening* to a new relational reality with God, called *Melchizedek.* Through *Awakening* in trust, the Path of Righteousness, also known as the Path of Peace, was opened. This connection to the Path of Righteousness and Peace was born from the *inner awakening* to trust in grace which brought about rest to the Soul. It was as if the Cherub that guarded the path with the flaming sword which turned in all directions, doused it with the waters of peace that grace offered, and rested in one direction, pointing to the Path of Life. This awakening began to spread in similar forms with increasing trust and understanding. What once felt distant was now realized much closer (as we see exemplified in the qualities called Isaac, Jacob, and Joseph). That said, there were still large aspects of the fragmented Vessel that still held to their fabricated beliefs regarding themselves, their gods, rituals, and justified violence. However, on occasion they too caught glimpses of their true selves, their Divine Nature, glistening with flashes of Son-Light through the dense atmosphere.

Creation Phase 5. Our egoistic struggle to let go of the Tree of the Knowledge of Good and Evil and walk the Path of the Tree of Life required further *clarification.* To the Ego it just doesn't make sense to embrace a Path of Love, Light, and Life, without some form of rules to attain it and judgment to maintain it.

This *Clarity* (Moses) was drawn from the same waters of peace that trust emerged. As clarity became prevalent between the two Trees, many of the fragments began to respond and followed through the seawaters of transformation to a higher elevation. Because we had moments of awakening and saw glimpses of the Creator we also had a sense our true self. Nonetheless, because of our Egoistic religious fears within the Vessel, the Soul hesitated (doubted) as it was awakening and filling with greater trust. Thus, a notable distinction of the two paths were becoming clear. There was the one of Law, judgment, blood sacrifice, and condemnation, which were seen in different forms throughout the nations, but now made extremely clear through the Law and its priesthood. However, though present, the *Awakened Trust,* known as *Melchizedek,* would remain concealed behind the thickening veil of *Aaron-Levi's* Egoism. Rather than increasing in our consciousness as an emanation of the limitless Source, the Ego thickened with more rules, rituals, and sacrifices. Yet, because there was a growing clarity of distinction, there were moments where we would step away from the dense laborious road of rules, blood sacrifice and judgment. By opening the Egoistic veil through surrender, we embraced the Path of Life through trusting grace and finding inner rest. Seeing the Path of Life through an *Awakened Clarified Trust* (David), one's heart began to beat in synchronicity with the Creator's.

Creation Phase 6. This *Clarified Trust* was free of rules, ritual, and judgment, and the Soul was once again reemerging with *Compassion, Grace,* and *inner Rest.* It became vividly clear that this was transforming into its fullness, removing the Egoistic veil, and overtly living as *Compassionate Selflessness,* the Image of God. Broad and complete this, *fullness of trust* was the revelation of *Compassionate Selflessness,* called **the Christ.**

At this point, the clarification of the two paths were so evident, that a choice was once again possible, like in the Garden between the two Trees. Finally, an aspect of the Vessel came forth as one embodying *Compassionate Selflessness.* This manifestation was called *Jesus.* When such was revealed, many began to awaken to a full liberty to trust in the Creator's grace, rather than its own effort to obey laws and sacrifices. The path of *Melchizedek,* the original priesthood of peace was revealed once again. This was a peace between all, both Creator and Creation. On the other hand, the distinction was so clear, the path of the Serpent with its condemning Law, was concerned it would lose its long-held recognition in the shattered Vessel. So, in the name of its religiously justified violence, it decided to rid itself of *Compassionate Selflessness* by scapegoating. It rationalized its actions by claiming they were for the greater good. "Better *Compassion's* liberty die, than the whole nation of Law, order and judgment." However, *Selfless Compassion* through *Grace* and *Rest,* had its Ego so tempered didn't need to resist or retaliate against any accusation. This enraged the system of Law and judgment with further condemnation. After all, when there's *Selfless Compassion,* there's no need for Law and rules to keep any form of order. To say this another way, there's no place for the Ego's pride, fear or wrath. Nonetheless, it violently took the revelation of *Selfless Compassion, the Christ,* condemned it and made it a scapegoat. It committed it to the emotional torment of ridicule, humiliation, and mockery, along with the physical pain of battery, torture, and eventually, the slow systematic murder of crucifixion. However! Because the fullness of trust was rooted in *Selfless Compassion,* whatever the Egoistic world of Law, judgment, and condemnation did, they couldn't destroy *the Tree of Life Realities* it lived in.

Creation Phase 7. Seemingly crucified to dead silence, *Selfless Compassion* awoke, rising from Egoism's grave and emanating its *Unified-Likeness* of the Creator and Creation. This resurrection and revealing is called *the Limitless Christ,* also known as *the Last Adam,* the *Alpha and Omega,* and *the Beginning and the End.* Because *Selfless Compassion* was part of the shattered Vessel, other fragments were awakening as well, and the renewed *order of Melchizedek* took center stage. This awakening was happening in various ways, but it was happening, and was unstoppable! The fragments began realizing that the path of *the Limitless Christ* was far more fulfilling because it *Reflected the Light,* rather than Egoistically consuming It. Once again filling the earth like a flood, fragments of the Soul were awakening to the emanation of *Unified-Likeness* within them. This stirring would occur because they would meet another who was stirring as well, like two heart cells when separated beat each to their own rhythm, yet when they touch they beat in synchronicity. Sometimes it was otherworldly, as if they heard a voice within and awoke as if the Creator called to them by name. Sometimes, one would hear aspects of the message of grace, rest, trust, and *Selfless Compassion,* which would be enough to realize *the Limitless Christ* was within. Regardless of any perceived external method that would stir one to awake, the concealing grave of Egoism could not contain what was being unveiled.

This inner awakening to *the Limitless Christ* restored the *Desire to Receive and Reflect.* This restoration is called *the Ekklesia* (the Called Out), not to be confused with Christendom's present definition of "the Church." Rather, it's the realization of the true-self and its Oneness with the Creator and Creation. It's the *Calling-Out* into one's true identity as part of *the Limitless Christ.* By choosing to live in *Selfless Compassion,* it causes us to see the path of *Melchizedek,* which leads to the vastness of its *Tree of Life Realities.* Now we can discern the difference between the Serpentine-Tree of Knowing Good and Evil as one that "consumes and conceals,", and *the Limitless Christ's Tree of Life* as one that "receives and reveals." Both dynamics seemingly acquire a type of awareness because we, the Creature, the living Soul, were created that way from the beginning. However, one is truly awake, aware of its limitless I AM-ness, at one with Creation and Creator. The other is unconscious in the illusion of its fabricated self-realization, separated and autocratic. Even so, it's within the beautiful privilege of choice that we acquire true fulfillment and find our connection to Divinity and Identity. In the end, the Ekklesia in its fullness is simply another way of saying the Soul has reached maturity, fully self-aware, yet through *Selfless Compassion.* The Soul is fully *Receiving and Reflecting,* it's emanating the Image and

Likeness of God, which means the two have become one because they are indistinguishable.

In summary, the process is something like this: we stir within our Soul as we see Grace for the first time, and yet we may struggle with Resting in it. However, as we continue to stir and catch glimpses of Grace, we find ourselves resting more, and we begin to Trust. This trust opens a different vista to us, a different path, one without Laws and Condemnation. Nonetheless, many times we need further clarification of the two paths, because our Ego, rather than transforming into *Compassion,* would much rather beguile itself into believing that Grace and Law, as well as Rest and Judgment, can live together happily-ever-after. In truth, we can't combine Grace, Trust, and Rest with Law, Judgment, and Condemnation any more than we can combine oil with water. They are immiscible. This attempt to mingle the two keeps the Melchizedekian path concealed behind the imaginations of the Egoistic veil. However, as clarification of the comparison continues, it becomes evident that rules, judgments, blood sacrifices, and the like, only obscure our true self, and the stirring once again emerges. What was once seemingly second nature to us, pointing the finger, accusing, and condemning, is realized as the Adversary we created. Thus, if we created such an adversary, we can also be its undoing. This means that in *the Melchizedekian* way of thinking—in other words, in the true *Ekklesia* way of thinking—if one stumbles along the path, it's no longer seen as failure or sinful, but part of learning, growing, and discovering the new living way. Regardless of where one is on the spectrum of consciousness, our Oneness with the Light, Life, and Love of the Creator, and our Union with the entire Vessel, from its Head to its toe, is sure and secure. Realizing we are part of, and an emanation of, *the Limitless Christ,* is a wonderful process of both personal and corporate discovery.

Part 2: The Path of the Tree of the Knowledge of Good and Evil.

All we've talked about in the first volume and in this volume was to bring us to this point. The purpose of the previous section was to present the idea that our fashioning and partaking of the Tree of the Knowledge of Good and Evil wasn't some diabolical plan of the devil, nor an evil trying to overthrow Heaven, nor a private Tree that God owned and was unwilling to share with others. Most importantly, it wasn't a Fall as we've understood it. Only from its own point of view does it appear as a disobedient, defiant Fall. In other words, because we, the Adam, partook of the Tree of the Knowledge of Good and Evil, we view our actions from a good and evil point of view. In other words, after partaking of the Tree, we view ourselves from the same unconscious mindset it brings. However, when viewed from the panorama of the Tree of Life, the Fall wasn't a disaster. Rather, the choice to eat from it came from the ignorance we occupied while we *Desired* to fulfill our purpose. Though we were already the Image and Likeness of God, or better said, an emanation of the Creator, we were unaware, unconscious, ignorant of what that meant in its entirety. We understood "choice" from the first time we decided to *Receive for Ourselves Alone,* but we were still unaware of what it meant to be the Image and Reflection of God. At this point, we were only self-aware through our *Desire to Receive for Ourselves Alone,* which was quickly cultivated into selfishness. However, how does one become self-aware and yet, like God, exist as Selfless? To say this in more conventional terms, how does one Love like God as depicted in the Trinitarian model? We would have to become fully aware of what it is to be equal in quality to God. In Christendom, if there's a message that's connected to the truth, it's that we were created for an intimate relationship with God. If so, then we must face that truth with this, intimacy isn't possible unless all components of the relationship are equal.

In the Trinitarian model, we have three equal persons selflessly loving and empowering the other, hence, *perichoresis.* However, as we pointed out earlier, if we're to follow the revelation of both the Trinity and the person of Christ to its fullness, the Divine Design isn't just about Three in One, but All in One. In Genesis, we see these qualities being revealed with the Father, the masculine quality, the Spirit, the feminine quality (Genesis 1:26), and the two in union manifesting the third, the Son, the Christ, embodied in the Adam (Romans 5:14). The Son, in true fullness, is found in the union and balance of both the masculine and feminine qualities. Hence, the fullness of the Son is found in His forthcoming Bride (John 3:29). However, for that balance to occur, the two dynamics had to be fully realized: in other words, consciously aware. The masculine aspect, called the Son, and the feminine aspect, His Bride (Ephesians 5:26 & 32), fill out Creation, also called the Ekklesia. This counterpart taken from His side, in other words, an expression of and yet a distinction, fills out the union because the Bride is conscious of their equality. The "conclusion" is to be equal in quality so the *perichoresis* is realized in its truest and fullest form. We see the Bride equated as the feminine aspect of the Spirit, and yet in union with the masculine, in the following verses:

> *"One of the seven angels who had the seven bowls full of the seven last plagues came and said to me, 'Come, I will show you the bride, the wife of the Lamb.' ... The Spirit and the bride say, 'Come!" And let him who hears say, 'Come!' Whoever is thirsty, let him come; and whoever wishes, let him take the free gift of the water of life."*
>
> *(Revelation 21:9, 22:17/NIV)*

It's important to realize we created the Tree of Contrasts, Good and Evil, Right and Wrong and so on, from our Egoism. That phrase alone can seem horrible and confusing, at least to the Ego. But from a Tree of Life vista, it's the beginning of the path to fullness. What appears as a failure from an Egoistic view, will become our riches. The "Death Sleep" we entered, obscuring the realm of Life, filled with our delusions of grandeur and illusions of a fabricated world, was the path we fashioned which would eventually give way to a consciousness of *Compassionate Selflessness.* This journey leads to our awakening of being an emanation of the Divine Nature. We, the Adam, as both masculine and feminine attributes of God, had to discover this ourselves or there

619

would be no realization of true Image and Likeness. Remember the spiritual qualities of which we speak have nothing to do with physical gender, but spiritual balance. We can't be an equal partner in quality with God if we don't know from the core of our being what that means. That kind of "knowing" from *Compassionate Selfless* equal quality, is how we find ourselves among the Divine Pleasure of *perichoresis.* What's profound is that none of this was God controlling, manipulating, or demanding our obedience to a predestined course. Though our course is "to be conformed to His Likeness" (Romans 8:29), God's surface invisibility to our perception in the physical world **is God fully aware of our need for irrevocable liberty to choose and discover our identity for ourselves.** The invisibility of God to the Ego is the release of our will into the freedom of choice. This doesn't mean God abandoned us to our own demise. To the contrary! The reality of the Living God, though egoistically concealed within us, couldn't be crucified and buried to linger in the chains of our Egoistic inner grave. No! Once again, the example *of us,* Jesus, proved this! At every stirring, every crossroad, every momentary glimpse that broke through to the eyes of our unconsciousness, God in Christ was shining, Loving, caring, and Life-Giving. In truth, whether we use the Biblical metaphors of Light shining out of darkness, or the Word of God piercing through between soul and spirit, or being a seed that's put in the ground and comes forth bearing much fruit, the reality of the Divine Nature within us is why we exist. It gives us the privilege of choice to awaken. The reason for this liberty to create the Ego, and choose its fruit of Knowing Good and Evil, was for our freedom to discover why we exist and the value of it. At each moment of stirring, God would respond in the proportion of our willingness to see. This wasn't a horrific Fall, nor a spiritual disaster that ends in a fiery garbage dump labeled *toxic sinful waste*, but the liberty to understand what was missed in order to become conscious of what fulfillment means. Consider this Tree of Life vista in the Apostle Paul's words regarding "the Fall" of Israel:

> *"Now I ask myself, 'Was this fall of theirs an utter disaster? It was not! For through their failure the benefit of salvation has passed to the Gentiles with the result that Israel is made to see and feel what is has missed. For if their failure has so enriched the world, and their defection proved such a benefit to the Gentiles, think what tremendous advantage their fulfilling of God's plan could mean."*
> *(Romans 11:11-12/PHILLIPS)*

In the initial phase of our creation as *the Desire to Receive*, which included a choice to emanate Divine Light, Life, and Love, we were completely free to give in return whatever measure we desired. This liberty is where it all started and were it all ends! This Alpha and Omega is not to be visualized as a straight line from beginning and end, but a cyclical one, where the beginning and end are at the same point. As Isaiah says, *"From face to face telling the end from the beginning..."* (Isaiah 46:10). In other words, **the end of an action is always in the initial thought,** and in God's economy this is the substance of Reality. The beginning always has the end within it. From a world of time and space, we see this as a prophetic outlook, one that points to an end in the future. From a *World Above* view, the conclusion is a transfiguration in our awareness of quality from the beginning. It's irrelevant whether it took a millisecond or a millennium in the intermediate *World Below*. Consider Jesus on the "Mount of Transfiguration" (Matthew 17:2). He never actually changed. The brightness that He emanated was always there. Rather, His true self was realized by those who were present, momentarily peering into Reality. Jesus's Beginning was the brightness of being the Light shining, and so was His Conclusion. The intermediate, concealed between the Beginning and the End, is the physical form which His disciples and the people saw. Theologically, we've come to call this *the incarnation*. On occasion, there would be a momentary stirring to consciousness, whether it was on the Mount with Peter, James, and John, or simply Peter realizing from the Father that Jesus was the Christ (Matthew 16:16). In the same manner that Peter, James, and John, had momentary stirrings and could see the brightness of *the Limitless Christ,* so do we regarding the Reality of Christ within us. To say this another way, because the End is in the Beginning, just as *the Limitless Christ* whose brightness was within the intermediate person of Jesus, the same applies to us. Our Beginning was the brightness of *the Limitless Life* in the Garden of Pleasure, and so is our End. Though fashioned by and being an emanation of the Light, our Beginning was in ignorance of it. Nonetheless, this intermediate journey of Divine concealment through the Tree of the Knowledge of Good and Evil was freely given to us as a choice to discover by "unbound will" who we really are. The result is our End in transformational awareness of what always Was, Is, and Shall Be: the *Likeness* of *the Limitless Christ* within ALL OF US!

To make the point a bit clearer, while the End found in the Beginning is very important, the focus was the liberty to "choose" to *Reflect* those qualities. The key was the complete **freedom** to choose. It bears repeating that in one of the very first epistles ever written, the Apostle Paul says:

> *"It is for freedom that Christ has set us free. Stand firm, then, and do not let yourselves be burdened again by a yoke of slavery."*   *(Galatians 5:1/NIV)*

In modern Christendom, we interpret this to mean that by accepting Jesus's substitutionary sacrifice, we're free from sin, meaning we're Heaven bound, can access all Biblical promises, and can resist the lust to sin morally again. Furthermore, in this interpretation, being enslaved to sin after being freed from it, we would reopen the door to God's wrath and the devil, until forgiveness is requested based on Jesus's blood sacrifice. This definition, and others like it, is the yoke of slavery the Apostle Paul was speaking of. This is no different than a reworked version of God sending confusion, curses, and destruction (Deut. 28:20), saying in summary, "You shall do this, and if you do, all these blessings will come upon you," and, "You shall not do this, but if you do, these curses will come upon you." Rather than reworking the Vassal covenant of Moses and giving it a Jesus label, the Apostle Paul was speaking of total freedom from that way of thinking.

From the beginning there were two dynamics that emanated from the One: the Creator and the Creature (same Hebrew word as *Soul* **נֶפֶשׁ** [nephesh]). Because the End is within the Beginning, the conclusion is for the Creature, the Soul, to realize equal quality with the Creator, yet selflessly. From a *World Below* perspective, to hear that we're equal in quality as God, and created to be so, we seem to refuse the notion, seizing up in a type of spiritual paralysis, thus revealing our imprisonment in the Knowledge of Good and Evil. In other words, regardless of how Egoistically we fashion ourselves, saying, "We're not like God," and using any moral code of right and wrong to prove it, *we can't escape being who we are and who we were truly created to be.* It's as if our choice to exist in this world was to prove that we're not like God, nor ever can be. Even so, by choosing this path, *it was our Divine equality that empowered us to make that choice!* In truth, our Divine identity is hidden in plain sight, and for the moment, it's imperceptible by our choice. Thus, in our unconsciousness, if we're Ego-Centered, we can only perceive we're not like God, or arrogantly, the lord of our own universe. We've contrived ourselves as something else, a merely flawed Human. However, as we empty ourselves of that fabricated self, we "find Ourselves" in full equality within the *perichoresis* of Divine Oneness, which is what it is to be fully Human.

Without such equality, there isn't a true relational union. As a rabbi once said in a lecture I attended, "You cannot be in union with something you rule over." This harkens back to what the Baal Shem Tov said, "To grasp a part of the nondivisible union is to grasp the whole." Jesus made this very clear when He spoke of Himself and the Father being One, then adding that we were to become aware of our Oneness with them as well. To achieve this, we had to become conscious of our equal quality to the Father, Spirit, and Son, awakened through humility. This is what the New Testament calls the *Mind of Christ.* In a Tree of Life consciousness *(the Mind of Christ),* it's easy to see throughout the book of Genesis and the Gospels that God didn't desire to rule over anyone, rather, He desired to Love everyone. For example, when Jesus bowed down and washed the disciples' feet, He revealed the Father's definition of His Love and Divine posture. In other words, in Jesus's act of washing feet, He reveals to humanity that the Supreme Ruler of the Universe is humbly on bended knee, lovingly elevating us to our place of equality. You could say, God Most High truly sits on His throne after He's done kneeling to elevate us to sit on it with Him (Revelation 3:21). Moreover, Jesus adds, *"...do as I have done..."* (John 13:15). He didn't say, "Because I am your holy teacher, Lord, and God Most High, only I can do this." To the contrary, the teacher, Lord and God Most High, showed us on His knees who He is, and who we are as His Likeness. Thus, every time we're on our knees, both in heart and practice of elevating another, we reveal God Most High.

Extending the definition of such Divine Love is the attribute of Life; we find it in the Bible as eternal Life, everlasting Life, or absolute Life. Because God, the Trinity, Loves, They give of Themselves. In other words, in sharing Love, They give Life, and such Life begets Life. In union, these qualities are called Light. Hence, when the Spirit of God fluttered over the face of the abyss, the Love that fluttered through Her brought forth Life. This combination of Love and Life manifested as Light, changing the quality of the abyss. You could say, the abyss became conscious. The abyss is a type of the Creature's, *the Soul's,* status in unconscious darkness as the simple *Desire to Receive.* However, from the utterance of "Light Be!" (Genesis 1:3), and through the seven phases of creative development spreading through it, the abyss emerges as the Creator's Image and Likeness, who finds Rest in Their Living Temple as One. Thus, the abyss reflected the Light that shined, and Life emerged from Love. This is what Divine Life does; it perpetually gives Life. It's not just occasionally giving Life, when necessary, but like yeast in dough, it spreads and expands, transforming the quality of whatever it touches. It permeates every aspect, causing it to *rise* from unconsciousness. Eventually this Love, Life, and Light expression resulted in conscious Likeness. When this was achieved, *the Soul* found rest in Their union with the Creator.

As we discussed in the first volume, something changed on the Day of Pentecost when the Spirit was once again poured out. Like the Light shining in unconscious darkness, then spreading through it to total consciousness, the Day of Pentecost shows us another aspect of that development. Unlike most holy days when unleavened bread is used (which most assume symbolized sinlessness), on Pentecost there's a change. Now, we use "leavened bread" (Leviticus 23:17). Why? Because that day represents our awakening to a Tree of Life consciousness, *the Mind of Christ.* It was then *Compassionate Selflessness, the Limitless Christ,* was revealed within the 120 in the upper room. Thus, in a Tree of Life panorama, what was once perceived as breaking the Law in a Tree of the Knowledge of Good and Evil mindset, is no longer perceived that way. What was once our arrogant, legalistic perception, which was and is "the old leaven," is now transformed by the eyes of *Grace* as part of the process of our awakening. Therefore, the way of the Serpent and the Tree of the Knowledge of Good and Evil, wasn't a "sinful disaster" as we might suppose. Instead, when we see it for what it is, it becomes a path which transforms into the riches of our consciousness; it becomes a component in learning our self-awareness. What started in selfish unconsciousness, the abyss of our Egoism, became an awakening to our identity found in *Grace* and *Rest*. Accordingly, we loosen ourselves from the Knowledge of Good and Evil, the old leaven, becoming conscious of our true Divine identity in *Compassionate Selflessness,* embracing Tree of Life realities. Once again, it was as if the Spirit fluttered over us and said, "Light Be!" and the leaven of Light permeated through us in the fullness of *perichoresis.* Thus, we've purged ourselves of the old leaven and, now unleavened from the old, we can receive the leaven of the new, the leaven of Life, full of *Grace* and Truth.

As a side note, it's interesting to point out that the Torah never actually says that unleavened bread is a symbol of sinlessness. This is our religious presumption about what leavened and unleavened means. The Torah only says that unleavened bread symbolizes the haste in which the children of Israel were liberated from the affliction of Egypt (Exodus 12:39; Deuteronomy 16:3). The closest we come to equating sin and unleavened bread is when the Torah says that if a holy man doesn't keep the ritual properly at the appointed time, this is considered a sin by him (Numbers 9:13). We then presume from a Serpentine Tree perspective, that when Paul says, *"...a little leaven leavens the whole lump..."* he's referring to sin. But not so! The leaven of which he speaks is the arrogance of legalistic, judgmental religion. He says to be circumcised once again as the Law demands, as some so-called Christians from Antioch were espousing, was to be infused once more with the old leaven (Galatians 5:1-12). Thus, this leaven of the Knowledge of Good and Evil will permeate through the whole, bewitching us to set aside the *Grace* of God (Galatians 2:21-3:3). This didn't just apply to the religiosity of Pharisaical thinking, but also the religions of paganism. This is expounded on by Paul to the Corinthians, when he points out that they've become proud, boastful, malicious, and wicked in their mindset. There was a painful situation among the people, one which was acceptable in their previous paganistic practice (1 Corinthians 5:1-2). Now however, in Christ such selfish behavior is no longer acceptable, especially if it's hurting the family and the congregation. The result was that the offending brother who refused to stop his actions was, out of necessity, told to leave the congregation. However, rather than the Corinthians mourning over this—and not just over the offense, but the loss of their brother—they were aloof and arrogant about it (1 Corinthians 5:2, 6-8). Paul is clear, the leaven isn't the painful situation, though that's clearly an agonizing problem, but the acute religious pride of the Corinthian's response, *"Your boasting is not good."* Hence, whether it's pagan religious tradition, or the legalism and ritual practices of Torah Law, it's all *old leaven*. So, old leaven is the religious mindset of what is presumed as Good or Evil, rather than one infused with *Grace,* freedom, sincerity, and truth (Galatians 5:4; 5:13; 1 Corinthians 5:8).

Let's explore this path from another side of the block for further clarity. In physics, when light is absorbed by an object rather than being reflected or allowed to pass through it, the absorbed light turns to heat. This receiving and not reflecting can be regarded as the blazing heat of selfishness (Hosea 7:4-6). If you like, we can also call this the burning Hell in which we live. It becomes an insatiable lust that's never satisfied, thus never ending and forever raging. One would think taking in all the Light for ourselves would be totally fulfilling, but not so. We were, as we've said many times, designed to *Receive ALL the Pleasure* the *infinite Creator* desires to give. In other words, if the infinite Giver is giving, then the one receiving must be capable of *infinitely Receiving.* Within the design to *Receive* was also the liberty of *choice* to *Reflect* what was received; this is what gave *the Soul* equality in God Likeness. In the state of *Reflection* and transmission, we're an emanation of the Light, to which any observer would say, "There's no difference." Consider, when Jesus called God, *Father,* that made Him equal with God (John 5:18). But then, when Jesus teaches us to pray (Luke 11:2), He tells us to call God, *Father.* So what does that make us? The same: equal in quality through humility. (Stop for a moment and pause in realizing this. Let's not let our Egoistic inner Pharisee pick up stones to throw at our true self [John 8:59]).

In functioning according to our Divine design, we find the fullness of fulfillment because the pleasure is infinite. By receiving and reflecting, we're forever filled and being filled, thus our cup runs over (Psalms 23:5). On the other hand, when we're in a state of selfishness, we receive momentary pleasure from the consumed Light, but are unable to receive all it has to offer. The result is that we burn for more yet, because of our selfishness, we seriously limit our capacity. Therefore, our burning desire is perpetually unfulfilled. It's an interesting paradox. Though we were created to *Receive infinitely,* when we live Egoistically we exist unfulfilled in exile in a finite world. How can this be? Because the way we *Receive limitlessly* is to raise our anti-egoistic *Reflecting screen,* the מסך (masach), and start Giving to all Creation. In this state of being, we *Receive* more by *Giving,* rather than just *Receiving for Ourselves.* Jesus calls this the abundance of absolute Life (John 10:10).

In our first form, we were ignorant of what the choice meant, though we had the right to choose. You could say, because of our ignorance, we hadn't yet fully realized what it meant to freely Love. This is just another way of saying that, as His Image and Likeness, we hadn't yet comprehended who we really were, though we were already fully His emanation. Having only existed in a state of fulfillment, this didn't mean we grasped its value. So, when we chose to *Receive for Ourselves Only,* we became aware of a lack of fulfillment. This was a new experience, having never understood lack before. King David shows us what it is to be in a state of *Receiving and Reflecting.* *"The Lord is my shepherd, I shall not want,"* (Psalms

23:1/NRSV). In that mindset, we *Receive and Reflect* because we're focused solely on the Source from which we emanate. On the other hand, the option is to say religiously, "I believe in a Great Shepherd, but it's up to me to find the green pastures and still waters He's provided," and so, we always want. It's as if there are two groups of sheep. The first are perpetually *Receiving,* eating, drinking, and joyously sharing with other sheep, *Reflecting,* because their focus is on their union with the Shepherd. Thus, both the still waters and green pastures are always effortlessly presenting themselves. The other group are Egoistic sheep, those who *Receive for themselves Alone.* They consume the grass and water, but only see grass and water while they "believe in a Shepherd." Because their focus is only on what's before them, their provision disappears as they consume it and they live in constant fear of lack. They keep "believing" and praying for more provision, rather than *Resting* in the *Grace* of being One with the Shepherd.

In our initial state, we were ignorant of lack, but we didn't understand fulfillment either. Because we had the privilege to choose to *Receive for Ourselves Only,* we experienced the result of our selfishness. In that new form of selfishness, we understood fulfillment from our memory, though now acquainted with lack through fear. Furthermore, because we created selfishness, we were also ignorant about returning to a place of fulfillment. It's as if, as sheep, we ran from one patch of grass to another, consuming all we could in fear of losing it. It wasn't that we were hungry, but that we were afraid of not having. The same could be said of the still waters. It wasn't that we were thirsty, but were afraid our thirst would not be quenched when it manifested. Thus, both our hunger and thirst exist because of a selfish fear of lack, not because we're truly hungry and thirsty. We can then add to this scenario the dreaded fear of another sheep possibly eating and drinking nearby, which could potentially take our perceived provision, increasing our fear of lack. Thus, we see the Ego that drives us from one patch of grass to another, and one puddle of water to another, as our provider, rather than the Shepherd. We feel that the fear our selfishness created will somehow save us from lack. Therefore, when we burn with Egoistic desire, the fear of letting go of it overwhelms us. Nonetheless, the Creator showed us what letting go looks like and how the choice reemerges. In like manner, when Jesus kneeled down and washed the disciples' feet, God showed us Love by Their choice to bend down toward the dust of the ground, which was us in our first phase of selfishness realization. When They chose to reach down into us and breathe into us the Breath of Life, we experienced what Love's choice was like.

We were breathing, inhaling and exhaling, *Receiving* the Life of God and *Giving* it in return; we were once again a *Living Soul.* Previously, when we chose to *Receive for Ourselves Alone,* we went from a place of being ignorant of what the choice meant, to being self-aware through our selfishness. Yet we hadn't discovered what it meant to choose the Divine Nature, to Love. Thus, in our burning torment of selfishness, God showed us what *Divine Compassion* looked like by humbly kneeling, picking us up, and restoring us as a *Living Soul.* In other words, He showed us what it was to choose Love. As we will see later, herein is the beginning of the powerful truth in the Apostle John's words, *"We love because he first loved us,"* (1 John 4:19/NIV). Nonetheless, till this point, we had only known fulfillment in ignorance and how to choose selfishness.

From a textual aspect, throughout the first chapter of Genesis we see this phrase at the end of each phase of Creation, *"And God saw that it was good."* In the sixth phase of Creation, after God creates the Adam, we find this phrase:

> *"Then God saw everything that He had made, and indeed it was very good."*　　*(Genesis 1:31/NKJV)*

The phrase, *"and indeed it was very good"* in Hebrew is:

והנה טוב מאד

(v^ehinneh tov m^eod)
And lo, good [functioning according to design] exceedingly.

Everything in Creation was functioning according to design, in other words, things were exceedingly good by the time God finishes and rests in the seventh phase. However, when we move into the second chapter, and God recounts the history of Creation's events, we find a powerful statement which points us to what we're discussing. God did create the Adam, and it was exceedingly good, however, for the first time we see this phrase after God reaches into the Egoistic *"dust of the ground"*:

> *"The Lord God said, 'It is not good for the man to be*
> *alone.'"* *(Genesis 2:18/NIV)*

Wait, stop! When did it become *"not good"?* The Hebrew is emphatic here. It sounds nice and poetic when we bring this over into English, but what is it saying?

ויאמר יהוה אלהים לא טוב היות האדם לבדו

(Vayyomer Yahweh Elohyim lo tov heyot ha'adam
l^ebaddo)

And said, Yahweh, the Powers, "Not good [not functioning according to design] exists the Adam to separation [aloneness, divided, destruction] him.

The final word in that phrase is לבדו (l^ebaddo). The word בדד (badad) means *aloneness* in the worst sense. To be alone means to be separated. How did the Adam separate himself? This is also the word for אבדון (abaddon), *destruction, to wander away, to lose oneself.* We find this version of the word in the following verses:

> *"Naked is Sheol before Him, and **Abaddon** has no*
> *covering."* *(Job 26:6/NASU)*

> *"Is your love declared in the grave, your faithfulness*
> *in **Destruction**?"* *(Psalms 88:11/NIV)*

*"Hell and **Destruction** are before the Lord..."*

(Proverbs 15:11/NKJV)

*"Sheol and **destruction** are not satisfied, and the eyes of man are not satisfied." (Proverbs 27:20/YLT)*

And most famously in:

*"And they had as king over them the angel of the bottomless pit, whose name in Hebrew is **Abaddon,** but in Greek he has the name Apollyon."*

(Revelation 9:11/NKJV)

We talked about this extensively in the first volume in, "Chapter 16 - Heaven and Hell Worlds Apart in the Same Place? Part Three: Fire and Water." Here's a segment:

"When you add the **א** (aleph) to the beginning of the word, you have, **אבד** (abad), which means, *lost.* Consider the words of Jesus: *"... for the Son of Man has come to seek and to save that which was lost,"* (Luke 19:10/NKJV). It's more illuminating to know that the word *lost* in the verse is ἀπολωλός (apoloolos), a verb form of *Apollyon.* The idea of destruction, or lost-ness, or worse yet, *eternal aloneness,* is what Jesus was speaking of when He taught of being in *outer darkness."*

(Melchizedek: Our Gracious King-Priesthood in Christ, pp. 447-448. Compass Rose Press.)

Separation, aloneness, or more emphatically, our *lost-ness,* is the illusion we created when we chose to *Receive for Ourselves Alone.* The Light, the Creator, the Christ, was clearly shining, but we, the Adam, were consuming it without reflection, and never satisfied. As stated in Proverbs, *"Sheol and destruction are not satisfied, and the eyes of man [the Adam] are not satisfied."* It's at this point that God, the eternal Christ, reaches into the dust of the ground, breathes into it the Breath of Life, and restores that which was *lost.* In the same way we see God bending down to the ground and saw Jesus bend down to wash the disciples' feet, we now see God breathing into our lost-ness the Breath of Life, just as we see Jesus *breathe on the disciples and say, "Receive the Holy Spirit,"* (John 20:22).

In this restored form through the Breath of Life, we hadn't yet chosen to *Love* from our self-awareness. We experienced God's *Divine Love* and graciousness, but from the viewpoint of our selfishness. This was the only aspect of self-awareness we had chosen to this point. Herein is a powerful paradox. We hadn't yet comprehended our ability to choose to return *Love,* though it was fully present within us to do so. All the same, that didn't hinder God from *Loving* us perpetually. Our self-awareness, regardless of what stage we're in, never changes God's heart toward us. This paradox opened to us the next aspect of the path we'd choose to walk. Though breathing the Breath of Life, the Ego was still present. God didn't remove what we experienced, knowing full well it was necessary for us to learn to choose; we had to discover through our self-awareness what it meant to be in Their Image and Likeness. Hence, even the Adam breathing the Breath of Life still had a sense of separation and aloneness from his Egoism. One may think, "Why didn't God cleanse us or remove our sinful Ego?" For two reasons. First and most important, the only one who can remove selfishness is the one who created it: *us.* With that in mind, the second is that Ego finds its root in the *Desire to Receive.* Therefore, for God to remove our newly fashioned Ego, the Trinity would have to tear apart and uproot a central aspect of what makes us a Living Soul: the *Desire to Receive.* Jesus speaks to this when He says, "*...lest in gathering the weeds you root up the wheat along with them,*" (Matthew 13:29/ESV). To tear apart, or uproot in that manner, is contrary to the very nature of God revealed in the Trinitarian model. This would revoke the central ingredient that grants us the ability to *Love* and be Like God, the dynamic of choice. For us to be self-aware as an emanation of God, the choices we've made, including the selfish ones (or to use a more traditional term, our sinful ones), become part of our process that stirs us to consciousness. It was at this point we were to care for the ground and cultivate Life-Giving Pleasure from it. This is a way of saying that we're to care for our Soul, our *Desire to Receive,* and what we're cultivating, or sowing, in it. Genesis 2:15 uses the phrases that we were to *till* or *enslave* it, and to *keep* or *guard* it. We were now making choices about what to cultivate and what not to. Though fully being the Image and Likeness of God, we were first ignorant of its value. Now in this form, we were self-aware through our Egoism, having experienced the privilege of choosing it. For God, the focus wasn't the Ego, because what appeared to be a failure will become a benefit in the long run (which Paul implies regarding Israel). Our choice of selfishness became an ingredient of becoming self-aware. We were cultivating Life and Pleasure and were to guard ourselves from our own selfish desires. The only difference between selfish desire and Life-Giving Pleasure is the choice of how we choose to *Receive*. Do we *Receive for Ourselves,* or *Receive* and joyously *Give* as well?

Thus, we cultivated the ground and caused what was planted in the Garden to grow. However, part of this growth was our newly formed Egoistic Seed. From God's perspective we were cultivating an honest definition of what it means to choose between selfishness and *Love,* and above all being self-aware when we do it. When we're fully self-aware and choose to *Love* without selfishness, we've truly realized what it means to be an emanation of God. The moment we Love with a diminished sense of selfishness, we open ourselves to realizing our participation in *perichoresis,* or as the Baal Shem Tov says, "To grasp a part of the nondivisible union is to grasp the whole."

Finally, all the trees of our desires in the Garden grew to their fullness. Self-awareness was the tallest of the trees, reaching deep and receiving an abundance of the Divine Waters (Ezekiel 31:7). The more it grew, the more aspects of Creation made their home in it. The more it drew the Divine Waters to itself, the less it shared with the rest of the trees in the Garden. In its self-awareness of its own greatness, its selfishness began bearing fruit, and envy began spreading throughout all the trees of the Garden (Ezekiel 31:9). Thus, a little leaven leavens the whole lump. We were given the choice to share and receive from all the trees in the Garden in perpetual

Divine Pleasure (Genesis 2:16-17). However, we were also warned against consuming from the Tree of our selfishness. Because of our self-awareness thus far, we understood what it meant to *Receive for Ourselves Alone,* and also to resist it for the sake of more Pleasure. But we hadn't transformed our selfishness into the choice of *Divine Love, Compassion.* When we resist *Receiving for Ourselves* with the objective of experiencing more Pleasure, there's still a form of selfishness at the root. It's still an Egoistic calculation. We hadn't yet discovered the infinite joy in letting go of what we've *Received,* and to *Give* because we *Love.* As Jesus says, *"Freely you have received, freely give,"* (Matthew 10:8).

As we've said previously, in Hebrew, the word for Earth, *the Desire to Receive* ארץ (erets), is the root for רצון (ratson), the *Desire to Receive Pleasure.* In Ezekiel, when discussing the Tree that became full of itself in the Garden, it calls it a *cedar.* In Hebrew, cedar is ארז (erez), pronounced effectively the same as ארץ (erets). In both words, we find an illustration of *firmness.* ארץ (erets) the *Desire to Receive,* is the strong, firm foundation from which all things grow. The other, ארז (erez), is the potent, firm fruit which grows from it. ארז (erez) can be a beautiful strength, like King David's house and the appearance of Solomon (1 Chronicles 7:1, Song of Solomon 5:15). Or it can be a proud, stubborn arrogance, like the description of the Assyrian and the shepherds of Jordan (Ezekiel 31:1; Zechariah 11:1-3). In all these examples, there's

the choice to bear beautiful or arrogant fruit. As Jesus and
James said:

> *"For there is no good tree which produces corrupt*
> *fruit, nor a corrupt tree which produces good fruit;*
> *for every tree is known by its own fruit, for figs are*
> *not gathered from thorns, nor grapes vintaged from*
> *a bramble."*   *(Luke 6:43-44/Darby)*

> *"With the tongue we praise our Lord and Father,*
> *and with it we curse men, who have been made in*
> *God's likeness. Out of the same mouth come praise*
> *and cursing. My brothers, this should not be. Can*
> *both fresh water and salt water flow from the same*
> *spring? My brothers, can a fig tree bear olives, or a*
> *grapevine bear figs? Neither can a salt spring*
> *produce fresh water."*   *(James 3:9-12/NIV)*

While no tree should be bearing "contrary fruit," James says,
"Out of the same mouth come praise and cursing. My brothers,
this should not be." Yet here we are praising and cursing, and
it's no wonder. What we've been cultivating within our Ego is
a Tree that will Knowingly bear two contrary types of fruit,
Good and Evil. Our Ego began growing as we saw all Creation
nestling in our greatness. As in the allegory in Ezekiel, the
birds of the air, the beasts of the field, the great nations,
gathered to us, and our branches were growing greater than
the other cedars. It was what should've happened, yet
shouldn't have at the same time. In the realm of the Tree of
Life, allowing Creation to feast on who we are, thus giving to

nourish and encourage, is because we Love Creation and take joy in sharing ourselves. We continue to grow so we all can be blessed together. In that symbiosis, we enjoy the fullness of Pleasure, which is a cyclical form of perpetual Life. However, from a Serpentine-Egoistic view, which was emerging at this point, we took pride in Creation feasting on who we'd become, and we selfishly loved that! We chose to grow at the expense of the other trees, taking the waters of Life (no different than consuming the Light), so we could grow bigger and stronger so more of Creation could come and give us increasingly more pleasure. In this selfish-awareness came an Egoistic evaluation, "This is a desire that's good, this is a desire that's pleasant, and these are desires for which I'm the wiser," (Genesis 3:6). So, we ate and consumed that newly formed fruit of Good and Evil, and like a fig leaf covering one who's naked, the Divine Nature was concealed. We shrouded the Wisdom of Life to embrace our own Egoistic Knowledge of Good and Evil. However, that didn't stop the nature of God living and speaking within us. *Love* never failed. In reaching out to bring our self-awareness to a higher place of consciousness, the Spirit of God within asked us whether we partook of the Selfish Tree we were to guard against. In our strengthened Egoism, we became aware that we partook of what we should've been resisting. In the inner conflict of our Knowledge of Good and Evil, we judged ourselves, and through that sensation we fashioned another. For the first time, we felt shame; hence, the fig leaf. Nonetheless, we weren't finished with our Egoistic calculations. To address the one, we made another. To avoid the sensation of shame, we judged again. Now we created blame. We created an external enemy, someone else who was responsible and culpable. To expound on the point, our first realization was to blame ourselves. But the shame was such a horrible sensation that we began another Egoistic calculation, and like lightening falls from heaven, we told ourselves it really wasn't our fault, it was another aspect of ourselves that was to blame (Genesis 3:12; Luke 10:18). It wasn't our doing, it was what God gave us; ultimately, it was God's fault! We externalized the blame, claiming that because the Creator gave us the choice to walk this path, it was the Creator's fault that we were in this horrible situation! Rather than address the shame we felt, we continued with blaming "the other" with another calculation. We justified ourselves as to why our blame was valid. Thus, we felt our Egoistic self-awareness growing from shame, to blame, to self-justification. Then the final calculation occurred in our garment to cover over our shame and to distance ourselves from the perceived cause; we created a scapegoat. With this displaced focus, we separated ourselves from our true selves. We accused the Source of our identity as being the problem and covered over our true self with an Egoistic fig leaf. In that moment, the physical world we now know started to form. It was our doing. What followed was only "the course of nature" we set in motion (James 3:6). We fell unconscious in the Garden of God, clothed in flesh and unable to perceive what was in plain sight. We could say, from an egoistic standpoint, that when God called to the Adam, *"Where are you?"* mission accomplished. Finally, I know something God doesn't know and am in control of my own life, even though I was afraid when I heard Him.

In our new level of selfish-awareness, with the growing fruit of our Knowing Good and Evil, we concealed our awareness of God, as well as any trace of our Likeness. We became our own gods and any connection to Creation was dissolved. Any so-called dominion we had over it, which was originally to enliven it, became our ability to destroy it. Think of all the religions of history, and even our current depictions on television and in the cinema. What defines a "god" is its ability to destroy. Thus, subjects worship them in hope of blessing on the surface, but underneath that worship, they fear the god's destructive wrath. We truly made the gods in our own image. Of course, there are good gods and evil ones, but then who's evil and who's good is based upon the tribal religion we're connected to.

The inner struggle we discussed within all the previous chapters prevailed. The potency of our Egoistic illusion grew, and the intensity of our struggle with Good and Evil also increased. However, something also occurred in the reverse. The Love of God could not be constrained. We couldn't suppress the impression of the Garden regardless of our Egoistic attempts through our illusions and delusions. Why? Because our memory of it prevailed as a phantasm in the darkness. In our calculations of Good and Evil, it didn't make sense that God's Love, inner presence, and acceptance, hadn't changed. The memory of our origins created a desire for infinite Peace, Love, and Life. Our wonderful Garden of Pleasure was still there, just darkly shrouded by the shade of our inner Egoistic Tree of Good and Evil. What once gave pleasant shade to Creation now shaded us from both Creation and the Creator. Throughout time and space, we would sense the memory of the One who once kneeled, reached into our selfishness, raised us up, and breathed into us the Breath of Life. These memories came as apparitions, but, in another sense, they were so real, more real than the illusions we created. Thus, from them we made stories and myths. We gave them mythological names, locations, and events. Some were based on real people and places, others invisible forces. However, in all those myths, the ends were sadly similar. The character of Love and Life would be killed by the gods of wrath in some sacrificial cruciform manner. Still, there was something wonderful happening. Through these memory myths, a new desire was forming. Despite our land of thorns and thistles, a lovely rose (like the one in Sharon) was budding; there was a stirring to a new type of choice. Through the manifestation of Jesus and what followed, the fruition of the inner memories were realized. God once again kneeled in the form of a selfless man and came to the dust of the Earth, but this time He didn't raise us up like the first. No! This time, it was something of a higher consciousness. It was to offer us the original choice, like from the beginning, with a new perspective of awareness, a clearer choice. Being we've been traveling this fabricated world of Good and Evil for millennia, the choice was either this death sleep of Good and Evil, or the liberty of Life. Why? Because we were now ready for it. It was the one that was always there, but now could be realized in a manner unlike before.

Part 3: The Path to the Tree of Life

We chose the Path of the Tree of the Knowledge of Good and Evil, whose calculations were intended to further feed our selfish gratifications. However, it wasn't a failure as one would suppose. Rather, as we pointed out that the Apostle Paul tells us, what can appear to be a failure, a disaster, and a defection from God, has within it the potential to be a true benefit and enrichment. We were, and still are, given the full opportunity to choose our path, both individually and corporately. The notion that we have such power to create and make our own decisions, can be horrific to our Egos. Just like when the man threw both God and his counterpart under the proverbial bus, saying it was the fault of *"...the woman YOU gave to be with me..."* (Genesis 3:12). He did it to justify himself regarding their choices and actions.

In the pagan world, the gods were always in control of what happened in human affairs. We were at the mercy of the decisions that the gods made. Nonetheless, if we see the events in Genesis as spiritual truth, and the precedent that set everything in motion, God chose not to be in control; for that matter, God relinquished control to give us the complete freedom to choose our path. This liberty is intrinsically necessary for us to be the Image and Likeness of God and, most importantly, to *Love* like God. Yet, what we've done, in the development of our Christian theology, is return to a pagan system of belief, which at its root caters to our Egoism with its calculations of Knowing Good and Evil. Within 1000 years of the resurrection, the notion of the Sovereignty of God started to regain what both the Bible and Jesus, in particular, didn't teach. Eventually, the notion of the Sovereignty of God began to include lofty theological terms such as predestination, annihilation, and eternal damnation, which made these ideas seem so definitive. Note how we're back to what makes a god a god, is the ability to control and destroy. Nonetheless, all these notions of sovereignty were reduced for the average Christian to this simple phrase, "God is in control." While this "belief" may comfort our Egoistic fears as we look at whatever mayhem is happening to us or around us, it's a misunderstanding of God's wonderful gift to fashion us as Their Likeness. What does this mean? Once again, we can't change who we were created to be, even if we "choose" to believe otherwise; we are who we are. What's before us could be construed this way: we are the "self-centered gods" of this world who are in control and keep making havoc for themselves and everyone else. In other words, as we continue to choose Egoistic paths of our contrived ideas of Good and Evil, we create all kinds of mayhem along with all the violence and destruction that goes with it.

Despite our choices spawning from our selfish-awareness, there's another sensitivity developing. The more we're consumed by our oscillating calculations of Good and Evil, we also become aware of another sensation, called suffering. Within the context of partaking of the Serpent's Tree, in an Egoistic world of self-justification, accusation, and the pursuit of external pleasures, there are many times we don't receive the desired good we believe we should. Rather, there are many unpleasantries, ranging from the discomfort of an unfulfilled desire to serious psychological and physical pain. Whether we define these experiences as "not good" or "pure evil," our Egos will focus on them. We'll contemplate, question, resist, and accuse as to why we're experiencing the pain we are. From fear, to anger, to tears, we're not just experiencing the sharp stab of the initial pain, but because of it, and the way our Ego functions, we've entered the unavoidable place of suffering. Pain is real, regardless in what form we experience it, and the more we become engrossed by it, the more we suffer. In some cases, the painful suffering we experience isn't just brought upon us because of the choices we've made, but because of the choices others have made, and it's mostly a relative combination of both. As we discuss this, keep in mind we're not addressing the ills of a victim mentality or the like, we're simply stating that we suffer because of how the Ego responds to pain. For that matter, let's not be drawn into putting a value on whether our suffering, or someone else's, is right or wrong, deserved or imposed. The point is, in this *World Below,* in the realm of the Egoistic Knowledge of Good and Evil, we experience suffering because of pain. One may say that the worst aspect of living in this world is all the suffering we bring on ourselves and others. While that may be a harsh truth in one respect, there's another dynamic which develops that can change everything.

As we're being honest with ourselves, in our *World Below,* human suffering is inescapable. We can't ignore it, though for a moment we may try. Why? Because it's the one thing that the Ego exists to avoid. However, this is where the illusion of this world begins to crack. Like in Hans Christian Andersen's,

The Princess and the Pea, regardless of what she Egoistically did to find comfort, the presence of her discomfort would cause her to stir, regardless of how small it was. In many cases, this is the other reason we stir to consciousness, as the Light shines through our inner window. The stirring that comes through suffering from the pain we've created and inflicted on each other isn't the Light, but it will cause enough discomfort where we may open our eyes, even for a moment, and catch a glimpse of *Divine Love* as it is. When it comes to us experiencing pain, all the avoidance through our questioning God, accusing the devil, finger pointing as to why, and blaming others, doesn't change its presence. Actually, it only causes more suffering. Sometimes, sooner than later, our Egos start giving up and cry out for help. In that moment, a powerful dynamic emerges with two facets: the desire for help to remove our suffering, and as we progress in our awareness, the desire to help remove it from others. Within the first is an inclination that the way of separation and independence is an insufficient way of existing. Within the second comes something deeper, from a realm where Egoism doesn't exist, and a stirring to a higher consciousness does. With the first comes a realization that being connected to others is part of our identity and design. With the second comes a stirring from our true nature, from a selfless *Desire to Give.* In both facets, we see our identity in Christ emerging.

The only true way to remove suffering from ourselves and others, is to awaken to our Divine design, the perichoresis. We were never created to believe in separation, nor to *Receive for Ourselves Alone.* Yet, to be the Image and Likeness of the

Creator, we had to have the total liberty to choose to discover this for ourselves, irrespective of any warning the Creator gave us. Notwithstanding, the way the Ego functions, when God told us that we shouldn't eat from our Egoistic Serpentine Tree, we had to have a bite. When we chose that path, we created an illusion that leaving the pleasures of our union with God would be good, pleasant, and wise as we continued to consume any desire we deemed Good and Right. However, what happened was that in our dream world of separation and independence, a clash of self-centered values with a hot pursuit for selfish pleasures occurred. Thus, we flung open the door to pain and suffering. We could say, we didn't open the door to the devil, but that we were the devil that opened the door. Yet, within our suffering, there's a stirring to awaken, and in that is the consideration of the same choice again. In other words, the stirring itself is the choice to stay asleep in our Egoistic illusions, or start awakening to the Divine Reality, the Light. It's important to reiterate that God isn't sending us the pain, and most definitely not creating it. Clearly, it was our creation from the beginning. However, when pain quickly becomes suffering, it is no longer unavoidable. In our suffering, we begin to reach out to "the other" for help, and even more so, having *Compassion* on another who suffers is the emerging of our Divine Likeness. To say this another way, our suffering begins to melt the strength of our self-centeredness, giving us the ability to open our eyes and see the original choice as something fresh and new.

In that light, there's a verse in the Book of Hebrews that lends itself to a misunderstanding, if we don't take a moment and unpack it at this point:

> *"Although he was a son, he learned obedience through the things he suffered."*
>
> *(Hebrews 5:8/NET)*

In the New English Translation there's a footnote that's worth considering. "There is a wordplay in the Greek text between the verbs *learned* ἔμαθεν (emathen) and *suffered* ἔπαθεν (epathen)." The misunderstanding that most of us read into the text is because the translators didn't grasp the wordplay, thus it doesn't come across to us, the reader. As a result, we read the passage as suggesting that Jesus didn't know obedience and had to yet learn it through His myriad of afflictions, both before and during the cross (especially if we include verses 9-10). This is most unreasonable if we just leave it as that in our thinking. Consider the times throughout the New Testament when the Father said, *"This is My beloved Son, in whom I am well pleased."* Four to be exact, and twice were in Matthew and Mark at the beginning of His public ministry. To consider that the Father was well pleased at the beginning of Jesus's ministry, but that Jesus didn't know much about being obedient until He started going through hardship, doesn't make the least bit of sense. This isn't to say He didn't go through hardships, or that the passion of the Cross wasn't seriously painful. Even if we left the verse as it's usually translated, we would have to come away with the idea that Jesus maintained His purpose despite what He suffered, not that he had yet to learn obedience through His suffering. Nonetheless, the way these words are used, they're better translated with this idea:

καίπερ ὢν υἱός, ἔμαθεν ἀφ' ὧν ἔπαθεν τὴν ὑπακοήν

(kaiper on huios emathen aph' hon epathen ten hupakoen)

Although (or Indeed) being a Son,
He was (internally) conscious (enlightened)
from whose (external) suffering He listened
intently.

The Greek phrase **ἔμαθεν ἀφ'** *He was (internally) conscious (enlightened),* comes directly from the philosophical teachings of Socrates and Plato. The word we usually translate as *learned* in the verse, actually meant to become *consciously aware,* or *enlightened,* not necessarily to learn in an academic or behavioral way (see the Theological Dictionary of the New Testament, Kittle and Friedrich). In other words, Jesus being the Son of God, hence, the Son of *Divine Love,* when He became *consciously aware* of the suffering of others *He listened intently* from His heart of *Compassion* and responded. We see this very clearly in the following verses:

"But when he saw the multitudes, he was moved with compassion for them, because they were distressed and scattered, as sheep not having a shepherd." (Matthew 9:36/ASV)

> *"And when Jesus went out He saw a great multitude; and He was moved with compassion for them, and healed their sick."* (Matthew 14:14/NKJV)

> *"Moved with compassion, Jesus reached out and touched him. 'I am willing,' he said. 'Be healed!'"* (Mark 1:41/NLT)

Regardless of the notion of "obedience" in Hebrews 5:8, the statement doesn't mean what we'd usually expect it to. Usually, when we see the words *obey* or *obedient*, we usually think of the word **πειθαρχεῖν** (peitharchein), meaning to *obey*, as in keeping the rules or being subject to a ruler or king (as in Titus 3:1). But not so in Hebrews 5:8. Rather, it's **ὑπακοήν** (hupakoen), *to listen intently*, or as the Mirror Translation points out, *"hearing from above."* There's a strong twofold meaning here. First, anything Jesus did, according to His own admission, was what He saw and heard the Father do within Him (John 5:19; 7:16; 8:28, 38; 12:49; 14:10). Thus, being moved by *Compassion* is what the Father was expressing. After all, *God IS Divine Love.* Hence, the reason He is the High Priest, according to Melchizedek, is that He was, and IS, the expression of the Father through *Compassion*, even to the point of the Cross.

The point is, when we observe someone suffering and are deeply moved within, this is the inner stirring of **μανθάνω** (manthanó), awareness, consciousness, enlightenment. To further the point, this consciousness doesn't come about by information or even a type of revelation, but through

Compassion. The arising of true *Compassion* is the greatest revelation, gnosis, or understanding we can awaken to. It is the eternal, infinite Source, the Father of Grace.

Consider the parable of the Good Samaritan (Luke 10:30-36). Much can be said about the priest and the Levite who passed by the man who was wounded on his way to Jericho. Going from Jerusalem to Jericho is a metaphor for someone who's seeking refuge for committing a serious wrong. Thus, the fact that he "fell," was stripped, and left half dead was, in the minds of the priest and the Levite, a consequence of his moral failure. In other words, he got what was coming to him. On the other hand, the unlikely half-breed Samaritan is the one through whom the Christ shines. It wasn't just what the Samaritan did, but what motivated him to do it: *Compassion.* In Judaism at the time, despite the man's moral failures, the priest and the Levite could have done a mitzvah, a good deed, though they were not morally obligated because of the man's sin. But for the Samaritan, it wasn't about morality or obligation; it wasn't a religious Egoistic calculation. Rather, it was something deeper and further reaching. For the Samaritan, being moved by *Compassion* was being moved by his true identity, his Divine Likeness. We may not be conscious of it yet, but there are moments we stir in our unconsciousness, when we're moved at the "Cross-roads" by human suffering and the inner rising of *Compassion.*

This deeper reality of Divine understanding opens to us why Jesus addressed the common people, in contrast to the religious leaders, the way He did. As in the parable of the Good

Samaritan, the priest and the Levite, who clearly knew their moral religious rhetoric, seem to miss the point, which is the point. If we take another look at who Jesus revealed as sinner and saint in the story, the man's painful condition was only relevant in regard to in whom it awoke *Compassion.* The man's moral dilemma was not relevant to that awakening. The focus was who left the *World Below* of religious moralism and through inner awakening ascended to the *World Above?* The Hebrew word for *sin,* חטאה (chattah), in simple definition means *to miss the mark.* In other words, *to miss the point.* Thus, the priests, Levites, Pharisees, and by extention our inadvertent descent into a delusional Christendom, putting moral correctness, Biblical certainty, and spiritual gifts as the point, is the חטאה (chattah), that which *misses the point!* It's no wonder why Jesus kept telling the religious community that when we focus on someone's so-called sin, *we miss the point,* and that unconsciousness remains! (John 9:41)

In a similar light, if we're the one who's suffering and someone is *Compassionate* toward us, that too has a transformational impact. To mention the verse earlier, *"We love Him because He FIRST loved us."* In some respects, the reason we learn the values of love is because we've experienced it, whether from a parent, a friend, or even a stranger. Nonetheless, the type of *Love* we are speaking of is not just what we've learned externally from someone else. More so, this is an ἔμαθεν (emathen), an *awareness* from a Divine quality within. This isn't an external experience, but an internal *awareness* that God first loved us, regardless of how our Ego views us. *Divine Compassion* isn't a respecter of laws, rules, good, evil, the righteous, or the unrighteous; *Compassion* is as Limitless as God, because they're one in the same. If Jesus, in the verses above, can be described as the *Compassion* of God, then we need to see the Living Eternal Christ, the Living Word, from a broader point of view. For that matter, we first see the definition of *Compassion* in Genesis:

> *"But he [Lot] hesitated, so because of the Lord's compassion for him, the men grabbed his hand, his wife's hand, and the hands of his two daughters. And they brought him out and left him outside the city.*
>
> *(Genesis 19:16/ASB)*

The men, or better said, the angels of **יהוה**, are revealed as having the Lord's *Compassion* (some translations use the words mercy or pity). Most importantly, the first time we see this description of God, it appears as other worldly, angelic manifestation. It wasn't a human who expressed it, but the Heavenly representatives, sent by God, revealed *Divine Compassion*. Thus, the *Love* or *Compassion* of God, *"...is not of this world,"* (John 18:36). However, the first time we see *Compassion* through a human being, it isn't expressed through a person who seemingly knew **יהוה**, or was in a covenant with God, nor was a recognized prophet heralding the Lord's name. Instead, it was one whom the average Bible reader would consider a pagan, an enemy of God, and enslaver of God's people. It was the daughter of Pharaoh, the princess of Egypt. Like the Samaritan, she was the most unlikely:

> *"Then the daughter of Pharaoh came down to bathe at the river. And her maidens walked along the riverside; and when she saw the ark among the reeds, she sent her maid to get it. And when she opened it, she saw the child, and behold, the baby wept. So **she had compassion** on him, and said, 'This is one of the Hebrews' children.'"*
>
> *(Exodus 2:5-6/NKJV)*

In that moment, the daughter of Pharaoh was the Living Christ, revealed in that situation. She understood the child was one of "those Hebrew slaves" of whom her father decreed, *"Every boy that is born to the Hebrews you shall throw into the Nile..."* (Exodus 1:22/NRSV). In that moment, this *Compassion* defied the rules, usurping not only Pharaoh, but also the voice of her natural father. In that moment, Princess Hatshepsut was as otherworldly as the angels that appeared to Lot and his family. If she hadn't been moved by *Compassion,* we would all still be under Egyptian rule and the Book of Exodus would be called the Short Book of Drowning, and the story ends there.

The days of Christendom believing that, in effect, we have exclusive rights, owning Father, Spirit, and Son, and only through our special version of the message over the last 500 years is Christ revealed, are coming to an end. Rather, like the first two centuries of Christianity, we are reawakening to the Reality that *"Christ is all and in all"* And that the preaching of the Gospel isn't about saving people from a torturous eternal damnation and, if they don't accept Christ as a substitutionary sacrifice to the Father, God is content with them going there.

No! The Gospel is awakening humanity to the Reality of Christ in them, their true "Divine Identity," and that sin, regardless of religious persuasion, is no longer an issue in any form. Rather, it's the Reality that we're all a living expression of the invisible God. That our choices between Good and Evil, really weren't choices at all, they're nothing more than the illusion of an Egoistic calculation. As Christopher Hitchens, Immanuel Kant, and yes, even Richard Dawkins point out, "Do I believe we have free will? *I have no choice!*" Such an oxymoron makes a strong point. Within the world of flesh and blood, the base nature, the Egoistic world of the Knowledge of Good and Evil, there's no true choice, only the illusion of it. There's only a calculation between which cravings for pleasure are stronger. Hence, the mind and emotions are the facilities we use to make the calculation to satisfy the Egoistic will. To make the point further, the calculation rises from the instinct of the Ego. As we've mentioned in other forms throughout these two volumes, sitting at a restaurant and ordering from a menu with a myriad of choices comes down to a calculation of craving and desire. There are times we'll choose something of a lesser desire because a greater pleasure is more attractive. "No, I'm not going to have the cheeseburger, I'm going to have a salad. I need to lose weight because I want to be healthy and look good." In that moment, the Ego just repositioned itself in the calculation. "I am willing to agonize for the moment by having a salad, which I really don't want, so I can look better in the future." Just in case you were thinking, "Well, isn't that crucifying the Ego?" No, the Ego wasn't "crucified" in that calculation, it just repositioned itself based on desire. Where true choice enters the picture isn't in an Egoistic calculation of

Good or Evil, nor the contrast of pleasure or pain, but from a higher level of consciousness. True choice begins between the base nature, the Ego, and the Divine Nature, *Compassion.* To say this another way, true choice begins between the Knowledge of Good and Evil, or the Consciousness of the Tree of Life.

The stories and myths throughout the ages in all the religions of the world, culminating with the Gospel of Jesus Christ, all contained a peek at *Selfless Love.* What's amazing is, there was an awareness of such through all humanity. Thus, within the human condition is the inherent, enduring, and unchangeable *Reality* that we are the Image and Likeness of God, whether or not we have a full understanding of what that means. Take a moment to contemplate this. Selflessness doesn't mean we have no sense of self, but that the sense of self of which we speak is rooted in our original design, encompassing something that, to any Egoistic calculation, is otherworldly and incomprehensible. The Ego cannot perceive *Compassion,* while *Compassion* is aware of the Ego, especially if the Ego is very dense. It's like the difference between light and sound in physics. Both are waves, however, the criteria for them to be perceived are different. Light can traverse in both a vacuum and a material environment. Sound, on the other hand, can only traverse in a material world, requiring a medium like a solid, liquid, or gas. Yet, sound in a vacuum is imperceptible, it can't exist. What's most interesting is that the denser the material, the faster sound will travel, where light will slow down to the point of being obstructed. For example, a loudspeaker for an audio system will be partly made up of polypropylene, Kevlar, aluminum, or another material. These solid materials are what generates sound. However, though light is present and radiating, in general it can't pass through such materials. Why? They're too dense. On the other hand, in a vacuum sound simply can't exist; it's not even present. While light may be radiating in the densest environments, sound will not be present in a vacuum. For that matter, in the densest environments when light is focused, by what we call a laser beam, it will burn through and shine. Sound, on the other hand, regardless of how powerfully we increase the amplitude of the wave, it comes to a screeching halt where the vacuum begins. With respect to the superiority of light, in the environment of a vacuum, it will travel at speeds that transcend the fastest speed that sound can in a dense world.

The same is true with the Ego and *Compassion*. *Compassion* can exist in both *the World Above* and *the World Below*. However, the denser the Ego, though *Compassion* is present, it is diminished even to the point of obscurity. This is what we've been calling unconsciousness. Nonetheless, as humility increases, which is simply the reduction of Egoism, *Compassion* becomes more radiant. Hence, *Divine Love* in its most radiant form has no resistance because the Ego as we understand it is no longer present. However, when we observe human suffering, something will happen when we're ready. Like light that can be focused into a laser beam, burning through any dense obstruction, the same is true with *Compassion*.

When faced with human suffering, regardless of how dense our Ego, like a laser, *Compassion* will break through and move us, even if momentarily. When this happens, like light shining through a window at dawn, we're never the same. Even in the darkest, densest situations, like a laser encased in a steel box, when it pierces through and makes the smallest hole, the opening remains. From that point forward, even if the box sits in the darkest of rooms, when we turn off the laser and have just a small, 5-watt LED light shining within that same box, it will illuminate through the little opening, affecting everything. The light shining through that tiny hole becomes the obvious illumination in the entire room, and draws our attention to itself. Think of it, in a completely dark room with nothing in it but a light shining in a steel box with a tiny hole in its side, our eyes are drawn to the tiny light. Again, the same is true with *Divine Compassion*. Once that point in the heart breaks through, we will be stirring, no matter how hard we try to go back to sleep. Even our Egoistic dreams will be affected by an awareness of it. Thus, all it takes is a point in the heart to shine with *Compassion* to begin our awakening. When we respond to that point in our heart, we become conscious of something greater than ourselves, and the one we touch is also stirred. In that moment the two are one—the one who suffers and the one who touches. This is what makes the crucifixion such an anomaly.

While we perceive Jesus's suffering on the Cross, because of the horrible pain crucifixion brings, or because we think He became our sin and took all the judgment of God, as in Penal Substitution, He didn't suffer in the same manner as Egoistic man. You could say, on one hand, His pain was more excruciating, and on the other hand, He didn't suffer at all as either of the thieves who hung beside Him. They suffered because they broke the Law of their God and Man on the basis of right and wrong, good and evil, thus as fragmented men. But not so with Jesus. He was different. He never broke the Law of His God, through fulfilling the Law of Love (Romans 13:8-10), and never violated Man because of it. His suffering was because of union with God and Man. He suffered as a Whole Man, one without a sense of separation from the Father or Creation. Yet, "we saw Him" not only as separate from us, but as if we were doing God a favor by crucifying Him. We crucified Christ erroneously, believing it was the Will of God that He be afflicted (Isaiah 53:4). If we look at the crucifixion closely, Christ didn't suffer *as* an Egoistic Man with a delusion of separation from God, but *because* of Egoistic Man, who had a delusion of being separated from God. The Cross is where those two worlds collide, *the World Above* and *the World Below*, and through it, the two become One. From an upper world perspective, the one who suffers isn't really Jesus, but unconscious Man who is touched with the Father's *Compassionate* forgiveness; and the two are made One. From a lower world perspective, the One who suffers is Jesus, and in our realization that we caused the affliction, we're stirred with anguish as *Compassion* is awakened. In that awakening, we're moved by seeing the innocent suffering, and we *will* Him to live; thus, the two are made One. Herein is the Divine mystery of those who suffer: One is conscious, the others unconscious. One suffers because of *Compassion*, while the others who caused the suffering are awakened by

Compassion; thus, the two are made One. The One who suffers is willed by the ones who caused the suffering to awaken and live again. This is more than just a resurrection that comes forth from the grave, but the Christ coming forth from the inner grave within us.

Of all the important statements Jesus made while He hung on the Cross, there are two that stand out regarding our topic. The first is the famous, *"My God, My God why have You forsaken me!"* (Psalms 22:1). Many from the Penal Substitution belief would say this is where the Father turned His back on Jesus because God infused our sin upon Him, and being that God is holy, He could not look upon sin. In that moment, Jesus then experienced God's wrath and judgment as a sinner. But to the contrary, the entire context of Psalm 22, is not about separation from God, but trust in God's faithfulness. To set the stage of the Psalm, it begins with this statement:

"To the Chief Musician. Set to 'Deer of the Dawn'."

למנצח על אילת השחר

(lamnatseeach al ayelet ha'smachar)

According to the Jerusalem Talmud Baerachot 1:1, the phrase "Deer of the Dawn" means, *the dawn of the morning light appearing on the horizon.* The entire notion is about the dawning of a new day. In keeping with all the other Hebraic metaphors regarding the masculine and feminine, and death and rebirth, what makes this interesting is that it's in the feminine gender. According to the Talmudic understanding, the notion of the "Deer of the Dawn" depicts how the sun's rays beam like a "male deer's antlers," however, being in the feminine implies that the womb of Earth's horizon is giving birth to a new Man. This echoes Genesis 1:1 where the Divine Feminine is pregnant with life. This also echoes Genesis 3:20, where **Ζωή** *(Zoe;* Septuagint) **חוה** *(Chavah,* Hebrew) is the mother and giver of **כל־חי** (cāl-chaiy) *all-life* and Whose Seed will crush the Serpentine-Ego. This echoes the forthtelling prophecy of Isaiah 7:14, where a young woman will bear a son named, **עמנו אל** (Imanu-El, *God with us).* This points us to the Gospel of Luke, where the *Star in the East* (the place of the horizon) signifies the birth of the new King. This points us to Mary, her miraculous virgin birth, and the angelic chorus with glorious light that shone to the shepherds, proclaiming there was born that day, Christ the Lord. This points directly to Mark 16:2-6, which tells that early in the morning, on the first day of the week, the women came to the tomb when the sun had risen, and entering the tomb, they saw a young man clothed in a long white robe who said to them, *"Do not be alarmed. You seek Jesus of Nazareth, who was crucified. He is risen! He is not here."* As we shared in the previous volume, and the book, *The Divine Womb,* the picture of the empty tomb, glistening in the morning light, with angels proclaiming the resurrection, all speak of a tomb transformed into Earth's womb, giving birth to a new Man and a New Day. This is the *"Deer of the Dawn."* The suffering Christ, the dawn of a new day that arises within our hearts (2 Peter 1:19). Therefore, Jesus on the Cross chooses and proclaims the prophetic Psalm by David, Psalm 22. While Mankind believes God is forsaking the one hung on the Cross, a man of sorrows acquainted with grief, one from whom we hid our face, believing He was smitten and afflicted by God, where we thought it pleased God to bruise Him (Isaiah 53). NO! Rather, it was God embracing us on the Cross, a Whole Man acquainted with *Compassion* and *Grace,* One who would not turn His face from us, believing, forgiving, and healing us. It was there it pleased the Eternal Creator to reconcile us to Himself, concluding for generations past, present, and future, *"They will proclaim his righteousness to a people yet unborn — for he has done it."* (Psalms 22:31/NIV)

The second powerful statement defines His wholeness and awareness. His suffering is *Divine Compassion* revealed. Rather than reciprocate in kind, or retaliate to those who accused, abused, and afflicted Him, He saw them as they truly were, those who suffer in their unconsciousness. *"Father forgive them they're unconscious in their doing."* Nonetheless, herein is the paradox. Through being aware of *Compassion's* suffering, many of us are moved as well. As we see the suffering Christ, the point in our heart breaks through as we stir to awareness, and our *Compassion* is realized. This is also why Christ identifies with the naked, hungry, thirsty, sick, and imprisoned in Matthew 25:35-40. His identification is more than a literal one, but that in their suffering, those who clothe, feed, and visit, are moved into *Compassionate* action. Hence, the Christ is again revealed in us. Furthermore, we also realize it was our Egoistic selfishness that caused the suffering. In that moment, a type of resurrection occurs that's eternal and internal. Not only can such a *Compassion* rise from the grave on the third day, as the Gospel story tells us, but it's resurrected within our hearts like a laser breaking through an Egoistic steel box.

Now as we read the events and exhortations of both Old and New Testaments, we see with Christlike eyes. Verses no longer simply testify of Abraham, Isaac, Jacob, Joseph, David, and even Jesus. Rather, now we can say as Jesus said, *"These are they that testify of ME!"* The inspiration of the writers, the Mind of Christ behind the verses, is speaking within us. It no longer matters if there was a "real" ark built by a man called Noah, nor if Abraham ate bread and wine with a physical man named Melchizedek, nor if a King named David fully understood in his Psalm that the Melchizedekian priesthood would be revived through a coming Messiah. If I may be so bold, it doesn't even matter if we can prove with perfectly accurate apologetics, foolproof archeology, fully recovered relics, and an infallible, inerrant Testament that a godman named Jesus lived, died, and resurrected 2000 years ago. Why? Because the point in the heart of *Divine Compassion* has awakened and is radiating within us. In comparison, the powerful point in the heart is more real, more true, more tangible, than any supposed inerrant Bible story or archeological found relic. You ask again, "Why?" Because it doesn't exist upon the authority of any natural external finding, story, or argument. *It's the consciousness of the resurrected Christ within us!* Now we're roused, bathing in "Horizon's Dawning Light," which is the Light of Mankind (John 1:4). We were Ego, flesh, that's now consciously being made Word. We behold the Glory within us, as one begotten of the Father, aware of Grace and Truth. Now we see Divine reality in real time because we're born from the bosom of the Father and can truly declare Him.

The revelation of Our true self is a dynamic radiating the Divine Union, which permeates all Creation. It's an awareness, which is a Living expression that fills All in All. The darkness of inner ignorance vanishes in the Light of Our true identity. Now there's a new choice, a different calculation because something of a greater reality has entered the equation. Without the component of *Compassion,* without an awareness of our Divine Nature, regardless of what good we do Egoistically, we still fall short (Romans 3:23). Nonetheless, with *Compassion* radiating in our heart, the equation completely changes. In the consciousness of our emanating the Divine Nature, we no longer only see Good and Evil where there's none righteous, no not one (Romans 3:10). Rather, now we see with illuminated eyes. The choice now is between the Knowing of Good and Evil, or the Consciousness of Divine Life. The amazing beauty of choosing the Tree of Life, the source of the gracious priesthood of Melchizedek, is that a righteousness is revealed apart from any government, kingdom, nation, or law, of any religion of any kind (Romans 3:21). This doesn't mean we forget the understanding of Good and Evil our Ego once held, it's just understood now in a very different "Light." What was once Good and Evil is now dissolved into *Receiving* and *Giving, Reflecting* and *Emanating.* Like the messengers who took Lot's family by the hand, the *Compassion* of the Creator is truly otherworldly. It's found in the Loving gaze of the Light of Christ clothed in Us in human form. This is where the Kingdom of God breathes in Us and through Us. It's found in the revelation of Peace to Us and through Us, breathing on anyone We encounter. Thus, the priesthood of the King of Righteousness and King of Peace, Melchizedek, is found in the conclusion of expressed *Compassion.*

The CONCLUSION is found in its beginning: infinite Life expressed through never-ending Love. Creation began because of Love, and its conclusion is in its seal of Love. The righteousness of God is found in Love, emanated through *Compassion,* and expressed throughout Creation. We are of the order of Melchizedek! In other words, we are of the order of *Gracious Compassionate Humility,* approaching humanity with the refreshing, restoring, bread and wine of Divine Oneness. We are of an eternal priesthood, because we are the emanation of *Gracious Compassionate Humility,* which is eternal, never-ending, and forever expanding. We are expressions of both *the World Above* and a reconciled *World Below.* We are a presence of Divine Light, radiating in the outer darkness of Humanity's Hell. We are a presence of Divine Love, radiating to the unawareness of Humanity's self-inflicted condemnation. We are a presence of Divine Life, radiating to the unconsciousness of Humanity's Egoistic Death Sleep. We are the "BODY of Christ." We are the eternal INCARNATION of the Infinite Creator. His story is now OUR story. He and Us are One. Now there's only WE.

Therefore, when WE came into the world, WE said:

"Sacrifice and offering You did not desire;
But a BODY You have prepared for ME.
MY ears You have opened.
Burnt offering and sin offering You did not require.
Then I said, "Behold, I HAVE COME;
In the scroll of THE BOOK IS WRITTEN OF ME.
I delight to do Your will, O MY God,
And Your LIVING WORD is within MY HEART."

(Psalms 40:6-8 and Hebrews 10:5-7
NKJV - Modified for clarity)

WE ARE THE CONCLUSION.

ABOUT THE AUTHOR

DR. JOHN has been an ordained minister for over forty years. His underlying call is to empower seasoned spiritual leaders and those just beginning their journey of discovery. His message at large is, as Christ said, *"...that they all may be one, as You Father, are in Me, and I in You; that they may be one in Us..."* He ministers across denominational lines, speaking in different seminar venues across the United States, the United Kingdom, Europe, and Africa. He was the founding pastor of Oasis of the Valley in 1985. His wife and partner, Karen, has been the senior pastor for the last decade, while Dr. John has traveled the world speaking and writing. Together they founded Foundation Rock Ministries International, a place of fellowship and spiritual development for leaders. For more information, visit www.MastroMin.com, www.TogetherAsOne.net, and www.toOasis.com.

Made in the USA
Las Vegas, NV
19 November 2023

81194510R00392